contents

A sizzling red door with a brass kickplate punctuates this home's nostalgic front-porch invitation.
See Plan J-86140 on page 63.
Design by Larry James & Associates, Inc.
Photo by Mark Englund/HomeStyles

When was the last time you examined your countertop options?
Photo by Koeschel Peterson
Design by Connie Gustafson, CKD

Before you realize your dreams—finance!
Illustration by Matthew Korsmo

EDITORIAL Brian Boese, Steven Gramins, Laura Lentz, Jason Miller, Pamela Robertson **PRODUCTION** Matthew Korsmo, Todd Monge, Leon Thompson **MARKETING** Dan Brown, Kris Donnelly, Brian Medenwaldt, Shelley Safratowich **TELERELATIONS** Heather Anderson, Jennifer Banks, Laurie Benke, Heidi Bjorlo, Bill Breen, Erika Brewer, Natasha Dilday, Bonny Duffney, Michele Flaherty, Carol Green, Mark Kalar, Patrick Kowal, Erin Marsh, Debra Matei, Brenda McCalister, Jessica Miller, Elaine Ray, Julie Schaetzel, Karen Strong, Mikeya Strowder, Robert Tratz, Laura Voetberg, Rebecca Wadsworth, Narkeetha Warren **INFORMATION SYSTEMS** John Driscoll, Kevin Gellerman, Brad Olson **ACCOUNTING** Barbara Marquardt, Kellie Pierce, Robert Schultz **ADMINISTRATION** Kristy Walsh **HUMAN RESOURCES** Rick Erdmann **COMPANY LEADERS** Jeffrey B. Heegaard, Roger W. Heegaard **STRATEGIC LEADERS** Craig Bryan–Marketing, Nancy Ness–Finance/Administration/Publishing, Wayne Ramaker–Telerelations **OPERATIONAL LEADERS** Eric Englund–Editorial, John Herber–Information Systems, Diana Jasan–Multimedia, Dorothy Jordan–Joint-Venture Marketing, Bruce Krause–Production, Jeanne Marquardt–Accounting, Michael Romain–Telerelations

FOR INFORMATION ON ADVERTISING, CONTACT KEVIN MILLER **(800) 755-0288**   INTERNET ADDRESS: homestyles.com   Copyright 1997, HomeStyles Publishing and Marketing Inc. All rights reserved. Printed in U.S.A. The trademark HomeStyles is registered in the U.S. Patent and Trademark Office by Gruner and Jahr, Inc., and is used under license therefrom.

PUBLISHED BY HOMESTYLES
P.O. Box 75488
St. Paul, MN 55175-0488
TEL: (612) 602-5000   FAX: (612) 602-5001

HomeStyles®
THE HOME PLANS PEOPLE

Life is change. Our minds, bodies and spirits are in a state of constant flux. We pass through significant phases and move on and up to, hopefully, bigger and better endeavors. It comes as no surprise that our need for shelter should change periodically also, and that our homes should grow and improve.

In this issue, you'll find an impressive variety of homes that are just waiting for you to build them and move in. Commonly called "move-up" homes, they are designed to meet your changing needs as you pass from stage to stage. Ranging from 1,500 to 2,500 square feet, they offer abundant opportunities to unwind, crunch numbers,

prepare elaborate feasts, strengthen business relationships and grow closer to loved ones.

To help you prepare financially for the changes ahead, turn to page eight and read Jessica Tolliver's feature on financing your home. On page four, Laura Lentz investigates the world of countertop finishes and points out the options you need to be aware of as you make decisions that affect both your budget and your lifestyle.

Change is inevitable. If you currently live in your first home and are sensing the need to "move up," your next home just might be found in these pages. It's time to begin your search.

Photo by Mark England/HomeStyles

Jason Miller

Editor

E-mail: jmiller@homestyles.com

A GLOSSARY OF BUILDING TERMS:
TO AID IN YOUR SEARCH FOR A HOME, LEARN THE LINGO

Bay - a projection formed by three windows joined at obtuse angles

Bow - a curved projection formed by at least five windows joined at obtuse angles

Clerestory - an outside wall of a room or building that rises above an adjoining roof and contains windows

Dentil - one of a series of small projecting rectangular blocks forming a molding under an overhang, most common in Colonial-style homes

Dormer - a gable-topped structure projecting from a roof, containing a window

Footprint - the outline of a home's foundation; this measures the home's outermost points and is used for site planning

Gable - the vertical triangular end of a building or part of a building, from the eaves to the ridge

Gable roof - a roof consisting of two rectanglular planes sloping up to a ridge, forming gables on both ends

Gambrel roof - a roof with a lower, steeper slope and an upper, less steep slope on each of its two sides

Hip roof - a roof with sloping ends and sloping sides that meet at a ridge

Keystone - a wedge-shaped detail at the crown of an arch

Lanai - a patio or veranda

Loggia - a roofed open gallery, often on an upper level

Palladian window - a window arrangement with a half-round window on top of a wider rectangular window

Pediment - a triangular space formed in the middle of a gable; also used as a decoration above a door

Porte cochere - a covered, drive-through structure that extends from the side of a home, providing shelter for people getting in and out of vehicles

Portico - a roof supported by columns; often used at an entry

Quoin - a large, square stone set into the corner of a masonry building; distinguished from the adjoining walls by material, texture or projection

Sidelight - a vertical window beside a door or another window

Transom window - a narrow horizontal window above a window or door, named for the cross bar on which it rests

Tray ceiling - a recessed ceiling resembling an upside-down tray; also referred to as a stepped ceiling

Turret - a small tower usually on the corner of a building, most common in Victorian-style homes

Vaulted ceiling - a ceiling that slopes up to a peak

Volume ceiling - any ceiling higher than the standard 8 feet

Topping expectations

kitchen countertops increase your options

You expect a lot from your kitchen. More than a practical

space for meal preparation and chores, it can be the heart

of afternoon gatherings and late-night conversations.

Naturally, a space that hosts so much activity needs to cook

up a combination of convenience and inviting good looks.

Countertops hold a key to your kitchen's atmosphere and performance. This deceptively simple detail can make the difference between an attractive, inviting work space and an area that fails to live up to your high standards.

There exist five basic kinds of countertop materials: laminate, solid surfacing, natural stone, ceramic tile and wood. Before making a decision that will affect your kitchen for years to come, familiarize yourself with the different aspects of these materials and choose the one that will best suit your family's needs.

Probably the most popular countertop surface in America, laminate supplies a tough, inexpensive covering with an extensive range of color and pattern choices. Constructed of plywood or particle board covered by a thin layer of laminate (layers of melamine and phenolic resin-impregnated paper fused together by heat and high pressure), this surface offers plenty of stain, abrasion and moisture resistance. It is, however, susceptible to scorching by hot items and damage from sharp objects, and it can be difficult to repair.

Laminate countertops can be finished with either a high-gloss or a flat finish, though the high-gloss option tends to highlight scratches and other damage. Edge treatments are another important design consideration. The conspicuous brown joint line in the edges of laminate countertops can be eliminated by adding a decorative molding or de-emphasized by other special edge treatments.

Versatility, in its wide range of color and finishing choices, defines solid surfacing, another prevalent countertop material. Made of a combination of acrylics and polyesters, this material has an appearance and texture similar to that of stone, and it offers the advantage of repairability. Minor damage, such as scratches and burns, can be buffed out with an abrasive pad or fine sandpaper. Solid surfacing is the only countertop surface in which one isolated area can be repaired without replacing the whole countertop. Further, its seamlessness looks attractive and simplifies maintenance.

Design possibilities are endless with solid surfacing. In addition to a range of color options, this material allows all sorts of creativity. Connie Gustafson, a Certified Kitchen Designer (CKD) at Minneapolis-based Sawhill Custom Kitchens & Design, Inc., encourages home owners to use their imaginations and make the most of solid surfacing's flexibility. Combinations of blocks of different colors can breathe vibrant life into a neutral kitchen; unique patterns can be incorporated for personal flair. As with laminate countertops, the high-gloss finishes tend to show scratches more readily and, therefore, should be avoided in high-use kitchens.

Natural stone, such as granite, marble or slate, presents a third option for countertop elegance. One of the most expensive countertop materials to buy and install, it is strikingly attractive, long-lasting and extremely heat resistant. Some stone counters are available in ¾-inch slabs, but 1¼-inch slabs will allow enough support for 12-inch stone overhangs, and they'll be less likely to become damaged during shipment.

With natural stone countertops, scratches and other damages are difficult to remove or repair, though granite countertops are not as susceptible to scratches as are marble countertops. Further, these porous surfaces are subject to staining. Sealing them may help to protect against the damage of everyday use.

Ceramic tile, the price of which varies widely, offers a virtually limitless array of color, texture and shape possibilities. Because it can be painted by hand or styled in any number of ways, ceramic tile serves as an ideal accent material; for example, as a decorative backsplash. Because it is heat and scratch resistant, tile can also be a practical choice for the countertop itself. You can place a hot pan from the stove directly on the surface, as well as cut directly on it.

Photo courtesy of DuPont Corian®

Photo and design by Sawhill Custom Kitchens & Design, Inc.

Photo by Mark Englund/HomeStyles; Plan J-9307 by Larry James & Associates, Inc.

The main disadvantages of tile are its susceptibility to cracking and chipping, and the fact that its grout lines are porous and likely to stain. If the grout is not sealed, it may also discolor and accumulate bacteria. According to Kari Hedstrom of Minneapolis-based Fantasia Showrooms, anything porous should be sealed. She explains that ceramic tile must cure for a couple of weeks after installation (during which time care should be taken not to spill on it and stain the grout) and then the grout can be sealed.

The warm sheen of wood countertops can add a nice glow to any kitchen. Not only do wood countertops exude a rich visual texture, they also offer plenty of flexibility. They can be finished, left unfinished, refinished now and then, and cut and sanded to different angles or levels of smoothness. These surfaces are somewhat fragile, however. They scratch, stain and burn easily; they are very susceptible to heat and water damage (causing warps and cracks); and they can be unsanitary unless disinfected, allowing bacteria to build up.

With the variety of countertop materials and treatments available on the market comes the knowledge that there are no right or wrong choices. Gustafson reminds her clients that a decision about countertops is very personal; what works well for one family may not be the best choice for the family living next door. She advises those who are considering building, remodeling or redecorating a home to consider the following factors as they weigh their many options: function, budget and aesthetics.

Choose products that will work for—not against—your family's lifestyle. Allow your budget to guide your decision, but remember that a more significant initial investment will most likely pay off over time and the life of your home. Finally, remember that even the most budget-conscious products are available in a plethora of colors and textures. You should be able to tailor your countertop to fit your needs perfectly and achieve a look that lives up to your expectations.

—*Laura Lentz*

Photo courtesy of Saari & Forral Photography
Design by Susan K. Palmquist, CKD

Sources: Connie Gustafson, CKD, and Tim Aden, CKD, CBD, Sawhill Custom Kitchens & Design, Inc.; Kari Hedstrom, Fantasia Showrooms; American HomeStyle Kitchens and Baths, Kitchen & Bath Custom Planner, Fall 1995; National Kitchen & Bath Association (NKBA); DuPont Corian®; Wilsonart International.

Realize *your dreams*

A Guide to Financing Your New Home

You've just spent weeks, months or even years traipsing through neighborhood after neighborhood. You've poked around closets, bedrooms and kitchens, knocked on water pipes and inspected roof shingles. After all the open houses and long evenings with real estate agents, you've found the perfect home.

You love the neighborhood, the yard, the schools and shops nearby and the house—even with those few quirks you hadn't anticipated. Your dream home has fairly new windows, a high-quality gas heater and maybe even a new appliance or two.

Before you move forward you need to make sure you have good financing. Precious few people can afford to pay for a new home in full, so take the time now to ensure that you secure a loan you can live with for years to come.

After all, you spent plenty of time and energy choosing your home, and most likely you will have the loan for as long as you have the home. So use the same care financing your home as you did choosing it.

The first step in the financing process actually starts long before your search for a home, when you decide how much you are able to spend. Traditional recommendations range from two to two-and-one-half times your annual salary. Other standards dictate that homeowners spend about 38 percent of their annual salaries (after taxes) on total housing costs—including mortgage, insurance and utilities.

You need to be the judge of how much your family can afford. Do you anticipate your income will stay the same, increase or decrease over the years? Will your monthly costs level out, decrease when children move out on their own, or increase with a growing family or added education costs?

Your lender will also review how much you can afford to spend. To make that decision the lender will want to review some of your financial documents. Those documents could include the purchase contract for the house, bank account numbers, bank branch addresses, recent bank statements, pay stubs, W-2 forms, information about all loans, debts and credit cards, mortgage or rental payment receipts and a Certificate of Eligibility from the Veterans Administration if you want a VA-guaranteed loan. If you are self-employed, the lender may also want to review business tax returns and balance sheets from the past two or three years.

In the past, the majority of consumers secured 30-year fixed-rate mortgages (FRMs) to finance a home purchase. Today's market, however, offers consumers a number of different types of loans.

A conventional FRM carries the same interest rate and the same monthly payments throughout the life of the loan. These loans generally offered in 15- or 30-year terms.

Two obvious benefits of a 15-year term are an earlier payoff date and a significantly lower overall interest charge. The monthly payments on a 15-year loan will be higher than those on a 30-year loan, though.

Because interest rates fluctuate from week to week and even from day to day, the rate a lender quotes when you are shopping around could be very different from the rate available when you finalize. Those rates can also increase after you apply for the loan, but before finalization. A few percentage points can dramatically increase (or decrease) the total interest you pay over the life of the loan.

Many lenders offer a lock-in on a quoted interest rate and sometimes on the number of points quoted. (A point equals one percent of the amount borrowed. Points are usually due at closing to secure the loan.) The lock-in ensures that if interest rates increase before finalization, the borrower can still secure the loan at the terms previously discussed.

How to Calculate Your Monthly Payments

Interest Rate	7.00%	7.50%	8.00%	8.50%	9.00%	9.50%	10.00%
15-Year	$8.99	$9.27	$9.56	$9.85	$10.15	$10.45	$10.75
30-Year	$6.65	$6.99	$7.34	$7.69	$8.05	$8.41	$8.78

The above figures show approximate principal and interest payments for every $1,000 borrowed on a 15- or 30-year fixed-rate loan. To calculate a payment, divide the amount borrowed by 1,000 and multiply the result by the figure in the chart.

A lock-in can also prevent the borrower from securing a lower rate if interest rates drop during that period. Some lenders, however, are willing to lock in at the lower rate.

Lenders often charge a fee for the lock-in, which lasts for a pre-determined amount of time—usually between 30 and 60 days.

Written documentation that details the terms of a lock-in helps the borrower understand all the elements. A tangible record is also helpful if a dispute occurs between the borrower and the lender.

An increasingly common type of home financing is the adjustable-rate mortgage (ARM). The interest rate of an ARM adjusts periodically throughout the life of the loan.

Many lenders advertise ARM interest rates that are much lower than those for fixed-rate mortgages. Those rates often last for a short time and, after that initial period, the rates are adjusted on a regular basis. The time between rate changes—called the adjustment period—is usually one year. Three- and five-year adjustment periods are also available.

Lenders base those adjustments on a variety of indexes that fluctuate with the general movement of interest rates. Common indexes include the rates on Treasury securities, and the national or regional average cost of funds to savings and loan associations.

Be sure to find out the index used by your lender and take a look at that index's history.

The lender then tacks a few percentage points onto the index rate to determine the final interest rate. That margin varies from lender to lender, so find out those terms also. The difference between a two- and a three-percent margin could mean thousands of dollars to you in the long run.

An ARM allows borrowers to take advantage of low initial rates. If interest rates drop over the life of the loan, you could also save money over an FRM.

Interest rates rise as often as they drop, though. A borrower who secures an ARM takes on the risk that interest rates could go up. Before assuming an ARM, evaluate how your finances will change in upcoming years. Can you afford monthly payments that could be higher than those you started with?

Lenders offer some options that reduce the risk assumed by ARM borrowers. Some ARMs also include the option to convert the loan to an FRM at a specified later date.

Federal regulations require that all ARMs include an overall cap on how much an interest rate can increase over the life of the loan.

Periodic interest-rate caps limit the increases between adjustment periods. Some ARMs limit the increase of your actual monthly payment from one adjustment period to the next.

While a payment cap can keep down monthly costs, it can also cost you money down the road.

If a cap keeps your monthly payments down as interest rates increase, your mortgage balance could also increase.

This negative amortization happens when your monthly payments are too small to cover the monthly interest. The difference is then tacked on to your debt. Some ARMs limit how much negative amortization a loan can accrue.

The key to finding the best mortgage for you and your family is to shop around, ask questions and seek professional advice. Talk to your real estate agent, your lender and, if possible, a real estate lawyer. Keep an eye on the shelter section of local and national newspapers to monitor the going rates.

A mortgage could be the most important—and the longest-lasting—financial decision you will ever make. A little time and education could make the difference between a catastrophe and a wise investment in your future.

—Jessica Tolliver

Adjustable-Rate Mortgage - ARM; a mortgage where the interest rate changes during the life of the loan; also referred to as Adjustable Mortgage Loan or Variable-Rate Mortgage.

Amortization - When monthly payments are large enough to pay the interest and also reduce the principal on a mortgage; negative amortization occurs when monthly payments do not cover interest costs so the balance due increases.

Annual Percentage Rate - APR; a measure of the cost of credit, expressed as a yearly rate, including interest as well as other charges; this rate provides a good basis for comparing costs of loans.

Cap - A limit on how much the interest rate or the monthly payment can change, either at each adjustment or during the life of a mortgage.

Conversion Clause - A provision in some ARMs that allows you to change the ARM to a fixed-rate loan at some point during the term; usually allowed at the end of the first adjustment period.

Equity - A buyer's initial and increasing ownership rights in a house as he/she pays off the mortgage; buyer has 100 percent equity when the mortgage is paid in full.

Farmers Home Administration - Government loans; available to citizens with limited incomes in rural communities.

Federal Housing Authority - Insures loans made by banks and other lenders; sets a maximum mortgage limit and usually requires a lower down payment than a traditional loan.

Fixed-Rate Mortgage - FRM; a mortgage where the interest rate stays the same throughout the life of the loan; usually paid over 15- or 30-year terms.

Index - The measure of interest rates.

Lock-in - A lender's promise to hold a certain interest rate and a certain number of points for the borrower, usually for a specific amount of time; also called a rate-lock or a rate commitment.

Margin - The number of percentage points the lender adds to the index rate to calculate the ARM interest rate at each adjustment.

Points - One percent of the principal amount of a mortgage; lenders often charge points to increase the yield on a mortgage and to cover loan closing costs; the home buyer, seller or both can assume this cost, usually due at closing.

Veterans Administration - VA; insures loans made by lenders for eligible veterans and their spouses; encourages lenders to write loans for people with lower incomes.

Modern Charmer

- This attractive plan combines country-style charm with a modern floor plan.
- The central foyer ushers guests past a study and on into the huge living room, which is highlighted by an 11-ft. ceiling, a corner fireplace and access to a big, covered backyard porch.
- An angled snack bar joins the living room to the bayed nook and the efficient kitchen. The formal dining room is easily reached from the kitchen and the foyer. A utility room and a half-bath are just off the garage entrance.
- The master suite, isolated for privacy, boasts a magnificent bath with a garden tub, a separate shower, double vanities and two walk-in closets.
- Two more bedrooms are located on the opposite side of the home and are separated by a hall bath.
- Ceilings in all rooms are at least 9 ft. high for added spaciousness.

REAR VIEW

Plan VL-2069

Bedrooms: 3	Baths: 2½
Living Area:	
Main floor	2,069 sq. ft.
Total Living Area:	**2,069 sq. ft.**
Garage	460 sq. ft.
Exterior Wall Framing:	2x4

Foundation Options:
Crawlspace
Slab
(All plans can be built with your choice of foundation and framing. A generic conversion diagram is available. See order form.)

BLUEPRINT PRICE CODE: **C**

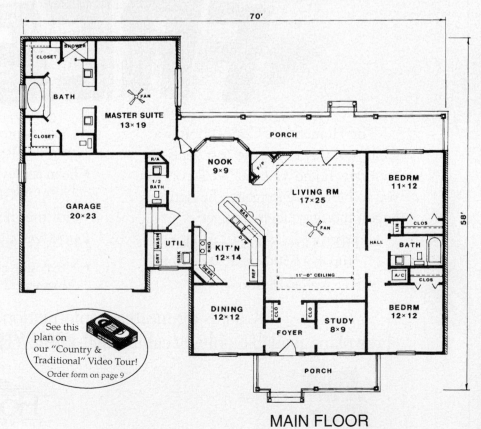

See this plan on our "Country & Traditional" Video Tour!
Order form on page 9

MAIN FLOOR

ORDER BLUEPRINTS ANYTIME!
CALL TOLL-FREE 1-888-626-2026

Plan VL-2069

PRICES AND DETAILS
ON PAGES 13-15

OUR BLUEPRINTS INCLUDE

HomeStyles construction blueprints are detailed, clear and concise. All blueprints are designed by licensed architects or members of the American Institute of Building Design (AIBD), and each plan is designed to meet one of the nationally recognized building codes (the Uniform Building Code, Standard Building Code or Basic Building Code) at the time and place they were drawn.

The blueprints for most home designs include the following elements, but the presentation of these elements may vary depending on the size and complexity of the home and the style of the individual designer:

1. **EXTERIOR ELEVATIONS** show the front, rear and sides of the house, including exterior materials, details and measurements.

2. **FOUNDATION PLANS** include drawings for a standard, daylight or partial basement, crawlspace, pole, pier, or slab foundation. All necessary notations and dimensions are included. (Foundation options will vary for each plan. If the home you want does not have the type of foundation you desire, a generic foundation conversion diagram is available from HomeStyles.)

3. **INTERIOR ELEVATIONS** show the specific details of cabinets (kitchen, bathroom, and utility room), fireplaces, built-in units, and other special interior features, depending on the nature and complexity of the item. *NOTE: To save money and to accommodate your own style and taste, we suggest contacting local cabinet and fireplace distributors for sizes and styles.*

4. **ROOF DETAILS** show slope, pitch and location of dormers, gables and other roof elements, including clerestory windows and skylights. These details may be shown on the elevation sheet or on a separate diagram. *NOTE: If trusses are used, we suggest using a local truss manufacturer to design your trusses to comply with your local codes and regulations.*

5. **SCHEMATIC ELECTRICAL LAYOUTS** show the suggested locations for switches, fixtures and outlets. These details may be shown on the floor plan or on a separate diagram.

6. **DETAILED FLOOR PLANS** show the placement of interior walls and the dimensions for rooms, doors, windows, stairways, etc., of each level of the house.

7. **CROSS SECTIONS** show details of the house as though it were cut in slices from the roof to the foundation. The cross sections specify the home's construction, insulation, flooring and roofing details.

8. **GENERAL SPECIFICATION** provide general instructions and information regarding structure, excavating and grading, masonry and concrete work, carpentry and wood, thermal and moisture protection, and specifications about drywall, tile, flooring, glazing, caulking and sealants.

OTHER HELPFUL BUILDING ITEMS

Every set of plans that you order will contain the details your builder needs. However, HomeStyles provides additional guides and information that you may order, as follows:

1. **REPRODUCIBLE SET** is useful if you plan to make changes to the stock home plan you've chosen. This set consists of line drawings produced on erasable, reproducible paper for the purpose of modification. When alterations are complete, working copies can be made. See chart on next page for availability.

2. **MIRROR-REVERSED PLANS** (available on all plans) are used when building the home in reverse of the illustrated floor plan. Reversed plans are available for an additional one-time surcharge. Since the lettering and dimensions will read backwards, we recommend that you order only one or two reversed sets in addition to the regular-reading sets.

3. **ITEMIZED LIST OF MATERIALS** details the quantity, type and size of basic materials needed to build your home. This list is helpful in acquiring an accurate construction estimate. See chart on next page for availability.

4. **DESCRIPTION OF MATERIALS** describes the type and quality of materials suggested for the home. This form may be required for obtaining FHA or VA financing. See chart on next page for availability.

5. **GENERIC "HOW-TO" DIAGRAMS**—**Plumbing, Wiring, Solar Heating, and Framing and Foundation Conversion Diagrams.** Each of these diagrams details the basic tools and techniques needed to plumb; wire; install a solar heating system; convert plans with 2x4 exterior walls to 2x6 (or vice versa); or adapt a plan for a basement, crawlspace or slab foundation. *NOTE: These diagrams are generic and not specific to any one plan.*

NOTE: Due to regional variations, local availability of materials, local codes, methods of installation, and individual preferences, it is impossible to include much detail on heating, plumbing, and electrical work on your plans. The duct work, venting, and other details will vary depending on the type of heating and cooling system (forced air, hot water, electric, solar) and the type of energy (gas, oil, electricity, solar) that you use. These details and specifications are easily obtained from your builder, contractor, and/or local suppliers.

BEFORE YOU ORDER, PLEASE READ

BLUEPRINT PRICES
Our pricing schedule is based on "Total heated living space." Garages, porches, decks and unfinished basements are not included.

EXCHANGE INFORMATION
We want you to be happy with your blueprint purchase. If, for some reason, the blueprints that you ordered cannot be used, we will be pleased to exchange them within 30 days of the purchase date. Please note that a handling fee will be assessed for all exchanges. For more information, call us toll-free. *NOTE:* **Reproducible sets cannot be exchanged for any reason.**

LICENSE AGREEMENT, COPY RESTRICTIONS AND COPYRIGHT INFORMATION
When you purchase a HomeStyles blueprint or reproducible set, we, as Licensor, grant you, as Licensee, the right to use these documents **to construct a single unit.** All of the plans in the publication are protected under the Federal Copyright Act, Title XVII of the United States Code and Chapter 37 of the Code of Federal Regulations. Each HomeStyles designer retains title and ownership of the original documents. The blueprints licensed to you cannot be resold or used by any other person, copied, or reproduced by any means. When you purchase a reproducible set, you reserve the right to modify and reproduce the plan. Reproducible sets cannot be resold or used by any other person.

ESTIMATING BUILDING COSTS
Building costs vary widely depending on style, size, type of finishing materials you select, and the local rates for labor and building materials. A local average cost per square foot of construction can give you a rough estimate. To get the average cost per square foot in your area, you can call a local contractor, your state or local builders association, the National Association of Home Builders (NAHB), or the American Institute of Building Design (AIBD). A more accurate estimate will require a professional review of the working blueprints and the types of materials you will be using.

FOUNDATION OPTIONS & EXTERIOR CONSTRUCTION
Depending on your location and climate, your home will normally be built with a slab, crawlspace or basement foundation; the exterior walls will usually be of 2x4 or 2x6 framing. Most professional contractors and builders can easily adapt a home to meet the foundation and exterior wall requirements that you desire.

If the home that you select does not offer the foundation or exterior wall requirements that you prefer, HomeStyles offers a typical foundation and framing conversion diagram. (See order form.)

Every state, county and municipality has its own codes, zoning requirements, ordinances, and building regulations. Modifications may be necessary to comply with your specific requirements—snow loads, energy codes, seismic zones, etc.

REVISIONS, MODIFICATIONS AND CUSTOMIZING
The tremendous variety of designs available from HomeStyles allows you to choose the home that best suits your lifestyle, budget and building site. Through your choice of siding, roof, trim, decorating, color, etc., your home can be customized easily.

Minor changes and material substitutions can be made by any professional builder without the need for expensive blueprint revisions. However, if you will be making major changes, we strongly recommend that you order a reproducible set and seek the services of an architect or professional designer.

COMPLIANCE WITH CODES
Depending on where you live, you may need to modify your plans to comply with local building requirements—snow loads, energy codes, seismic zones, etc. All HomeStyles plans are designed to meet the specifications of seismic zones I or II. HomeStyles authorizes the use of our blueprints expressly conditioned upon your obligation and agreement to strictly comply with all local building codes, ordinances, regulations, and requirements—including permits and inspections at the time of construction.

ARCHITECTURAL AND ENGINEERING SEALS
The increased concern over energy costs and safety has prompted many cities and states to require an architect or engineer to review and "seal" a blueprint prior to construction. There may be a fee for this service. Please contact your local lumber yard, municipal building department, builders association, or local chapter of the American Institute of Building Design (AIBD) or the American Institute of Architects (AIA).

NOTE: (Plans for homes to be built in Nevada may have to be re-drawn and sealed by a Nevada-licensed design professional.)

HOW MANY SETS TO ORDER? BLUEPRINT CHECKLIST

- Owner (**1 SET**)
- Lending Institution (usually **1 SET** for conventional mortgage; **3 SETS** for FHA or VA loans)
- Builder (usually requires at least **3 SETS**)
- Building Permit Department (at least **1 SET**)

PLAN PREFIX	Reproducible Set	Itemized List of Materials	Description of Materials
A	●		
AG	●		
AGH	●		
AH	●	●	
AHP	●	●	●
AM	●		
APS	●	*	
AX	●	*	
B	●	*	
BOD	●	*	
BRF	●		
C	●	●	●
CAR	●		
CC	●	●	
CDG	*	*	
CH	●		
CPS	●	●	
DCL	●		
DD	●	*	
DW	●	●	●
E	●	●	
EOF	●		
FB	●		
G	●		
GA	●		
GL	●		
GSA	●	●	
H	●	●	●
HDS	●		
HFL	●		
HOM	●	*	
I		*	
IDG	●	●	
J	●	●	●
JWA	●		
JWB	●		
K	●	●	●
KD	●		
KLF	●		
KY	●		
L	●	*	
LMB		*	
LRD	●	●	
LS	●		
M	●		
NBV	●		
NW		*	
OH	●		
P	●	●	●
PH	●	●	●
PI	●		
Q	●		
R	●		
RD	●		
S	●	●	
SAN	●		
SD	●		
SDG	●		
SG		*	
SUL	●		
SUN	●		
THD	●		
TS	●		
U	●		
UD	●		
UDA	●		
UDG	●		
V	●		
VL		●	●
WH	●	●	
YS		●	●

*Call for availability

Blueprint Order Form

OPEN 24 HOURS!

HOMESTYLES®
THE HOME PLANS PEOPLE

Visit our Web site at: homestyles.com

FOR FAST 24-HOUR SERVICE CALL TOLL-FREE:

1-888-626-2026

Source Code HD11

OR MAIL TO:

HomeStyles Plan Service
P.O. Box 75488
St. Paul, MN 55175-0488

OR FAX TO:
1-612-602-5002

☐ I do not wish to receive future mailings.

Plan Number

| HD11 |

PRICE CODE _____

FOUNDATION _____
Carefully review the foundation option(s) available for your plan—basement, crawlspace, pole, pier, or slab. If several options are offered, *choose only one.*

NO. OF SETS (See Blueprint Chart below)
☐ ONE SET   ☐ FOUR SETS   ☐ SEVEN SETS
☐ ONE REPRODUCIBLE SET (See availability chart on opposite page.) $_____

ADDITIONAL SETS ($40 each) _____ $_____

MIRROR-REVERSED SETS ($50 one-time surcharge) _____ $_____
(Available on all plans)

ITEMIZED LIST OF MATERIALS ($50; $15 for each additional) _____ $_____
(See availability chart on opposite page.)

DESCRIPTION OF MATERIALS ($50 for two sets) $_____
(See availability chart on opposite page.)

GENERIC HOW-TO DIAGRAMS $_____
(One set $20. Two sets $30. Three sets $40. All four only $45.)
☐ PLUMBING   ☐ WIRING   ☐ SOLAR HEATING   ☐ FRAMING & FOUNDATION CONVERSION

SUBTOTAL $_____

Minnesota Residents Only: Add 6.5% Sales Tax $_____

(See chart below) **SHIPPING/HANDLING** $_____

TOTAL $_____

Make checks payable to: **HomeStyles Plan Service**
☐ Check/Money Order enclosed (in U.S. funds)
☐ VISA ☐ MasterCard ☐ AmEx ☐ Discover

CREDIT CARD NUMBER _____   EXPIRATION DATE _____

NAME _____

ADDRESS _____   CITY _____

STATE _____   COUNTRY _____   ZIP _____

DAYTIME PHONE NUMBER _____   FAX NUMBER _____
☐ Please check if you are a builder   •For international orders, please indicate fax number.

Source Code HD11

BLUEPRINTS
(PRICES SUBJECT TO CHANGE)

Price Code	1 Set	4 Sets	7 Sets	Reproducible Set*
AAA	$245	$295	$330	$430
AA	$285	$335	$370	$470
A	$365	$415	$450	$550
B	$405	$455	$490	$590
C	$445	$495	$530	$630
B	$485	$535	$570	$670
E	$525	$575	$610	$710
F	$565	$615	$650	$750
G	$605	$655	$690	$790
H	$645	$695	$730	$830
I	$685	$735	$770	$870

ADDITIONAL ITEMS

MIRROR-REVERSED PLANS: A $50 surcharge. From the total number of sets you order, choose the number of these that you want to be reversed. Pay only $50.
NOTE: All writing on mirror-reversed plans is backward. We recommend ordering only one or two reversed sets in addition to the regular-reading sets.

*ITEMIZED LIST OF MATERIALS: Available for $50; each additional set is $15.
Details the quantity, type and size of basic materials needed to build your home.

*DESCRIPTION OF MATERIALS: Sold only in set of two for $50.
(For use in obtaining FHA or VA financing.)

*Refer to availability chart on opposite page or call for further information.

SHIPPING & HANDLING

	1-3 sets	4-6 sets	7 sets or more	Reproducible Set
U.S. Regular (5-6 business days)	$17.50	$20.00	$22.50	$17.50
U.S. Express (2-3 business days)	$29.50	$32.50	$35.00	$29.50
Canada Regular (2-3 weeks)	$20.00	$22.50	$25.00	$20.00
Canada Express (5-6 business days)	$35.00	$40.00	$45.00	$35.00
Overseas/Airmail (7-10 business days)	$57.50	$67.50	$77.50	$57.50

15

Flexible Cottage

- This charming cottage is big enough to be a permanent home, yet small enough to fit on a narrow or lakeside lot.
- If you love to entertain, imagine the events you can host in the L-shaped living room! A two-sided fireplace serves as the focal point, while a corner window seat is great for conversation.
- Move the party into the glass-embraced dining room for a light meal or even a surprise birthday cake.
- A French door leads to a third party venue—your lovely backyard. Throw some horseshoes, fire up the barbecue or show off your prized fruit trees.
- Do you like to cook? Then you'll adore the open, U-shaped kitchen, complete with a pantry closet, double ovens and a brick cooktop.
- Was your nest recently emptied? You'll appreciate the main-floor master suite, with its vast sleeping area. The well-designed private bath opens to the backyard through a French door.
- Upstairs, children, boarders or guests are nicely accommodated by two bedrooms and a full bath.

Plan L-818-CSA

Bedrooms: 3	Baths: 2½
Living Area:	
Upper floor	486 sq. ft.
Main floor	1,330 sq. ft.
Total Living Area:	**1,816 sq. ft.**
Exterior Wall Framing:	2x4

Foundation Options:

Slab

(All plans can be built with your choice of foundation and framing. A generic conversion diagram is available. See order form.)

BLUEPRINT PRICE CODE: **B**

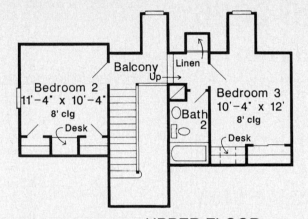

UPPER FLOOR

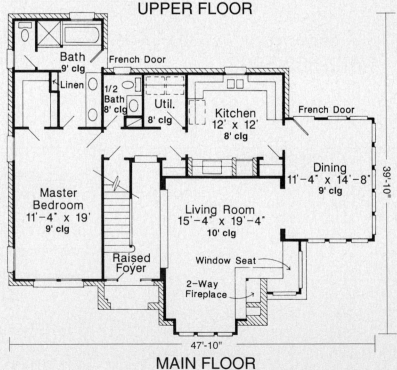

MAIN FLOOR

Plan L-818-CSA

PRICES AND DETAILS
ON PAGES 13-15

home

a dream of comfort

a gathering of memories

a place of solitude and relaxation

HOMESTYLES® **has the perfect home plan for you.**

Panoramic Prow View

- This glass-filled prow gable design is almost as spectacular as the panoramic view from inside.
- French doors open from the front deck to the dining room. A stunning window wall illuminates the adjoining living room, which flaunts a 20-ft.-high cathedral ceiling.

- The open, corner kitchen is perfectly angled to service the dining room and the family room, while offering views of the front and rear decks.
- A handy utility/laundry room opens to the rear deck. Two bedrooms share a full bath, to complete the main floor.
- A dramatic, open-railed stairway leads up to the secluded master bedroom, which boasts a dressing room and a private bath with a dual-sink vanity and a separate tub and shower.

Plan NW-196	
Bedrooms: 3	**Baths:** 2
Living Area:	
Upper floor	394 sq. ft.
Main floor	1,317 sq. ft.
Total Living Area:	**1,711 sq. ft.**
Exterior Wall Framing:	2x6
Foundation Options:	

Crawlspace
(All plans can be built with your choice of foundation and framing. A generic conversion diagram is available. See order form.)

BLUEPRINT PRICE CODE:	B

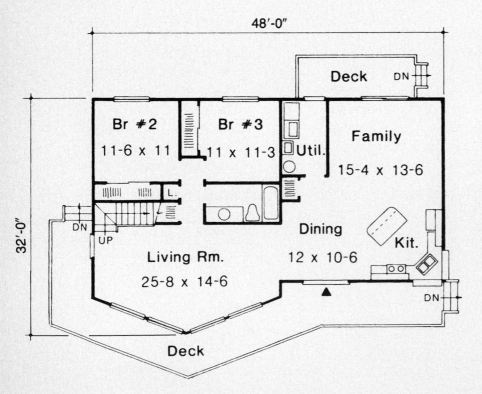

MAIN FLOOR

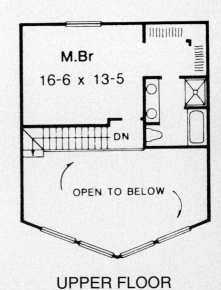

UPPER FLOOR

Plan NW-196

PRICES AND DETAILS
ON PAGES 13-15

Need to Make Plan Changes?

You've purchased your dream home plans, but the bids coming back from local builders are giving you sticker shock . . .

Your family has narrowed down the choices in your search for the perfect dream home plan to build, but there are a few things you wish were different about the plans . . .

Sound familiar? You're not alone. Most home plans buyers love their design, but need to make some changes, whether to add or delete square footage, make regional changes to satisfy code requirements or just rearrange rooms to better meet their family's lifestyle needs.

The good news is that any plan can be modified to your exact requirements. Your family doesn't have to settle for "close." To modify a plan, you need to purchase a reproducible plan set from HomeStyles, which allows changes to be made from the original.

Once you have a reproducible copy of your dream home plan, you can have the plans modified at an additional cost either locally by a design professional or nationally by a company like **LifeStyle HomeDesign Services** of St. Paul, Minnesota. LifeStyle offers quick, cost-effective modifications to any plan, many of which are drawn on a computer and can be changed easily.

Make your dream home perfect. Call LifeStyle toll-free at **1-888-2MODIFY** for a free, no-obligation quote for the cost, and expected delivery time for modifications.

Want the power of a nationally recognized home design and modification company working for you? Get to know **LifeStyle**.

LifeStyle HOME**DESIGN** SERVICES

Tradition Updated

- The nostalgic exterior of this home gives way to dramatic cathedral ceilings and illuminating skylights inside.
- The covered front porch welcomes guests into the stone-tiled foyer, which flows into the living spaces.
- The living and dining rooms merge, forming a spacious, front-oriented entertaining area.

See this plan on our "Country & Traditional" Video Tour!
Order form on page 9

- A large three-sided fireplace situated between the living room and the family room may be enjoyed in both areas.
- The skylighted family room is also brightened by sliding glass doors that access a rear patio.
- The sunny island kitchen offers a nice breakfast nook and easy access to the laundry room and the garage.
- The master suite boasts a walk-in closet and a skylighted bath with a dual-sink vanity, a soaking tub and a separate shower. Two additional bedrooms share another full bath.

Plan AX-90303-A

Bedrooms: 3	**Baths:** 2

Living Area:	
Main floor	1,615 sq. ft.
Total Living Area:	**1,615 sq. ft.**
Basement	1,615 sq. ft.
Garage	412 sq. ft.

Exterior Wall Framing: 2x4

Foundation Options:
Daylight basement
Standard basement
Crawlspace
Slab
(All plans can be built with your choice of foundation and framing. A generic conversion diagram is available. See order form.)

BLUEPRINT PRICE CODE:	B

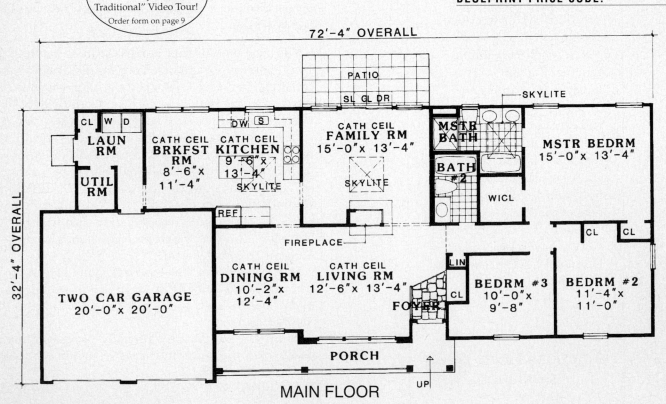

MAIN FLOOR

Sophisticated Farmhouse

- This traditional farmhouse design boasts elegant extras.
- A wraparound veranda welcomes guests in style.
- A warm fireplace brightens the spacious living room.
- A U-shaped kitchen easily serves the formal dining room, the bayed breakfast nook and the central family room.
- Walk-in closets are found in all three bedrooms. The master suite features a bayed sitting area.
- The optional basement (not shown) offers a second fireplace in a recreation room spanning the entire left side of the home. The remainder of the basement consists of a huge area for general use.

**NOTE: The above photographed home may have been modified by the homeowner. Please refer to floor plan and/or drawn elevation shown for actual blueprint details.

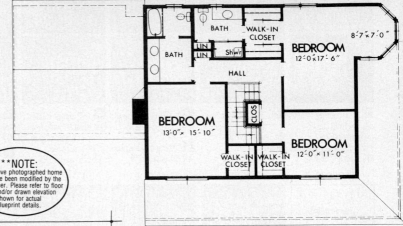

UPPER FLOOR

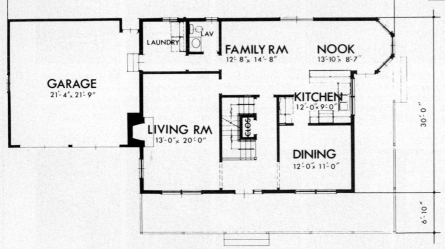

MAIN FLOOR

Plans H-1414-1 & -1A

Bedrooms: 3		**Baths:** 2½
Living Area:		
Upper floor		1,103 sq. ft.
Main floor		1,138 sq. ft.
Standard basement		1,080 sq. ft.
Total Living Area:		**2,241/3,321 sq. ft.**
Garage		464 sq. ft.
Exterior Wall Framing:		2x6
Foundation Options:		**Plan #**
Standard basement		H-1414-1
Crawlspace		H-1414-1A

(Typical foundation & framing conversion diagram available—see order form.)

BLUEPRINT PRICE CODE: C/E

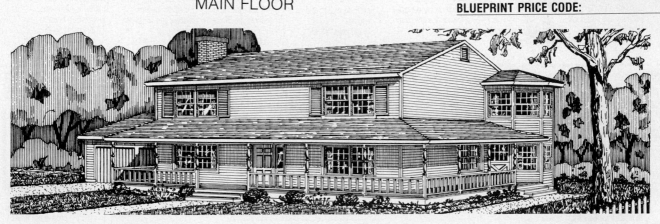

Poised and Pure

- This pure country-style home stands poised with plenty of eye-catching features to grab your attention.
- Relaxation is the rule on the railed veranda in front; on starry summer nights it's the perfect place to cuddle up with your loved ones.
- From the raised foyer you can step down to the living room or dining room. The living room features a cozy boxed-out window and a pleasant fireplace to cheer up the large space.
- The dining room also contains a boxed-out window, and is just a step from the island kitchen, which helps to make serving and cleaning up meals fast and easy.
- Sunshine pours into the corner breakfast nook via two walls of windows. Sit down and enjoy the great views or step outside via a handy French door.
- French doors are also a key feature in the beautiful master suite—they invite you to a private patio. Other highlights include a huge bath and an equally spacious walk-in closet.
- Two more bedrooms complete the main floor. A large game room upstairs converts easily to a fourth bedroom.

Plan L-284-VB

Bedrooms: 3+	Baths: 3
Living Area:	
Upper floor	445 sq. ft.
Main floor	1,837 sq. ft.
Total Living Area:	**2,282 sq. ft.**
Exterior Wall Framing:	2x4

Foundation Options:

Slab

(All plans can be built with your choice of foundation and framing. A generic conversion diagram is available. See order form.)

BLUEPRINT PRICE CODE:	C

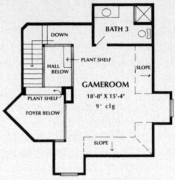

UPPER FLOOR

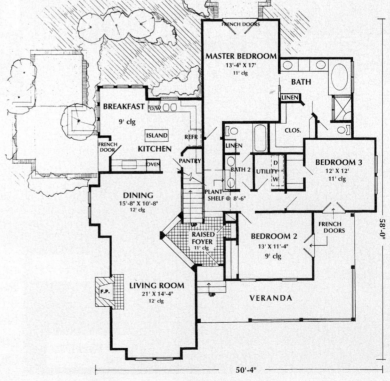

MAIN FLOOR

Plan L-284-VB

PRICES AND DETAILS
ON PAGES 13-15

Colonial with a Contemporary Touch

- Open, flowing rooms highlighted by a two-story round-top window combine to give this colonial design a contemporary, today touch.
- To the left of the elegant, two-story foyer lies the living room, which flows into the rear-facing family room with fireplace.
- The centrally located kitchen serves both the formal dining room and the dinette, with a view of the family room beyond.
- All four bedrooms are located upstairs. The master suite includes a walk-in closet and private bath with double vanities, separate shower and whirlpool tub under skylights.

Plan AHP-9020

Bedrooms: 4	Baths: 2 ½
Space:	
Upper floor	1,021 sq. ft.
Main floor	1,125 sq. ft.
Total Living Area	**2,146 sq. ft.**
Basement	1,032 sq. ft.
Garage	480 sq. ft.
Exterior Wall Framing	**2x6**

Foundation options:
Standard Basement
Slab
(Foundation & framing conversion diagram available—see order form.)

Blueprint Price Code	**C**

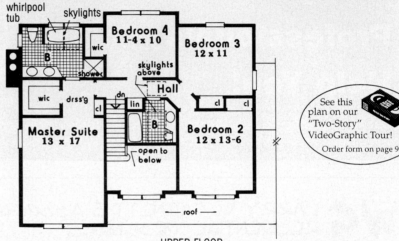

See this plan on our "Two-Story" VideoGraphic Tour!
Order form on page 9

UPPER FLOOR

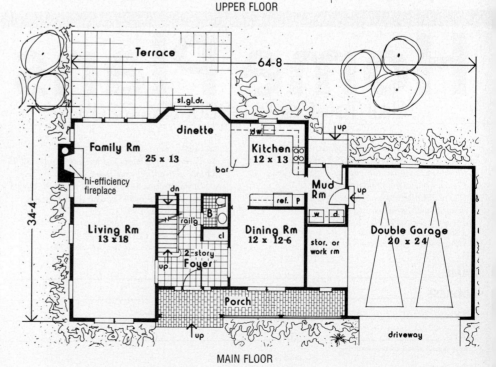

MAIN FLOOR

Plan B-7743

Bedrooms: 3-4	**Baths:** 2½

Space:
Upper floor: 1,080 sq. ft.
Main floor: 1,364 sq. ft.

Total living area: 2,444 sq. ft.
Basement: +/– 1,364 sq. ft.
Garage: 677 sq. ft.

Exterior Wall Framing: 2x4

Foundation options:
Standard basement.
(Foundation & framing conversion diagram available — see order form.)

Blueprint Price Code: C

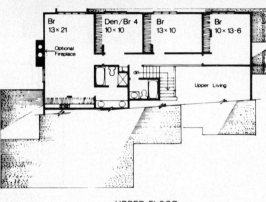

UPPER FLOOR

Family-Style Contemporary

● This home offers plenty of space for an active, growing family.
● Large family room connects directly to spacious nook/kitchen/deck area.
● Living and dining rooms pair up to create large space for entertaining.
● Living room features high, vaulted ceiling and large front windows.
● Upstairs offers three or four bedrooms, two baths.
● Master suite includes private bath with both tub and shower, plus a large closet and optional fireplace.
● Standard basement is easily modified for sloping lot, and garage level can be lowered to fit slope.

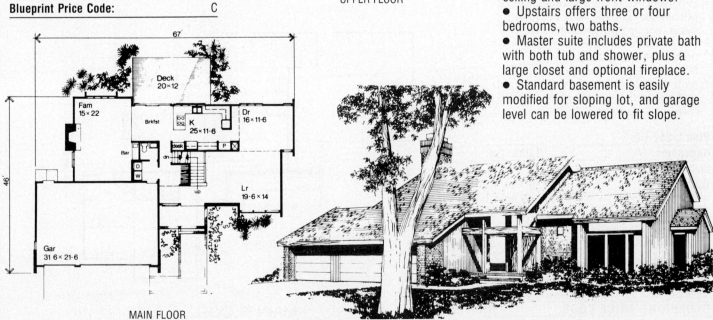

MAIN FLOOR

Fairy-Tale Feel

- Charming and whimsical, this comfy cottage jumps right out of the pages of your favorite fairy tale.
- Back in the real world, the home's inside spaces offer every modern convenience.
- Flowing from the foyer, the dining and living rooms are separated only by a lovely staircase. Imagine the parties you can host in this vast expanse! A nice fireplace adds ambience, while a French door opens onto a sunny patio.
- The open kitchen boasts an unusual layout; a central wet bar with a built-in wine rack facilitates the serving of refreshing beverages. Handy laundry facilities are nearby.
- The grocery shopper of the family will love the kitchen's proximity to the oversized two-car garage.
- The master suite is a relaxing haven. Its private bath and big walk-in closet make morning preparation easy.
- The children have their own space upstairs. A skylighted loft with bookshelves is a cozy spot to curl up with that favorite story. Walk-in closets and a shared, split bath give everyone a measure of comfort.

Plan L-867-HA

Bedrooms: 3	Baths: 2½
Living Area:	
Upper floor	603 sq. ft.
Main floor	1,262 sq. ft.
Total Living Area:	**1,865 sq. ft.**
Garage	478 sq. ft.
Exterior Wall Framing:	2x4

Foundation Options:

Slab

(All plans can be built with your choice of foundation and framing. A generic conversion diagram is available. See order form.)

BLUEPRINT PRICE CODE:	B

REAR VIEW

UPPER FLOOR

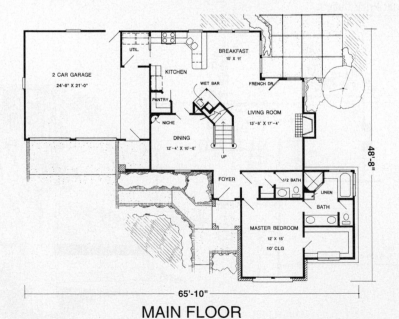

MAIN FLOOR

Plan L-867-HA

PRICES AND DETAILS
ON PAGES 13-15

Photo by Anthony James Dugal

Single-Story with Sparkle

See this plan on our "Best-Sellers" VideoGraphic Tour! Order form on page 9

NOTE: The above photographed home may have been modified by the homeowner. Please refer to floor plan and/or drawn elevation shown for actual blueprint details.

- A lovely front porch with a cameo front door, decorative posts, bay windows and dormers give this country-style home extra sparkle.
- The Great Room is at the center of the floor plan, where it merges with the dining room and the screened porch. The Great Room features a 10-ft. tray ceiling, a fireplace, a built-in wet bar and a wall of windows to the patio.
- The eat-in kitchen has a half-wall that keeps it open to the Great Room and hallway. The dining room offers a half-wall facing the foyer and a bay window overlooking the front porch.
- The delectable master suite is isolated from the other bedrooms and includes a charming bay window, a 10-ft. tray ceiling and a luxurious private bath.
- The two smaller bedrooms are off the main foyer and separated by a full bath.
- A mudroom with a washer and dryer is accessible from the two-car garage, disguised with another bay window.

Plan AX-91312

Bedrooms: 3	**Baths:** 2

Living Area:

Main floor	1,595 sq. ft.
Total Living Area:	**1,595 sq. ft.**
Screened porch	178 sq. ft.
Basement	1,595 sq. ft.
Garage, storage and utility	508 sq. ft.
Exterior Wall Framing:	2x4

Foundation Options:

Daylight basement

Standard basement

Slab

(All plans can be built with your choice of foundation and framing. A generic conversion diagram is available. See order form.)

BLUEPRINT PRICE CODE: **B**

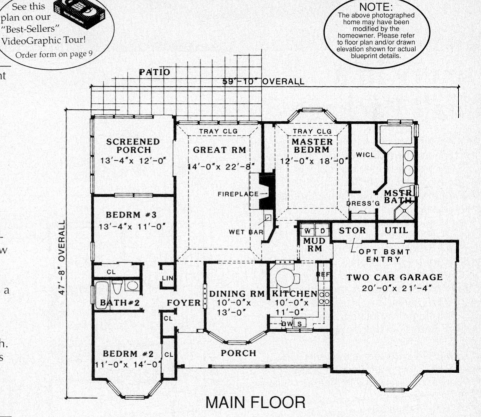

MAIN FLOOR

- PATIO
- 59'-10" OVERALL
- 47'-8" OVERALL
- SCREENED PORCH 13'-4" x 12'-0"
- TRAY CLG
- GREAT RM 14'-0" x 22'-8"
- TRAY CLG
- MASTER BEDRM 12'-0" x 18'-0"
- WICL
- MSTR BATH
- DRESS'G
- FIREPLACE
- BEDRM #3 13'-4" x 11'-0"
- WET BAR
- W D
- STOR
- UTIL
- MUD RM
- OPT BSMT ENTRY
- CL
- LIN
- REF
- TWO CAR GARAGE 20'-0" x 21'-4"
- BATH #2
- FOYER
- DINING RM 10'-0" x 13'-0"
- KITCHEN 10'-0" x 11'-0"
- CL
- CL
- DW S
- BEDRM #2 11'-0" x 14'-0"
- CL
- PORCH

VIEW INTO GREAT ROOM

TOUR THIS HOME BEFORE YOU BUILD!

See page 9 for details on Interactive Floor Plans.

Plan AX-91312

Luxury in a Small Package

- The elegant exterior of this design sets the tone for the luxurious spaces within.
- The foyer opens to the centrally located living room, which features a 15-ft. cathedral ceiling, a handsome fireplace and access to a lovely rear terrace.
- The unusual kitchen design includes an angled snack bar that lies between the bayed breakfast den and the formal dining room. Sliding glass doors open to another terrace.
- The master suite is a dream come true, with its romantic fireplace, built-in desk and 9-ft.-high tray ceiling. The private bath includes a whirlpool tub and a dual-sink vanity.
- Another full bath serves the remaining two bedrooms, one of which boasts a cathedral ceiling and a beautiful arched window.

Plan AHP-9300

Bedrooms: 3	Baths: 2
Living Area:	
Main floor	1,513 sq. ft.
Total Living Area:	**1,513 sq. ft.**
Standard basement	1,360 sq. ft.
Garage	400 sq. ft.
Exterior Wall Framing:	2x4 or 2x6

Foundation Options:

Standard basement
Crawlspace
Slab

(All plans can be built with your choice of foundation and framing. A generic conversion diagram is available. See order form.)

BLUEPRINT PRICE CODE: B

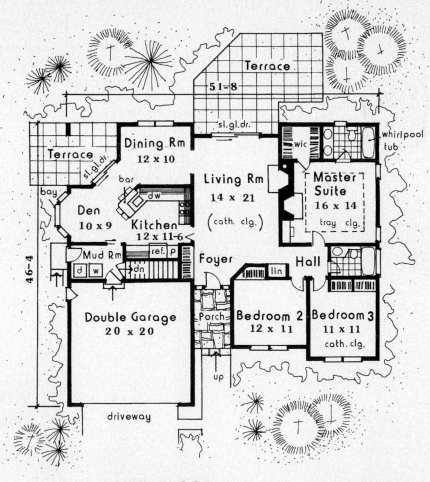

MAIN FLOOR

See this plan on our "One-Story" VideoGraphic Tour!
Order form on page 9

Authentic Charm

- Intricate fretwork, turned spindles and copper-topped bays lend authentic charm to this one-story home.
- Its unique shape and projecting gables make it aesthetically adaptable to nearly any lot orientation or size.
- The wraparound veranda ends at an angled entry and foyer; functional niches to the left and right provide display space for art or memorabilia.
- Handsome columns set off the central living room, with its corner fireplace and radiant window wall.
- A boxed-out bay and an attractive built-in hutch add interest and dimension to the formal dining room.
- Bifold doors close off the galley-style kitchen, where a snack bar and breakfast nook offer casual dining options. French doors entice you to dine outdoors on the porch.
- This same porch winds along to the master suite and its roomy garden bath. Two more bedrooms share a second full bath in the same wing.

Plan L-755-VA	
Bedrooms: 3	**Baths:** 2
Living Area:	
Main floor	1,753 sq. ft.
Total Living Area:	**1,753 sq. ft.**
Exterior Wall Framing:	2x4

Foundation Options:

Slab

(All plans can be built with your choice of foundation and framing. A generic conversion diagram is available. See order form.)

BLUEPRINT PRICE CODE:	B

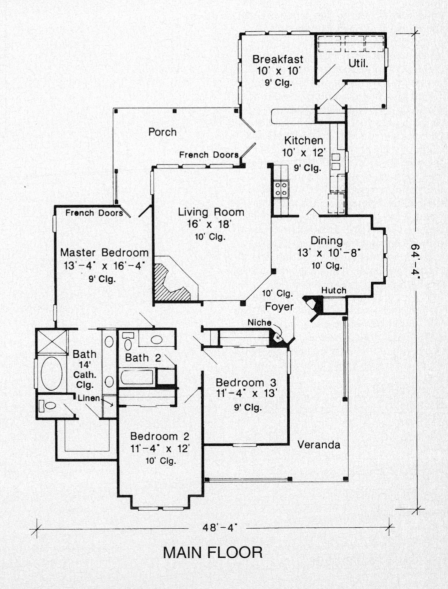

MAIN FLOOR

Peaceful Days

- This beautiful home's wraparound veranda and adjacent piazza recall the peaceful days of the past when friends spent restful afternoons mingling at pretty garden parties.
- Inside, a series of handsome columns create a dignified gallery that ushers guests into the living and dining rooms. When appearances count, serve dinner in the dining room. Afterwards, step out to the piazza for a breath of night air.
- Day-to-day, the kitchen and breakfast nook will bustle with activity. Perfect for family meals, the nook is also a great spot for a student to do homework under the watchful eye of a parent in the kitchen. Nearby access to the garage saves steps when unloading groceries.
- In the master suite, a number of perks provide special treatment for the home owners. Access to the veranda offers a romantic escape, while a Jacuzzi tub in the bath pampers a weary spirit.
- Upstairs, all three bedrooms include sizable walk-in closets. The front-facing bedroom also boasts a soaring vaulted ceiling and a separate vanity.
- A convenient laundry chute in the hall helps keep kids' bedrooms neat.

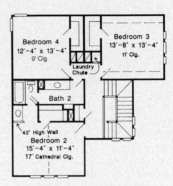

UPPER FLOOR

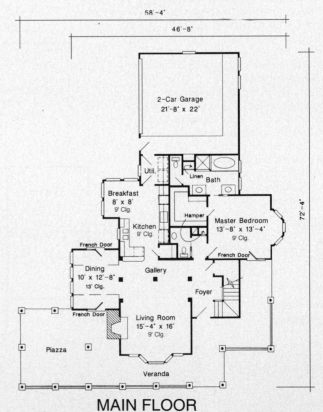

MAIN FLOOR

Plan L-215-VSB

Bedrooms: 4	Baths: 2½
Living Area:	
Upper floor	862 sq. ft.
Main floor	1,351 sq. ft.
Total Living Area:	**2,213 sq. ft.**
Garage	477 sq. ft.
Exterior Wall Framing:	2x4

Foundation Options:
Slab
(All plans can be built with your choice of foundation and framing. A generic conversion diagram is available. See order form.)

BLUEPRINT PRICE CODE:	**C**

Classic Country-Style

- At the center of this rustic country-style home is an enormous living room with a flat beamed ceiling, a massive stone fireplace and access to a patio and a covered rear porch.
- The adjoining eating area and kitchen provide plenty of room for casual dining and meal preparation. The eating area is visually enhanced by a 14-ft. sloped ceiling with false beams. The kitchen includes a snack bar, a pantry closet and a built-in spice cabinet.
- The formal dining room gets plenty of pizzazz from the stone-faced wall and arched planter facing the living room.
- The secluded master suite has it all, including a private bath, a separate dressing area and a large walk-in closet with built-in shelves.
- The two remaining bedrooms have big closets and easy access to a full bath.

Plan E-1808

Bedrooms: 3	Baths: 2
Living Area:	
Main floor	1,800 sq. ft.
Total Living Area:	**1,800 sq. ft.**
Garage	605 sq. ft.
Exterior Wall Framing:	2x4

Foundation Options:

Crawlspace
Slab
(All plans can be built with your choice of foundation and framing. A generic conversion diagram is available. See order form.)

BLUEPRINT PRICE CODE:	**B**

See this plan on our "One-Story" VideoGraphic Tour!
Order form on page 9

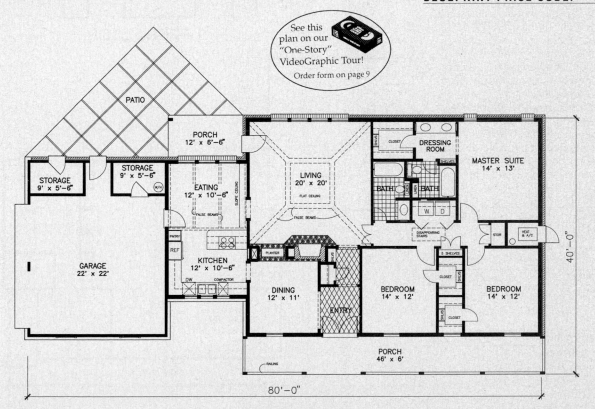

MAIN FLOOR

Sunny Comfort

- A covered wraparound porch and lovely arched windows give this home a comfortable country style.
- Inside, an elegant columned archway introduces the formal dining room.
- The huge Great Room features an 18-ft. vaulted ceiling, a dramatic wall of windows and two built-in wall units on either side of the fireplace.
- Ample counter space and a convenient work island allow maximum use of the roomy kitchen.
- The sunny breakfast nook opens to a porch through sliding glass doors.
- On the other side of the home, a dramatic bay window and a 10-ft. ceiling highlight the master bedroom. The enormous master bath features a luxurious whirlpool tub.
- Unless otherwise noted, all main-floor rooms have 9-ft. ceilings.
- Open stairs lead up to a balcony with a magnificent view of the Great Room. Two upstairs bedrooms, one with an 11-ft. vaulted ceiling, share a bath.

Plan AX-94317

Bedrooms: 3	Baths: 2½
Living Area:	
Upper floor	525 sq. ft.
Main floor	1,720 sq. ft.
Total Living Area:	**2,245 sq. ft.**
Standard basement	1,720 sq. ft.
Garage	502 sq. ft.
Storage/utility	51 sq. ft.
Exterior Wall Framing:	2x4

Foundation Options:

Standard basement

Crawlspace

Slab

(All plans can be built with your choice of foundation and framing. A generic conversion diagram is available. See order form.)

BLUEPRINT PRICE CODE: C

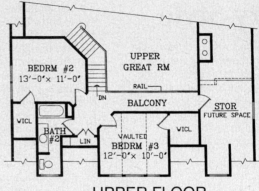

UPPER FLOOR

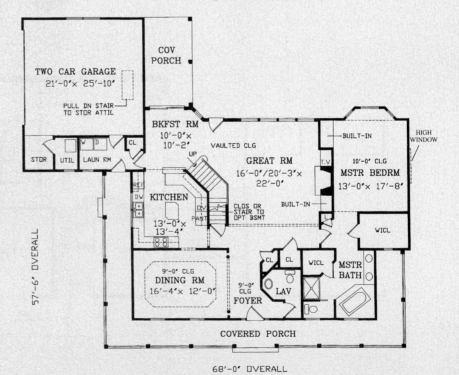

MAIN FLOOR

ORDER BLUEPRINTS ANYTIME!
CALL TOLL-FREE 1-888-626-2026

Plan AX-94317

PRICES AND DETAILS
ON PAGES 13-15

Rustic, Relaxed Living

- The screened porch of this rustic home offers a cool place to dine on warm summer days. The covered front porch provides an inviting welcome and a place for pure relaxation.
- With its warm fireplace and surrounding windows, the home's spacious living room is ideal for unwinding indoors. The living room unfolds to a nice-sized dining area that overlooks a backyard patio and opens to the screened porch.
- The U-shaped kitchen is centrally located and features a nice windowed sink. A handy pantry and a laundry room adjoin to the right.
- Three large bedrooms make up the home's sleeping wing. The master bedroom boasts a roomy private bath with a step-up spa tub, a separate shower and two walk-in closets.
- The secondary bedrooms share a compartmentalized hall bath.

Plan C-8650	
Bedrooms: 3	**Baths:** 2
Living Area:	
Main floor	1,773 sq. ft.
Total Living Area:	**1,773 sq. ft.**
Daylight basement	1,773 sq. ft.
Garage	441 sq. ft.
Exterior Wall Framing:	2 x 4
Foundation Options:	

Daylight basement
Crawlspace
Slab

(All plans can be built with your choice of foundation and framing. A generic conversion diagram is available. See order form.)

BLUEPRINT PRICE CODE:	B

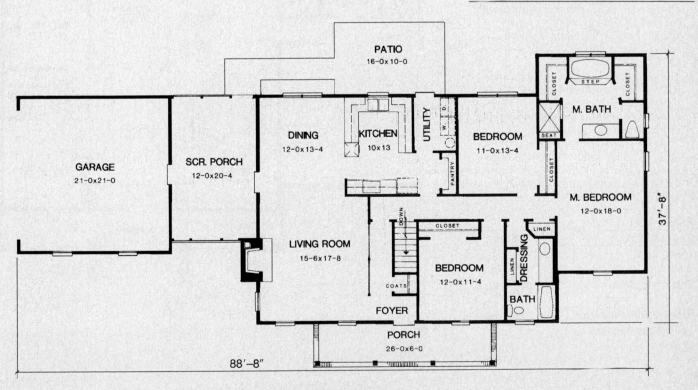

MAIN FLOOR

Masterful Master Suite

- This gorgeous home features front and rear covered porches and a master suite so luxurious it deserves its own wing.
- The expansive entry welcomes visitors into a spacious, skylighted living room, which boasts a handsome fireplace. The adjacent formal dining room overlooks the front porch.
- Designed for efficiency, the kitchen features an angled snack bar, a bayed eating area and views of the porch. An all-purpose utility room is conveniently located off the kitchen.
- The kitchen, eating area, living room and dining room are all heightened by 12-ft. ceilings.
- The sumptuous and secluded master suite features a tub and a separate shower, a double-sink vanity, a walk-in closet with built-in shelves and a compartmentalized toilet.
- The two secondary bedrooms share a hall bath at the other end of the home. The rear bedroom offers porch access.
- The garage features built-in storage and access to unfinished attic space.

Plan E-1811

Bedrooms: 3	Baths: 2

Living Area:

Main floor	1,800 sq. ft.
Total Living Area:	**1,800 sq. ft.**
Garage and storage	634 sq. ft.
Exterior Wall Framing:	2x6

Foundation Options:

Crawlspace
Slab
(All plans can be built with your choice of foundation and framing. A generic conversion diagram is available. See order form.)

BLUEPRINT PRICE CODE:	**B**

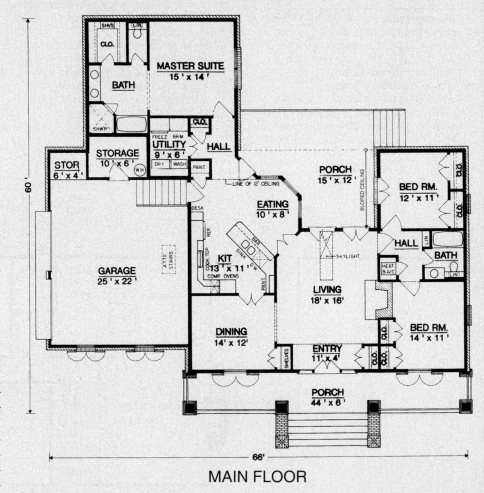

MAIN FLOOR

Fresh Air

- With its nostalgic look and country style, this lovely home brings a breath of fresh air into any neighborhood.
- Past the inviting wraparound porch, the foyer is brightened by an arched transom window above the front door.
- The adjoining formal dining room is defined by decorative columns and features a 9-ft., 4-in. stepped ceiling.
- The bright and airy kitchen includes a pantry, a windowed sink and a sunny breakfast area with porch access.
- Enhanced by an 11-ft stepped ceiling, the spacious Great Room is warmed by a fireplace flanked by sliding glass doors to a covered back porch.
- The lush master bedroom boasts an 11-ft. tray ceiling and a bayed sitting area. The master bath showcases a circular spa tub with a glass-block wall.
- The two remaining bedrooms are serviced by a second bath and a nearby laundry room. The protruding bedroom has a 12-ft. vaulted ceiling.
- Additional living space can be made available by finishing the upper floor.

Plan AX-93308

Bedrooms: 3+	Baths: 2
Living Area:	
Main floor	1,793 sq. ft.
Total Living Area:	**1,793 sq. ft.**
Standard basement	1,793 sq. ft.
Unfinished upper floor	779 sq. ft.
Garage and utility	471 sq. ft.
Exterior Wall Framing:	2x4

Foundation Options:

Standard basement

Crawlspace

Slab

(All plans can be built with your choice of foundation and framing. A generic conversion diagram is available. See order form.)

BLUEPRINT PRICE CODE: B

VIEW INTO GREAT ROOM

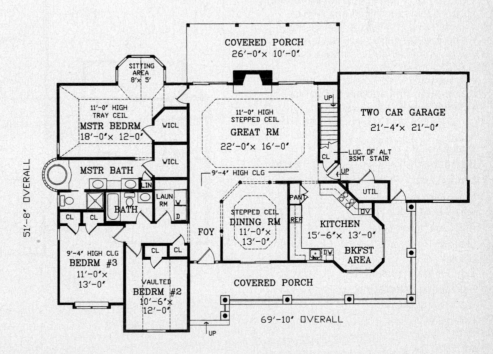

MAIN FLOOR

FRONT VIEW

Free-Flowing Floor Plan

- A fluid floor plan with open indoor/outdoor living spaces characterizes this exciting luxury home.
- The stylish columned porch opens to a spacious living room and dining room expanse that overlooks the outdoor spaces. The breathtaking view also includes a dramatic corner fireplace.
- The dining area opens to a bright kitchen with an angled eating bar. The overall spaciousness of the living areas is increased with high 12-ft. ceilings.
- A sunny, informal eating area adjoins the kitchen, and an angled set of doors opens to a convenient main-floor laundry room near the garage entrance.
- The vaulted master bedroom has a walk-in closet and a sumptuous bath with an oval tub.
- A separate wing houses two additional bedrooms and another full bath.
- Attic space is accessible from stairs in the garage and in the bedroom wing.

Plan E-1710

Bedrooms: 3	**Baths:** 2

Living Area:	
Main floor	1,792 sq. ft.
Total Living Area:	**1,792 sq. ft.**
Standard basement	1,792 sq. ft.
Garage	484 sq. ft.
Storage	96 sq. ft.
Exterior Wall Framing:	2x6

Foundation Options:
Standard basement
Crawlspace
Slab
(All plans can be built with your choice of foundation and framing. A generic conversion diagram is available. See order form.)

BLUEPRINT PRICE CODE: B

REAR VIEW

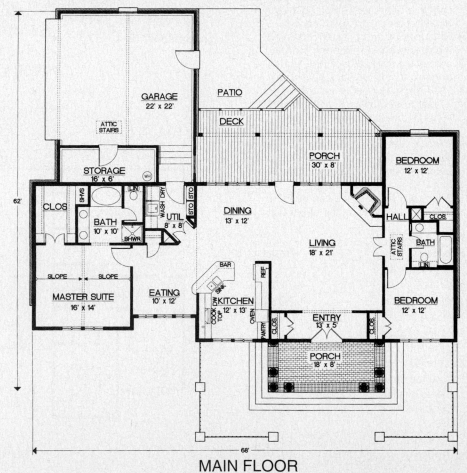

MAIN FLOOR

Plan E-1710

PRICES AND DETAILS
ON PAGES 13-15

Angled Solar Design

- This passive-solar design with a six-sided core is angled to capture as much sunlight as possible.
- Finished in natural vertical cedar planks and stone veneer, this contemporary three-bedroom requires a minimum of maintenance.
- Double doors at the entry open into the spacious living and dining areas.

- The formal area features a 14-ft. domed ceiling with skylights, a freestanding fireplace and three sets of sliding glass doors. The central sliding doors lead to a glass-enclosed sun room.
- The bright eat-in kitchen merges with the den, where sliding glass doors lead to one of three backyard terraces.
- The master bedroom, in the quiet sleeping wing, boasts ample closets, a private terrace and a luxurious bath, complete with a whirlpool tub.
- The two secondary bedrooms share a convenient hall bath.

Plan K-534-L

Bedrooms: 3	Baths: 2
Living Area:	
Main floor	1,647 sq. ft.
Total Living Area:	**1,647 sq. ft.**
Standard basement	1,505 sq. ft.
Garage	400 sq. ft.
Exterior Wall Framing:	2x4 or 2x6

Foundation Options:

Standard basement

Slab

(All plans can be built with your choice of foundation and framing. A generic conversion diagram is available. See order form.)

BLUEPRINT PRICE CODE: B

See this plan on our "Best-Sellers" VideoGraphic Tour! Order form on page 9

VIEW INTO LIVING ROOM AND DINING ROOM

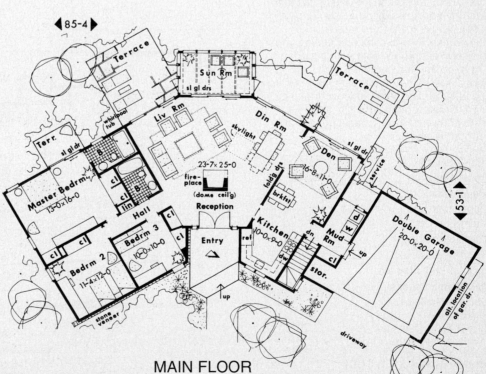

MAIN FLOOR

Classic Victorian

- This classic exterior is built around an interior that offers all the amenities desired by today's families.
- In from the covered front porch, the entry features a curved stairway and a glass-block wall to the dining room.
- A step down from the entry, the Great Room boasts a dramatic 24½-ft. cathedral ceiling and provides ample space for large family gatherings.
- The formal dining room is available for special occasions, while the 13-ft.-high breakfast nook serves everyday needs.
- The adjoining island kitchen offers plenty of counter space and opens to a handy utility room and a powder room.
- The deluxe main-floor master suite features a 14½-ft. cathedral ceiling and an opulent private bath with a garden spa tub and a separate shower.
- Upstairs, two secondary bedrooms share a full bath and a balcony overlooking the Great Room below.
- Plans for a two-car garage are available upon request.

Plan DW-2112

Bedrooms: 3	Baths: 2½
Living Area:	
Upper floor	514 sq. ft.
Main floor	1,598 sq. ft.
Total Living Area:	**2,112 sq. ft.**
Standard basement	1,598 sq. ft.
Exterior Wall Framing:	2x4

Foundation Options:
Standard basement
Crawlspace
Slab
(All plans can be built with your choice of foundation and framing. A generic conversion diagram is available. See order form.)

BLUEPRINT PRICE CODE:	C

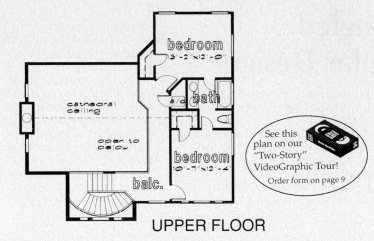

See this plan on our "Two-Story" VideoGraphic Tour! Order form on page 9

UPPER FLOOR

bedroom 13'-2"x12'-0"

cathedral ceiling

bath

open to below

bedroom 10'-7"x12'-4"

balc.

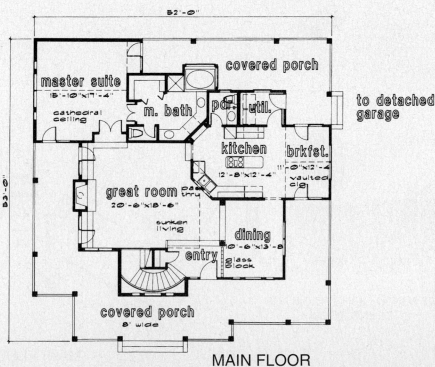

MAIN FLOOR

52'-0"

53'-0"

master suite 15'-10"x17'-4"

cathedral ceiling

covered porch

to detached garage

m. bath

pdr.

util.

kitchen 12'-8"x12'-4"

brkfst. 11'-0"x12'-4"

vaulted clg.

great room 20'-6"x18'-6"

pass thru

sunken living

dining 10'-6"x13'-8"

entry

glass block

covered porch 8' wide

Stylish and Compact

- This country-style home has a classic exterior and a space-saving and compact interior.
- A quaint covered porch extends along the front of the home. The oval-glassed front door opens to the entry, which leads to the spacious living room with a handsome fireplace, windows at either end and access to a big screened porch.
- The formal dining room flows from the living room and is easily served by the convenient U-shaped kitchen.
- A nice-sized laundry room and a full bath are nearby. The two-car garage offers a super storage area.
- The deluxe master suite features a huge walk-in closet. A separate dressing area leads to an adjoining, dual-access bath.
- The upper floor offers two more bedrooms and another full bath. Each bedroom has generous closet space and independent access to attic space.

Plan E-1626

Bedrooms: 3	Baths: 2
Living Area:	
Upper floor	464 sq. ft.
Main floor	1,136 sq. ft.
Total Living Area:	**1,600 sq. ft.**
Garage	462 sq. ft.
Exterior Wall Framing:	2x6

Foundation Options:

Crawlspace
Slab
(All plans can be built with your choice of foundation and framing. A generic conversion diagram is available. See order form.)

BLUEPRINT PRICE CODE: **B**

NOTE: The above photographed home may have been modified by the homeowner. Please refer to floor plan and/or drawn elevation shown for actual blueprint details.

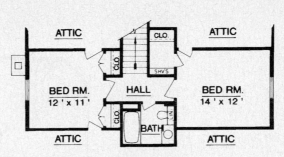

UPPER FLOOR

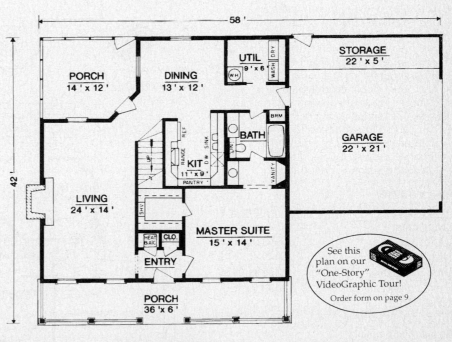

MAIN FLOOR

See this plan on our "One-Story" VideoGraphic Tour! Order form on page 9

Photo by Joshua McClure

Panoramic Porch

- A gracious, ornately rounded front porch and a two-story turreted bay lend Victorian charm to this home.
- A two-story foyer with round-top transom windows and a plant ledge above greets guests at the entry.
- The living room enjoys a 13-ft.-high ceiling and a panoramic view overlooking the front porch and yard.
- The formal dining room and den each feature a bay window for added style.
- The sunny kitchen incorporates an angled island cooktop with an eating bar to the bayed breakfast room.
- A step down, the family room offers a corner fireplace that may be enjoyed throughout the casual living spaces.
- The upper floor is highlighted by a stunning master suite, which flaunts an octagonal sitting area with a 10-ft. tray ceiling and turreted bay. The master bath offers a corner spa tub and a separate shower. Two additional bedrooms share another full bath.

Plan AX-90307

Bedrooms: 3+	Baths: 3
Living Area:	
Upper floor	956 sq. ft.
Main floor	1,499 sq. ft.
Total Living Area:	**2,455 sq. ft.**
Standard basement	1,499 sq. ft.
Garage	410 sq. ft.
Exterior Wall Framing:	2x4

Foundation Options:
Standard basement
Slab
(All plans can be built with your choice of foundation and framing.
A generic conversion diagram is available. See order form.)

BLUEPRINT PRICE CODE: C

NOTE:
The above photographed home may have been modified by the homeowner. Please refer to floor plan and/or drawn elevation shown for actual blueprint details.

See this plan on our "Best-Sellers" VideoGraphic Tour!
Order form on page 9

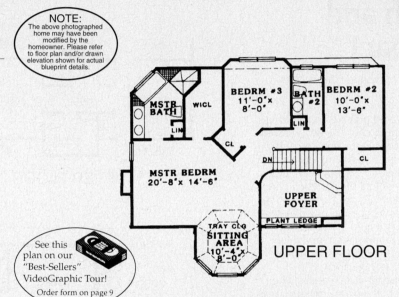

UPPER FLOOR

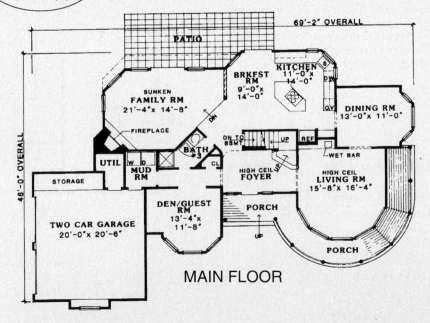

MAIN FLOOR

ORDER BLUEPRINTS ANYTIME!
CALL TOLL-FREE 1-888-626-2026

Plan AX-90307

*PRICES AND DETAILS
ON PAGES 13-15*

Luxurious Master Suite

- The inviting facade of this gorgeous one-story design boasts a sheltered porch, symmetrical architecture and elegant window treatments.
- Inside, beautiful arched openings frame the living room, which features a 12-ft. ceiling, a dramatic fireplace and a wet bar that is open to the deluxe kitchen.
- The roomy kitchen is highlighted by an island cooktop, a built-in desk and a snack bar that faces the bayed eating area and the covered back porch.
- Isolated to the rear of the home, the master suite is a romantic retreat, offering an intimate sitting area and a luxurious bath. Entered through elegant double doors, the private bath showcases a skylighted corner tub, a separate shower, his-and-hers vanities, and a huge walk-in closet.
- The two remaining bedrooms have walk-in closets and share a hall bath.
- Unless otherwise specified, the home has 9-ft. ceilings throughout.

Plan E-2106

Bedrooms: 3	Baths: 2
Living Area:	
Main floor	2,177 sq. ft.
Total Living Area:	**2,177 sq. ft.**
Standard basement	2,177 sq. ft.
Garage and storage	570 sq. ft.
Exterior Wall Framing:	2x4

Foundation Options:

Standard basement

Crawlspace

Slab

(All plans can be built with your choice of foundation and framing. A generic conversion diagram is available. See order form.)

BLUEPRINT PRICE CODE: C

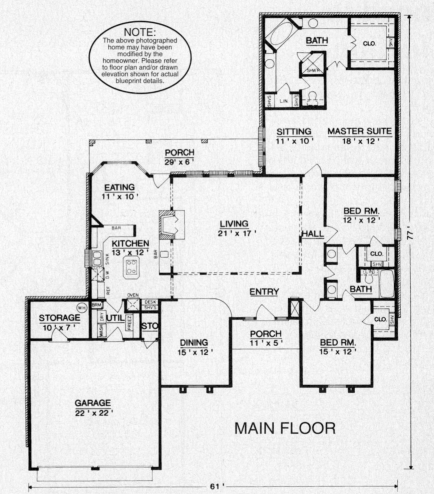

NOTE: The above photographed home may have been modified by the homeowner. Please refer to floor plan and/or drawn elevation shown for actual blueprint details.

MAIN FLOOR

BATH — CLO.

SITTING 11' x 10'   MASTER SUITE 18' x 12'

PORCH 29' x 6'

EATING 11' x 10'

LIVING 21' x 17'

BED RM. 12' x 12'

HALL

BAR

KITCHEN 13' x 12'

REF DW SINK

CLO.

ENTRY

BATH

STORAGE 10' x 7'

UTIL

STO

OVEN DESK

DINING 15' x 12'

PORCH 11' x 5'

BED RM. 15' x 12'

CLO.

GARAGE 22' x 22'

61'

77'

See this plan on our "Best-Sellers" VideoGraphic Tour!

Order form on page 9

Planned to Perfection

- This attractive and stylish home offers an interior design that is planned to perfection.
- The covered entry and vaulted foyer create an impressive welcome.
- The vaulted Great Room features a corner fireplace, a wet bar and lots of windows. The adjoining dining room offers a bay window and access to a covered patio.
- The gourmet kitchen includes an island cooktop, a garden window above the sink and a built-in desk. The attached nook is surrounded by windows that overlook a delightful planter.
- The master suite boasts a tray ceiling that rises to 9½ ft. and a peaceful reading area that accesses a private patio. The superb master bath features a garden tub and a separate shower.
- Two secondary bedrooms share a compartmentalized bath.

Plan S-4789

Bedrooms: 3	Baths: 2
Living Area:	
Main floor	1,665 sq. ft.
Total Living Area:	**1,665 sq. ft.**
Standard basement	1,665 sq. ft.
Garage	400 sq. ft.
Exterior Wall Framing:	2x6

Foundation Options:
Standard basement
Crawlspace
Slab
(All plans can be built with your choice of foundation and framing. A generic conversion diagram is available. See order form.)

BLUEPRINT PRICE CODE: B

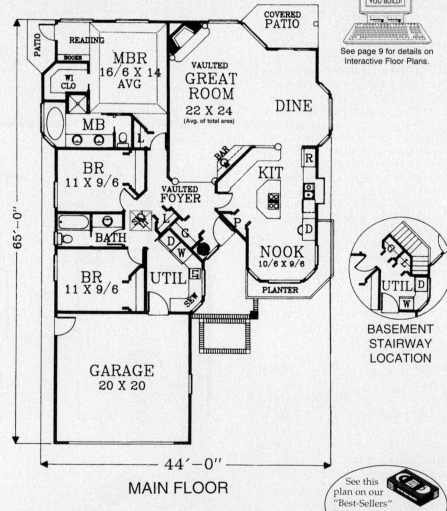

MAIN FLOOR

TOUR THIS HOME BEFORE YOU BUILD!

See page 9 for details on Interactive Floor Plans.

BASEMENT STAIRWAY LOCATION

See this plan on our "Best-Sellers" VideoGraphic Tour! Order form on page 9

Designed for Livability

- As you enter this excitingly spacious traditional home, you see through the extensive windows to the backyard.
- This four-bedroom home was designed for the livability of the maturing family with the separation of the master suite.
- The formal dining room expands spatially to the living room while being set off by a decorative column and plant shelves.
- The bay that creates the morning room and the sitting area for the master suite also adds excitement to this plan, both inside and out.
- The master bath offers an exciting oval tub under glass and a separate shower, as well as a spacious walk-in closet and a dressing area.

Plan DD-1696

Bedrooms: 4	Baths: 2
Living Area:	
Main floor	1,748 sq. ft.
Total Living Area:	**1,748 sq. ft.**
Standard basement	1,748 sq. ft.
Garage	393 sq. ft.
Exterior Wall Framing:	2x4

Foundation Options:

Standard basement

Crawlspace

Slab

(All plans can be built with your choice of foundation and framing. A generic conversion diagram is available. See order form.)

BLUEPRINT PRICE CODE:	B

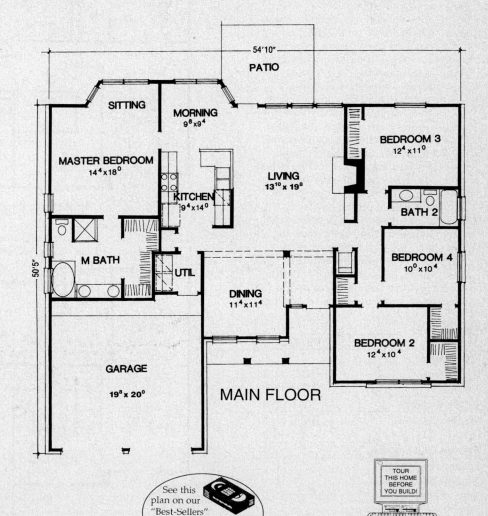

MAIN FLOOR

See this plan on our "Best-Sellers" VideoGraphic Tour! Order form on page 9

TOUR THIS HOME BEFORE YOU BUILD!

See page 9 for details on Interactive Floor Plans.

NOTE: The photographed home may have been modified by the homeowner. Please refer to floor plan and/or drawn elevation shown for actual blueprint details.

High Honors

- Because this home includes living spaces for all your needs—from formal evenings to quiet nights—it makes the grade as a family retreat.
- Inside, the two-story foyer ushers guests into the living room on the left. The close proximity of the living room to the dining room makes dinner parties flow simply and smoothly.
- Well suited to serve its role as the busiest room in the home, the kitchen features an island workstation. A wall of windows and a French door make the breakfast nook a cheery spot for coffee.
- For everyday life, the two-story family room provides the perfect setting. When the kids need a place to work on a school project or watch a movie with friends, this room fits the bill.
- The master suite upstairs beckons you to take a little extra time in the morning and enjoy. A 9-ft. tray ceiling lends elegance to the bedroom, while an 11-ft. ceiling adds drama to the bath.
- A 10-ft. vaulted ceiling opens up the good-sized fourth bedroom.

Plan FB-2055

Bedrooms: 4	Baths: 2½
Living Area:	
Upper floor	1,041 sq. ft.
Main floor	1,014 sq. ft.
Total Living Area:	**2,055 sq. ft.**
Daylight basement	1,014 sq. ft.
Garage	422 sq. ft.
Exterior Wall Framing:	2x4

Foundation Options:

Daylight basement
Crawlspace
Slab

(All plans can be built with your choice of foundation and framing. A generic conversion diagram is available. See order form.)

BLUEPRINT PRICE CODE:	C

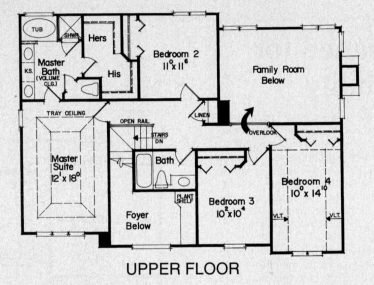

UPPER FLOOR

MAIN FLOOR

High Luxury in One Story

NOTE:
The above photographed home may have been modified by the homeowner. Please refer to floor plan and/or drawn elevation shown for actual blueprint details.

- Beautiful arched windows lend a luxurious feeling to the exterior of this one-story home.
- Soaring 12-ft. ceilings add volume to both the wide entry area and the central living room, which boasts a large fireplace and access to a covered porch and the patio beyond.
- Double doors separate the formal dining room from the corridor-style kitchen. Features of the kitchen include a pantry and an angled eating bar. The sunny, bayed eating area is perfect for casual family meals.
- The plush master suite has amazing amenities: a walk-in closet, a skylighted, angled whirlpool tub, a separate shower and private access to the laundry/utility room and the patio.
- Three good-sized bedrooms and a full bath are situated across the home.

Plan E-2302

Bedrooms: 4	Baths: 2
Living Area:	
Main floor	2,396 sq. ft.
Total Living Area:	**2,396 sq. ft.**
Standard basement	2,396 sq. ft.
Garage	484 sq. ft.
Exterior Wall Framing:	2x6

Foundation Options:

Standard basement

Crawlspace

Slab

(All plans can be built with your choice of foundation and framing. A generic conversion diagram is available. See order form.)

BLUEPRINT PRICE CODE: C

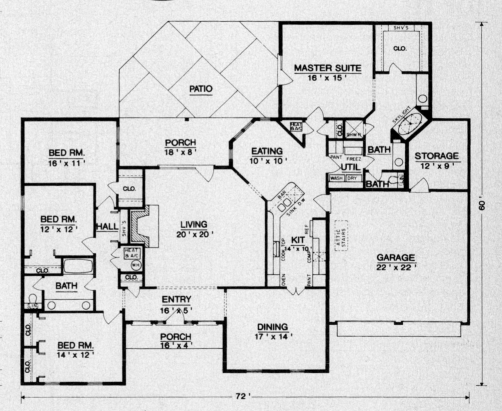

MAIN FLOOR

See this plan on our "Best-Sellers" VideoGraphic Tour!
Order form on page 9

You Asked for It!

- Our most popular plan in recent years, E-3000, has now been downsized for affordability, without sacrificing character or excitement.
- Exterior appeal is created with a covered front porch with decorative columns, triple dormers and rail-topped bay windows.
- The floor plan offers one spacious family room with corner fireplace, which flows into the dining room through a columned gallery.
- The kitchen serves the breakfast room over an angled snack bar, and features a huge pantry.
- The stunning main-floor master suite offers a private sitting area, a walk-in closet and a dramatic, angled bath.
- There are two large bedrooms upstairs accessible via a curved staircase with bridge balcony.

Plan E-2307

Bedrooms: 3	Baths: 2½
Living Area:	
Upper floor	595 sq. ft.
Main floor	1,765 sq. ft.
Total Living Area:	**2,360 sq. ft.**
Standard basement	1,765 sq. ft.
Garage	484 sq. ft.
Storage	44 sq. ft.
Exterior Wall Framing:	2x6

Foundation Options:

Standard basement
Crawlspace
Slab

(All plans can be built with your choice of foundation and framing. A generic conversion diagram is available. See order form.)

BLUEPRINT PRICE CODE: C

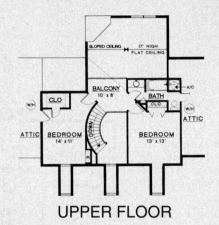

See this plan on our "Best-Sellers" VideoGraphic Tour!
Order form on page 9

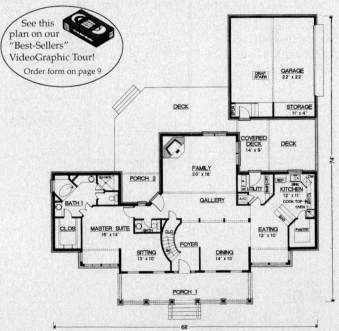

UPPER FLOOR

MAIN FLOOR

PLANS H-3711-1 & -1A
WITH GARAGE

PLANS H-3711-2 & -2A
WITHOUT GARAGE

All-American Country Home

- The covered wraparound porch of this popular all-American home creates an old-fashioned country appeal.
- Off the entryway is the generous-sized living room, which offers a fireplace and French doors that open to the porch.
- The large adjoining dining room further expands the entertaining area.
- The country kitchen has a handy island and flows into the cozy family room, which is enhanced by exposed beams. A handsome fireplace warms the entire informal area, while windows overlook the porch.
- The quiet upper floor hosts four good-sized bedrooms and two baths. The master suite includes a walk-in closet, a dressing area and a private bath with a sit-down shower.
- This home is available with or without a basement and with or without a garage.

See this plan on our "Best-Sellers" VideoGraphic Tour!
Order form on page 9

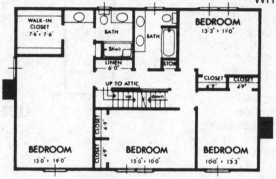

UPPER FLOOR

Plans H-3711-1, -1A, -2 & -2A

Bedrooms: 4	Baths: 2½
Living Area:	
Upper floor	1,176 sq. ft.
Main floor	1,288 sq. ft.
Total Living Area:	**2,464 sq. ft.**
Standard basement	1,176 sq. ft.
Garage	505 sq. ft.
Exterior Wall Framing:	2x6
Foundation Options:	**Plan #**
Basement with garage	H-3711-1
Basement without garage	H-3711-2
Crawlspace with garage	H-3711-1A
Crawlspace without garage	H-3711-2A

(All plans can be built with your choice of foundation and framing. A generic conversion diagram is available. See order form.)

BLUEPRINT PRICE CODE: C

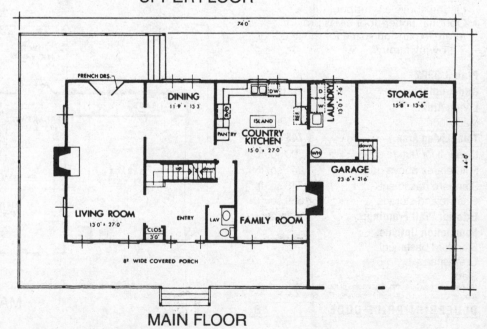

MAIN FLOOR

Breathtaking Open Space

- Soaring ceilings and an open floor plan add breathtaking volume to this charming country-style home.
- The inviting covered-porch entrance opens into the spacious living room, which boasts a spectacular 17-ft.-high cathedral ceiling. Two overhead dormers fill the area with natural light, while a fireplace adds warmth.
- Also under the cathedral ceiling, the kitchen and bayed breakfast room share an eating bar. Skylights brighten the convenient laundry room and the computer room, which provides access to a covered rear porch.
- The secluded master bedroom offers private access to another covered porch. The skylighted master bath has a walk-in closet and a 10-ft. sloped ceiling above a whirlpool tub.
- Optional upper-floor areas provide future expansion space for the needs of a growing family.

Plan J-9302

Bedrooms: 3+	Baths: 2
Living Area:	
Main floor	1,745 sq. ft.
Total Living Area:	**1,745 sq. ft.**
Upper floor (future area)	500 sq. ft.
Future area above garage	241 sq. ft.
Standard basement	1,745 sq. ft.
Garage and storage	559 sq. ft.
Exterior Wall Framing:	2x4

Foundation Options:

Standard basement

Crawlspace

Slab

(All plans can be built with your choice of foundation and framing. A generic conversion diagram is available. See order form.)

BLUEPRINT PRICE CODE:	B

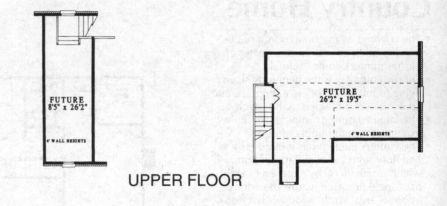

UPPER FLOOR

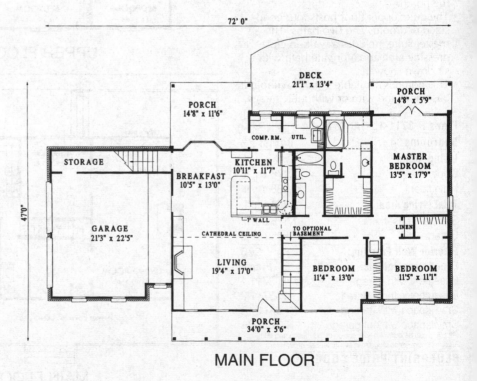

MAIN FLOOR

ORDER BLUEPRINTS ANYTIME!
CALL TOLL-FREE 1-888-626-2026

Plan J-9302

PRICES AND DETAILS
ON PAGES 13-15

Indoor/Outdoor Delights

- A curved porch in the front and a garden sun room in the back make this home an indoor/outdoor delight.
- Inside, a roomy kitchen is open to a five-sided, glassed-in dining room that views out to the porch.
- The living room features a fireplace along a glass wall that adjoins the gloriously sunny garden room.

- Wrapped in windows, the garden room accesses the backyard as well as a large storage area in the unobtrusive, side-entry garage.
- The master suite is no less luxurious, featuring a a sumptuous master bath with a garden spa tub, a corner shower and a walk-in closet.
- Each of the two remaining bedrooms has a boxed-out window and a walk-in closet. A full bath with a corner shower and a dual-sink vanity is close by.
- A stairway leads to the attic, which provides more potential living space.

Plan DD-1852	
Bedrooms: 3	**Baths:** 2
Living Area:	
Main floor	1,852 sq. ft.
Total Living Area:	**1,852 sq. ft.**
Standard basement	1,852 sq. ft.
Garage	528 sq. ft.
Exterior Wall Framing:	2x4
Foundation Options:	
Standard basement	
Crawlspace	
Slab	

(All plans can be built with your choice of foundation and framing. A generic conversion diagram is available. See order form.)

BLUEPRINT PRICE CODE:	B

Floor Plan

72⁶ wide × 52⁶ deep

GARDEN ROOM 24⁰ X 10⁰

STORAGE

M. BATH LINEN

MASTER BEDROOM 12⁴ X 15⁴

ATTIC

LIVING 20⁸ X 20⁰

GARAGE 22⁰ X 24⁰

UTIL.

BASEMENT

BEDROOM 3 11⁰ X 13⁰

BATH 2 LINEN

KITCHEN 12⁴ X 11⁴

DINING 12⁰ X 12⁰

ENTRY

BEDROOM 2 13⁰ X 11⁰

PORCH

MAIN FLOOR

Stunning Style

- The stunning detailing of this three-bedroom stucco home includes a stately roofline, round louvers and a sidelighted entry door topped with a half-round transom.
- The open floor plan begins at the foyer, where a decorative column is all that separates the dining room from the living room. Lovely French doors and windows overlook the backyard, while a 13½-ft. ceiling creates a dramatic effect for this spacious area.

- A sunny breakfast room and a great kitchen with a huge serving bar adjoin a 14½-ft.-high vaulted family room.
- A laundry/mudroom lies near the garage, which is supplemented by a handy storage or shop area.
- The opulent master suite has an 11-ft. tray ceiling, a rear window wall and a French door to the outdoors. The master bath includes a spa tub, a separate shower, a spacious walk-in closet and a dual-sink vanity with a sit-down makeup area. Another full bath serves the two remaining bedrooms.

Plan FB-1802	
Bedrooms: 3	**Baths: 2**
Living Area:	
Main floor	1,802 sq. ft.
Total Living Area:	**1,802 sq. ft.**
Garage and storage	492 sq. ft.
Exterior Wall Framing:	2x4

Foundation Options:

Crawlspace
Slab
(All plans can be built with your choice of foundation and framing. A generic conversion diagram is available. See order form.)

BLUEPRINT PRICE CODE: B

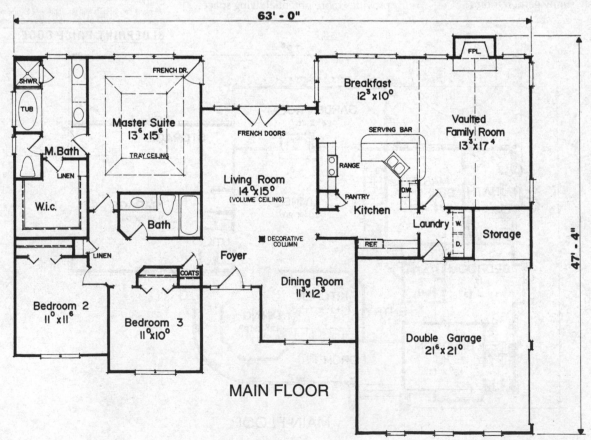

MAIN FLOOR

Plan FB-1802

PRICES AND DETAILS
ON PAGES 13-15

Interior Angles Add Excitement

- Interior angles add a touch of excitement to this one-story home.
- A pleasantly charming exterior combines wood and stone to give the plan a solid, comfortable look for any neighborhood.
- Formal living and dining rooms flank the entry, which leads into the large family room, featuring a fireplace, a

19-ft. high vaulted ceiling and built-in bookshelves. A covered porch and a sunny patio are just steps away.
- The adjoining eating area with a built-in china cabinet angles off the roomy kitchen. Note the pantry and the convenient utility room.
- The master bedroom suite is both spacious and private, and includes a dressing room, a large walk-in closet and a secluded bath.
- The three secondary bedrooms are also zoned for privacy, and share a compartmentalized bath.

Plan E-1904	
Bedrooms: 4	**Baths:** 2½
Living Area:	
Main floor	1,997 sq. ft.
Total Living Area:	**1,997 sq. ft.**
Garage	484 sq. ft.
Storage	104 sq. ft.
Exterior Wall Framing:	2x4
Foundation Options:	

Crawlspace
Slab
(All plans can be built with your choice of foundation and framing. A generic conversion diagram is available. See order form.)

BLUEPRINT PRICE CODE:	B

MAIN FLOOR

Nicely Done!

- An inviting window-covered exterior, coupled with an interior designed to give a sunny, open feel, will have you saying, "Nicely done!"
- Two eye-catching dormers, front-facing gables and two stately columns on the covered porch add a balanced sense of high style.
- The gallery, with its 13-ft. ceiling, presents guests with a dramatic entrance, and offers a gorgeous view into the huge Great Room through three elegantly inviting openings.

- The island kitchen will lure any gourmet. Nestled between the formal dining room and the breakfast room, it stands ready for all types of meals. Just steps away, the mudroom lets you keep an eye on the laundry while you cook.
- The lovely master bedroom greets you with an abundance of charms: an enormous walk-in closet, a private bath with a dual-sink vanity and a garden tub, plus convenient access to the large covered patio in back.
- That patio, you'll find, is the stuff of dreams—allowing you to enjoy outdoor meals come rain or shine!

Plan DD-2228

Bedrooms: 3	Baths: 2
Living Area:	
Main floor	2,228 sq. ft.
Total Living Area:	**2,228 sq. ft.**
Standard basement	2,228 sq. ft.
Garage	431 sq. ft.
Exterior Wall Framing:	2x4

Foundation Options:
Standard basement
Crawlspace
Slab
(All plans can be built with your choice of foundation and framing. A generic conversion diagram is available. See order form.)

BLUEPRINT PRICE CODE: C

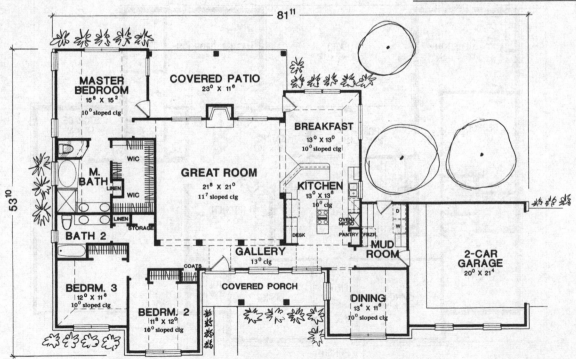

MAIN FLOOR

Plan DD-2228

Farmhouse for Today

- An inviting covered porch and decorative dormer windows lend traditional warmth and charm to this attractive design.
- The up-to-date interior includes ample space for entertaining as well as for daily family activities.
- The elegant foyer is flanked on one side by the formal, sunken living room and on the other by a sunken family room with a fireplace and an entertainment center. Each room features an 8½-ft. tray ceiling and views of the porch.
- The dining room flows from the living room to increase the entertaining space.
- The kitchen/nook/laundry area forms a large expanse for casual family living and domestic chores.
- Upstairs, the grand master suite includes a large closet and a private bath with a garden tub, a designer shower and a private deck.

Plan U-87-203

Bedrooms: 3	Baths: 2½
Living Area:	
Upper floor	857 sq. ft.
Main floor	1,064 sq. ft.
Total Living Area:	**1,921 sq. ft.**
Standard basement	1,064 sq. ft.
Garage	552 sq. ft.
Exterior Wall Framing:	2x4 or 2x6

Foundation Options:

Standard basement
Crawlspace
Slab

(All plans can be built with your choice of foundation and framing. A generic conversion diagram is available. See order form.)

BLUEPRINT PRICE CODE: B

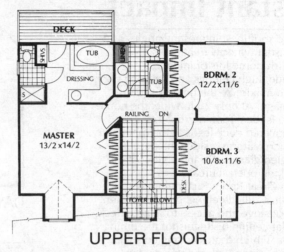

UPPER FLOOR

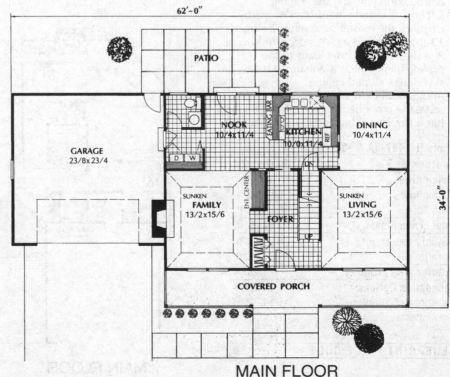

MAIN FLOOR

Instant Impact

- Bold rooflines, interesting angles and unusual window treatments give this stylish home lots of impact.
- Inside, high ceilings and an open floor plan maximize the home's square footage. At only 28 ft. wide, the home also is ideal for a narrow lot.
- A covered deck leads to the main entry, which features a sidelighted door, angled glass walls and a view of the striking open staircase.
- The Great Room is stunning, with its 16-ft. vaulted ceiling, energy-efficient woodstove and access to a large deck.
- A flat ceiling distinguishes the dining area, which shares an angled snack bar/cooktop with the step-saving kitchen. A laundry/mudroom is nearby.
- Upstairs, the master suite offers a sloped 13-ft. ceiling and a clerestory window. A walk-through closet leads to the private bath, which is enhanced by a skylighted, sloped ceiling.
- Another full bath and plenty of storage serve the other bedrooms, one of which has a sloped ceiling and a dual closet.

Plans H-1427-3A & -3B

Bedrooms: 3	Baths: 2½
Living Area:	
Upper floor	880 sq. ft.
Main floor	810 sq. ft.
Total Living Area:	**1,690 sq. ft.**
Daylight basement	810 sq. ft.
Garage	409 sq. ft.
Exterior Wall Framing:	**2x4**
Foundation Options:	**Plan #**
Daylight basement	H-1427-3B
Crawlspace	H-1427-3A

(All plans can be built with your choice of foundation and framing. A generic conversion diagram is available. See order form.)

BLUEPRINT PRICE CODE:	**B**

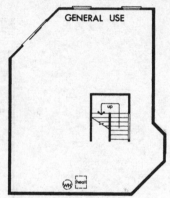

DAYLIGHT BASEMENT

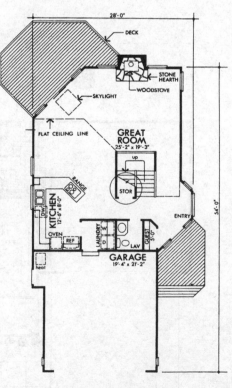

MAIN FLOOR

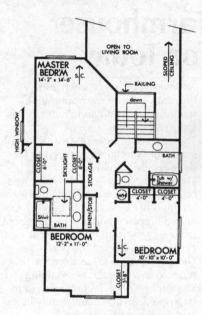

UPPER FLOOR

BASEMENT STAIRWAY LOCATION

See this plan on our "Best-Sellers" VideoGraphic Tour!
Order form on page 9

TOUR THIS HOME BEFORE YOU BUILD!

See page 9 for details on Interactive Floor Plans.

Elements of Elegance

- Elegant details adorn both the facade and the interior of this delightful home.
- A nostalgic covered porch introduces the sidelighted entry, which spills into the formal and informal gathering areas.
- To the left, the dramatic formal dining room is perfect for special meals.
- Double doors lead to a quiet study, warmed by its handsome fireplace and boxed-out window with curtains thrown open to the sun.
- Straight ahead, the ambience of the spacious family room is enhanced by a rustic corner fireplace and a stunning cathedral ceiling. French doors open to a comfortable screened porch, which accesses a deck only steps away.
- The island kitchen includes a long work island with a cooktop and generous cabinet space.
- A tray ceiling tops the master bedroom, which boasts private deck access. The master bath has a whirlpool garden tub separated from a shower by glass blocks.
- Two secondary bedrooms occupy the opposite side of the home.

Plan SDG-30616

Bedrooms: 3+	Baths: 2½
Living Area:	
Main floor	2,173 sq. ft.
Total Living Area:	**2,173 sq. ft.**
Screened porch	204 sq. ft.
Garage and storage	556 sq. ft.
Exterior Wall Framing:	2x4

Foundation Options:

Slab
(All plans can be built with your choice of foundation and framing.
A generic conversion diagram is available. See order form.)

BLUEPRINT PRICE CODE: C

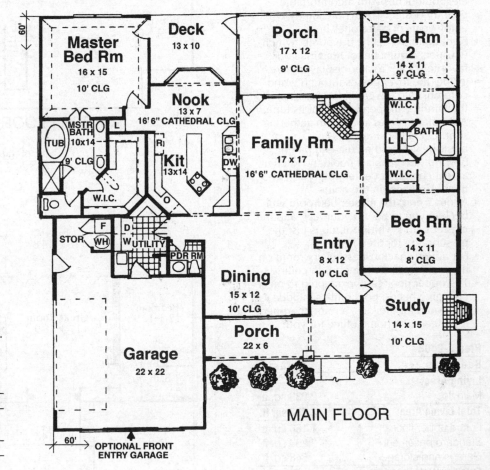

MAIN FLOOR

Family Values

- This family home masterfully blends elegant touches with a comfortable country design. The whole family will enjoy years of milestones here.
- Eight columns define the porch, which whispers a quiet hello. Imagine your favorite wicker rocker displayed here.
- Inside, the foyer passes through grand columns into the Great Room, where the family will spend much of its time. A fireplace serves as a warm gathering spot. On either side, built-in bookshelves hold media equipment.
- Beyond the breakfast nook and kitchen, a neat computer center could turn into the busiest spot in the home.
- At day's end, the master bedroom will beckon you to put up your feet, and the master bath's whirlpool tub is just the prescription for tired bones.
- For added spaciousness, every room on the main floor includes a 9-ft. ceiling.
- The upper floor can be adapted to meet changing needs; possibilities include a playroom for the kids, a mini-apartment for a teen or a home office for you.

Plan J-9408

Bedrooms: 3+	Baths: 2
Living Area:	
Main floor	2,233 sq. ft.
Total Living Area:	**2,233 sq. ft.**
Future upper floor	1,168 sq. ft.
Standard basement	2,233 sq. ft.
Garage and storage	548 sq. ft.
Exterior Wall Framing:	2x4

Foundation Options:

Standard basement

Crawlspace

Slab

(All plans can be built with your choice of foundation and framing. A generic conversion diagram is available. See order form.)

BLUEPRINT PRICE CODE:	C

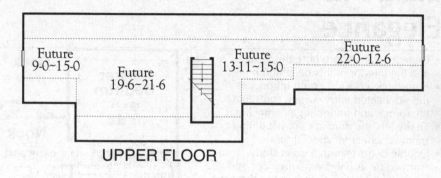

UPPER FLOOR

Future 9-0~15-0
Future 19-6~21-6
Future 13-11~15-0
Future 22-0~12-6

MAIN FLOOR

69-0

61-6

Patio 18-0~14-8
Master Bedroom 14-9~16-2
M.Bath 8-5~13-2
Bedroom 12-3~12-9
Great Room 17-3~18-9
Breakfast 10-6~10-4
Laun. 6-2~9-5
Comp. Desk
Storage 10-10~4-6
Kitchen 13-5~11-4
Bath
Garage 21-8~21-3
Bedroom 16-9~12-1
Foyer 8-8~14-9
Dining 13-5~12-1
Porch 29-0~6-6

Wonderful Windows

- This one-story's striking stucco and stone facade is enhanced by great gables and wonderful windows.
- A beautiful bay augments the living room/den, which can be closed off.
- A wall of windows lets sunbeams brighten the exquisite formal dining room, which is defined by decorative columns and a high 14-ft. ceiling.
- The spacious family room offers a handsome fireplace flanked by glass.
- The kitchen boasts a large pantry, a corner sink and two convenient serving bars. A 13-ft. vaulted ceiling presides over the adjoining breakfast room.
- A lovely window seat highlights one of the two secondary bedrooms, which are serviced by a full bath with a 13-ft., 10-in. vaulted ceiling.
- The magnificent master suite features a symmetrical tray ceiling that sets off an attractive round-top window. The elegant master bath offers a 15-ft.-high vaulted ceiling, a garden tub and dual vanities, one with knee space.
- Ceilings not specified are 9 ft. high.

Plan FB-5009-CHAD

Bedrooms: 3	Baths: 2
Living Area:	
Main floor	2,115 sq. ft.
Total Living Area:	**2,115 sq. ft.**
Daylight basement	2,115 sq. ft.
Garage and storage	535 sq. ft.
Exterior Wall Framing:	2x4
Foundation Options:	
Daylight basement	
Slab	

(All plans can be built with your choice of foundation and framing. A generic conversion diagram is available. See order form.)

BLUEPRINT PRICE CODE: C

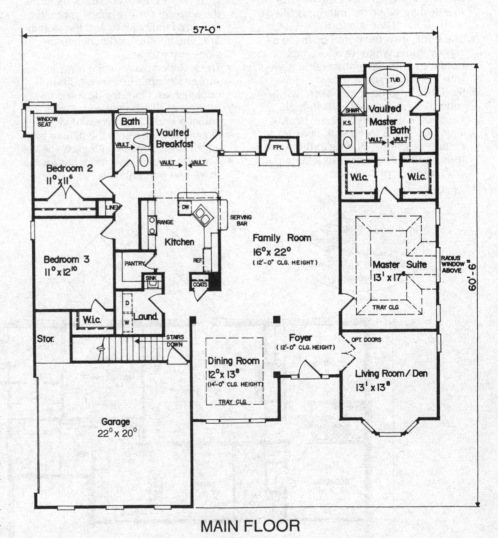

MAIN FLOOR

Rustic Comfort

- Rustic charm highlights the exterior of this design, while the interior is filled with all the latest comforts.
- The wide, covered porch opens to a roomy entry, where two 7-ft.-high openings with decorative railings view into the dining room.
- Straight ahead lies the sunken living room, which features a 16-ft.-high vaulted ceiling with exposed beams. The fireplace is faced with floor-to-ceiling fieldstone, adding to the rustic look. A rear door opens to a large patio with luscious plant areas.

- The large and functional U-shaped kitchen features a china niche with glass shelves. Other bonuses include the adjacent sewing/hobby room, the oversized utility room and the storage area and built-in workbench in the side-entry garage.
- The secluded master suite hosts a sunken sleeping area with built-in bookshelves. One step up is a cozy sitting area that is defined by brick columns and a railed room divider. Double doors open to the deluxe bath, which offers a niche with glass shelves.
- Across the home, two more bedrooms share a second full bath.

Plan E-1607

Bedrooms: 3	**Baths: 2**

Living Area:	
Main floor	1,600 sq. ft.
Total Living Area:	**1,600 sq. ft.**
Standard basement	1,600 sq. ft.
Garage	484 sq. ft.
Storage	132 sq. ft.
Exterior Wall Framing:	2x6

Foundation Options:
Standard basement
Crawlspace
Slab
(All plans can be built with your choice of foundation and framing. A generic conversion diagram is available. See order form.)

BLUEPRINT PRICE CODE: **B**

See this plan on our "Country & Traditional" Video Tour! Order form on page 9

MAIN FLOOR

Dramatic
Interior Spaces

- This home's design utilizes unique shapes and angles to create a dramatic and dynamic interior.
- Skylights brighten the impressive two-story entry from high above, as it flows to the formal living areas.
- The sunken Great Room features a massive stone-hearthed fireplace with flanking windows, plus a 19-ft. vaulted ceiling. Sliding glass doors open the formal dining room to a backyard patio.
- The spacious kitchen features an oversized island, plenty of counter space and a sunny breakfast nook.
- A den or third bedroom shares a full bath with another secondary bedroom to complete the main floor.
- An incredible bayed master suite takes up the entire upper floor of the home. The skylighted master bath features a bright walk-in closet, a dual-sink vanity, a sunken tub and a separate shower.

Plans P-6580-3A & -3D

Bedrooms: 2+	Baths: 2
Living Area:	
Upper floor	705 sq. ft.
Main floor	1,738 sq. ft.
Total Living Area:	**2,443 sq. ft.**
Daylight basement	1,738 sq. ft.
Garage	512 sq. ft.
Exterior Wall Framing:	2x4
Foundation Options:	**Plan #**
Daylight basement	P-6580-3D
Crawlspace	P-6580-3A

(All plans can be built with your choice of foundation and framing. A generic conversion diagram is available. See order form.)

BLUEPRINT PRICE CODE:	C

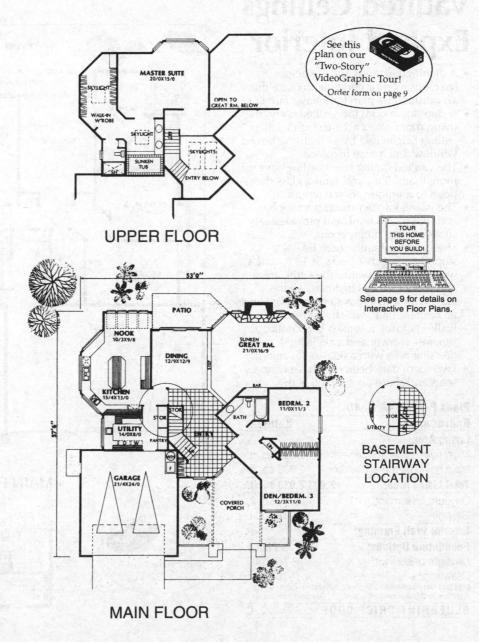

UPPER FLOOR

MAIN FLOOR

See this plan on our "Two-Story" VideoGraphic Tour!
Order form on page 9

TOUR THIS HOME BEFORE YOU BUILD!
See page 9 for details on Interactive Floor Plans.

BASEMENT STAIRWAY LOCATION

Vaulted Ceilings Expand Interior

- A dignified exterior and a gracious, spacious interior combine to make this an outstanding plan for today's families.
- A step down from the vaulted entry, the living room offers a 12-ft.-high vaulted ceiling brightened by an arch-top boxed window and a nice fireplace.
- The vaulted dining room ceiling rises to more than 15 ft., and sliding glass doors open to a unique central atrium.
- The island kitchen shares a snack bar with the bayed nook and provides easy service to the dining room.
- The spacious family room boasts a sloped ceiling that peaks at 18 ft. and a woodstove that warms the entire area.
- The master suite is first-class all the way, with a spacious sleeping room and an opulent bath, which features a walk-in closet, a sunken garden tub, a separate shower and a skylighted dressing area with a dual-sink vanity.
- Two secondary bedrooms have window seats and share another full bath.

Plans P-7697-4A & -4D

Bedrooms: 3	Baths: 2

Living Area:

Main floor (crawlspace version)	2,003 sq. ft.
Main floor (basement version)	2,030 sq. ft.
Total Living Area:	**2,003/2,030 sq. ft.**
Daylight basement	2,015 sq. ft.
Garage	647 sq. ft.
Exterior Wall Framing:	**2x6**

Foundation Options:	**Plan #**
Daylight basement	P-7697-4D
Crawlspace	P-7697-4A

(All plans can be built with your choice of foundation and framing. A generic conversion diagram is available. See order form.)

BLUEPRINT PRICE CODE: **C**

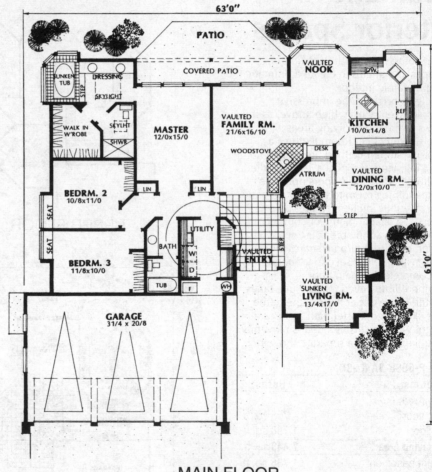

MAIN FLOOR

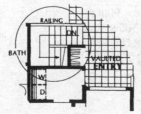

See this plan on our "Best-Sellers" VideoGraphic Tour! Order form on page 9

BASEMENT STAIRWAY LOCATION

Plans P-7697-4A & -4D

PRICES AND DETAILS
ON PAGES 13-15

Spacious Country-Style

- This distinctive country-style home is highlighted by a wide front porch and multi-paned windows with shutters.
- Inside, the dining room is off the foyer and open to the living room, but is defined by elegant columns and beams above.
- The central living room boasts a 12-ft. cathedral ceiling, a fireplace and French doors to the rear patio.
- The delightful kitchen/nook area is spacious and well planned for both work and play.
- A handy utility room and a half-bath are on either side of a short hallway leading to the carport, which includes a large storage area.
- The master suite offers his-and-hers walk-in closets and an incredible bath that incorporates a plant shelf above the raised spa tub.
- The two remaining bedrooms share a hall bath that is compartmentalized to allow more than one user at a time.

Plan J-86140

Bedrooms: 3	Baths: 2½
Living Area:	
Main floor	2,177 sq. ft.
Total Living Area:	**2,177 sq. ft.**
Standard basement	2,177 sq. ft.
Carport	440 sq. ft.
Storage	120 sq. ft.
Exterior Wall Framing:	2x4
Foundation Options:	
Standard basement	
Crawlspace	
Slab	

(All plans can be built with your choice of foundation and framing. A generic conversion diagram is available. See order form.)

BLUEPRINT PRICE CODE: C

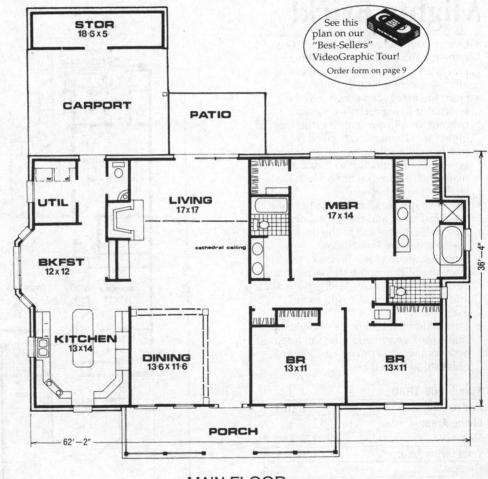

MAIN FLOOR

Mighty Cozy, Mighty Brick!

- Cozier confines can't be found! This one-story brick design's warmth and practicality will be mighty appealing to any prospective home owner.
- From the foyer, step down into the enormous living room—a natural magnet for all your family gatherings. Its impressive fireplace is flanked by a handy media center, while a convenient serving bar connects it to the kitchen. A plant shelf above the bar adds the charm of lush greenery.
- The U-shaped kitchen serves both the breakfast nook and the formal dining area, which steps out to the back patio via an attractive French door.
- A huge walk-in closet is one of the many highlights in the stylish master bedroom. A luxurious, and private, bath and access to the patio add to its excitement.
- Two additional bedrooms allow enough space for a growing family; the foremost bedroom would convert easily into a quiet study if need be.

Plan L-509-TRAD

Bedrooms: 2+	Baths: 2
Living Area:	
Main floor	1,529 sq. ft.
Total Living Area:	**1,529 sq. ft.**
Garage	452 sq. ft.
Exterior Wall Framing:	2x4

Foundation Options:

Slab

(All plans can be built with your choice of foundation and framing. A generic conversion diagram is available. See order form.)

BLUEPRINT PRICE CODE: B

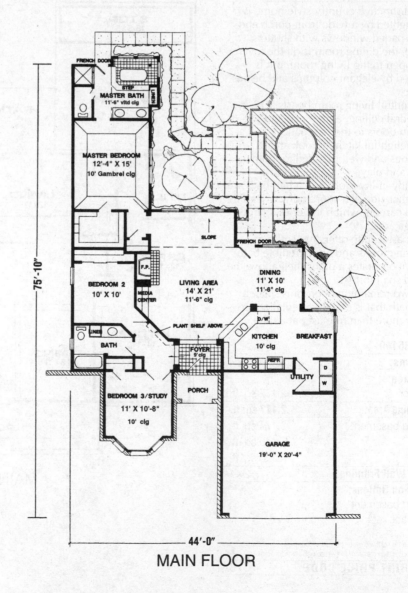

MAIN FLOOR

ORDER BLUEPRINTS ANYTIME!
CALL TOLL-FREE 1-888-626-2026

Plan L-509-TRAD

PRICES AND DETAILS
ON PAGES 13-15

Living on Four Levels

- Perfect for a narrow or side-sloping lot, this charming transitional home offers four levels of excitement.
- The entry, and the combined living and dining rooms share a 16-ft. vaulted ceiling on the home's main level.
- The adjacent kitchen includes a great snack bar and a pantry. An open railing in the adjoining bay-windowed breakfast nook overlooks the family room. The nook also provides a convenient built-in desk.

- The family room boasts a 17-ft. vaulted ceiling and a handsome fireplace as it sits one level below the dining room and nook. Sliding glass doors open to a backyard patio. A half-bath and access to the garage are nearby.
- Upstairs, a railed balcony bridge overlooks the family and living rooms.
- Two bedrooms with window seats are serviced by a full bath. The convenient upper-floor laundry room minimizes trips up and down the stairs.
- Double doors lead into the secluded master suite of the highest level. The master bath flaunts a soothing whirlpool tub, a separate shower and a roomy walk-in closet.

Plan AG-1902

Bedrooms: 3	Baths: 2½
Living Area:	
Upper floor	860 sq. ft.
Main floor	1,070 sq. ft.
Total Living Area:	**1,930 sq. ft.**
Partial basement	800 sq. ft.
Garage	424 sq. ft.
Exterior Wall Framing:	2x4

Foundation Options:

Partial basement
(All plans can be built with your choice of foundation and framing. A generic conversion diagram is available. See order form.)

BLUEPRINT PRICE CODE:	B

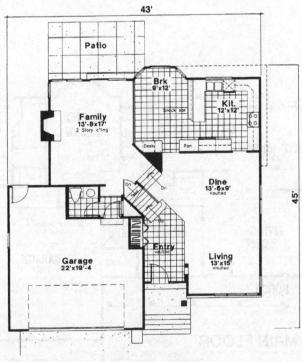

MAIN FLOOR

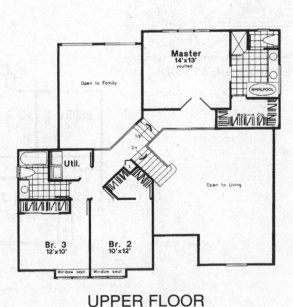

UPPER FLOOR

While Away an Afternoon

- The pretty porch that stretches along the front of this traditional home provides plenty of room for sitting and whiling away an afternoon. Try a porch swing on one end and a cluster of comfortable wicker furniture on the other.
- Inside, handsome columns introduce the living room and the dining room, on either side of the foyer. A 10-ft. tray ceiling lends a touch of elegance to the living room, while the open relationship to the dining room consolidates formal affairs in one impressive space.
- At the rear, the Great Room, the breakfast nook and the kitchen flow into one another, creating an easygoing, casual spot for family fun. In the Great Room, a neat media wall holds the TV, the VCR and the stereo. An angled fireplace adds a bit of rustic charm to the setting.
- Tucked away for privacy, the master bedroom provides a pleasant retreat. A stepped ceiling crowns the room, while a bay window serves as a sitting area.

Plan AX-5374	
Bedrooms: 3	**Baths:** 2
Living Area:	
Main floor	1,902 sq. ft.
Total Living Area:	**1,902 sq. ft.**
Standard basement	1,925 sq. ft.
Garage and storage	552 sq. ft.
Exterior Wall Framing:	2x4

Foundation Options:
Standard basement
Crawlspace
Slab
(All plans can be built with your choice of foundation and framing. A generic conversion diagram is available. See order form.)

BLUEPRINT PRICE CODE:	B

VIEW INTO GREAT ROOM

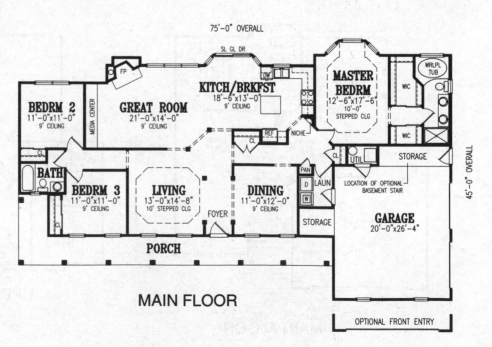

MAIN FLOOR

Plan AX-5374

PRICES AND DETAILS
ON PAGES 13-15

Sensible and Sun-Drenched!

- This brilliant design combines lots of open, vaulted space with an abundance of windows to maximize its exquisite sun-drenched feel.
- The well-equipped kitchen features a handy snack bar, plus easy access to the dinette and the formal dining room, both of which are highlighted by warmly elegant, curved glass walls.
- Laundry facilities are conveniently located in the handy mudroom just off the kitchen.
- Your favorite room may well be the vaulted family room, with its cozy fireplace, adjoining terrace and romantic skylight.
- Clerestory windows above provide an interesting and dramatic use of light for the dining and living rooms.
- A private terrace is a unique feature of the deluxe master suite, which also includes a large walk-in closet and a secluded bath boasting a whirlpool tub.
- A full bath services two secondary bedrooms, which are brightened by large, beautiful boxed-out windows.

Plan K-818-D

Bedrooms: 3	Baths: 2½
Living Area:	
Main floor	1,674 sq. ft.
Total Living Area:	**1,674 sq. ft.**
Standard basement	1,627 sq. ft.
Garage	486 sq. ft.
Exterior Wall Framing:	2x4 or 2x6

Foundation Options:

Standard basement

Slab

(All plans can be built with your choice of foundation and framing. A generic conversion diagram is available. See order form.)

BLUEPRINT PRICE CODE:	B

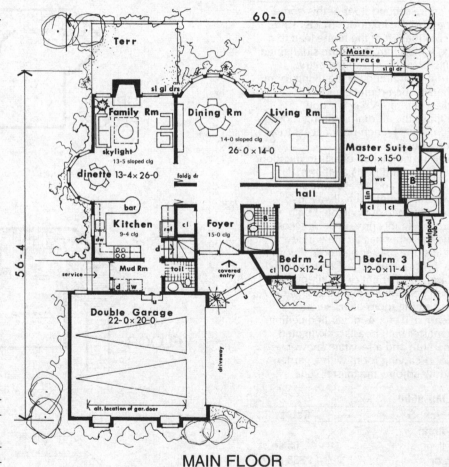

MAIN FLOOR

Masterful Suite

- The entire second floor of this home belongs to the luxurious master suite!
- Stairs to the left of the home lead to a deck, which introduces the sidelighted, 12-ft., 11-in.-high vaulted entry.
- Natural light drenches the living room, with its rustic fireplace and 17-ft., 5-in. vaulted ceiling. A bay window beautifies the adjoining dining room, which offers French-door access to a second deck.
- The gourmet kitchen boasts tremendous space. Its island hosts an informal breakfast bar and a vegetable sink.
- Down the skylighted hallway, two bedrooms share a skylighted bath. One bedroom flaunts private deck access, while the other has a cute window seat.
- Upstairs, the master bedroom enjoys a cozy fireplace under a 12½-ft. vaulted ceiling. To the right of the fireplace, a French door opens to a private deck. A bayed sitting room offers serenity beneath a 10-ft., 4-in. vaulted ceiling.
- The master bath boasts a skylighted garden tub and a separate shower.
- A wood-carving room with a garden window adjoins the master suite.

Plan LMB-9600

Bedrooms: 3	Baths: 2½

Living Area:

Upper floor	763 sq. ft.
Main floor	1,338 sq. ft.
Daylight basement	68 sq. ft.
Total Living Area:	**2,169 sq. ft.**
Tuck-under garage and storage	780 sq. ft.
Exterior Wall Framing:	2x6

Foundation Options:

Daylight basement

(All plans can be built with your choice of foundation and framing. A generic conversion diagram is available. See order form.)

BLUEPRINT PRICE CODE:	C

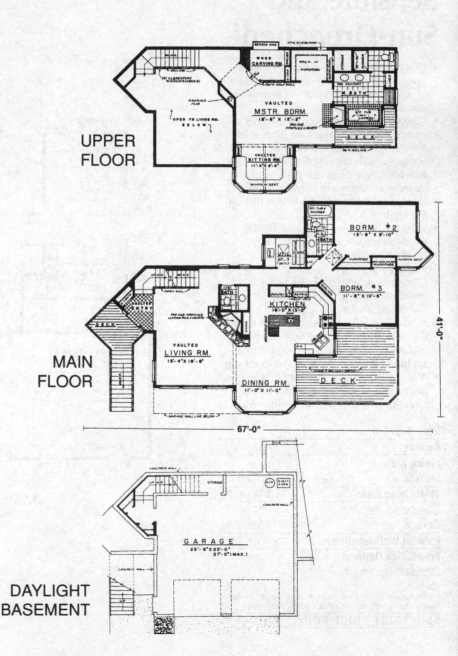

UPPER FLOOR

MAIN FLOOR

DAYLIGHT BASEMENT

Deluxe Suite!

- Decorative corner quoins, arched windows and a sleek hip roofline give this charming home a European look.
- The inviting foyer extends its 12-ft. ceiling into the formal spaces. The airy living room is brightened by high half- and quarter-round windows.
- The adjoining formal dining room is set off with elegant columned openings and high plant shelves.
- The island kitchen features a pantry and a sunny breakfast bay. A pass-through over the sink serves the family room.
- Boasting a 17-ft. vaulted ceiling and a glass-flanked fireplace, the family room also enjoys backyard access.
- The deluxe master suite includes a private sitting room. Both the bedroom and the sitting room have an 11-ft. tray ceiling and a view of a romantic two-sided fireplace. The master bath boasts a 13½-ft. vaulted ceiling, a garden tub, a three-sided mirror and a dual-sink vanity with knee space.
- A second bath is shared by the two remaining bedrooms.
- Unless otherwise noted, all rooms have 9-ft. ceilings.

Plan FB-5154-GEOR

Bedrooms: 3	Baths: 2½
Living Area:	
Main floor	2,236 sq. ft.
Total Living Area:	**2,236 sq. ft.**
Daylight basement	2,236 sq. ft.
Garage	483 sq. ft.
Exterior Wall Framing:	2x4

Foundation Options:

Daylight basement

Crawlspace

(All plans can be built with your choice of foundation and framing. A generic conversion diagram is available. See order form.)

BLUEPRINT PRICE CODE:	C

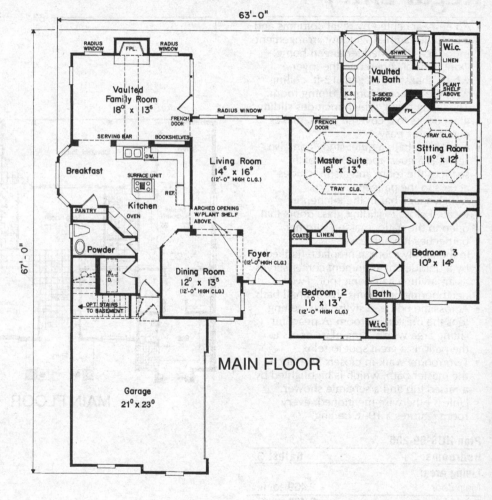

MAIN FLOOR

Regal Entry

- An entry accented by regal columns and a beautiful arched window arrangement introduces this Mediterranean home.
- Double doors open into the foyer, which shares an elegant 12-ft. ceiling with the adjacent formal dining room. The living room, which includes sliding glass doors to a covered patio, makes entertaining easy.
- Across the hall, a quiet study can also serve as a guest room. A full bath services the room and also includes access to the patio.
- A high snack bar in the kitchen is located close to sliding glass doors that open to the patio, making summer barbecues fun and easy.
- In the family room, a fireplace flanked by a unique entertainment center serves as an inviting gathering spot. Two neighboring bedrooms share a hall bath.
- Across the home, a stylish tray ceiling tops the master bedroom. A peaceful sitting area with sliding glass doors to the patio is a great spot to relax.
- Two roomy walk-in closets introduce the master bath, which is highlighted by a raised tub and a separate shower.
- Unless otherwise mentioned, every room features a 10-ft. ceiling.

Plan HDS-99-205

Bedrooms: 3+	Baths: 3
Living Area:	
Main floor	2,409 sq. ft.
Total Living Area:	**2,409 sq. ft.**
Garage	495 sq. ft.
Exterior Wall Framing:	8-in. concrete block

Foundation Options:

Slab
(All plans can be built with your choice of foundation and framing. A generic conversion diagram is available. See order form.)

BLUEPRINT PRICE CODE: **C**

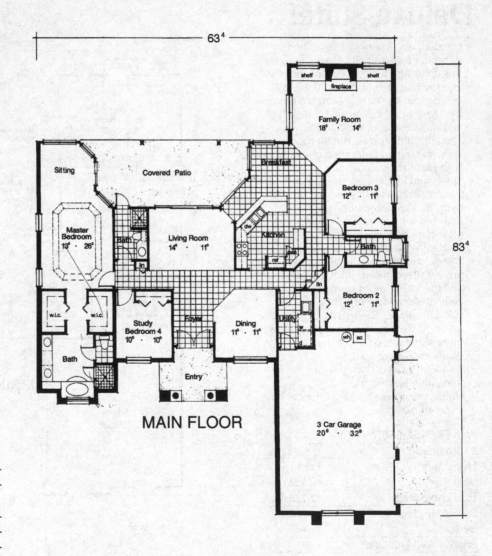

MAIN FLOOR

Cozy Covered Porches

- Twin dormers give this raised one-story design the appearance of a two-story. Two covered porches and a deck supplement the main living areas with plenty of outdoor entertaining space.
- The large central living room features a dramatic fireplace, a 12-ft. ceiling with a skylight and access to both porch areas.
- Double doors open to a bayed eating area, which overlooks the adjoining deck and includes a sloped ceiling that rises to 12 ft. in the kitchen. An angled snack bar and a pantry are also featured.
- The elegant master suite is tucked to one side of the home and also overlooks the backyard and deck. Laundry facilities and garage access are nearby.
- Across the home, two additional bedrooms share another full bath.

Plan E-1826

Bedrooms: 3	Baths: 2
Living Area:	
Main floor	1,800 sq. ft.
Total Living Area:	**1,800 sq. ft.**
Garage	550 sq. ft.
Storage	84 sq. ft.
Exterior Wall Framing:	2x6

Foundation Options:

Crawlspace
Slab
(All plans can be built with your choice of foundation and framing. A generic conversion diagram is available. See order form.)

BLUEPRINT PRICE CODE:	B

MAIN FLOOR

See this plan on our "Country & Traditional" Video Tour! Order form on page 9

Classic Styling

- Classic styling transcends the exterior and interior of this sprawling one-story.
- Outside, sweeping rooflines, arched windows and brick planters combine for an elegant curb appeal.
- The angled entry opens to a tiled foyer, which overlooks the spacious central living room. A handsome fireplace and a string of windows lend light and volume to this high-profile area.

- Unfolding to the right, the kitchen and dining room flow together, making the space seem even larger. A snack counter, bar sink and corner pantry are attractive kitchen efficiencies.
- The master suite is drenched in luxury with a romantic fireplace, a private porch and a grand Jacuzzi bath with lush surrounding plant shelves.
- Two good-sized secondary bedrooms share another full bath.
- Extra storage is offered in the garage.

Plan L-824-EMB

Bedrooms: 3	**Baths:** 2

Living Area:

Main floor	1,826 sq. ft.
Total Living Area:	**1,826 sq. ft.**
Garage and storage	534 sq. ft.
Exterior Wall Framing:	2x4

Foundation Options:

Slab
(All plans can be built with your choice of foundation and framing. A generic conversion diagram is available. See order form.)

BLUEPRINT PRICE CODE:	**B**

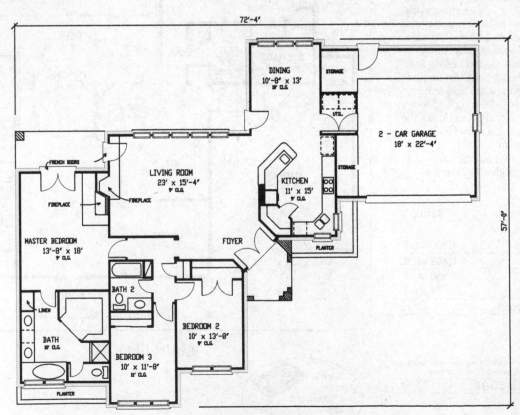

MAIN FLOOR

Plan L-824-EMB

PRICES AND DETAILS
ON PAGES 13-15

High Interest!

- Angles, high ceilings and an excellent use of space add interest and volume to the living areas of this efficient four-bedroom home.

- Beyond the beautiful stucco facade, the spacious central living room extends a warm welcome with its handsome fireplace; a French door whisks you outside to the covered back porch.

- The kitchen and breakfast room's unique designs ensure easy access and mobility for the family.

- A giant-sized walk-in closet, a separate dressing room and an adjoining bath pamper you in the secluded master suite. The bath conveniently opens to the utility room, which houses the washer and dryer and an extra freezer.

- Three more bedrooms share another bath at the opposite end of the home.

- To the rear of the garage, a handy storage room and a built-in workbench help to organize your lawn and maintenance equipment.

Plan E-1828

Bedrooms: 4	Baths: 2
Living Area:	
Main floor	1,828 sq. ft.
Total Living Area:	**1,828 sq. ft.**
Standard basement	1,828 sq. ft.
Garage	605 sq. ft.
Storage	120 sq. ft.
Exterior Wall Framing:	2x6

Foundation Options:

Standard basement

Crawlspace

Slab

(All plans can be built with your choice of foundation and framing. A generic conversion diagram is available. See order form.)

BLUEPRINT PRICE CODE: B

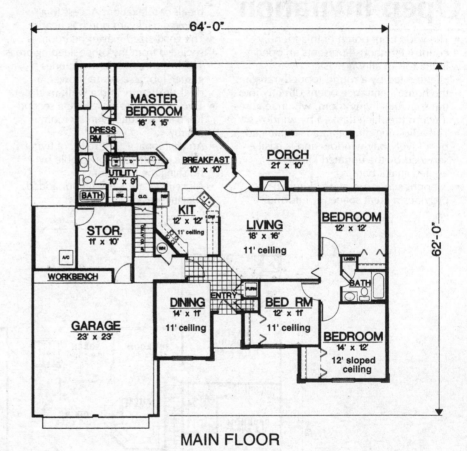

MAIN FLOOR

Open Invitation

- The wide front porch of this friendly country farmhouse presents an open invitation to all who visit.
- Highlighted by a round-topped transom, the home's entrance opens directly into the spacious living room, which features a warm fireplace flanked by windows.
- The adjoining dining area is enhanced by a lovely bay window and is easily serviced by the updated kitchen's angled snack bar.
- A bright sun room off the kitchen provides a great space for informal

meals or relaxation. Access to a covered backyard porch is nearby.
- The good-sized master bedroom is secluded from the other sleeping areas. The lavish master bath includes a garden tub, a separate shower, a dual-sink vanity and a walk-in closet.
- Two more bedrooms share a second full bath. A laundry/utility room is nearby.
- An additional 1,007 sq. ft. of living space can be made available by finishing the upper floor.
- All ceilings are 9 ft. high for added spaciousness.

Plan J-91078	
Bedrooms: 3	**Baths: 2**
Living Area:	
Main floor	1,846 sq. ft.
Total Living Area:	**1,846 sq. ft.**
Future upper floor	1,007 sq. ft.
Standard basement	1,846 sq. ft.
Garage	484 sq. ft.
Exterior Wall Framing:	2x6

Foundation Options:
Standard basement
Crawlspace
Slab
(All plans can be built with your choice of foundation and framing. A generic conversion diagram is available. See order form.)

BLUEPRINT PRICE CODE:	B

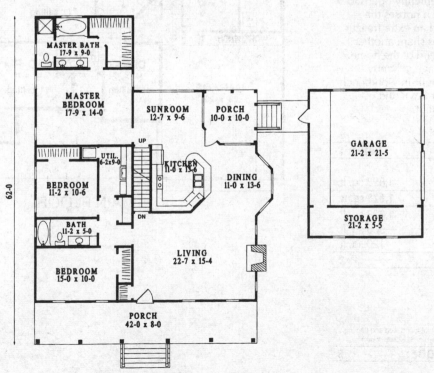

MAIN FLOOR

Plan J-91078

PRICES AND DETAILS
ON PAGES 13-15

Strength of Character

- The solid, permanent feel of brick and the intelligent, efficient floor plan of this stately one story home give it an obvious strength of character.
- Guests are welcomed inside by an attractive raised foyer, from which virtually any room can be reached with just a few steps.
- With a high ceiling, a built-in bookcase, a gorgeous fireplace and French doors that lead to the backyard, the centrally located living room is well equipped to serve as a hub of activity.
- Smartly designed and positioned, the galley-style kitchen easily serves the cozy breakfast nook and the formal dining room.
- The beautiful master bedroom provides a nice blend of elegance and seclusion, and features a striking stepped ceiling, a large walk-in closet, a private bath and its own access to the backyard.
- Two additional bedrooms feature walk-in closets and share a full-sized bath.

Plan L-851-A

Bedrooms: 3	Baths: 2
Living Area:	
Main floor	1,849 sq. ft.
Total Living Area:	**1,849 sq. ft.**
Garage	437 sq. ft.
Exterior Wall Framing:	2x4

Foundation Options:
Slab
(All plans can be built with your choice of foundation and framing. A generic conversion diagram is available. See order form.)

BLUEPRINT PRICE CODE: B

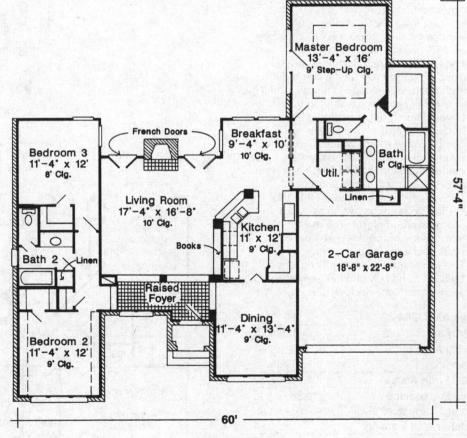

MAIN FLOOR

Bedroom 3
11'-4" x 12'
8' Clg.

French Doors

Breakfast
9'-4" x 10'
10' Clg.

Master Bedroom
13'-4" x 16'
9' Step-Up Clg.

Bath
8' Clg.

Util.

Linen

Living Room
17'-4" x 16'-8"
10' Clg.

Kitchen
11' x 12'
9' Clg.

Books

Bath 2

Linen

2-Car Garage
18'-8" x 22'-8"

Raised Foyer

Bedroom 2
11'-4" x 12'
9' Clg.

Dining
11'-4" x 13'-4"
9' Clg.

60'

57'-4"

Classic Ranch

- With decorative brick quoins, a columned porch and stylish dormers, the exterior of this classic one-story provides an interesting blend of Early American and European design.
- Flowing from the foyer, the bay-windowed dining room is enhanced by an 11½-ft.-high stepped ceiling.
- The spacious Great Room, separated from the dining room by a columned arch, features a stepped ceiling, a built-in media center and a striking fireplace. Lovely French doors lead to a big backyard patio.
- The breakfast room, which shares an eating bar with the kitchen, boasts a ceiling that slopes to 12 feet. French doors access a covered rear porch.
- The master bedroom has a 10-ft. tray ceiling, a sunny bay window and a roomy walk-in closet. The master bath features a whirlpool tub in a bayed nook and a separate shower.
- The front-facing bedroom is enhanced by a 10-ft.-high vaulted area over an arched transom window.

Plan AX-93304

Bedrooms: 3	Baths: 2
Living Area:	
Main floor	1,860 sq. ft.
Total Living Area:	**1,860 sq. ft.**
Standard basement	1,860 sq. ft.
Garage/utility/storage	434 sq. ft.
Exterior Wall Framing:	2x4

Foundation Options:
Standard basement
Crawlspace
Slab
(All plans can be built with your choice of foundation and framing. A generic conversion diagram is available. See order form.)

BLUEPRINT PRICE CODE:	B

VIEW INTO GREAT ROOM

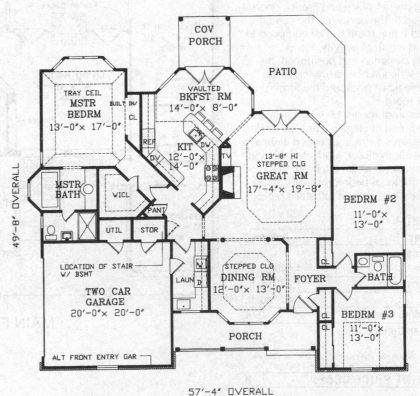

MAIN FLOOR

Plan AX-93304

PRICES AND DETAILS
ON PAGES 13-15

Impressive Master Suite

- This attractive one-story home features an impressive master suite located apart from the secondary bedrooms.
- A lovely front porch opens to the entry, which flows to the formal dining room, the rear-oriented living room and the secondary bedroom wing.
- The living room boasts a large corner fireplace, a ceiling that slopes to 11 ft. and access to a backyard patio.
- A U-shaped kitchen services the dining room and its own eating area. It also boasts a built-in desk, a handy pantry closet and access to the nearby laundry room and carport.
- The wide master bedroom hosts a lavish master bath with a spa tub, a separate shower and his-and-hers dressing areas.
- Across the home, the two secondary bedrooms share another full bath.

Plan E-1818

Bedrooms: 3	Baths: 2
Living Area:	
Main floor	1,868 sq. ft.
Total Living Area:	**1,868 sq. ft.**
Carport	484 sq. ft.
Storage	132 sq. ft.
Exterior Wall Framing:	2x6

Foundation Options:

Crawlspace

Slab

(All plans can be built with your choice of foundation and framing. A generic conversion diagram is available. See order form.)

BLUEPRINT PRICE CODE: B

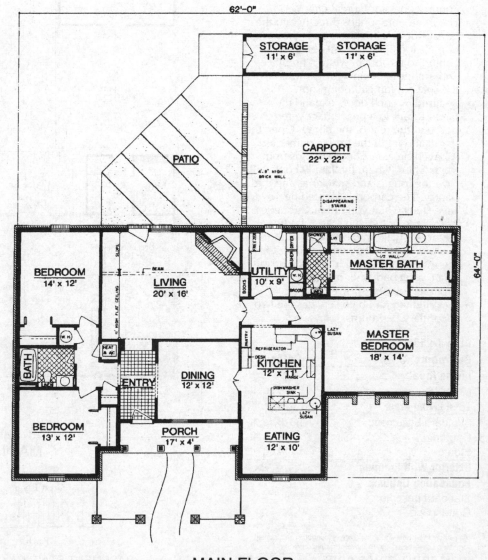

MAIN FLOOR

Plan E-1818

PRICES AND DETAILS
ON PAGES 13-15

A Real Charmer

- A tranquil railed porch makes this country one-story a real charmer.
- The main entry opens directly into the Great Room, which serves as the home's focal point. A 14-ft. cathedral ceiling soars above, while a fireplace and a built-in cabinet for games make the space a fun gathering spot.
- Beautiful French doors expand the Great Room to a peaceful covered porch at the rear of the home. Open the doors and let in the fresh summer air!
- A bayed breakfast nook unfolds from the kitchen, where the family cook will love the long island snack bar and the pantry. The carport is located nearby to save steps when you unload groceries.
- Across the home, the master bedroom features a walk-in closet with built-in shelves. A 10-ft. cathedral ceiling tops the master bath, which boasts a private toilet, a second walk-in closet and a separate tub and shower.
- A skylighted hall bath services the two secondary bedrooms.

Plan J-9508

Bedrooms: 3	Baths: 2½
Living Area:	
Main floor	1,875 sq. ft.
Total Living Area:	**1,875 sq. ft.**
Standard basement	1,875 sq. ft.
Carport	418 sq. ft.
Storage	114 sq. ft.
Exterior Wall Framing:	2x4

Foundation Options:

Standard basement
Crawlspace
Slab
(All plans can be built with your choice of foundation and framing. A generic conversion diagram is available. See order form.)

BLUEPRINT PRICE CODE:	**B**

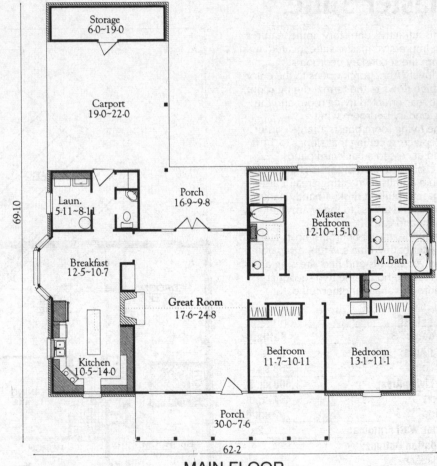

MAIN FLOOR

Storage
6-0~19-0

Carport
19-0~22-0

Porch
16-9~9-8

Laun.
5-11~8-11

Master Bedroom
12-10~15-10

M.Bath

Breakfast
12-5~10-7

Great Room
17-6~24-8

Kitchen
10-5~14-0

Bedroom
11-7~10-11

Bedroom
13-1~11-1

Porch
30-0~7-6

69-10

62-2

Great Room
17-6~20-7

Porch

BASEMENT STAIRWAY LOCATION

ORDER BLUEPRINTS ANYTIME!
CALL TOLL-FREE 1-888-626-2026

Plan J-9508

PRICES AND DETAILS
ON PAGES 13-15

Country Living

- A covered porch, half-round transom windows and three dormers give this home its warm, nostalgic appeal. Shuttered windows and a louvered vent beautify the side-entry, two-car garage.

- Designed for the ultimate in country living, the floor plan starts off with a dynamic Great Room that flows to a bayed dining area. A nice fireplace adds warmth, while a French door provides access to a backyard covered porch. A powder room is just steps away.

- A 12-ft., 4-in. vaulted ceiling presides over the large country kitchen, which offers a bayed nook, an oversized breakfast bar and a convenient pass-through to the rear porch.

- The exquisite master suite boasts a tray ceiling, a bay window and an alcove for built-in shelves or extra closet space. Other amenities include a large walk-in closet and a compartmentalized bath.

- Upstairs, 9-ft. ceilings enhance two more bedrooms and a second full bath. Each bedroom boasts a cozy dormer window and two closets.

Plan AX-93311

Bedrooms: 3	Baths: 2½
Living Area:	
Upper floor	570 sq. ft.
Main floor	1,375 sq. ft.
Total Living Area:	**1,945 sq. ft.**
Standard basement	1,280 sq. ft.
Garage	450 sq. ft.
Exterior Wall Framing:	2x4

Foundation Options:
Standard basement
Crawlspace
Slab
(All plans can be built with your choice of foundation and framing. A generic conversion diagram is available. See order form.)

BLUEPRINT PRICE CODE: B

VIEW INTO GREAT ROOM

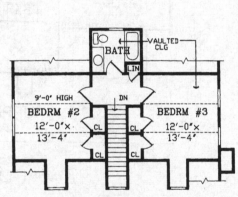

UPPER FLOOR

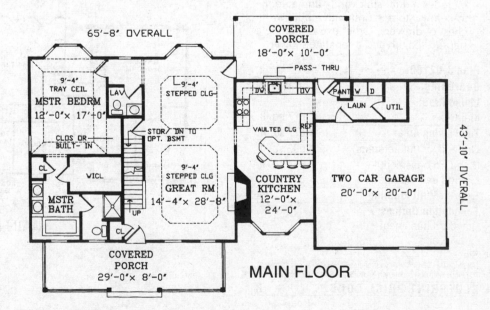

MAIN FLOOR

Plan AX-93311

PRICES AND DETAILS
ON PAGES 13-15

Upscale Charm

- Country charm and the very latest in conveniences mark this upscale home. To add extra appeal, all of the living areas are housed on one floor, yet may be expanded to the upper floor later.
- Set off from the foyer, the dining room is embraced by elegant columns. Arched windows in the dining room and in the bedroom across the hall echo the delicate detailing of the covered front porch.
- Straight ahead, the family room flaunts a wall of French doors overlooking a covered back porch and a large deck.
- A curved island snack bar smoothly connects the gourmet kitchen to the sunny breakfast area, which features a dramatic 13-ft. vaulted ceiling brightened by skylights. All other rooms have 9-ft. ceilings. A nearby computer room and a laundry/utility room with a recycling center are other amenities.
- The master bedroom's private bath includes a dual-sink vanity and a floor-to-ceiling storage unit with a built-in chest of drawers. Other extras include a step-up spa tub and a separate shower.

Plan J-92100

Bedrooms: 3+	Baths: 2
Living Area:	
Main floor	1,877 sq. ft.
Total Living Area:	**1,877 sq. ft.**
Upper floor (future areas)	1,500 sq. ft.
Standard basement	1,877 sq. ft.
Garage and storage	551 sq. ft.
Exterior Wall Framing:	2x4

Foundation Options:
Standard basement
Crawlspace
Slab
(All plans can be built with your choice of foundation and framing. A generic conversion diagram is available. See order form.)

BLUEPRINT PRICE CODE:	**B**

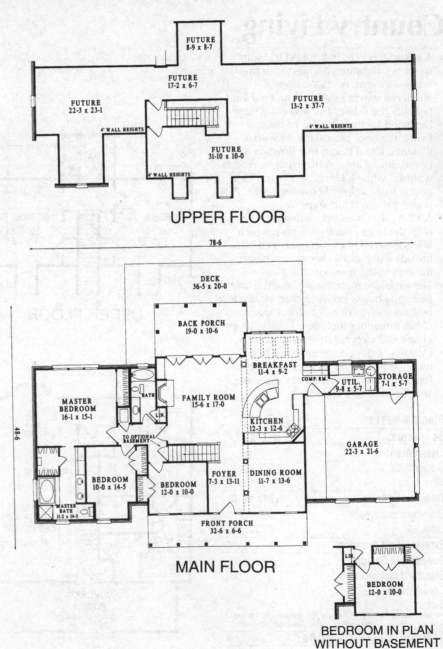

UPPER FLOOR

MAIN FLOOR

BEDROOM IN PLAN WITHOUT BASEMENT

Plan J-92100

PRICES AND DETAILS ***ON PAGES 13-15***

Irresistible Master Suite

- This traditional three-bedroom home features a main-floor master suite that is hard to resist, with an inviting window seat and a delightful bath.
- The home is introduced by a covered front entry, topped by a dormer with a half-round window.
- Just off the front entry, the formal dining room is distinguished by a tray ceiling and a large picture window overlooking the front porch.
- Straight back, the Great Room features a 16-ft.-high vaulted ceiling with a window wall facing the backyard. The fireplace can be enjoyed from the adjoining kitchen and breakfast area.
- The gourmet kitchen includes a corner sink, an island cooktop and a walk-in pantry. A 12-ft. vaulted ceiling expands the breakfast nook, which features a built-in desk and backyard deck access.
- The spacious master suite offers a 14-ft. vaulted ceiling and a luxurious private bath with a walk-in closet, a garden tub, a separate shower and a dual-sink vanity with a sit-down makeup area.
- An open-railed stairway leads up to another full bath that serves two additional bedrooms.

Plan B-89061

Bedrooms: 3	Baths: 2½
Living Area:	
Upper floor	436 sq. ft.
Main floor	1,490 sq. ft.
Total Living Area:	**1,926 sq. ft.**
Standard basement	1,490 sq. ft.
Garage	400 sq. ft.
Exterior Wall Framing:	2x4
Foundation Options:	
Standard basement	

(All plans can be built with your choice of foundation and framing. A generic conversion diagram is available. See order form.)

BLUEPRINT PRICE CODE:	**B**

UPPER FLOOR

Br 2
11-8x11

open to below

DN

Br 3
11-8x10-4

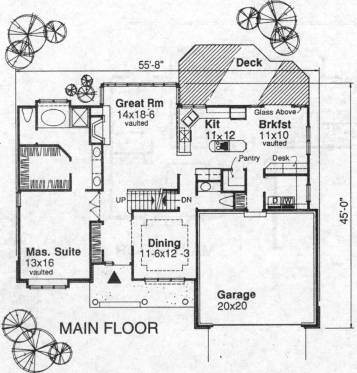

MAIN FLOOR

55'-8"

Deck

Great Rm
14x18-6
vaulted

Glass Above

Kit
11x12

Brkfst
11x10
vaulted

Pantry

Desk

45'-0"

UP   DN

D W

Mas. Suite
13x16
vaulted

Dining
11-6x12 -3

Garage
20x20

Plan B-89061

PRICES AND DETAILS ON PAGES 13-15

Meant to Be

- One glimpse of the beautiful front view will tempt you, and a good look at the stunning rear view will convince you, that this home was meant to be yours!
- The vaulted, skylighted entry ushers you to the Great Room, which vaults up to 10 feet and features an inspiring fireplace. Sliding glass doors provide speedy access to an incredible wraparound deck.
- Equipped for any sudden culinary inspirations, the well-planned kitchen features its own pantry. You'll also appreciate its close proximity to the garage when it's time to unload those heavy grocery bags.
- The master suite will take your breath away, with its walk-in closet and a secluded bath with dual sinks and a spa tub. Exquisite French doors create easy access to the deck.
- Imagine magical nights on the deck. With the kids at Grandma's house, put on some soft music and use the deck as your own private dance floor!
- A vast unfinished area in the daylight basement promises excitement. Turn it into a game room for the ultimate in entertainment! A fourth bedroom and a full bath complete the space.

Plan SUN-1310-C

Bedrooms: 4	Baths: 3½
Living Area:	
Main floor	1,636 sq. ft.
Daylight basement (finished)	315 sq. ft.
Total Living Area:	**1,951 sq. ft.**
Daylight basement (unfinished)	730 sq. ft.
Garage	759 sq. ft.
Exterior Wall Framing:	2x6

Foundation Options:
Daylight basement
Crawlspace
Slab
(All plans can be built with your choice of foundation and framing. A generic conversion diagram is available. See order form.)

BLUEPRINT PRICE CODE:	B

MAIN FLOOR

70'-0"
45'-0"

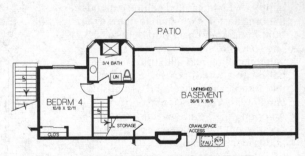

DAYLIGHT BASEMENT

REAR VIEW

Plan SUN-1310-C

A Splash of Style

- Eye-catching keystones, arched window arrangements and a varied roofline give this home a refreshing splash of style.
- Inside, the 10-ft., 8-in.-high entry leads to the dining room and the Great Room. A 12-ft. sloped ceiling expands the Great Room, which features a brick fireplace that soars to the ceiling.
- A sunny bay brightens the cheery breakfast nook and the adjacent kitchen. A built-in desk, a pantry, an island workstation and a nearby powder room make the most of this busy area.
- A split staircase at the center of the plan leads to the upper-floor bedrooms.
- A 13-ft., 4-in. cathedral ceiling, a sunny bay and a plant ledge spice up the master bedroom. The private bath boasts a whirlpool tub under an 11-ft., 4-in. sloped ceiling. Two vanities and a separate shower are also included.
- The secondary bedrooms share a split hall bath. The front bedroom has a built-in bookcase and an 11-ft., 4-in. sloped ceiling; the left, rear bedroom has a 13-ft., 10-in. cathedral ceiling.

Plan CC-1990-M

Bedrooms: 4	Baths: 2½
Living Area:	
Upper floor	967 sq. ft.
Main floor	1,023 sq. ft.
Total Living Area:	**1,990 sq. ft.**
Standard basement	1,023 sq. ft.
Garage	685 sq. ft.
Exterior Wall Framing:	2x4

Foundation Options:
Standard basement
(All plans can be built with your choice of foundation and framing. A generic conversion diagram is available. See order form.)

BLUEPRINT PRICE CODE:	B

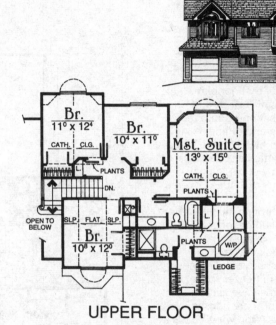

REAR VIEW

UPPER FLOOR

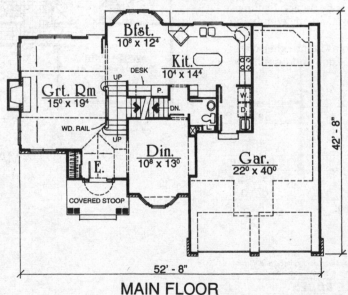

MAIN FLOOR

French Garden Design

- A creative, angular design gives this traditional French garden home an exciting, open and airy floor plan.
- Guests enter through a covered, columned porch that opens into the large, angled living and dining rooms.
- High 12-ft. ceilings highlight the living and dining area, which also features corner windows, a wet bar, a cozy fireplace and access to a huge covered backyard porch.
- The angled walk-through kitchen, also with a 12-ft.-high ceiling, offers plenty of work space and an adjoining informal eating nook that faces a delightful private courtyard. The nearby utility area has extra freezer space, a walk-in pantry and garage access.
- The home's bedrooms are housed in two separate wings. One wing boasts a luxurious master suite, which features a large walk-in closet, an angled tub and a separate shower.
- Two large bedrooms in the other wing share a hall bath. Each bedroom has a walk-in closet.

Plan E-2004

Bedrooms: 3	Baths: 2
Living Area:	
Main floor	2,023 sq. ft.
Total Living Area:	**2,023 sq. ft.**
Garage	484 sq. ft.
Storage	87 sq. ft.
Exterior Wall Framing:	2x6

Foundation Options:

Crawlspace

Slab

(All plans can be built with your choice of foundation and framing. A generic conversion diagram is available. See order form.)

BLUEPRINT PRICE CODE: C

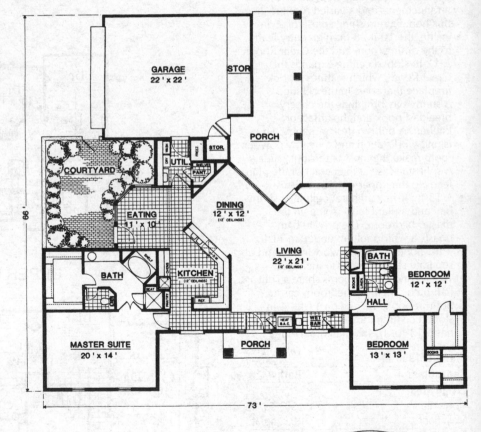

MAIN FLOOR

See this plan on our "One-Story" VideoGraphic Tour!

Order form on page 9

ORDER BLUEPRINTS ANYTIME!
CALL TOLL-FREE 1-888-626-2026

Plan E-2004

PRICES AND DETAILS
ON PAGES 13-15

Elaborate Entry

- This home's important-looking covered entry greets guests with heavy, banded support columns, sunburst transom windows and dual sidelights.

- Once inside the home, the 15-ft.-high foyer is flanked by the formal living and dining rooms, which have 10½-ft. vaulted ceilings. Straight ahead and beyond five decorative columns lies the spacious family room.

- Surrounded by 8-ft.-high walls, the family room features a 13-ft. vaulted ceiling, a fireplace and sliding doors to a covered patio. A neat plant shelf above the fireplace adds style.

- The bright and airy kitchen has a 13-ft. ceiling and serves the family room and the breakfast area, which is enhanced by a corner window and a French door.

- The master suite enjoys a 13-ft. vaulted ceiling and features French-door patio access, a large walk-in closet and a private bath with a corner platform tub and a separate shower.

- Across the home, three secondary bedrooms share a hall bath, which boasts private access to the patio.

Plan HDS-90-806

Bedrooms: 4	Baths: 2

Living Area:	
Main floor	2,056 sq. ft.
Total Living Area:	**2,056 sq. ft.**
Garage	452 sq. ft.

Exterior Wall Framing:
2x4 or 8-in. concrete block

Foundation Options:
Slab
(All plans can be built with your choice of foundation and framing. A generic conversion diagram is available. See order form.)

BLUEPRINT PRICE CODE: C

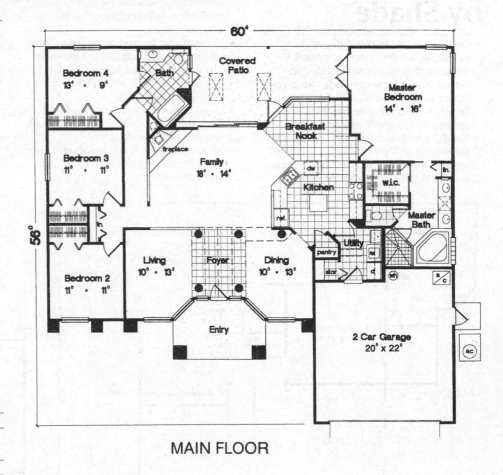

MAIN FLOOR

Surrounded by Shade

- Comfort reigns in this delightful domicile, which boasts a shaded veranda that nearly surrounds the home. There's enough room for a porch hammock! When it rains during the family reunion, the festivities can be moved to this glorious covered area.
- Inside, a fireplace-blessed living room joins seamlessly with the welcoming foyer. Opposite, the big dining room will hold the largest dinner parties.

- Your whole family can participate in meal preparation, since the kitchen and connecting breakfast room flow into each other. A French door gives veranda access.
- In the master bedroom, an atrium door offers private passage to the veranda. The private bath includes a bubbly tub, a separate shower and a planter for your lush greenery.
- Upstairs, two more bedrooms flank a peaceful sitting area. A large split bath features a dual-sink vanity.
- All rooms in the home are topped by airy 9-ft. ceilings, for added spaciousness.

Plan L-88-VB	
Bedrooms: 3	**Baths:** 2½
Living Area:	
Upper floor	751 sq. ft.
Main floor	1,308 sq. ft.
Total Living Area:	**2,059 sq. ft.**
Detached two-car garage	505 sq. ft.
Exterior Wall Framing:	2x4
Foundation Options:	

Slab
(All plans can be built with your choice of foundation and framing. A generic conversion diagram is available. See order form.)

BLUEPRINT PRICE CODE: C

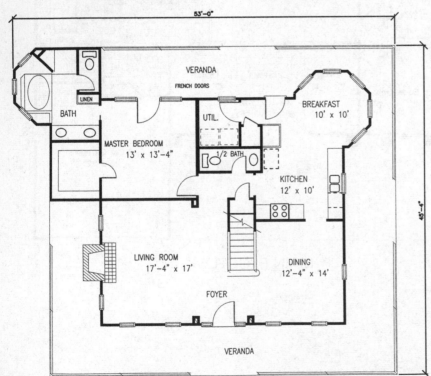

MAIN FLOOR

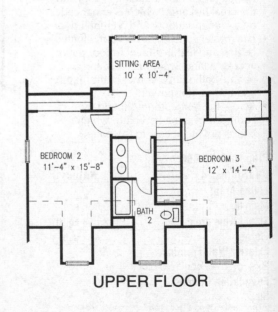

UPPER FLOOR

Treasure It

- Without a doubt, you'll treasure the years you spend in this home, which is stocked with pleasing amenities.
- Inside, the two-story foyer creates an elegant first impression for visitors. To its right, meals take on a special flavor in the dining room. After a fine supper, move outside to the porch, or across the foyer to the living room.
- Casual activities have a place of their own in the family room. Whether enjoying Disney's latest release, or reading a novel by the fireplace, comfort takes precedence here.
- The sunny breakfast nook leads the way to the island kitchen. Plenty of room is available for holiday baking parties.
- Unless otherwise noted, all main-floor rooms include 9-ft. ceilings.
- Upstairs, the stylish master suite boasts a 10-ft., 8-in. tray ceiling. In the master bath, a 12-ft. vaulted ceiling brings a touch of splendor to mundane rituals.
- An alternate upper-floor plan includes a versatile bonus room that can be adapted to meet your specific needs.

Plan FB-1786

Bedrooms: 3+	Baths: 2½
Living Area:	
Upper floor	824 sq. ft.
Main floor	962 sq. ft.
Bonus room	282 sq. ft.
Total Living Area:	**2,068 sq. ft.**
Daylight basement	962 sq. ft.
Garage and storage	440 sq. ft.
Exterior Wall Framing:	2x4

Foundation Options:

Daylight basement

Slab

(All plans can be built with your choice of foundation and framing. A generic conversion diagram is available. See order form.)

BLUEPRINT PRICE CODE: C

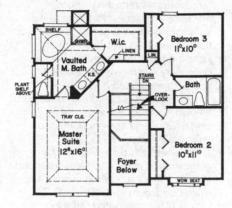

UPPER FLOOR

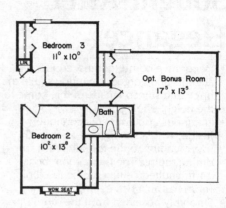

ALTERNATE
UPPER FLOOR

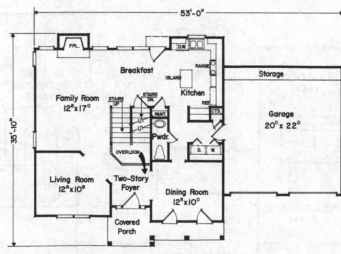

MAIN FLOOR

Sought-After Elegance

- Decorative corner quoins, copper accents and gorgeous windows take the brick and stucco facade of this home to the height of elegance.
- Luxurious appointments continue inside, with a sidelighted 11-ft.-high foyer leading to the formal living and dining rooms. The living room boasts a 14-ft. vaulted ceiling, while the dining room has an 11-ft. ceiling.
- Smoothly accessed from the dining room, the flow-through kitchen offers a serving counter to the breakfast nook. Bright windows light the two areas, which share an 11-ft. vaulted ceiling.

- Adjacent to the nook, the luxurious family room sports a handsome fireplace and access to a sprawling backyard deck. A fancy fan hangs from the soaring 14-ft. vaulted ceiling.
- Just off the family room, two roomy secondary bedrooms share a nice compartmentalized bath.
- The sumptuous master bedroom flaunts its own deck access, a quaint morning porch for quiet cups of coffee and a large walk-in closet.
- The master bath is highlighted by a plant shelf, a garden tub and a separate shower. An 11-ft. ceiling crowns the master bedroom and bath.
- Unless otherwise noted, all rooms have 9-ft. ceilings.
- A bonus room above the garage offers expansion possibilities.

Plan APS-2018	
Bedrooms: 3+	Baths: 2½
Living Area:	
Main floor	2,088 sq. ft.
Total Living Area:	**2,088 sq. ft.**
Bonus room (unfinished)	282 sq. ft.
Daylight basement	2,088 sq. ft.
Garage	460 sq. ft.
Storage	35 sq. ft.
Exterior Wall Framing:	2x4
Foundation Options:	
Daylight basement	

(All plans can be built with your choice of foundation and framing. A generic conversion diagram is available. See order form.)

BLUEPRINT PRICE CODE: C

MAIN FLOOR

Picture Perfect!

- With graceful arches, columns and railings, the wonderful front porch makes this home the picture of country charm. Decorative chimneys, shutters and quaint dormers add more style.
- Inside, the foyer shows off sidelights and a fantail transom. The foyer is flanked by the dining room and a bedroom, both of which boast porch views and arched transoms. All three areas are expanded by 10-ft. ceilings.
- The living room also flaunts a 10-ft. ceiling, plus a fireplace and French doors that open to a skylighted porch. The remaining rooms offer 9-ft. ceilings.
- The L-shaped kitchen has an island cooktop and a sunny breakfast nook.
- A Palladian window arrangement brightens the sitting alcove in the master suite. Other highlights include porch access and a fantastic bath with a garden tub and a separate shower.
- The upper floor is perfect for future expansion space.

Plan J-9401

Bedrooms: 3+	Baths: 2½
Living Area:	
Main floor	2,089 sq. ft.
Total Living Area:	**2,089 sq. ft.**
Upper floor (unfinished)	878 sq. ft.
Standard basement	2,089 sq. ft.
Garage and storage	530 sq. ft.
Exterior Wall Framing:	2x4

Foundation Options:

Standard basement
Crawlspace
Slab
(All plans can be built with your choice of foundation and framing. A generic conversion diagram is available. See order form.)

BLUEPRINT PRICE CODE: C

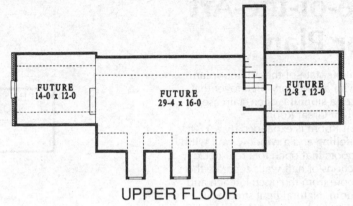

UPPER FLOOR

MAIN FLOOR

State-of-the-Art Floor Plan

- This design's state-of-the-art floor plan begins with a two-story-high foyer that introduces a stunning open staircase and a bright Great Room.
- The Great Room is expanded by a 17-ft. vaulted ceiling and a window wall with French doors that open to a rear deck.
- Short sections of half-walls separate the Great Room from the open kitchen and dining room. Natural light streams in through a greenhouse window above the sink and lots of glass facing the deck.
- The main-floor master suite has a 9-ft. coved ceiling and private access to an inviting hot tub on the deck. Walk-in closets frame the entrance to the luxurious bath, highlighted by a 10-ft. vaulted ceiling and an arched window above a raised spa tub.
- Upstairs, a balcony hall leads to two bedrooms and a continental bath, plus a den and a storage room.

Plan S-2100

Bedrooms: 3+	Baths: 2½
Living Area:	
Upper floor	660 sq. ft.
Main floor	1,440 sq. ft.
Total Living Area:	**2,100 sq. ft.**
Standard basement	1,440 sq. ft.
Garage	552 sq. ft.
Exterior Wall Framing:	2x6

Foundation Options:

Standard basement
Crawlspace
Slab

(All plans can be built with your choice of foundation and framing. A generic conversion diagram is available. See order form.)

BLUEPRINT PRICE CODE:	C

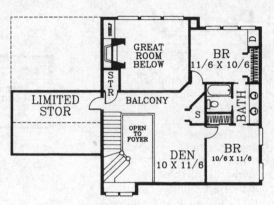

UPPER FLOOR

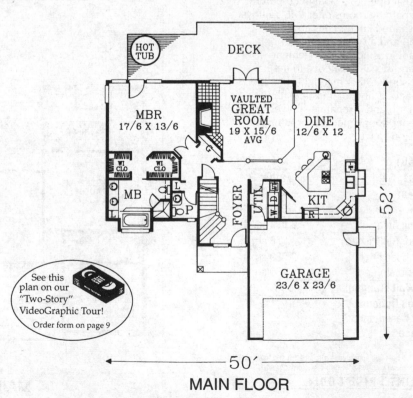

See this plan on our "Two-Story" VideoGraphic Tour! Order form on page 9

MAIN FLOOR

LEFT VIEW

Mediterranean Splendor

- This splendid Mediterranean design has sunny living spaces both inside and out.
- Handsome double doors open to a huge covered porch/loggia. French doors beyond escort you into the tiled foyer. Windows along the left wall overlook a dramatic courtyard/arbor.
- Stately columns and overhead plant shelves accent the living and dining rooms, which are designed to view the courtyard. The living room features a built-in media center and a fireplace.
- The kitchen boasts a pantry, a Jenn-Air range, a serving counter and a sunny breakfast nook. A wet bar serves both the indoor and outdoor entertainment areas.
- The gorgeous master bedroom, crowned by a 9-ft. ceiling, shares a rotating entertainment cabinet and a see-through fireplace with the luxurious master bath. The bath includes a sunken bathing area and a huge walk-in closet.
- A second bedroom features a peaceful window seat, a walk-in closet and private bath access. The third bedroom also has a walk-in closet.
- For added spaciousness, all ceilings are 10 ft. high unless otherwise specified.

Plan L-2176-MC

Bedrooms: 3	Baths: 2
Living Area:	
Main floor	2,176 sq. ft.
Total Living Area:	**2,176 sq. ft.**
Garage	549 sq. ft.
Exterior Wall Framing:	2x4

Foundation Options:

Slab

(All plans can be built with your choice of foundation and framing. A generic conversion diagram is available. See order form.)

BLUEPRINT PRICE CODE:	C

FRONT VIEW

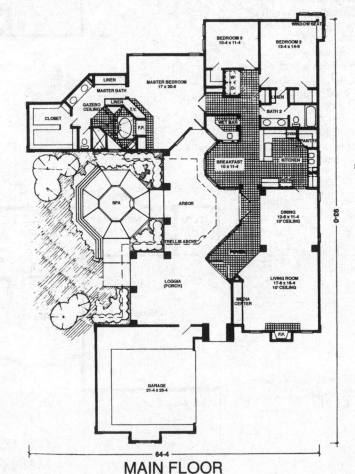

MAIN FLOOR

TOUR THIS HOME BEFORE YOU BUILD!

See page 9 for details on Interactive Floor Plans.

Country Kitchen

- A lovely front porch, dormers and shutters give this home a country-style exterior and complement its comfortable and informal interior.
- The roomy country kitchen connects with the sunny breakfast nook and the formal dining room.
- The central portion of the home consists of a large family room with a handsome fireplace and easy access to a backyard deck.
- The main-floor master suite, particularly impressive for a home of this size, features a majestic master bath with a corner garden tub, two walk-in closets and a dual-sink vanity with knee space.
- Upstairs, you will find two more good-sized bedrooms, a double bath and a large storage area.

Plan C-8645

Bedrooms: 3	Baths: 2½
Living Area:	
Upper floor	704 sq. ft.
Main floor	1,477 sq. ft.
Total Living Area:	**2,181 sq. ft.**
Daylight basement	1,400 sq. ft.
Garage and storage	561 sq. ft.
Exterior Wall Framing:	2x4

Foundation Options:

Daylight basement
Crawlspace
Slab

(All plans can be built with your choice of foundation and framing. A generic conversion diagram is available. See order form.)

BLUEPRINT PRICE CODE:	**C**

See this plan on our "Country & Traditional" Video Tour! Order form on page 9

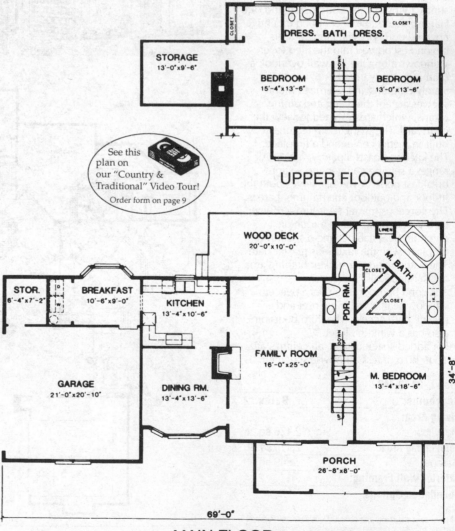

UPPER FLOOR

MAIN FLOOR

Plan C-8645

PRICES AND DETAILS
ON PAGES 13-15

Quiet Relaxation

- This elegant brick one-story home features a stunning master bedroom with a sunny morning porch for quiet relaxation. The bedroom's 11-ft. vaulted ceiling extends into the master bath, which boasts a corner garden tub and an attractive plant shelf.
- A few steps away, the open kitchen shares its 11-ft. ceiling and handy snack bar with the bright breakfast nook.
- A handsome fireplace warms the spacious family room, which is enhanced by a soaring 14-ft. ceiling. A striking French door provides access to a roomy deck that may also be reached from the master bedroom.
- The formal living areas flank the sidelighted foyer. The living room shows off a 14-ft. cathedral ceiling.
- Three secondary bedrooms with 9-ft. ceilings have easy access to a split bath. The center bedroom features a built-in desk with shelves above. Two of the bedrooms have walk-in closets.
- A convenient half-bath and a good-sized laundry room are located near the two-car garage, which offers additional storage space and excellent lighting from three bright windows.

Plan APS-2117	
Bedrooms: 4	**Baths:** 2½
Living Area:	
Main floor	2,187 sq. ft.
Total Living Area:	**2,187 sq. ft.**
Garage	460 sq. ft.
Exterior Wall Framing:	2x4

Foundation Options:

Crawlspace
(All plans can be built with your choice of foundation and framing. A generic conversion diagram is available. See order form.)

BLUEPRINT PRICE CODE: C

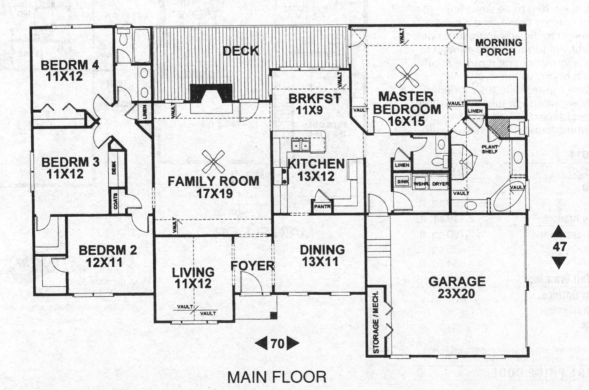

MAIN FLOOR

Versatile Sun Room

- This cozy country-style home offers an inviting front porch and an interior just as welcoming.
- The spacious living room features a warming fireplace and windows that overlook the porch.
- The living room opens to a dining area, where French doors access a covered porch and a sunny patio.
- The island kitchen has a sink view, plenty of counter space, and a handy pass-through to the adjoining sun room. The bright sun room is large enough to serve as a formal dining room, a family room or a hobby room.
- The private master suite is secluded to the rear. A garden spa tub, dual walk-in closets and separate dressing areas are nice features found in the master bath.

Plan J-90014

Bedrooms: 3	Baths: 2½
Living Area:	
Main floor	2,190 sq. ft.
Total Living Area:	**2,190 sq. ft.**
Standard basement	2,190 sq. ft.
Garage	465 sq. ft.
Storage	34 sq. ft.
Exterior Wall Framing:	2x6

Foundation Options:

Standard basement

Crawlspace

Slab

(All plans can be built with your choice of foundation and framing. A generic conversion diagram is available. See order form.)

BLUEPRINT PRICE CODE: C

MAIN FLOOR

See this plan on our "One-Story" VideoGraphic Tour!
Order form on page 9

ORDER BLUEPRINTS ANYTIME!
CALL TOLL-FREE 1-888-626-2026

Plan J-90014

PRICES AND DETAILS
ON PAGES 13-15

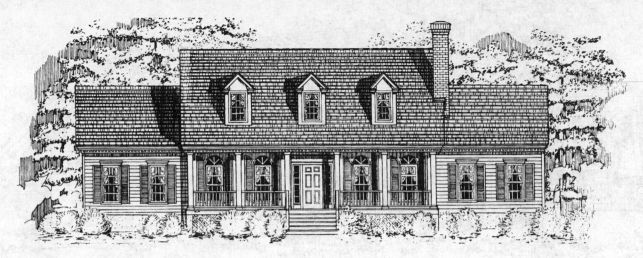

Graceful Facade

- Elegant half-round transoms spruce up the wood-shuttered facade of this charming traditional two-story.
- The wide front porch opens to a two-story foyer that flows between the formal dining room and a two-story-high library or guest room. Sliding French doors close off the library from the Great Room.
- Perfect for entertaining, the spacious Great Room shows off a handsome fireplace and a TV center. Beautiful French doors on either side extend the room to a large backyard deck.
- The adjoining dinette has its own view of the backyard through a stunning semi-circular glass wall, which sheds light on the nice-sized attached kitchen.
- A pantry and a laundry room are neatly housed near the two-car garage. The adjacent full bath could be downsized to a half-bath with storage space.
- The master suite and its private whirlpool bath are isolated from the three upper-floor bedrooms and features a 14-ft.-high cathedral ceiling.
- Unless otherwise specified, all main-floor ceilings are 9 ft. high.

Plan AHP-9490

Bedrooms: 4+	Baths: 2½-3
Living Area:	
Upper floor	722 sq. ft.
Main floor	1,497 sq. ft.
Total Living Area:	**2,219 sq. ft.**
Standard basement	1,165 sq. ft.
Garage	420 sq. ft.
Exterior Wall Framing:	2x4 or 2x6

Foundation Options:
Standard basement
Crawlspace
Slab
(All plans can be built with your choice of foundation and framing. A generic conversion diagram is available. See order form.)

BLUEPRINT PRICE CODE:	C

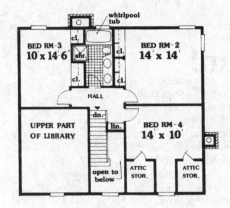

UPPER FLOOR

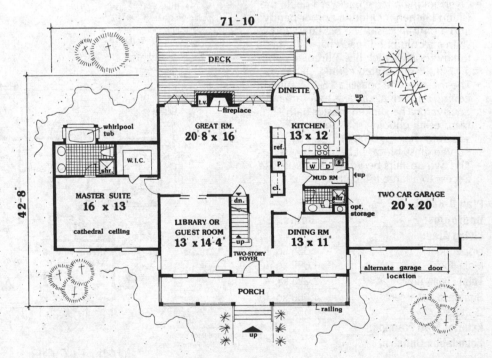

MAIN FLOOR

Fantastic Floor Plan!

- Featured on "Hometime," the popular PBS television program, this unique design combines a dynamic exterior with a fantastic floor plan.

- The barrel-vaulted entry leads into the vaulted foyer, which is outlined by elegant columns. To the left, the living room features a 13-ft. vaulted ceiling, a curved wall and corner windows. To the right, the formal dining room is enhanced by a tray ceiling.

- Overlooking a large backyard deck, the island kitchen includes a corner pantry and a built-in desk. The breakfast room shares a columned snack bar with the family room, which has a fireplace and a 17-ft., 8-in. vaulted ceiling.

- The master suite boasts a 15-ft. vaulted ceiling and private access to a romantic courtyard. The sunken master bath features an enticing spa tub and a separate shower, both encased by a curved glass-block wall.

- The two upstairs bedrooms have private access to a large full bath.

Plan B-88015

Bedrooms: 3	Baths: 2½
Living Area:	
Upper floor	534 sq. ft.
Main floor	1,689 sq. ft.
Total Living Area:	**2,223 sq. ft.**
Standard basement	1,689 sq. ft.
Garage	455 sq. ft.
Exterior Wall Framing:	2x4

Foundation Options:

Standard basement

(All plans can be built with your choice of foundation and framing. A generic conversion diagram is available. See order form.)

BLUEPRINT PRICE CODE: C

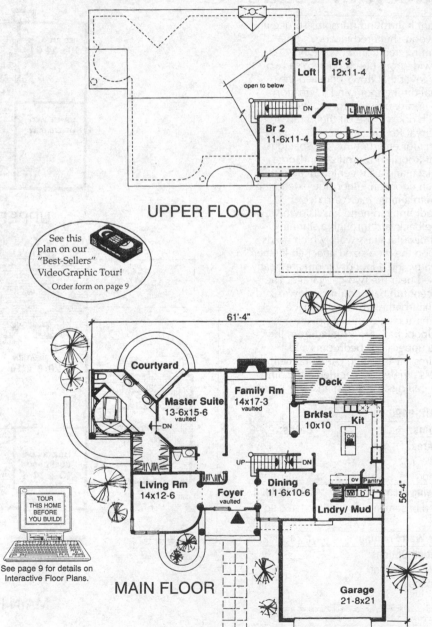

See this plan on our "Best-Sellers" VideoGraphic Tour! Order form on page 9

UPPER FLOOR

TOUR THIS HOME BEFORE YOU BUILD!

See page 9 for details on Interactive Floor Plans.

MAIN FLOOR

ORDER BLUEPRINTS ANYTIME!
CALL TOLL-FREE 1-888-626-2026

Plan B-88015

PRICES AND DETAILS
ON PAGES 13-15

Charming Chateau

- A two-story arched entry introduces this charming French chateau.
- To the left of the tiled foyer, the elegant formal dining room will impress friends when you entertain.
- In the kitchen, a handy island worktop and a step-in pantry take advantage of the unique space. The cheery breakfast nook is a great spot for family meals.
- A neat see-through fireplace and built-in bookshelves define the formal living room and the casual family room. Lovely French doors open to a quiet covered porch in back.
- The secluded master suite on the main floor boasts two enormous walk-in closets and a lush private bath with an inviting marble tub, a separate shower and his-and-hers vanities.
- The kitchen and the nook have 9- and 8-ft. ceilings, respectively. All other main-floor rooms are enhanced by soaring 10-ft. ceilings.
- On the upper floor, two bedrooms share a unique bath. The front bedroom offers a 10-ft. ceiling. A bonus room can be adapted to fit your future needs.

Plan RD-2225	
Bedrooms: 3+	**Baths:** 2½
Living Area:	
Upper floor	547 sq. ft.
Main floor	1,678 sq. ft.
Total Living Area:	**2,225 sq. ft.**
Bonus room (unfinished)	136 sq. ft.
Garage and storage	519 sq. ft.
Exterior Wall Framing:	2x4

Foundation Options:

Crawlspace
Slab

(All plans can be built with your choice of foundation and framing. A generic conversion diagram is available. See order form.)

BLUEPRINT PRICE CODE: C

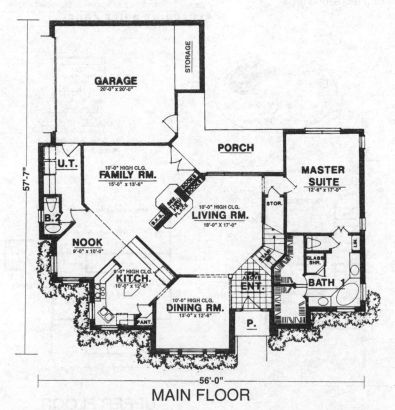

MAIN FLOOR

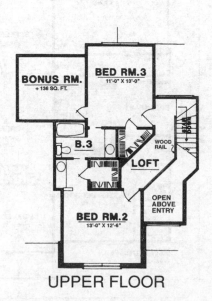

UPPER FLOOR

Gracious Traditional

- This traditional home is perfect for a corner lot, with a quaint facade and an attached garage around back.
- Tall windows, elegant dormers and a covered front porch welcome guests to the front entry and into the foyer.
- Just off the foyer, the formal dining room boasts a built-in hutch and views to the front porch.
- The expansive, skylighted Great Room features a wet bar, a 16-ft. vaulted

ceiling, a stunning fireplace and access to the screened back porch.
- The kitchen includes a large pantry and an eating bar to the bayed breakfast nook. A large utility room with garage access is nearby.
- The master bedroom offers a walk-in closet and a bath with a large corner tub and his-and-hers vanities.
- Two additional bedrooms have big walk-in closets, built-in desks and easy access to another full bath.
- Upstairs, a loft overlooks the Great Room and is perfect as an extra bedroom or a recreation area.

Plan C-8920

Bedrooms: 3+	Baths: 3
Living Area:	
Upper floor	305 sq. ft.
Main floor	1,996 sq. ft.
Total Living Area:	**2,301 sq. ft.**
Daylight basement	1,996 sq. ft.
Garage	469 sq. ft.
Exterior Wall Framing:	2x4

Foundation Options:

Daylight basement
Crawlspace
(All plans can be built with your choice of foundation and framing. A generic conversion diagram is available. See order form.)

BLUEPRINT PRICE CODE: C

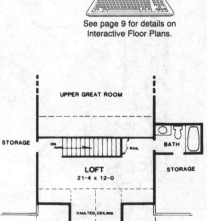

See this plan on our "Country & Traditional" Video Tour!
Order form on page 9

TOUR THIS HOME BEFORE YOU BUILD!

See page 9 for details on Interactive Floor Plans.

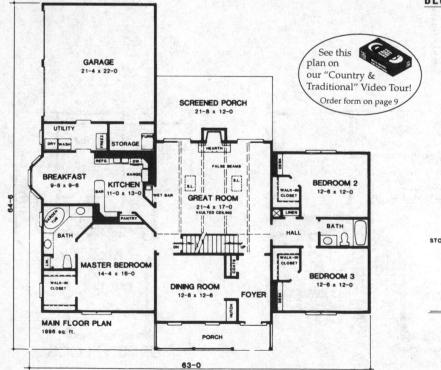

MAIN FLOOR

UPPER FLOOR

Place of Peace

- This elegant home's covered front and back porches promise moments of sweet tranquility.
- A vaulted turret dominates the home's facade, which serves as a sophisticated introduction to the interior.
- Straight ahead through the two-story foyer, the Great Room boasts a window wall overlooking the back porch and a fine fireplace for warmth and romance.
- The large breakfast room is the perfect complement to the walk-through kitchen. The path from the kitchen to the prowed dining room passes through a tidy butler's pantry.
- Solitude is the operative word in the master bedroom, which drapes you in warmth from its fireplace and grants passage to the back porch through sliding glass doors. The opulent bath delivers a whirlpool tub, a separate shower and a walk-in closet.

REAR VIEW

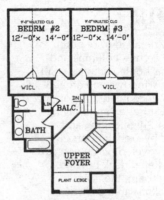

UPPER FLOOR

Plan AX-94329

Bedrooms: 3	Baths: 2½
Living Area:	
Upper floor	570 sq. ft.
Main floor	1,808 sq. ft.
Total Living Area:	**2,378 sq. ft.**
Standard basement	1,808 sq. ft.
Garage, storage and utility	461 sq. ft.
Exterior Wall Framing:	**2x4**

Foundation Options:

Standard basement
Crawlspace
Slab

(All plans can be built with your choice of foundation and framing. A generic conversion diagram is available. See order form.)

BLUEPRINT PRICE CODE: C

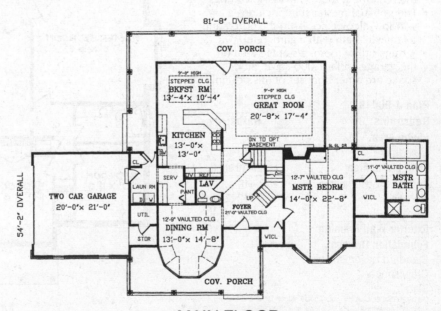

MAIN FLOOR

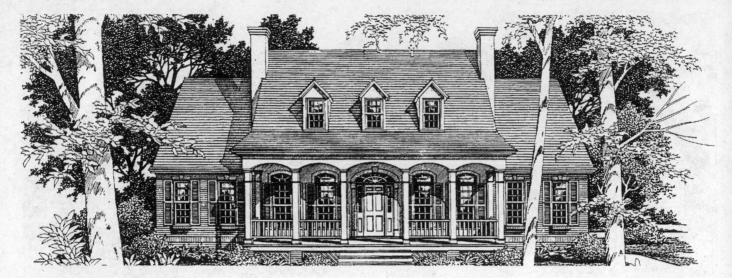

Wonderful Detailing

- The wonderfully detailed front porch, with its graceful arches, columns and railings, gives this home a character all its own. Dormer windows and arched transoms further accentuate the porch.
- The floor plan features a central living room with a 10-ft.-high ceiling and a fireplace framed by French doors. These doors open to a covered porch or a sun room, and a sheltered deck beyond.
- Just off the living room, the island kitchen and breakfast area provide a spacious place for family or guests. The nearby formal dining room has arched transom windows and a 10-ft. ceiling, as does the bedroom off the foyer. All of the remaining rooms have 9-ft. ceilings.
- The unusual master suite includes a window alcove, access to the porch and a fantastic bath with a garden tub.
- A huge utility room, a storage area off the garage and a 1,000-sq.-ft. attic space are other bonuses of this design.

Plan J-90019

Bedrooms: 3	Baths: 2½
Living Area:	
Main floor	2,410 sq. ft.
Total Living Area:	**2,410 sq. ft.**
Standard basement	2,410 sq. ft.
Garage	512 sq. ft.
Storage	86 sq. ft.
Exterior Wall Framing:	2x6

Foundation Options:

Standard basement
Crawlspace
Slab

(All plans can be built with your choice of foundation and framing. A generic conversion diagram is available. See order form.)

BLUEPRINT PRICE CODE:	C

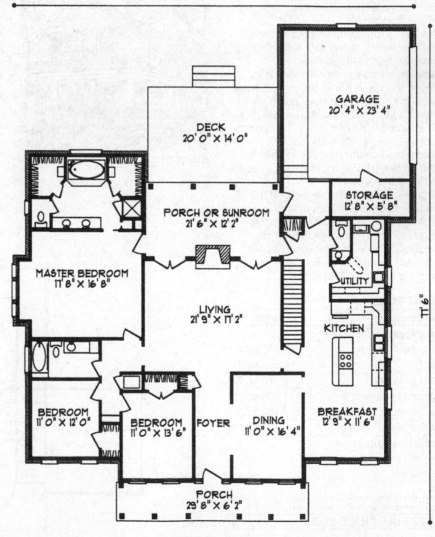

64' 4"

GARAGE
20' 4" X 23' 4"

DECK
20' 0" X 14' 0"

STORAGE
12' 8" X 5' 8"

PORCH OR SUNROOM
21' 6" X 12' 2"

UTILITY

MASTER BEDROOM
17' 8" X 16' 8"

LIVING
21' 9" X 17' 2"

KITCHEN

71' 6"

BEDROOM
11' 0" X 12' 0"

BEDROOM
11' 0" X 13' 6"

FOYER

DINING
11' 0" X 16' 4"

BREAKFAST
12' 9" X 11' 6"

PORCH
29' 8" X 6' 2"

MAIN FLOOR

Old-Fashioned Charm

- A trio of dormers add old-fashioned charm to this modern design.
- Both the living room and the dining room offer 12-ft.-high vaulted ceilings and flow together to create a sense of even more spaciousness.
- The open kitchen/nook/family room features a sunny alcove, a walk-in pantry and a woodstove.
- A first-floor den and a walk-through utility room are other big bonuses.
- Upstairs, the master suite includes an enormous walk-in closet and a deluxe bath with a refreshing spa tub and a separate shower and water closet.
- Two more bedrooms, each with a window seat, and a bonus room complete this stylish design.

Plan CDG-2004

Bedrooms: 3+	Baths: 2½
Living Area:	
Upper floor	928 sq. ft.
Main floor	1,317 sq. ft.
Bonus area	192 sq. ft.
Total Living Area:	**2,437 sq. ft.**
Partial daylight basement	780 sq. ft.
Garage	537 sq. ft.
Exterior Wall Framing:	2x6

Foundation Options:

Partial daylight basement
Crawlspace
(All plans can be built with your choice of foundation and framing.
A generic conversion diagram is available. See order form.)

BLUEPRINT PRICE CODE: C

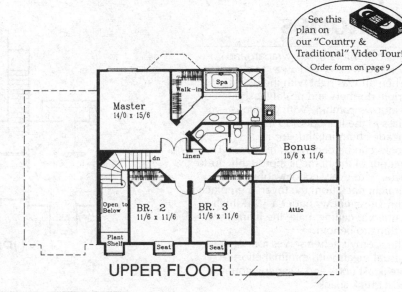

UPPER FLOOR

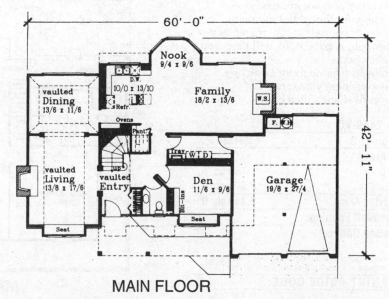

MAIN FLOOR

ORDER BLUEPRINTS ANYTIME!
CALL TOLL-FREE 1-888-626-2026

Plan CDG-2004

PRICES AND DETAILS
ON PAGES 13-15

101

Rapt in Country Memories

- This beautiful home's wraparound porch will carry you away to a time when all was right with the world.
- Triple dormers and nostalgic shuttered windows combine with gorgeous oval glass in the front door to make the facade charming indeed!
- Looks can be deceiving, however. The interior of the home is thoroughly up-to-date, with every conceivable feature.
- Straight back from the foyer, a fireplace and tall windows under a 19-ft.-high cathedral ceiling make the living room a thing to behold.
- The roomy kitchen serves formal or casual meals with minimal effort. A breakfast nook and a serving counter host quick snacks.
- Two corner porches are easily accessible for thoughtful moments.
- Or, refresh yourself in the master suite's garden tub. A good book will keep you there for hours.
- Upstairs, the game room's balcony offers sweeping views; two big bedrooms share a nice bath.

Plan L-2449-VC

Bedrooms: 3	Baths: 2½
Living Area:	
Upper floor	780 sq. ft.
Main floor	1,669 sq. ft.
Total Living Area:	**2,449 sq. ft.**
Exterior Wall Framing:	2x4

Foundation Options:

Slab

(All plans can be built with your choice of foundation and framing. A generic conversion diagram is available. See order form.)

BLUEPRINT PRICE CODE: **C**

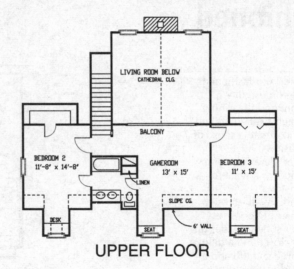

UPPER FLOOR

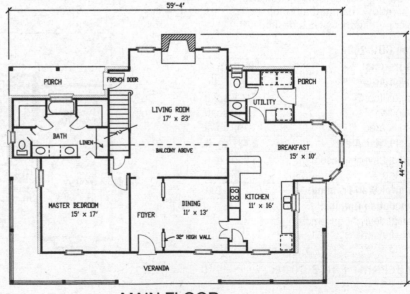

MAIN FLOOR

ORDER BLUEPRINTS ANYTIME! CALL TOLL-FREE 1-888-626-2026   Plan L-2449-VC   **PRICES AND DETAILS ON PAGES 13-15**

Large-Scale Living

- Eye-catching windows and an appealing wraparound porch highlight the exterior of this outstanding home.
- High ceilings and large-scale living spaces prevail inside, beginning with the two-story-high foyer.
- The spacious living room flows into the formal dining room, which accesses the front porch as well as an optional backyard deck.
- The island kitchen combines with a bright breakfast room, also with deck access. The fabulous family room offers a warm corner fireplace, a soaring 18-ft. vaulted ceiling and a wall of windows.
- Upstairs, the luxurious master bedroom boasts an 11-ft. vaulted ceiling, a magnificent arched window and two walk-in closets. The skylighted master bath features a spa tub, a separate shower and a dual-sink vanity.
- The three remaining bedrooms are reached via a balcony hall, which offers a stunning view of the family room.

Plan AX-93309

Bedrooms: 4	Baths: 2½
Living Area:	
Upper floor	1,180 sq. ft.
Main floor	1,290 sq. ft.
Total Living Area:	**2,470 sq. ft.**
Basement	1,290 sq. ft.
Garage	421 sq. ft.
Exterior Wall Framing:	2x4

Foundation Options:
Daylight basement
Standard basement
Slab
(All plans can be built with your choice of foundation and framing. A generic conversion diagram is available. See order form.)

BLUEPRINT PRICE CODE: C

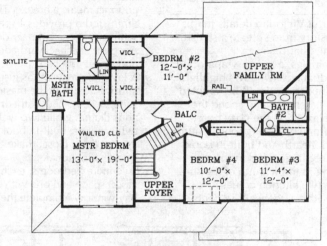

UPPER FLOOR

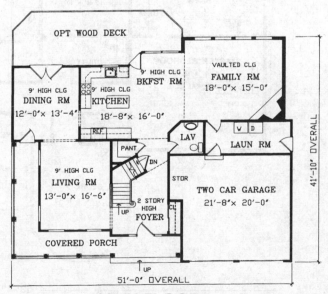

MAIN FLOOR

ORDER BLUEPRINTS ANYTIME!
CALL TOLL-FREE 1-888-626-2026

Plan AX-93309

PRICES AND DETAILS
ON PAGES 13-15

103

Details, Details!

- The wonderful Victorian details in this lovely one-story home create a stylish, yet practical, charm.
- Fishscale shingles, a railed wraparound porch and dual bay windows highlight the inviting exterior. You'll be tempted to stretch a hammock and spend the weekend relaxing on the cozy porch.
- Inside, the immense living room features a huge brick hearth and built-in book shelves. Three large windows in front help to bring in the warmth of the sun.
- The galley-style kitchen comes equipped with a large walk-in pantry

and enough conveniences to make gourmet meals a breeze. The bayed dining room provides a sparkling setting for those culinary delights. Access to the backyard adds a pleasant and useful touch.

- A lavish bath awaits as just one of the alluring details in the master bedroom suite. A 12-ft.-high cathedral ceiling adds drama, while two walk-in closets, twin vanities, built-in bookshelves and its own linen closet make the suite smartly functional.
- Two more bedrooms, each with ample closet space and one with a gorgeous bay window, complete the design.

Plan L-1659	
Bedrooms: 3	**Baths:** 2
Living Area:	
Main floor	1,659 sq. ft.
Total Living Area:	**1,659 sq. ft.**
Exterior Wall Framing:	2x4

Foundation Options:

Slab
(All plans can be built with your choice of foundation and framing. A generic conversion diagram is available. See order form.)

BLUEPRINT PRICE CODE: B

MAIN FLOOR

63'-4"

37'-10"

BATH

BEDROOM 3
10'-4" x 10'

LINEN

PANTRY

KITCHEN

REFR

D/W

DINING
15' x 10'

COOKTOP

OVEN

BOOKS

MASTER BEDROOM
15'-4" x 13'-4"
CATHEDRAL CLG.

SLOPE

D
W

UTILITY

BATH 2

LIVING ROOM
20' x 15'-4"
10'CLG.

FOYER

BRICK HEARTH

BEDROOM 2
11'-4" x 13'-8"

PORCH

Plan L-1659

PRICES AND DETAILS ON PAGES 13-15

Fine Dining

- This fine stucco home showcases a huge round-top window arrangement, which augments the central dining room with its 14½-ft. ceiling.
- A cute covered porch opens to the bright foyer, where a 13-ft.-high ceiling extends past a decorative column to the airy Great Room.
- The sunny dining room merges with the Great Room, which features a warm

fireplace, a kitchen pass-through and a French door to the backyard.
- The kitchen boasts a pantry closet, a nice serving bar and an angled sink. The vaulted breakfast nook with an optional bay hosts casual meals.
- The secluded master suite has a tray ceiling and a vaulted bath with a dual-sink vanity, a large garden tub and a separate shower. Across the home, two secondary bedrooms share another full bath.

Plan FB-5351-GENE

Bedrooms: 3	Baths: 2
Living Area:	
Main floor	1,670 sq. ft.
Total Living Area:	**1,670 sq. ft.**
Daylight basement	1,670 sq. ft.
Garage	400 sq. ft.
Exterior Wall Framing:	2x4

Foundation Options:

Daylight basement
Crawlspace
(All plans can be built with your choice of foundation and framing. A generic conversion diagram is available. See order form.)

BLUEPRINT PRICE CODE:	B

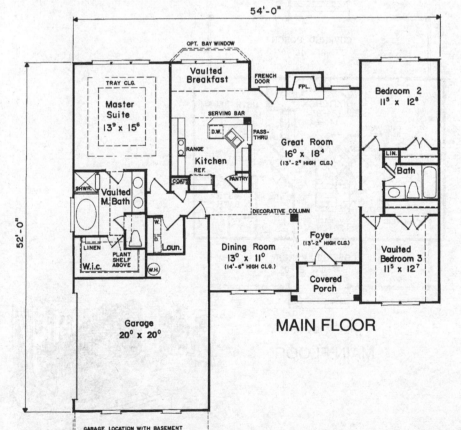

MAIN FLOOR

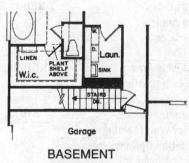

BASEMENT STAIRWAY LOCATION

ORDER BLUEPRINTS ANYTIME!
CALL TOLL-FREE 1-888-626-2026

Plan FB-5351-GENE

PRICES AND DETAILS
ON PAGES 13-15
105

Spacious Economy

- This economical country cottage features wide, angled spaces and 9-ft., 4-in. ceilings in both the Great Room and the master bedroom for roomy appeal and year-round comfort.

- The Great Room boasts a cozy fireplace with a raised hearth and a built-in niche for a TV, making this room perfect for winter gatherings. On warm nights, a homey covered porch at the rear can be accessed through sliding glass doors.

- Amenities in the luxurious master bedroom include a large walk-in closet, a private whirlpool bath and a dual-sink vanity.

- The nicely appointed kitchen offers nearby laundry facilities and porch access. A serving bar allows for casual dining and relaxed conversation.

- The optional daylight basement includes a tuck-under, two-car garage.

Plan AX-94322

Bedrooms: 3	Baths: 2½
Living Area:	
Upper floor	545 sq. ft.
Main floor	1,134 sq. ft.
Total Living Area:	**1,679 sq. ft.**
Daylight basement	618 sq. ft.
Standard basement	1,134 sq. ft.
Tuck-under garage	516 sq. ft.
Exterior Wall Framing:	2x4

Foundation Options:
Daylight basement
Standard basement
Crawlspace
Slab
(All plans can be built with your choice of foundation and framing. A generic conversion diagram is available. See order form.)

BLUEPRINT PRICE CODE: B

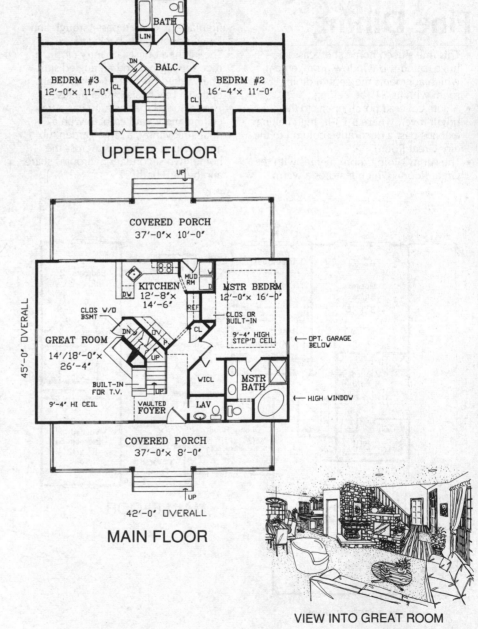

UPPER FLOOR

MAIN FLOOR

VIEW INTO GREAT ROOM

Plan AX-94322

PRICES AND DETAILS
ON PAGES 13-15

Plenty of Presence

- A stucco facade complemented by fieldstone, a dramatic roofline and handsome keystones accenting the window treatments gives this home plenty of presence.

- Inside, the two-story foyer boasts an open stairway with a balcony overlook. Straight ahead, the huge family room is expanded by a 16½-ft. vaulted ceiling, plus a tall window and a French door that frame the fireplace.

- The adjoining dining room flows into the kitchen and breakfast room, which feature an angled serving bar, a bright window wall and a French door that opens to a covered patio.

- The main-floor master suite is the pride of the floor plan, offering a 10-ft. tray ceiling. The deluxe master bath has a 14-ft. vaulted ceiling, a garden tub and a spacious walk-in closet.

- The upper floor offers two more bedrooms, a full bath and attic space.

Plan FB-1681

Bedrooms: 3	Baths: 2½
Living Area:	
Upper floor	449 sq. ft.
Main floor	1,232 sq. ft.
Total Living Area:	**1,681 sq. ft.**
Daylight basement	1,232 sq. ft.
Garage and storage	435 sq. ft.
Exterior Wall Framing:	2x4

Foundation Options:

Daylight basement
Crawlspace
(All plans can be built with your choice of foundation and framing. A generic conversion diagram is available. See order form.)

BLUEPRINT PRICE CODE: B

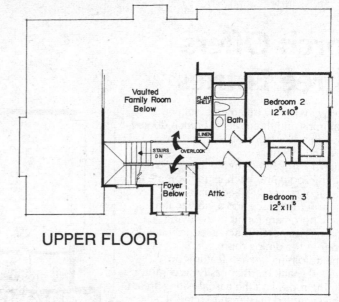

UPPER FLOOR

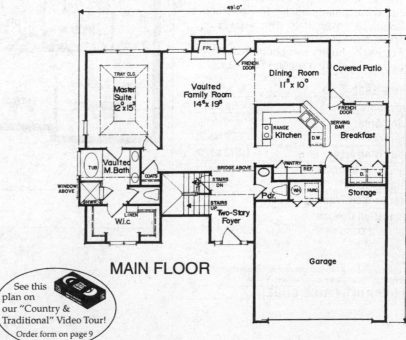

MAIN FLOOR

ORDER BLUEPRINTS ANYTIME!
CALL TOLL-FREE 1-888-626-2026

Plan FB-1681

PRICES AND DETAILS
ON PAGES 13-15

107

Porch Offers Three Entries

- Showy window treatments, stately columns and three sets of French doors give this Plantation-style home an inviting exterior.
- High 12-ft. ceilings in the living room, dining room and kitchen add volume to the economically-sized home.
- A corner fireplace and a view to the back porch are found in the living room. The porch is accessed from a door in the dining room.
- The adjoining kitchen features an angled snack bar that easily serves the dining room and the casual eating area.
- The secluded master suite offers a cathedral ceiling, a walk-in closet and a luxurious private bath with a spa tub and a separate shower.
- Across the home, two additional bedrooms share a second full bath.

Plan E-1602	
Bedrooms: 3	**Baths:** 2
Living Area:	
Main floor	1,672 sq. ft.
Total Living Area:	**1,672 sq. ft.**
Standard basement	1,672 sq. ft.
Garage	484 sq. ft.
Exterior Wall Framing:	2x6
Foundation Options:	
Standard basement	
Crawlspace	
Slab	

(All plans can be built with your choice of foundation and framing. A generic conversion diagram is available. See order form.)

BLUEPRINT PRICE CODE: B

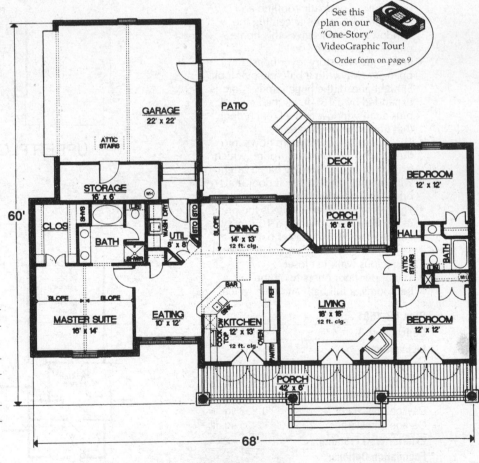

See this plan on our "One-Story" VideoGraphic Tour! Order form on page 9

MAIN FLOOR

Plan E-1602

Full of Dreams

- The thrill of owning a first home is one of the greatest of a lifetime. In this perfect two-story, all of those years of dreams will play out to their fullest.
- Out front, a covered porch protects guests from the elements when they arrive for dinner or a night of cards.
- Inside, a lush plant shelf ushers them into the formal dining room, which is great for life's many special occasions.
- Located just steps away, the kitchen provides fast, efficient service to even the most elaborate of meals. A pretty garden window over the sink brings a ray of sunshine to chores. Nearby, the morning room comfortably hosts breakfast and casual lunches.
- In the living room at the rear of the home, folks will gather to watch the evening news or read the latest bestseller. A French door leads outside to a patio—a soothing backdrop to a lazy summer afternoon.
- Nearby, a private bath and a walk-in closet distinguish the master suite. A window seat calls you to sit and reflect.
- Upstairs, an open loft gives the kids a place of their own, while still within earshot of parents downstairs.

Plan L-705-A

Bedrooms: 3	Baths: 2½
Living Area:	
Upper floor	540 sq. ft.
Main floor	1,163 sq. ft.
Total Living Area:	**1,703 sq. ft.**
Garage	494 sq. ft.
Exterior Wall Framing:	2x4

Foundation Options:

Slab

(All plans can be built with your choice of foundation and framing. A generic conversion diagram is available. See order form.)

BLUEPRINT PRICE CODE: B

UPPER FLOOR

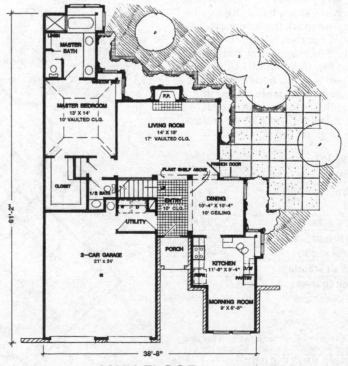

MAIN FLOOR

ORDER BLUEPRINTS ANYTIME!
CALL TOLL-FREE 1-888-626-2026

Plan L-705-A

PRICES AND DETAILS
ON PAGES 13-15

109

Perfect Repose

- This perfectly planned home is well suited to serve as the haven your family retreats to for repose and relaxation.
- Out front, a covered porch includes just the right amount of space for your favorite two rockers and a side table.
- Inside, the foyer flows right into the Great Room, which will serve as home base for family gatherings. A fireplace flanked by a media center turns this room into a home theater.
- Nearby, sunlight pours into the versatile dining room. Along one wall, a beautiful built-in cabinet holds linens, china and other fine collectibles.
- Afternoon treats take on a fun twist at the kitchen's snack bar. For easy serving, the snack bar extends to a peninsula counter.
- A 10-ft., 8-in. tray ceiling and a cheery bay window in the master suite turn this space into a stylish oasis. A dressing area with a vanity table for morning preening leads to the master bath, where a skylight and a 15-ft. vaulted ceiling brighten the room.

Plan AX-95347

Bedrooms: 3	**Baths:** 2½
Living Area:	
Main floor	1,709 sq. ft.
Total Living Area:	**1,709 sq. ft.**
Standard basement	1,709 sq. ft.
Garage and storage	448 sq. ft.
Exterior Wall Framing:	2x4
Foundation Options:	
Standard basement	
Crawlspace	
Slab	

(All plans can be built with your choice of foundation and framing. A generic conversion diagram is available. See order form.)

BLUEPRINT PRICE CODE: B

REAR VIEW

MAIN FLOOR

Plan AX-95347

PRICES AND DETAILS ON PAGES 13-15

Enchanting!

- This gracious French-style home is the picture of enchantment, with its striking Palladian window and its beautiful brick facade with lovely corner quoins.
- Beyond the leaded-glass front door, the open entry introduces the versatile living room. Guests will enjoy visiting for hours in front of the crackling fire!
- Visible over a half-wall, the formal dining room is worthy of any festive occasion. A wall of windows offers delightful views to a covered porch and your backyard's award-winning landscaping.

- The bayed morning room is the perfect spot for orange juice and waffles. If the weather permits, open the French door and dine alfresco on the porch!
- A handy snack bar highlights the gourmet kitchen. The sink is positioned for backyard views, to brighten those daily chores.
- The two-car garage is ideally located for easy unloading of groceries.
- Across the home, the master suite is a restful haven. Soak away your cares in the fabulous garden tub!
- Two secondary bedrooms, a nice hall bath and a central laundry room round out this enchanting plan.

Plan L-709-FA

Bedrooms: 3	**Baths:** 2

Living Area:

Main floor	1,707 sq. ft.
Total Living Area:	**1,707 sq. ft.**
Garage	572 sq. ft.
Exterior Wall Framing:	2x4

Foundation Options:

Slab
(All plans can be built with your choice of foundation and framing. A generic conversion diagram is available. See order form.)

BLUEPRINT PRICE CODE:	**B**

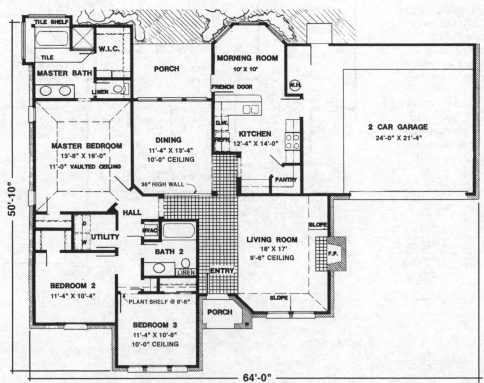

MAIN FLOOR

ORDER BLUEPRINTS ANYTIME!
CALL TOLL-FREE 1-888-626-2026

Plan L-709-FA

PRICES AND DETAILS
ON PAGES 13-15

111

Dramatic Dining Room

- The highlight of this lovely one-story design is its dramatic dining room, which boasts a 14-ft. ceiling and a soaring window wall.
- The airy foyer ushers guests through an arched opening and into the vaulted Great Room, which is warmed by an inviting fireplace. This room will easily host both formal receptions and casual evenings of conversation.
- The gourmet kitchen features a handy pantry, a versatile serving bar and a pass-through to the Great Room.
- The bright breakfast area offers a laundry closet and outdoor access.
- Two secondary bedrooms share a compartmentalized bath.
- Across the home, the removed master suite boasts a tray ceiling, overhead plant shelves and an adjoining vaulted sitting room. An exciting garden tub is found in the luxurious master bath.

Plan FB-5008-ALLE

Bedrooms: 3	Baths: 2
Living Area:	
Main floor	1,715 sq. ft.
Total Living Area:	**1,715 sq. ft.**
Daylight basement	1,715 sq. ft.
Garage	400 sq. ft.
Exterior Wall Framing:	2x4

Foundation Options:

Daylight basement
Crawlspace
Slab
(All plans can be built with your choice of foundation and framing. A generic conversion diagram is available. See order form.)

BLUEPRINT PRICE CODE:	B

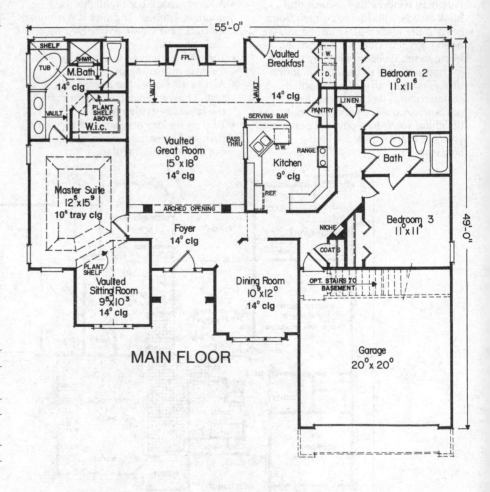

MAIN FLOOR

Plan FB-5008-ALLE

PRICES AND DETAILS
ON PAGES 13-15

Appealing, Angled Ranch

- This unique, angled ranch boasts a striking interior, which is highlighted by a dramatic domed ceiling at its center.
- The gabled entryway opens to a spacious pentagonal living area. A handsome fireplace, lots of glass and an adjoining backyard terrace are showcased, in addition to the 14-ft.-high domed ceiling.
- The dining room can be extended into the nearby den by opening the folding doors. The den features a 14-ft. sloped ceiling, an exciting solar bay and terrace access.
- A casual eating area and a nice-sized kitchen expand to the front of the home, ending at a windowed sink.
- The nearby mudroom area includes laundry facilities and an optional powder room.
- The sleeping wing offers four bedrooms, including an oversized master suite with a private terrace and a skylighted bath with dual sinks and a whirlpool tub. The secondary bedrooms share another full bath.

Plan K-669-N

Bedrooms: 4	Baths: 2-2½
Living Area:	
Main floor	1,728 sq. ft.
Total Living Area:	**1,728 sq. ft.**
Standard basement	1,545 sq. ft.
Garage and storage	468 sq. ft.
Exterior Wall Framing:	2x4 or 2x6

Foundation Options:

Standard basement
Slab

(All plans can be built with your choice of foundation and framing. A generic conversion diagram is available. See order form.)

BLUEPRINT PRICE CODE:	B

VIEW INTO DINING ROOM AND LIVING ROOM

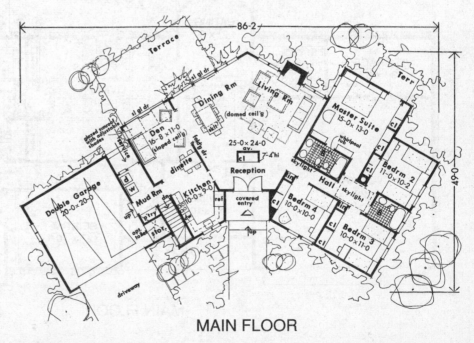

MAIN FLOOR

ORDER BLUEPRINTS ANYTIME!
CALL TOLL-FREE 1-888-626-2026

Plan K-669-N

PRICES AND DETAILS
ON PAGES 13-15

113

Simply Beautiful

- This four-bedroom design offers simplistic beauty, economical construction and ample space for both family life and formal entertaining—all on one floor.
- The charming cottage-style exterior gives way to a spacious interior. A 13-ft. vaulted, beamed ceiling soars above the huge living room, which features a massive fireplace, built-in bookshelves and access to a backyard patio.
- The efficient galley-style kitchen flows between a sunny bayed eating area and the formal dining room.
- The deluxe master suite includes a dressing room, a large walk-in closet and a private bath.
- The three remaining bedrooms are larger than average and offer ample closet space.
- A nice-sized storage area and a deluxe utility room are accessible from the two-car garage.

Plan E-1702

Bedrooms: 4	Baths: 2
Living Area:	
Main floor	1,751 sq. ft.
Total Living Area:	**1,751 sq. ft.**
Garage	484 sq. ft.
Storage	105 sq. ft.
Exterior Wall Framing:	2x4

Foundation Options:

Crawlspace
Slab

(All plans can be built with your choice of foundation and framing. A generic conversion diagram is available. See order form.)

BLUEPRINT PRICE CODE: **B**

See this plan on our "One-Story" VideoGraphic Tour! Order form on page 9

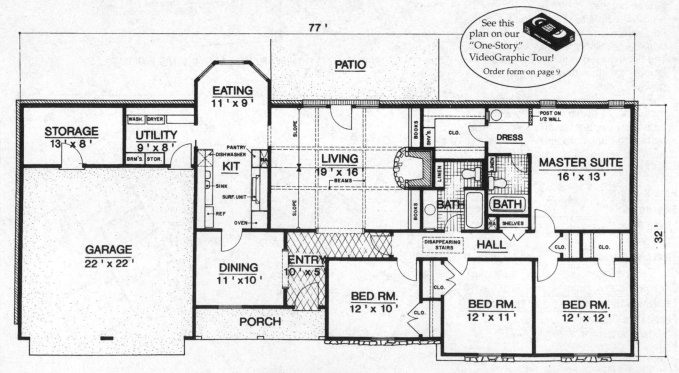

MAIN FLOOR

Rural Roots

- This nostalgic farmhouse reminds you of country life, bringing back memories or maybe just fond daydreams.
- Authentic Victorian details contribute to the comforting facade. Lovely fishscale shingles above the bay window and oval glass in the front door will command attention from visitors.
- Receive the long-awaited kinfolk on the delightful wraparound porch; you may want to sit a spell and catch up on family news!
- Then usher everyone into the family room, for memorable moments in front of the corner fireplace.

- When the feast is ready, eyes will sparkle as the turkey is presented in the bay-windowed dining room. A French door leads to the back porch for after-dinner chatting in the cool evening.
- The efficient kitchen handles meal preparation with ease. The "east" wall features a pantry and double ovens.
- The secluded master suite lets you unwind before a good night's rest. A fabulous bath and direct porch access make this suite really sweet!
- Two secondary bedrooms share a split bath. The bayed front bedroom boasts a 10-ft. ceiling and a walk-in closet.
- The blueprints include plans for a detached, two-car garage (not shown).

Plan L-1772

Bedrooms: 3	Baths: 2

Living Area:

Main floor	1,772 sq. ft.
Total Living Area:	**1,772 sq. ft.**
Detached garage	576 sq. ft.

Exterior Wall Framing: 2x4

Foundation Options:

Slab
(All plans can be built with your choice of foundation and framing. A generic conversion diagram is available. See order form.)

BLUEPRINT PRICE CODE: B

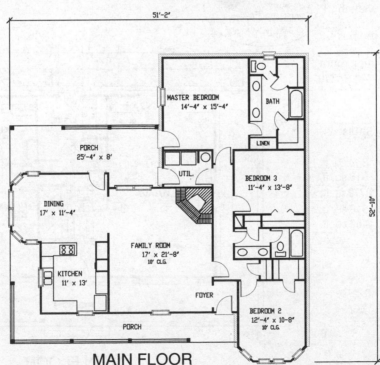

MAIN FLOOR

ORDER BLUEPRINTS ANYTIME!
CALL TOLL-FREE 1-888-626-2026

Plan L-1772

PRICES AND DETAILS
ON PAGES 13-15

115

Casual Country Living

- With its covered wraparound porch, this gracious design is ideal for warm summer days or starry evenings.
- The spacious living room boasts a handsome brick-hearth fireplace and built-in book and gun storage. A French door accesses the backyard.
- The open kitchen design provides plenty of space for food storage and preparation with its pantry and oversized central island.
- Two mirror-imaged baths service the three bedrooms on the upper floor. Each secondary bedroom features a window seat and two closets. The master bedroom has a large walk-in closet and a private bath.
- A versatile hobby or sewing room is also included.
- An optional carport off the dining room is available upon request. Please specify when ordering.

Plan J-8895

Bedrooms: 3	Baths: 2½
Living Area:	
Upper floor	860 sq. ft.
Main floor	919 sq. ft.
Total Living Area:	**1,779 sq. ft.**
Standard basement	919 sq. ft.
Optional carport	462 sq. ft.
Exterior Wall Framing:	2x4

Foundation Options:

Standard basement

Crawlspace

Slab

(All plans can be built with your choice of foundation and framing. A generic conversion diagram is available. See order form.)

BLUEPRINT PRICE CODE:	B

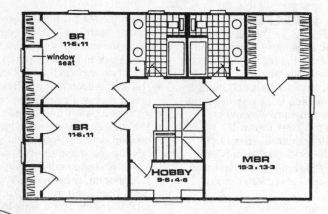

See this plan on our "Two-Story" VideoGraphic Tour! Order form on page 9

UPPER FLOOR

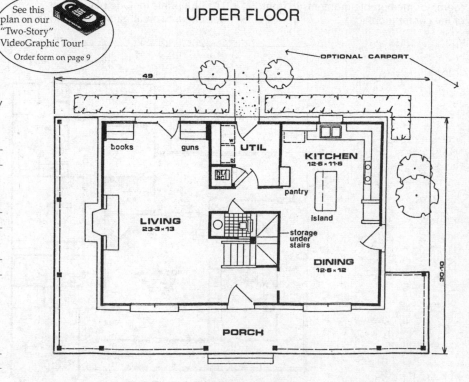

MAIN FLOOR

ORDER BLUEPRINTS ANYTIME!
CALL TOLL-FREE 1-888-626-2026

Plan J-8895

PRICES AND DETAILS
ON PAGES 13-15

Stunning Stucco

- A stunning columned porch and bright stucco adorn the exterior of this attractive one-story home.
- The bold foyer leads to the formal living room, which is set off with decorative half-walls and a high plant shelf. The room is further enhanced by a 14-ft. vaulted ceiling and an energy-efficient fireplace. A 36-in.-high counter to the right of the fireplace is open to the adjoining dining room.
- The spacious kitchen, which includes a space-saving island cooktop, merges with the cheery bayed breakfast nook.
- The nearby family room boasts a 13-ft. vaulted ceiling, a nice fireplace and a French door to an expansive rear patio.
- The lovely den located off the foyer could double as a guest room.
- Dramatic 10-ft. ceilings brighten the den, the kitchen and the breakfast nook.
- A 13-ft., 9-in. vaulted ceiling adorns the sun-drenched master suite, which features a huge walk-in closet. His-and-hers vanities and a platform garden tub highlight the private master bath.
- The second bedroom features a walk-in closet and a nearby full bath.

Plan B-93032

Bedrooms: 2+	Baths: 2½
Living Area:	
Main floor	2,029 sq. ft.
Total Living Area:	**2,029 sq. ft.**
Standard basement	2,029 sq. ft.
Garage	682 sq. ft.
Exterior Wall Framing:	2x6

Foundation Options:

Standard basement

(All plans can be built with your choice of foundation and framing. A generic conversion diagram is available. See order form.)

BLUEPRINT PRICE CODE: C

MAIN FLOOR

Traditional Treasure

- Arched windows lend elegance to the trio of dormers that accentuate this traditional treasure.
- Double doors off the covered front porch open to a dramatic two-story lobby with a curved stairway. The adjacent living room is set in a stunning glass alcove, lending sunlight and spaciousness to the design. A spectacular fireplace is angled to parallel the living room.
- The adjoining dining room offers sliding glass doors to a back terrace, which is perfect for outdoor dining or entertaining.
- The L-shaped island kitchen, the sunny dinette and the family room merge for a cozy ambience. A second fireplace enhances the comfortable feel. Sliding glass doors provide outdoor access.
- Off the upper-floor balcony are four bedrooms and two baths. The master bedroom offers a cathedral ceiling and a private balcony. The skylighted master bath has twin sinks and a bidet.

Plan K-690-D

Bedrooms: 4	Baths: 2½
Living Area:	
Upper floor	1,086 sq. ft.
Main floor	1,171 sq. ft.
Total Living Area:	**2,257 sq. ft.**
Standard basement	1,098 sq. ft.
Garage	420 sq. ft.
Exterior Wall Framing:	2x4 or 2x6

Foundation Options:

Standard basement
Slab
(Typical foundation & framing conversion diagram available—see order form.)

BLUEPRINT PRICE CODE: C

VIEW INTO THE LIVING ROOM
AND DINING ROOM

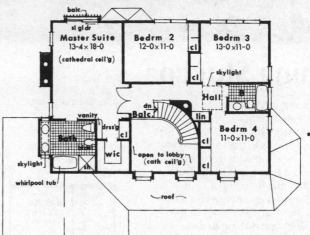

UPPER FLOOR

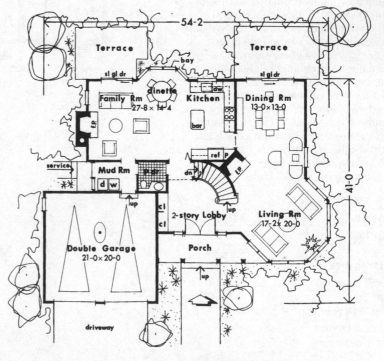

MAIN FLOOR

Sweet Nostalgia

- This two-story design conjures up sweet memories of simpler days, when home served as grand central for the family.
- A covered porch out front whispers a quiet welcome to visitors. On summer nights, pull up a chair to listen to the pitter-patter of the raindrops.
- Inside, the Great Room acts as home base for daily activities. An 18-ft. vaulted ceiling opens up the space, while a fireplace adds cheer.
- Finding someone to cook will be a snap once the family sees the kitchen. Even a master chef would envy the island cooktop and workstation.
- Across the home, a stylish 13½-ft. vaulted ceiling makes the master suite extra special. After a day of hiking, sink into the whirlpool tub to rejuvenate.
- Unless otherwise noted, every room on the main floor has a 9-ft. ceiling.
- Upstairs, the bath and front bedrooms include dormers under 10½-ft. ceilings. The family's students can turn these dormers into neat reading nooks.

Plan AHP-9550

Bedrooms: 4	Baths: 2½
Living Area:	
Upper floor	762 sq. ft.
Main floor	1,689 sq. ft.
Total Living Area:	**2,451 sq. ft.**
Standard basement	1,689 sq. ft.
Garage and storage	484 sq. ft.
Exterior Wall Framing:	2x4 or 2x6

Foundation Options:

Standard basement
Crawlspace
Slab

(All plans can be built with your choice of foundation and framing. A generic conversion diagram is available. See order form.)

BLUEPRINT PRICE CODE: **C**

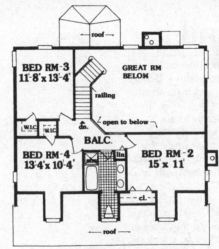

UPPER FLOOR

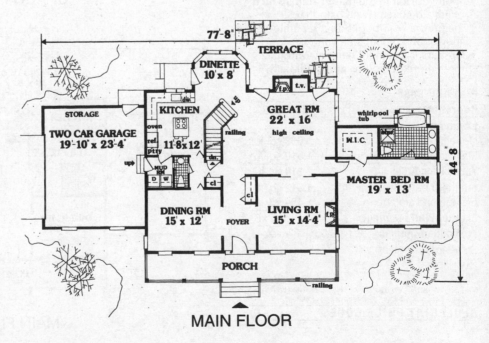

MAIN FLOOR

Splendor on the Land

- Plantation touches adorn the facade of this breathtaking home, making it a splendid companion to your pastoral tract of land.
- The columned porch leads to an exquisite interior. A cozy two-way fireplace and a fun wet bar unite the formal living room and the more casual Great Room. The media shelf will spice up your weekends!
- Mornings are glorious in the cozy bayed dinette. Access to a backyard terrace is just a step away. The adjoining kitchen boasts an island cooktop and snack bar, plus a cheery windowed sink.
- Spoil yourself in the master suite, which offers a deluxe private bath that includes a whirlpool tub, a separate shower and a dual-sink vanity.
- Upstairs, a beautiful balcony introduces three more bedrooms and a full bath.

Plan AHP-9605

Bedrooms: 4	Baths: 2½
Living Area:	
Upper floor	698 sq. ft.
Main floor	1,512 sq. ft.
Total Living Area:	**2,210 sq. ft.**
Standard basement	1,512 sq. ft.
Garage and storage	484 sq. ft.
Exterior Wall Framing:	2x4 or 2x6

Foundation Options:

Standard basement

Crawlspace

Slab

(All plans can be built with your choice of foundation and framing. A generic conversion diagram is available. See order form.)

BLUEPRINT PRICE CODE: C

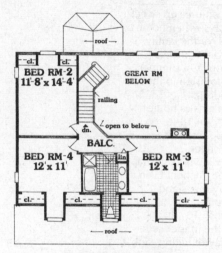

UPPER FLOOR

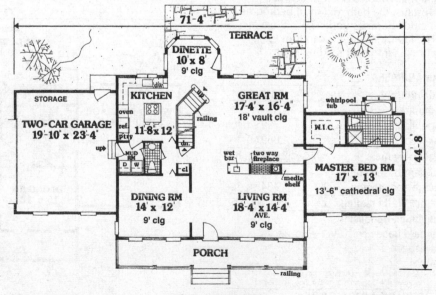

MAIN FLOOR

ORDER BLUEPRINTS ANYTIME!
CALL TOLL-FREE 1-888-626-2026

Plan AHP-9605

PRICES AND DETAILS
ON PAGES 13-15

UPPER FLOOR

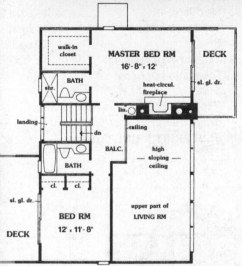

walk-in closet

MASTER BED RM
16'-8" x 12'

DECK

BATH
shr.

heat-circul. fireplace

sl. gl. dr.

lin.

landing

dn

railing

BALC.

high sloping ceiling

BATH

cl.   cl.

sl. gl. dr.

BED RM
12' x 11'-8"

upper part of LIVING RM

DECK

LOWER FLOOR

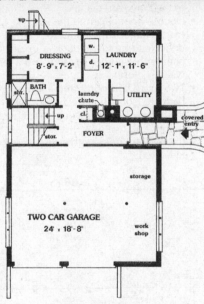

up

DRESSING
8'-9" x 7'-2"

w.
d.

LAUNDRY
12'-1" x 11'-6"

BATH
shr.

laundry chute

UTILITY

cl.

up

stor.

FOYER

covered entry

storage

TWO CAR GARAGE
24' x 18'-8"

work shop

MAIN FLOOR

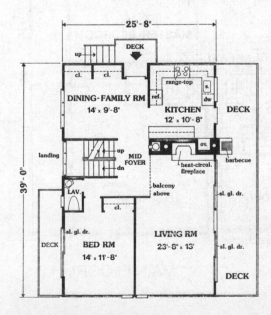

25'-8"

39'-0"

up

DECK

cl.   cl.

DINING-FAMILY RM
14' x 9'-8"

range-top

ref.

s.

dw

KITCHEN
12' x 10'-8"

DECK

landing

up

MID FOYER

dn

heat-circul. fireplace

ov.

barbecue

LAV.

balcony above

cl.

sl. gl. dr.

DECK

sl. gl. dr.

BED RM
14' x 11'-8"

LIVING RM
23'-8" x 13'

sl. gl. dr.

DECK

A Deck for Each Room

- Exciting outdoor living is possible in this three-level contemporary design.
- The front entrance and garage are located on the lower level, along with a dressing room, full bath and laundry facilities.
- The main level offers a spectacular two-story living room overlooked by an upper-level balcony; highlights include a massive stone wall with heat-circulating fireplace and two sets of sliding glass doors that offer entrance to the front deck that stretches to the kitchen.
- Outdoor dining can take place off the kitchen deck with barbecue or off the formal dining/family area.
- The main-level bedroom and pair of upper-level bedrooms each offer private decks.

Plan HFL-2176	
Bedrooms: 3	**Baths:** 3½
Space:	
Upper floor	712 sq. ft.
Main floor	1,001 sq. ft.
Lower floor	463 sq. ft.
Total Living Area	**2,176 sq. ft.**
Garage and storage	448 sq. ft.
Exterior Wall Framing	2x6
Foundation options:	
Slab (Foundation & framing conversion diagram available—see order form.)	
Blueprint Price Code	C

ORDER BLUEPRINTS ANYTIME!
CALL TOLL-FREE 1-888-626-2026

Plan HFL-2176

PRICES AND DETAILS
ON PAGES 13-15

121

Fantastic Family Living Space

- Luxury begins at the front door with this exciting one-story traditional home.
- The eye-catching front entry opens to an impressive vaulted foyer. Double doors open to an unusual living room that can be used as a den, home office or bedroom.
- The formal dining room offers a tray ceiling and has easy access to the combination kitchen, breakfast room

and family room. This fantastic family living space is punctuated by floor-to-ceiling windows, a fireplace and views to the backyard deck.
- Double doors open to the vaulted master suite, which features French doors leading to the deck, a luxurious bath with a corner spa tub, and a large walk-in closet.
- Two more bedrooms and another full bath are isolated at the other side of the home. This sprawling design is further enhanced by 9-ft. ceilings throughout, unless otherwise indicated.

Plan APS-1812

Bedrooms: 3-4	Baths: 2
Living Area:	
Main floor	1,886 sq. ft.
Total Living Area:	**1,886 sq. ft.**
Garage	400 sq. ft.
Exterior Wall Framing:	2x4

Foundation Options:

Slab

(Typical foundation & framing conversion diagram available—see order form.)

BLUEPRINT PRICE CODE:	B

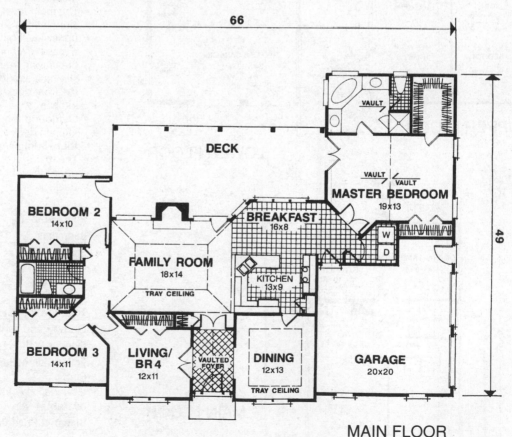

MAIN FLOOR

Plan APS-1812

PRICES AND DETAILS
ON PAGES 13-15

Stately but Affordable

- Stately columns set off transom windows and support an inviting porch in this well-planned design.
- French doors give classic charm to the central Great Room, which boasts a large fireplace.
- The formal dining room features access to a covered rear porch.

- The unique kitchen arrangement offers a bright, bayed breakfast nook. The peninsula counter allows the cook to view the outdoors while preparing meals or cleaning up.
- A perfect master suite is positioned for peace and quiet. It boasts backyard views, a walk-in closet and a private bath with a garden tub, a separate shower and a dual-sink vanity.
- The two remaining bedrooms feature porch views and walk-in closets, and share a compartmentalized bath.

Plan V-1595	
Bedrooms: 3	**Baths:** 2
Living Area:	
Main floor	1,595 sq. ft.
Total Living Area:	**1,595 sq. ft.**
Garage	473 sq. ft.
Exterior Wall Framing:	2x6
Foundation Options:	

Crawlspace
(All plans can be built with your choice of foundation and framing. A generic conversion diagram is available. See order form.)

| **BLUEPRINT PRICE CODE:** | **B** |

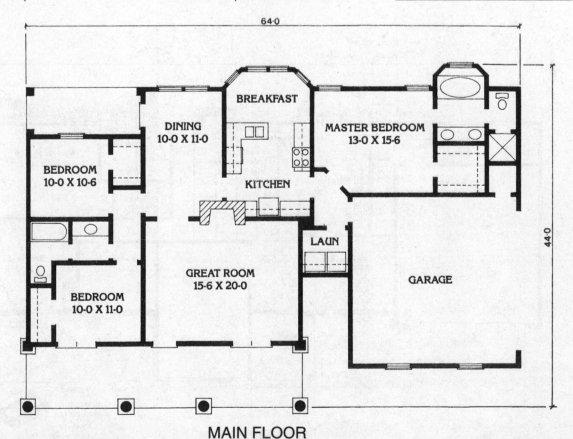

MAIN FLOOR

Outstanding One-Story

- This sharp one-story home has an outstanding floor plan, attractively enhanced by a stately brick facade.
- A vestibule introduces the foyer, which flows between the formal living spaces at the front of the home.
- The large living room features a 14-ft., 8-in. sloped ceiling and dramatic, high windows. The spacious dining room has easy access to the kitchen.

- The expansive family room is the focal point of the home, with a 16-ft. beamed cathedral ceiling, a slate-hearth fireplace and sliding glass doors to a backyard terrace.
- The adjoining kitchen has a snack bar and a sunny dinette framed by a curved window wall that overlooks the terrace.
- Included in the sleeping wing is a luxurious master suite with a private bath. A skylighted dressing room and a big walk-in closet are also featured.
- The two secondary bedrooms share a hall bath that has a dual-sink vanity. A half-bath is near the mud/laundry room.

Plan K-278-M	
Bedrooms: 3	**Baths:** 2½
Living Area:	
Main floor	1,803 sq. ft.
Total Living Area:	**1,803 sq. ft.**
Standard basement	1,778 sq. ft.
Garage and storage	586 sq. ft.
Exterior Wall Framing:	2x4 or 2x6
Foundation Options:	
Standard basement	
Slab	

(All plans can be built with your choice of foundation and framing. A generic conversion diagram is available. See order form.)

BLUEPRINT PRICE CODE:	B

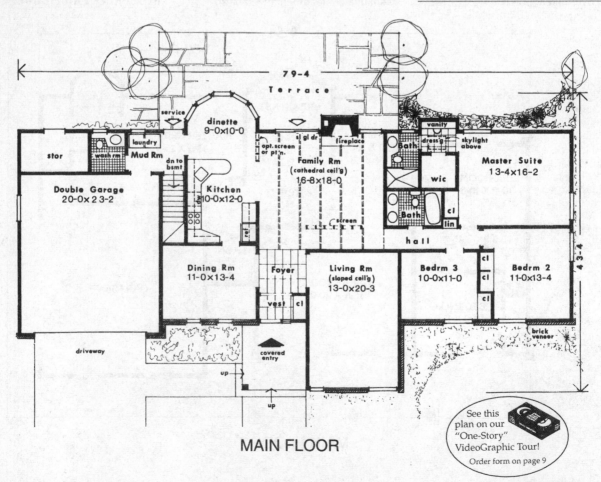

MAIN FLOOR

See this plan on our "One-Story" VideoGraphic Tour! Order form on page 9

Unique and Dramatic

- This home's unique interior and dramatic exterior make it perfect for a sloping, scenic lot.
- The expansive and impressive Great Room, warmed by a woodstove, flows into the island kitchen, which is completely open in design.
- The passive-solar sun room collects and stores heat from the sun, while offering a good view of the surroundings. Its ceiling rises to a height of 16 feet.
- Upstairs, a glamorous, skylighted master suite features an 11-ft. vaulted ceiling, a private bath and a huge walk-in closet.
- A skylighted hall bath serves the bright second bedroom. Both bedrooms open to the vaulted sun room below.
- The daylight basement adds a sunny sitting room, a third bedroom and a large recreation room.

Plans P-536-2A & -2D

Bedrooms: 2+	Baths: 2½-3½
Living Area:	
Upper floor	642 sq. ft.
Main floor	863 sq. ft.
Daylight basement	863 sq. ft.
Total Living Area:	**1,505/2,368 sq. ft.**
Garage	445 sq. ft.
Exterior Wall Framing:	2x6
Foundation Options:	**Plan #**
Daylight basement	P-536-2D
Crawlspace	P-536-2A

(All plans can be built with your choice of foundation and framing. A generic conversion diagram is available. See order form.)

BLUEPRINT PRICE CODE: B/C

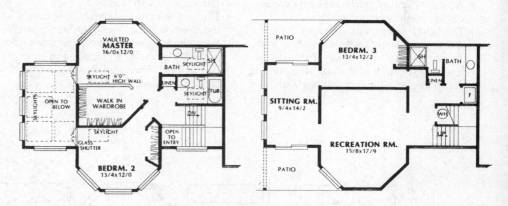

UPPER FLOOR   **DAYLIGHT BASEMENT**

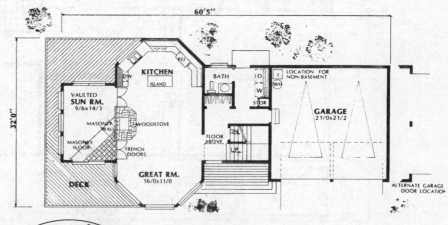

MAIN FLOOR

See this plan on our "Two-Story" VideoGraphic Tour! Order form on page 9

Plans P-536-2A & -2D

PRICES AND DETAILS
ON PAGES 13-15

Friendly Country Charm

- An inviting front porch welcomes you to this friendly one-story home.
- The porch opens to a spacious central living room with a warm fireplace and functional built-in storage shelves.
- The bay window of the adjoining dining room allows a view of the backyard.

The dining area also enjoys an eating bar provided by the adjacent walk-through kitchen.
- The nice-sized kitchen also has a windowed sink and easy access to the laundry room and carport.
- Three bedrooms and two baths occupy the sleeping wing. The oversized master bedroom features a lovely boxed-out window, two walk-in closets and a private bath. The secondary bedrooms share the second full bath.

Plan J-8692	
Bedrooms: 3	**Baths:** 2
Living Area:	
Main floor	1,633 sq. ft.
Total Living Area:	**1,633 sq. ft.**
Standard basement	1,633 sq. ft.
Carport	380 sq. ft.
Exterior Wall Framing:	2x4

Foundation Options:
Standard basement
Crawlspace
Slab
(All plans can be built with your choice of foundation and framing. A generic conversion diagram is available. See order form.)

BLUEPRINT PRICE CODE:	B

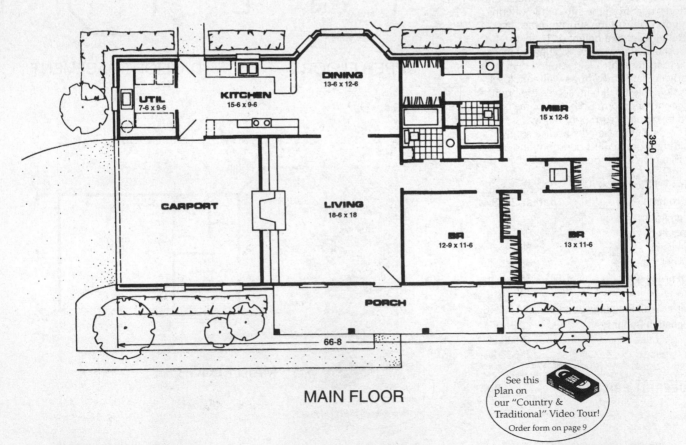

MAIN FLOOR

See this plan on our "Country & Traditional" Video Tour!
Order form on page 9

Easy and Wonderful!

- The easy, efficient style of this attractive one-story home will put a smile on any home owner's face; its practical floor plan provides a wonderful feeling of well-being.

- Protected from the elements, guests can wait in comfort on the front porch.

- With a stylish boxed ceiling, a handsome corner fireplace and access to the backyard, the nicely sized Great Room is a natural location for large gatherings and family events. A convenient snack bar holds chips and popcorn on movie nights.

- Elegant formal meals have a home in the bay-windowed dining room. If the occasion is casual, use the adjacent corner breakfast room. The nearby kitchen makes for quick setup and cleanup of either area.

- Impressively grand and surprisingly large is the master bedroom. Boasting a boxed ceiling, twin walk-in closets and a luscious private bath, it's a welcome dose of luxury!

Plan NBV-11396

Bedrooms: 3	Baths: 2
Living Area:	
Main floor	1,517 sq. ft.
Total Living Area:	**1,517 sq. ft.**
Garage	595 sq. ft.
Exterior Wall Framing:	2x4

Foundation Options:

Slab

(All plans can be built with your choice of foundation and framing. A generic conversion diagram is available. See order form.)

BLUEPRINT PRICE CODE: B

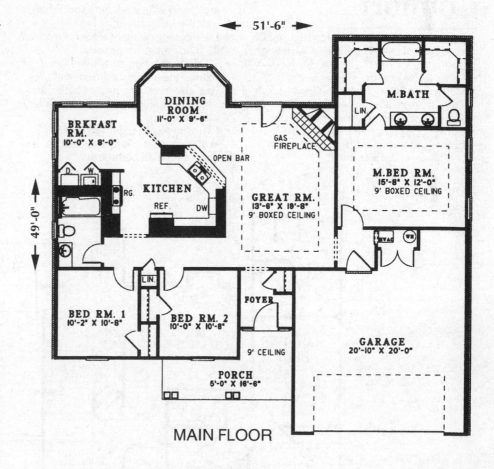

MAIN FLOOR

ORDER BLUEPRINTS ANYTIME!
CALL TOLL-FREE 1-888-626-2026

Plan NBV-11396

PRICES AND DETAILS
ON PAGES 13-15

127

Designed For Comfort

- With an eye-catching design focused on comfort, this home satisfies a variety of your family's needs.
- Enjoy a relaxing evening at home in front of a blazing fire in the living room. French doors lead out to the backyard, an ideal spot for a summer barbecue.
- Tucked into the front corner of the home, the formal dining room stands ready for a gourmet meal.

- The well-designed walk-through kitchen easily accesses both the formal dining room and the cozy breakfast nook, and shares a handy snack bar with the living room.
- The sleeping quarters are set apart from the living areas for privacy.
- Highlighted by an attractive sloped ceiling, the master bedroom captures your attention. The private bath offers a fabulous spa tub, dual sinks and a large walk-in closet.
- Two generously sized secondary bedrooms with plenty of closet space share a full hall bathroom.

Plan BOD-15-2A

Bedrooms: 3	**Baths: 2**
Living Area:	
Main floor	1,553 sq. ft.
Total Living Area:	**1,553 sq. ft.**
Garage and storage	482 sq. ft.
Exterior Wall Framing:	2x4

Foundation Options:

Crawlspace
Slab
(All plans can be built with your choice of foundation and framing. A generic conversion diagram is available. See order form.)

BLUEPRINT PRICE CODE:	B

MAIN FLOOR

61'-0"

44'-9"

MSTR BATH
KS

MASTER BEDRM
11-6x14-8
10 FT CLG
SLPE

BRKFST
8-0x11-6
10 FT CLG

STOR

D
W

LIVING
17-4x13-6
10 FT CLG

FP

42" LEDGE

KITCH
10-6x14-0
10 FT CLG

GARAGE
19-4x20-4

P

BATH 2

ENTRY

BEDRM 2
11-8x13-0

BEDRM 3
11-0x13-6

PORCH

DINING
10-6x12-0

Sunny Delight

- Sunny skylights and expanses of windows give this home a delightful focus on open spaces and scenic views.
- The barrel-vaulted entry opens to an 11-ft.-high gallery that flows nicely into the three sections of the home.
- Straight ahead, the formal dining room and living room share a vast space topped by a 13½-ft. sloped ceiling.
- A skylighted, boxed-out set of windows in the dining room reveals the panorama of the backyard. The living room's fireplace warms the entire formal area, and sliding glass doors lead to a gracious terrace.
- The U-shaped kitchen, with a windowed sink, is at the center of the casual zone. It serves both the cozy family room and the dinette, which includes sliding glass doors to a side terrace, perfect for dining alfresco.
- Across the home, the sleeping quarters make up their own wing. The lavish master suite showcases a bedroom with an 11½-ft. cathedral ceiling, plus a private bath with a whirlpool tub and a separate shower. Two additional bedrooms share a skylighted hall bath.

Plan K-810-S

Bedrooms: 3	Baths: 2
Living Area:	
Main floor	1,581 sq. ft.
Total Living Area:	**1,581 sq. ft.**
Standard basement	1,542 sq. ft.
Garage and storage	496 sq. ft.
Exterior Wall Framing:	2x4 or 2x6
Foundation Options:	
Standard basement	
Slab	

(All plans can be built with your choice of foundation and framing. A generic conversion diagram is available. See order form.)

BLUEPRINT PRICE CODE:	B

VIEW INTO DINING AND LIVING ROOMS

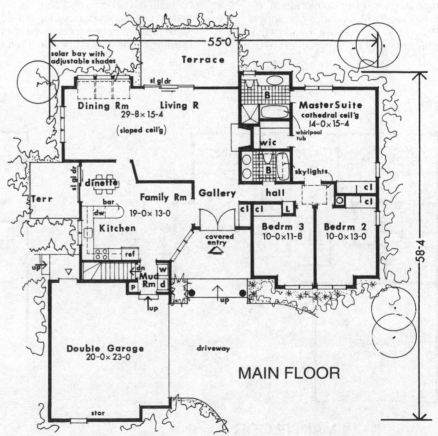

MAIN FLOOR

Favorite Sun

- Greet the sun each morning on this home's cute backyard patio. Sliding doors from the kitchen let you turn this quaint spot into a breakfast nook with connections to nature!
- The living and dining rooms are united by a 17-ft. vaulted ceiling, imparting a wide-open feel to their shared space. After supper, you and your guests may gather in front of the living room's fireplace for warm conversation. A boxed-out window adds eye appeal.
- Peace and comfort are found in the master bedroom, which offers two

pretty windows in the sleeping chamber. Two closets flank the passage to the private bath, where you'll find a zesty shower and room for your towels.
- A nice overlook to the entry and living room enhances the upper floor, which hosts two more bedrooms. The foremost bedroom is plenty big for the teenager who likes to spread out.
- A full bath serves the two bedrooms.
- The loft can become whatever you wish. As your family grows, you can turn it into a generously sized bedroom. Or consider making it a game room, a hobby room, an exciting learning center or your personal retreat!

Plan B-91041

Bedrooms: 3+	Baths: 2½
Living Area:	
Upper floor	581 sq. ft.
Main floor	1,052 sq. ft.
Total Living Area:	**1,633 sq. ft.**
Standard basement	1,052 sq. ft.
Garage	380 sq. ft.
Exterior Wall Framing:	2x4

Foundation Options:

Standard basement
Slab
(All plans can be built with your choice of foundation and framing. A generic conversion diagram is available. See order form.)

BLUEPRINT PRICE CODE:	B

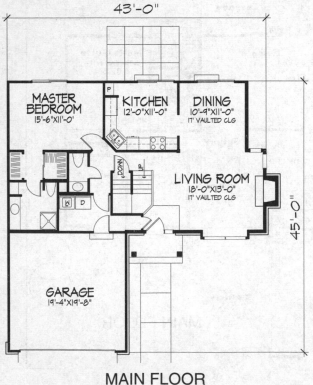

MAIN FLOOR

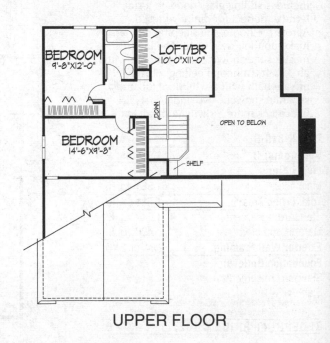

UPPER FLOOR

Comfortable Appeal

- One look at this home's smart layout will convince you that its comfort is both appealing and affordable.
- Sunlight graces the table in the formal dining room, which offers convenient access to the kitchen.
- Unique angles distinguish the kitchen from the other living areas. A handy snack bar holds healthy treats for after-school snacks.
- The sunny eating nook is just right for casual meals or everyday dining. A built-in desk on one end of the nook is framed by decorative niches.
- Simple and bright, the Great Room impresses you with its sense of spaciousness. Enjoy the warmth of a glowing fire with your loved one after the kids have gone to bed.
- Tucked into the rear corner of the home, the master bedroom promises to be a relaxing retreat. An inviting garden tub in the private bath will soothe those aching muscles.
- This home features 9-ft. ceilings in all the living areas.

Plan S-3295-F

Bedrooms: 3	Baths: 2
Living Area:	
Main floor	1,634 sq. ft.
Total Living Area:	**1,634 sq. ft.**
Garage	370 sq. ft.
Exterior Wall Framing:	2x6
Foundation Options:	

Crawlspace
(All plans can be built with your choice of foundation and framing. A generic conversion diagram is available. See order form.)

BLUEPRINT PRICE CODE:	**B**

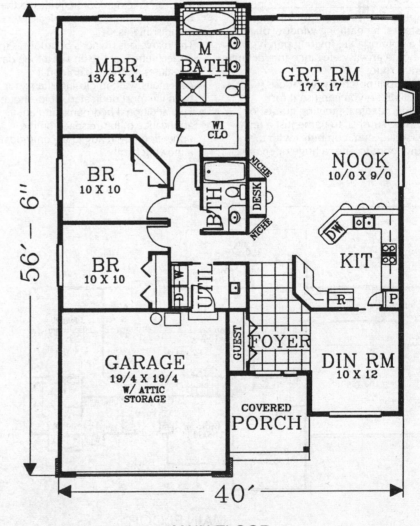

MAIN FLOOR

Easy Country Elegance

- A triplet of dormers, a sprinkling of keystones, a charming window planter and a comfortable, inviting porch give this home an easy elegance in a definite country style.
- A nice front porch always adds possibilities—you can use it for relaxing, reading, greeting guests, or watching sunsets, to name just a few.
- The Great Room combines with the dining room to offer a huge open area

great for entertaining big or small groups. A pass-through to the kitchen makes serving hors d'oeuvres during the party a breeze.
- You can take outdoor activities to the back porch/patio area on pleasant summer nights.
- The marvelous owner's bedroom is the perfect retreat at the end of a long day. It features a private bath and a cavernous walk-in closet suitable for even the most dedicated clotheshound.
- Two additional bedrooms and an abundance of future space on the upper floor are ready to accommodate a growing family.

Plan J-9417	
Bedrooms: 3+	**Baths: 2**
Living Area:	
Main floor	1,645 sq. ft.
Total Living Area:	**1,645 sq. ft.**
Future upper floor	563 sq. ft.
Standard basement	1,645 sq. ft.
Garage	441 sq. ft.
Storage	47 sq. ft.
Exterior Wall Framing:	**2x4**

Foundation Options:

Standard basement
Crawlspace
Slab

(All plans can be built with your choice of foundation and framing. A generic conversion diagram is available. See order form.)

BLUEPRINT PRICE CODE:	**B**

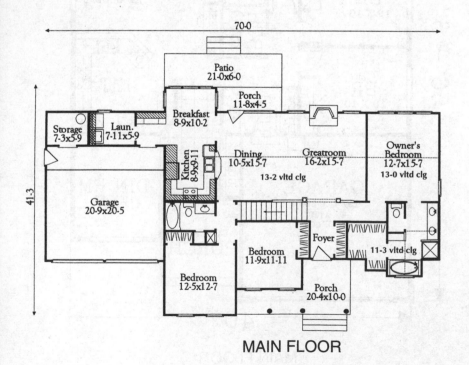

MAIN FLOOR

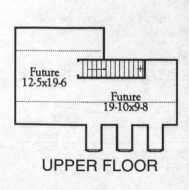

UPPER FLOOR

ORDER BLUEPRINTS ANYTIME!
CALL TOLL-FREE 1-888-626-2026

Plan J-9417

PRICES AND DETAILS
ON PAGES 13-15

Elegance for All

- With its modest square footage and versatile spaces, this stucco beauty offers elegance to all.
- French doors under an arched transom window introduce the open foyer.
- On the right, an arched opening frames the dining room, which is enhanced by a vaulted ceiling that rises to 11½ ft. in the adjoining Grand Room.
- Your family will really appreciate the comfortable Grand Room, with its wide alcove for an entertainment center. This room is great for hosting parties or for just relaxing and watching a video.
- The efficient kitchen and the bayed eating nook share an 11½-ft. vaulted ceiling. Imagine morning coffee and scrambled eggs in the cozy nook.
- For fresh-air dining or reading, how about the expansive lanai? It's accessible from four rooms!
- After a hard day, soak your cares away in the master suite's corner tub.
- Two more bedrooms share a second bath, while a quiet study would be perfect for a fourth bedroom.

Plan SG-6658

Bedrooms: 3+	**Baths:** 2

Living Area:

Main floor	1,647 sq. ft.
Total Living Area:	**1,647 sq. ft.**
Garage	427 sq. ft.

Exterior Wall Framing: 8-in. concrete block

Foundation Options:

Slab
(All plans can be built with your choice of foundation and framing. A generic conversion diagram is available. See order form.)

BLUEPRINT PRICE CODE: B

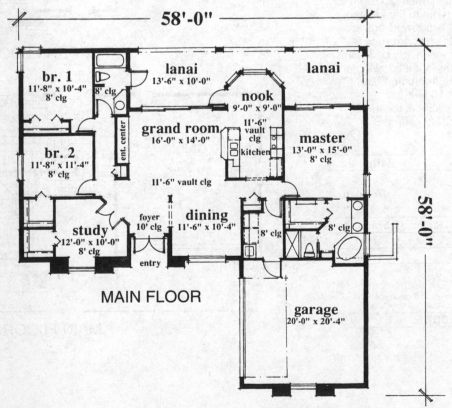

MAIN FLOOR

58'-0"

58'-0"

br. 1 — 11'-8" x 10'-4" — 8' clg
br. 2 — 11'-8" x 11'-4" — 8' clg
study — 12'-0" x 10'-0" — 8' clg
ent. center
lanai — 13'-6" x 10'-0"
grand room — 16'-0" x 14'-0"
11'-6" vault clg
nook — 9'-0" x 9'-0"
kitchen — 11'-6" vault clg
lanai
master — 13'-0" x 15'-0" — 8' clg
foyer — 10' clg
dining — 11'-6" x 10'-4"
entry
garage — 20'-0" x 20'-4"

ORDER BLUEPRINTS ANYTIME!
CALL TOLL-FREE 1-888-626-2026

Plan SG-6658

PRICES AND DETAILS
ON PAGES 13-15

133

Striking Sundries

- Louvered wood shutters and ornate detailing make this stately brick home beautifully striking.
- A lofty railed balcony and 18-ft.-high ceilings in the foyer and dining room create a dramatic first impression of the airy interior.
- The sprawling family room to the right of the foyer culminates at an attractive fireplace and media center, and could be partitioned to add a formal living space to the home.
- A sunny walk-through breakfast room bridges the family room to the kitchen, which has a lovely windowed sink area.
- Upstairs, the master bedroom suite is separated from the secondary bedrooms by the railed balcony. Vaulted ceilings above the master bedroom and bath slope to a height of 10 feet.
- Unless otherwise specified, the main-floor rooms feature 9-ft. ceilings.

Plan BRF-1678	
Bedrooms: 3	**Baths:** 2½
Living Area:	
Upper floor	878 sq. ft.
Main floor	800 sq. ft.
Total Living Area:	**1,678 sq. ft.**
Garage	477 sq. ft.
Exterior Wall Framing:	2x4
Foundation Options:	
Slab	
(All plans can be built with your choice of foundation and framing. A generic conversion diagram is available. See order form.)	
BLUEPRINT PRICE CODE:	B

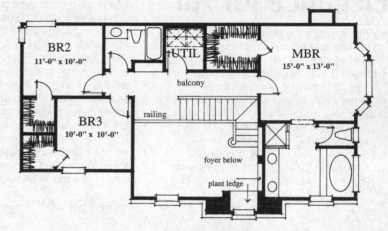

UPPER FLOOR

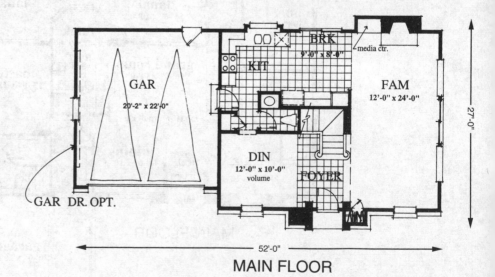

MAIN FLOOR

Plan BRF-1678

PRICES AND DETAILS
ON PAGES 13-15

Bold Stucco and Stone

- Stone and stucco join forces to create this dapper home's bold facade.
- Windows and high ceilings command attention inside and add a vertical dimension to the sprawling layout.
- The foyer's 20½-ft.-high vaulted ceiling is echoed by the family room ahead. Nestled between two windows, the family room's handsome fireplace further attracts your eye.
- At the center of the living spaces, the kitchen offers its users a stylish wraparound serving bar and a neat five-shelf pantry.
- Four bedrooms make up the sleeping wing. The foremost bedroom boasts a 15-ft. vaulted ceiling, while the master bedroom offers a 10-ft. tray ceiling.
- The master bath's 13-ft. vaulted ceiling hovers above a garden tub, a dual-sink vanity and a dramatic arched window.
- Unless otherwise mentioned, each room has a 9-ft. ceiling.

Plan FB-1688

Bedrooms: 4	**Baths:** 2

Living Area:	
Main floor	1,702 sq. ft.
Total Living Area:	**1,702 sq. ft.**
Daylight basement	1,702 sq. ft.
Garage	400 sq. ft.
Exterior Wall Framing:	2x4

Foundation Options:

Daylight basement
Crawlspace

(All plans can be built with your choice of foundation and framing. A generic conversion diagram is available. See order form.)

BLUEPRINT PRICE CODE:	B

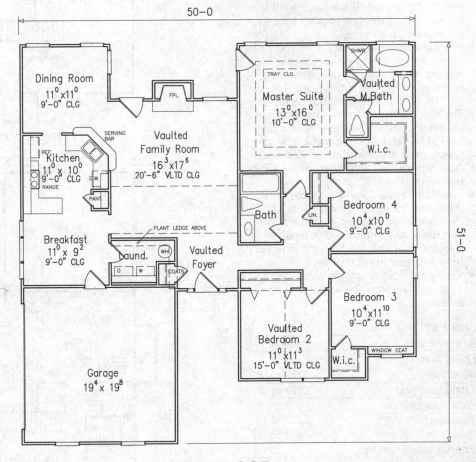

MAIN FLOOR

ORDER BLUEPRINTS ANYTIME!
CALL TOLL-FREE 1-888-626-2026

Plan FB-1688

PRICES AND DETAILS
ON PAGES 13-15

135

Lofty Dreams

- With triple dormers, a columned front porch and a lovely flower planter, this home's cozy presence inspires lofty dreams for your family.
- Past the foyer, the Great Room beckons family and guests to gather cheerily around its fireplace. A stepped ceiling and a window wall overlooking the back porch create a spacious feeling.
- The sunny dining room is easily served by the spectacular kitchen. With a large angled bar and a built-in desk, this area promises to become a hub of activity.
- Across from the laundry room, a walk-in pantry stocks extra supplies.
- Sweet privacy awaits at the other end of the home. Here, the owner's suite flaunts vaulted ceilings in the bedroom and bath. A whirlpool tub, a separate shower, dual sinks and a walk-in closet help to preserve your sanity.
- The upper floor is large enough to host a future playroom and an extra bedroom.

Plan J-9418

Bedrooms: 3	Baths: 2
Living Area:	
Main floor	1,727 sq. ft.
Total Living Area:	**1,727 sq. ft.**
Future upper floor	563 sq. ft.
Standard basement	1,727 sq. ft.
Garage and storage	531 sq. ft.
Exterior Wall Framing:	2x4

Foundation Options:

Standard basement
Crawlspace
Slab
(All plans can be built with your choice of foundation and framing. A generic conversion diagram is available. See order form.)

BLUEPRINT PRICE CODE: B

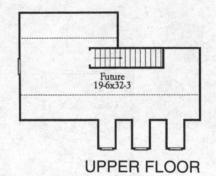

UPPER FLOOR

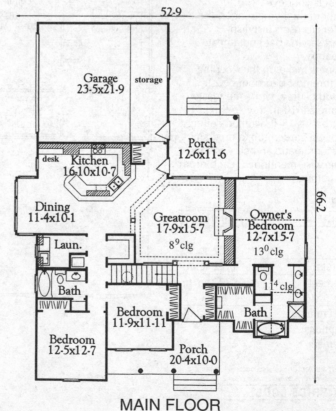

MAIN FLOOR

Plan J-9418

PRICES AND DETAILS
ON PAGES 13-15

Courtyard Retreat

- When you crave peace and relaxation, retreat to the private courtyard of this sweet one-story home. Nestled to the side of the design, this is an ideal spot for fun family gatherings or quiet time alone with a good book.
- Fishscale shingles and quaint detailing mark the front of the home and create a sense of friendly welcome.
- Inside, the roomy entry includes a door to the courtyard. A hallway leads past a lovely wall of windows to the living room, which boasts a grand fireplace and a convenient wet bar.
- The kitchen offers a pantry for extra supplies, as well as its own door to the backyard. The dining room hosts any occasion in style and features its own outdoor access.
- The master suite holds a 12-ft.-high skylighted bath with a garden tub, a separate shower, dual sinks, a walk-in closet and passage to the courtyard. A planter adds a bit of lush greenery.
- Unless otherwise specified, all rooms are topped by 9-ft. ceilings.

Plan E-1705

Bedrooms: 3	Baths: 2
Living Area:	
Main floor	1,732 sq. ft.
Total Living Area:	**1,732 sq. ft.**
Garage and storage	517 sq. ft.
Exterior Wall Framing:	2×4

Foundation Options:
Crawlspace
Slab
(All plans can be built with your choice of foundation and framing. A generic conversion diagram is available. See order form.)

BLUEPRINT PRICE CODE:	B

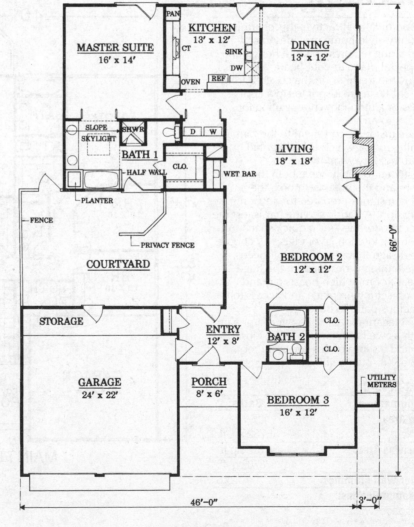

MAIN FLOOR

ORDER BLUEPRINTS ANYTIME!
CALL TOLL-FREE 1-888-626-2026

Plan E-1705

PRICES AND DETAILS
ON PAGES 13-15

137

Especially Endearing

- Economically attractive, this charming country-style home provides lots of endearing features that will help it find a special place in your heart.
- Enjoy the fresh air on the covered front porch! It's a great spot to sip a cool glass of lemonade while waiting for guests to arrive.
- Once inside, escort them to the formal dining room, which is highlighted by a beautiful bay window.
- Designed to easily serve both the dining room and the breakfast nook, the kitchen stands prepared for any culinary occasion. A handy serving bar is just the spot to offer the kids a quick snack. An alternate kitchen layout lets you choose the design that best suits your needs.
- Entertaining is destined for the huge Great Room, which boasts a grand, mood-setting fireplace and access to the spacious patio in back.
- The elegant master suite offers a private bath as well as a large walk-in closet.
- To add a sense of openness, all rooms have 9-ft.-high ceilings.

Plan S-3295-C

Bedrooms: 3	Baths: 2
Living Area:	
Main floor	1,732 sq. ft.
Total Living Area:	**1,732 sq. ft.**
Garage	370 sq. ft.
Exterior Wall Framing:	2x6

Foundation Options:

Crawlspace

(All plans can be built with your choice of foundation and framing. A generic conversion diagram is available. See order form.)

BLUEPRINT PRICE CODE:	B

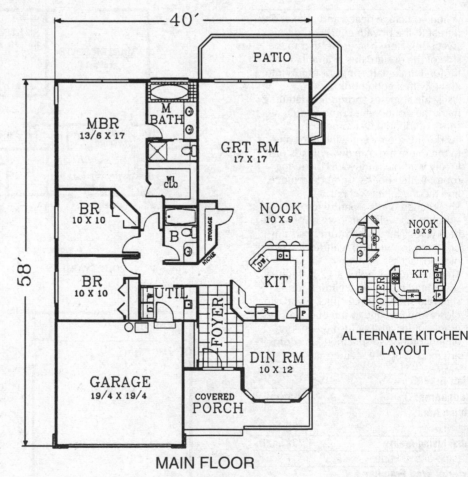

ALTERNATE KITCHEN LAYOUT

MAIN FLOOR

Plan S-3295-C

PRICES AND DETAILS
ON PAGES 13-15

Toward Perfection!

- This picturesque one-story home will bring you one step closer to the perfection you're looking for!
- The huge sundeck in back may be all you need on a cloudless summer day, but once the chilly days of fall and winter arrive, you'll be thankful for the warm, inviting interior as well.
- Past the foyer, you'll discover an enormous living room with a comfy corner fireplace and a beautiful view of the backyard.
- The adjacent dining area provides a nice spot for special meals. Steps away, the nice-sized kitchen boasts a handy island with a snack bar.
- Bask in the sunshine from the lovely bay-windowed nook. If the day is too irresistible, just step out to the sundeck and enjoy!
- Three bedrooms create plenty of space for a growing family. The master bedroom features a walk-in closet and a private bath.

Plan IDG-2021

Bedrooms: 3	Baths: 2
Living Area:	
Main floor	1,741 sq. ft.
Total Living Area:	**1,741 sq. ft.**
Daylight basement	1,741 sq. ft.
Garage	494 sq. ft.
Exterior Wall Framing:	2x6

Foundation Options:

Daylight basement

(All plans can be built with your choice of foundation and framing. A generic conversion diagram is available. See order form.)

BLUEPRINT PRICE CODE: B

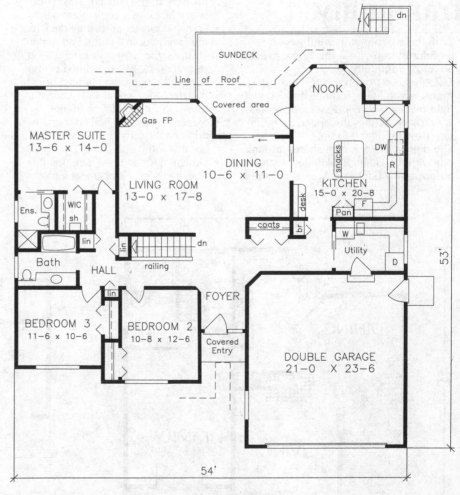

MAIN FLOOR

Air of Tranquility

- With its tall, roundtop windows and wonderful front deck, this home exudes an air of tranquility.
- Two steps up from the entry, the 16½-ft.-high vaulted living room is flooded with light from a high window arrangement. A fireplace defines this space from the free-flowing dining room.
- The dining room, which shares a snack bar with the U-shaped kitchen, features a door to the backyard or a rear patio.

- A windowed sink makes daily chores a pleasure in the kitchen. This work space includes a convenient pantry.
- French doors to an inviting deck make the family room a natural attraction.
- Upstairs, the master suite enables quiet relaxation. A 13½-ft. vaulted ceiling adorns the bedroom, and the private bath includes a dual-sink vanity for those hectic Monday mornings.
- Nearby, a balcony hall connects two additional bedrooms. They share another full bath.
- Designed for an up-sloping lot, this plan includes a tuck-under garage.

Plan AM-2113-A

Bedrooms: 3	**Baths:** 2½

Living Area:

Upper floor	813 sq. ft.
Main floor	1,022 sq. ft.
Total Living Area:	**1,835 sq. ft.**
Daylight basement/garage	994 sq. ft.
Exterior Wall Framing:	2x6

Foundation Options:

Daylight basement
(All plans can be built with your choice of foundation and framing. A generic conversion diagram is available. See order form.)

BLUEPRINT PRICE CODE: B

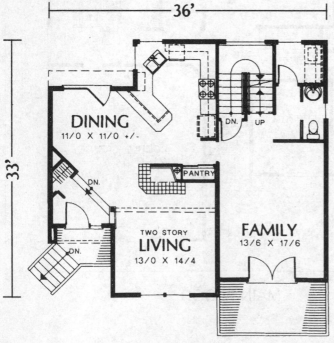

MAIN FLOOR

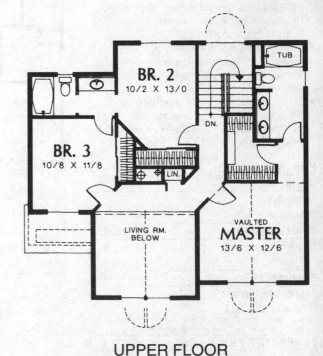

UPPER FLOOR

Elegance in One Story

- Decorative dormers, a columned front porch and high arched windows lined with soldier coursing lend elegance to this charming one-story home.
- Off the entry, the formal dining room sets the mood for fine meals and romantic, candlelit moments.
- A stunning three-way fireplace reigns at the center of the home. It glows merrily for all to see, while nicely dividing the formal living room from the rambling family room.
- The kitchen features a pantry closet and an angled bar overlooking the family room. Nearby, the boxed-out breakfast nook accommodates casual dining.
- Secluded to the rear of the home, the master suite provides plenty of privacy, plus an access to the covered patio. The master bath is a haven of comfort, with a lovely garden tub, a separate shower, a dual-sink vanity, a private toilet and a convenient walk-in closet.
- Across the home, two secondary bedrooms dwell in their own wing. They share a hall bath.

Plan KD-1918

Bedrooms: 3	Baths: 2
Living Area:	
Main floor	1,918 sq. ft.
Total Living Area:	**1,918 sq. ft.**
Garage and storage	496 sq. ft.
Exterior Wall Framing:	2x4

Foundation Options:

Slab
(All plans can be built with your choice of foundation and framing. A generic conversion diagram is available. See order form.)

BLUEPRINT PRICE CODE:	B

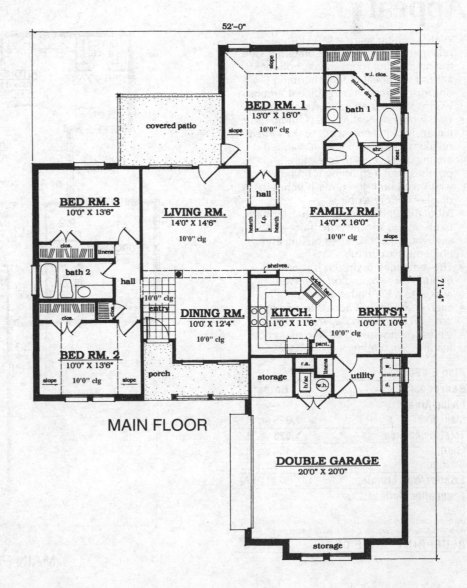

MAIN FLOOR

Refreshing Appeal

- With a ceiling soaring to 15½ ft. and relaxing covered porches on either side, the huge living room speaks volumes about the appeal of this charming one-story home. A magnificent fireplace warms the area on cold winter days.
- Two wonderful eating areas frame the expansive kitchen—a cozy, skylighted breakfast nook with a 12-ft. vaulted ceiling and access to one of the porches, and a stunning formal dining room with built-in corner hutches to display your fine china.
- Attractive and alluring, the master bath treats you to special amenities—a sunny skylight, a 12-ft. vaulted ceiling and a gorgeous garden tub.
- The remaining bedroom is roomy enough for two, and offers private access to a full bath.
- Each bedroom has access to one of the covered porches via a French door.
- Unless otherwise noted, the main floor features 9-ft. ceilings.

Plan E-1900

Bedrooms: 2	Baths: 2
Living Area:	
Main floor	1,928 sq. ft.
Total Living Area:	**1,928 sq. ft.**
Garage	484 sq. ft.
Storage	48 sq. ft.
Exterior Wall Framing:	2x6

Foundation Options:

Slab

(All plans can be built with your choice of foundation and framing. A generic conversion diagram is available. See order form.)

BLUEPRINT PRICE CODE:	**B**

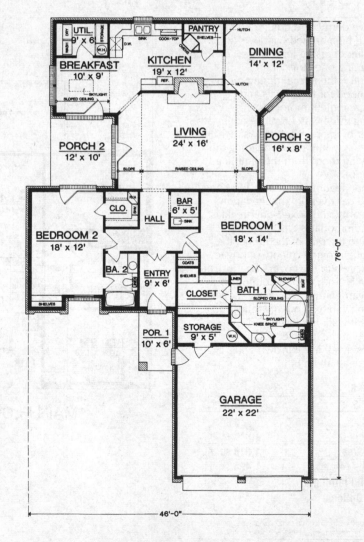

MAIN FLOOR

Plan E-1900

PRICES AND DETAILS
ON PAGES 13-15

Rave Reviews

- Even the toughest critics will applaud this dynamic design. Its striking exterior—with bold lines, shutters and keystone accents—sets the scene for an excellent plot inside.
- Formal and informal areas are separated by the entry. On the right side, the living room and dining room flow together nicely. A boxed-out window adds drama to the living room, and the dining room looks over a fresh garden.
- To the left of the entry, the sprawling family room boasts a fireplace and access to a pretty porch. It shares an angled snack bar with the kitchen.
- A breakfast nook, perfect for casual family meals, rounds out this wing.
- Secluded to the rear of the home, the master suite treats you like a star. The bedroom includes a bayed sitting area.
- A masterpiece in its own right, the private bath features a unique symmetrical layout and a number of amenities. These include dual sinks and vanities, a marble tub, a separate glass shower, a private toilet and an enormous walk-in closet.
- Two more bedrooms share a full bath.

Plan RD-2021

Bedrooms: 3	Baths: 2
Living Area:	
Main floor	2,021 sq. ft.
Total Living Area:	**2,021 sq. ft.**
Garage and storage	533 sq. ft.
Exterior Wall Framing:	2x4

Foundation Options:

Crawlspace

Slab

(All plans can be built with your choice of foundation and framing. A generic conversion diagram is available. See order form.)

BLUEPRINT PRICE CODE: C

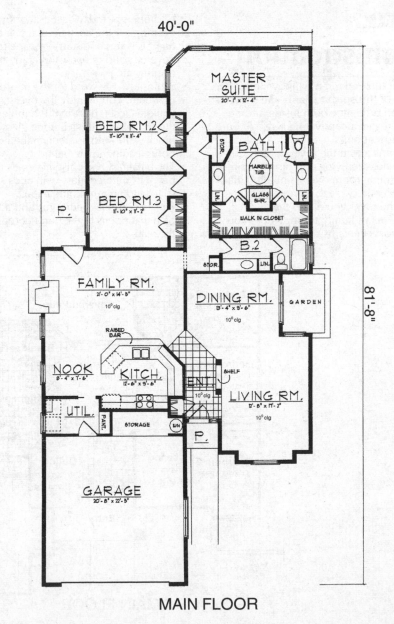

MAIN FLOOR

Pure Sophistication

- The grand Palladian window above the entry of this spectacular home showers lighted brilliance both inside and out, and creates a captivating sense of pure sophistication.
- Columns adorn the foyer, which separates the living and dining rooms. The dining room offers a mitered glass wall to add pizzazz to your meal.
- Past the foyer you'll find the magnificent family room, where you can host events of all sizes, from boisterous birthday bashes to intimate evenings by the cozy fireplace. If the night is warm and starry, escape to the covered patio in back and enjoy the evening air.
- Exquisite is the word for the master bedroom. You'll enjoy the oversized walk-in closet, bask in the bubbles of the spa tub—with its unique glass-block wall—and appreciate the French doors leading to the patio.
- The breakfast nook also accesses the patio. Its mitered glass wall adds sparkle to your morning meal.
- Three additional bedrooms and a full bath that opens to the patio complete the plan.

Plan HDS-99-255	
Bedrooms: 4	**Baths:** 2
Living Area:	
Main floor	2,060 sq. ft.
Total Living Area:	**2,060 sq. ft.**
Garage	478 sq. ft.
Exterior Wall Framing:	2x4

Foundation Options:
Slab
(All plans can be built with your choice of foundation and framing. A generic conversion diagram is available. See order form.)

BLUEPRINT PRICE CODE:	C

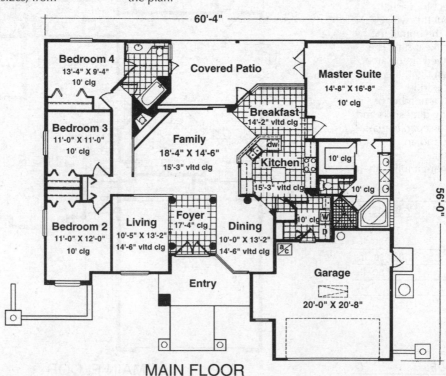

MAIN FLOOR

Vibrance Revisited

- This breathtaking Mediterranean-style home delivers a vibrant facade and an even more scintillating floor plan!
- Openly inviting living spaces greet you as you step into the foyer. Nothing but air joins the living and dining rooms. A stunning fireplace provides a focal point for the living room; near it, a door opens to a sweet patio that will prove to be a favorite early-morning spot.
- Walk through the kitchen to the breakfast nook, where three windows admit the day's first light or romantic moonglow at midnight.
- The master bedroom is an oasis of comfort and calm. Its private bath delivers your every desire, including a zesty tub, two walk-in closets and a sink for you and your spouse.
- Upstairs, a fun balcony hall leads to two more bedrooms.

Plan DD-2131	
Bedrooms: 3	**Baths: 2½**
Living Area:	
Upper floor	600 sq. ft.
Main floor	1,537 sq. ft.
Total Living Area:	**2,137 sq. ft.**
Standard basement	1,537 sq. ft.
Garage and storage	525 sq. ft.
Exterior Wall Framing:	2x4

Foundation Options:
Standard basement
Crawlspace
Slab

(All plans can be built with your choice of foundation and framing. A generic conversion diagram is available. See order form.)

BLUEPRINT PRICE CODE:	C

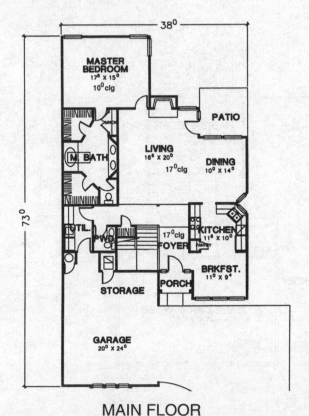

MAIN FLOOR

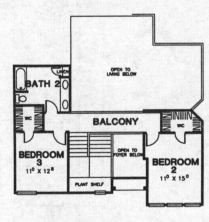

UPPER FLOOR

ORDER BLUEPRINTS ANYTIME!
CALL TOLL-FREE 1-888-626-2026

Plan DD-2131

PRICES AND DETAILS
ON PAGES 13-15

145

Spacious and Spanish

- With a facade reminiscent of a Spanish villa, this spacious home would look great in any neighborhood.
- A columned arch frames the sidelighted entry, which is further adorned with an arched transom window.
- Host a fiesta in the 14-ft.-high living room! A wall of windows gives guests a great view of your sprawling hacienda.

- The kitchen, nook and family room share a dramatic ceiling that rises to 13 ft. near the cozy fireplace. An angled island and a handy wet bar facilitate your entertaining. When the guests have left, how about a siesta on the covered backyard patio?
- A second patio belongs to the posh master suite, where a 13-ft. ceiling increases the elegant feel. Soak your worries away in the inviting corner tub.
- Two of the remaining bedrooms offer 10-ft. vaulted ceilings, while a 9-ft. ceiling graces the central bedroom.

Plan LS-95811-BJ

Bedrooms: 4	**Baths: 2**

Living Area:

Main floor	2,142 sq. ft.
Total Living Area:	**2,142 sq. ft.**
Garage	620 sq. ft.
Exterior Wall Framing:	2x6

Foundation Options:

Slab
(All plans can be built with your choice of foundation and framing. A generic conversion diagram is available. See order form.)

BLUEPRINT PRICE CODE:	**C**

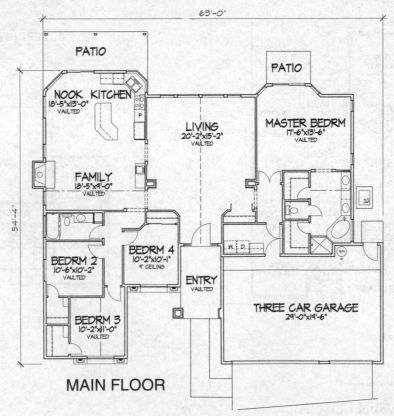

MAIN FLOOR

63'-0"

54'-4"

PATIO

NOOK 18'-5"x13'-0" VAULTED

KITCHEN

LIVING 20'-2"x15'-2" VAULTED

PATIO

MASTER BEDRM 17'-6"x13'-6" VAULTED

FAMILY 18'-5"x9'-0" VAULTED

BEDRM 2 10'-6"x10'-2" VAULTED

BEDRM 4 10'-2"x10'-1" 9' CEILING

ENTRY VAULTED

THREE CAR GARAGE 29'-0"x19'-6"

BEDRM 3 10'-2"x11'-0" VAULTED

Plan LS-95811-BJ

PRICES AND DETAILS
ON PAGES 13-15

Instant Impact

- Suitable for a compact lot, this two-story home makes an instant impact with its many-layered roofline and elegant arched windows.
- Inside, the foyer greets guests with a soaring 16-ft., 10-in. ceiling. Special occasions are celebrated in style in the dramatic living room, which includes a fireplace and a 15-ft. vaulted ceiling.
- Take formal meals in the dining room. A built-in china cabinet supplies a place to showcase family treasures.
- Meal preparation is a breeze in the spacious kitchen. A walk-in pantry

closet and a built-in desk number among its many conveniences.
- The bayed breakfast nook features a French door to a rear covered patio.
- Nearby, the family room inspires a comfortable ambience; its fireplace lends coziness to family movie nights.
- A unique staircase leads to the upper-floor sleeping quarters. Here, two secondary bedrooms share a full bath, and the master suite enjoys its own exclusive space.
- A sitting room and a private sun deck distinguish the master suite, as does its large bath with a spa tub, a separate shower and a dual-sink vanity.

Plan WH-9425

Bedrooms: 3+	**Baths: 2½**

Living Area:	
Upper floor	887 sq. ft.
Main floor	1,256 sq. ft.
Total Living Area:	**2,143 sq. ft.**
Standard basement	1,250 sq. ft.
Garage	415 sq. ft.
Exterior Wall Framing:	2x6

Foundation Options:

Standard basement
(All plans can be built with your choice of foundation and framing. A generic conversion diagram is available. See order form.)

BLUEPRINT PRICE CODE:	**C**

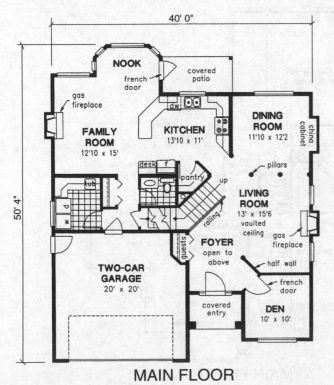

MAIN FLOOR

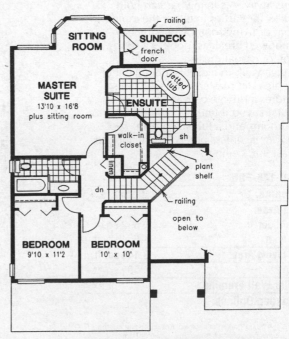

UPPER FLOOR

ORDER BLUEPRINTS ANYTIME!
CALL TOLL-FREE 1-888-626-2026

Plan WH-9425

PRICES AND DETAILS
ON PAGES 13-15

147

Contentment

- The carefree brick exterior, the smart and efficient floor plan and the special touches of style and convenience will bring that confident, contented feeling that every homeowner is looking for.
- With an 18-ft.-high ceiling, the raised foyer offers a grand welcome to guests.
- From the foyer, you can step down to the stylish living room and enjoy its many pleasures. A boxed-out window, a commanding fireplace and a lovely window seat at the beautiful corner window are signs of a well-planned, user-friendly approach to home design.
- The kitchen is at the hub of activity, which means dinner is always just a few steps away. A serving bar can hold snacks for parties in either the dining room or living room, while the bay-windowed breakfast nook is a sunny spot for casual meals.
- A huge walk-in closet is a highlight of the pleasant master suite, which also features a private bath.
- Upstairs, you'll find two additional bedrooms and a full-sized bath.
- All rooms, unless otherwise mentioned, boast 9-ft. ceilings.

Plan L-146-FSB

Bedrooms: 3	Baths: 2½
Living Area:	
Upper floor	592 sq. ft.
Main floor	1,554 sq. ft.
Total Living Area:	**2,146 sq. ft.**
Garage	591 sq. ft.
Exterior Wall Framing:	2x4

Foundation Options:
Slab
(All plans can be built with your choice of foundation and framing. A generic conversion diagram is available. See order form.)

BLUEPRINT PRICE CODE:	C

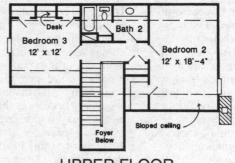

UPPER FLOOR

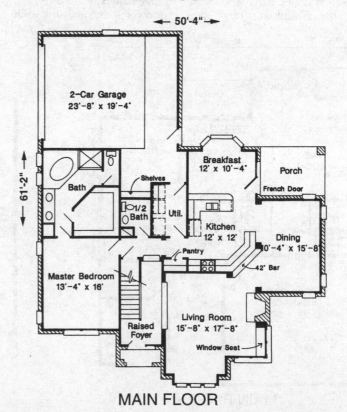

MAIN FLOOR

ORDER BLUEPRINTS ANYTIME!
CALL TOLL-FREE 1-888-626-2026

Plan L-146-FSB

PRICES AND DETAILS
ON PAGES 13-15

Sturdy Character

- This sturdy home's distinctly Georgian exterior proves a fitting companion to its interior, which fairly bursts with character and charm.
- The centerpiece of the home is its fabulous Great Room, which is warmed by a delightful corner fireplace and brightened by a pair of cheery windows. A door leads to the outdoors.

- Open flow marks the trio of the breakfast room, the kitchen and the dining room.
- Seclusion keeps the master bedroom quiet and peaceful. Its private bath pampers you with two walk-in closets, and a separate tub and shower.
- Upstairs, two bedrooms flank a quaint overlook to the foyer below. A full bath serves the rooms.
- You control the use of the room at the end of the hall. Marked as a rec room, it could become a fun media room or off-season storage.

Plan SUL-1322	
Bedrooms: 4+	Baths: 3
Living Area:	
Upper floor	760 sq. ft.
Main floor	1,388 sq. ft.
Total Living Area:	**2,148 sq. ft.**
Garage and storage	438 sq. ft.
Exterior Wall Framing:	2x4

Foundation Options:

Slab
(All plans can be built with your choice of foundation and framing. A generic conversion diagram is available. See order form.)

BLUEPRINT PRICE CODE:	**C**

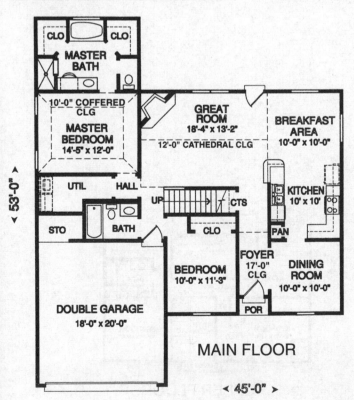

MAIN FLOOR

< 45'-0" >

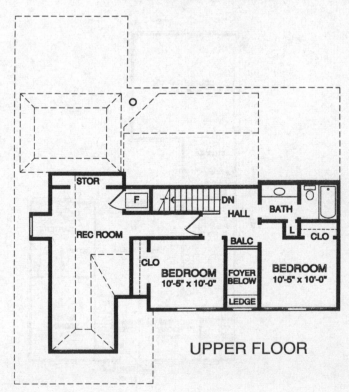

UPPER FLOOR

ORDER BLUEPRINTS ANYTIME!
CALL TOLL-FREE 1-888-626-2026

Plan SUL-1322

PRICES AND DETAILS
ON PAGES 13-15

149

Noble Presence

- Quoins, keystones, soldier coursing and an impeccable brick exterior give this two-story home a noble presence.
- Decorative lights, one on either side of the entry, as well as an arched window above, give guests a stately view as they approach.
- Inside, visitors will be greeted in style by the foyer's impressive 16-ft., 8-in. ceiling. If a formal meal is on the agenda, they can step directly into the lovely dining room on the left.

- Enjoy the rest of the evening in front of the fireplace in the adjoining family room; a dramatic 16-ft., 8-in. vaulted ceiling soars above.
- A coffered, 10-ft.-high ceiling in the breakfast nook adds a touch of elegance to your casual meals.
- The grand master bedroom boasts an oversized walk-in closet opposite the deluxe private bath, which is highlighted by an opulent corner tub.
- The upper floor holds two additional bedrooms, a full bath and a balcony overlooking the family room.

Plan SUL-1522

Bedrooms: 3	**Baths: 2½**
Living Area:	
Upper floor	673 sq. ft.
Main floor	1,483 sq. ft.
Total Living Area:	**2,156 sq. ft.**
Garage and storage	586 sq. ft.
Exterior Wall Framing:	2x4

Foundation Options:

Slab
(All plans can be built with your choice of foundation and framing. A generic conversion diagram is available. See order form.)

BLUEPRINT PRICE CODE:	**C**

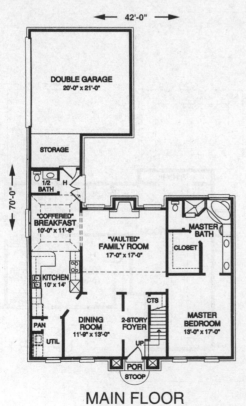

MAIN FLOOR

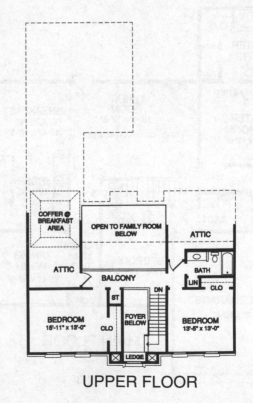

UPPER FLOOR

Plan SUL-1522

PRICES AND DETAILS ON PAGES 13-15

Striking Symmetry

- Bold lines and keystone accents mark this elegant one-story home. The exterior draws attention to its striking, symmetrical entry.
- Beyond the covered porch, a gallery leads to all areas of the home. Ahead, the Great Room boasts a cozy fireplace flanked by windows on each side.
- Afternoon snacks will be bathed in light, and evening affairs will be lit by stars in the boxed-out dining room. A door to the rear patio allows summer meals to be served alfresco.
- The galley-style kitchen includes a pantry closet and an angled snack bar.
- Facing the front of the home, a versatile flex room offers outdoor access and a nicely sized window.
- A home office down the hall provides a quiet place to work or study. A separate entrance from the outside creates a professional image for clients.
- The sleeping quarters are secluded in their own wing. The master suite features a walk-in closet and a spa bath with dual sinks and a private toilet decorated by a plant shelf.

Plan DD-2167	
Bedrooms: 3+	**Baths:** 3
Living Area:	
Main floor	2,167 sq. ft.
Total Living Area:	**2,167 sq. ft.**
Standard basement	2,167 sq. ft.
Garage	369 sq. ft.
Exterior Wall Framing:	2x4

Foundation Options:
Standard basement
Crawlspace
Slab
(All plans can be built with your choice of foundation and framing. A generic conversion diagram is available. See order form.)

BLUEPRINT PRICE CODE:	C

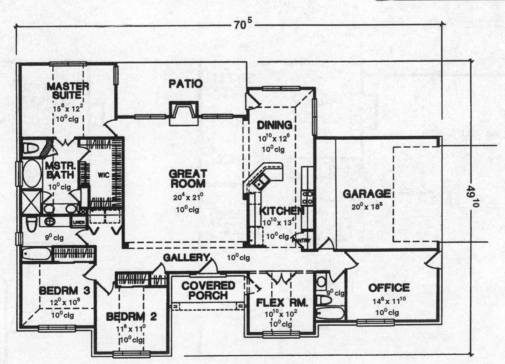

MAIN FLOOR

ORDER BLUEPRINTS ANYTIME!
CALL TOLL-FREE 1-888-626-2026

Plan DD-2167

PRICES AND DETAILS
ON PAGES 13-15

151

Classic Tailoring

- Tailored to fit the needs of today's families, this home displays classic good looks and a well-designed interior.
- The formal areas are arranged toward the front of the home. The sunken living room features two impressive window arrangements and a 19-ft.-high vaulted ceiling. Nearby, the dining room is defined by a number of stately columns and an elegant stepped ceiling.
- A hallway to a utility room, a half-bath and the three-car garage marks the transition to the rambling, casual areas. Family times reign here, especially near the fireplace in the family room.
- Sunshine from the bayed breakfast nook adds cheer to every meal, and a windowed sink in the kitchen makes daily chores a pleasure.
- Unless otherwise noted, all main-floor rooms have 9-ft. ceilings.
- Luxurious privacy awaits in the master suite upstairs. A huge walk-in closet and another ample closet flank the entrance to the luscious bath, which includes a corner tub, a separate shower and a dual-sink vanity.
- Two secondary bedrooms share another full bath nearby.

Plan LS-95921-MC	
Bedrooms: 3	**Baths:** 2½
Living Area:	
Upper floor	942 sq. ft.
Main floor	1,265 sq. ft.
Total Living Area:	**2,207 sq. ft.**
Standard basement	1,265 sq. ft.
Garage	775 sq. ft.
Exterior Wall Framing:	2x6

Foundation Options:

Standard basement
(All plans can be built with your choice of foundation and framing. A generic conversion diagram is available. See order form.)

BLUEPRINT PRICE CODE: **C**

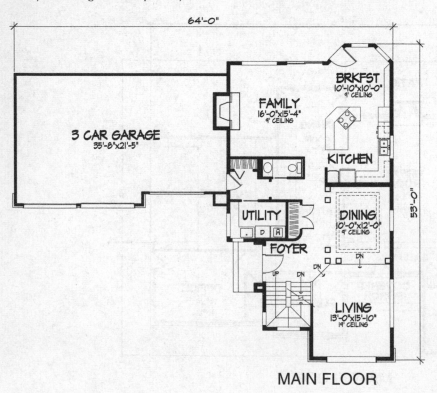

MAIN FLOOR

UPPER FLOOR

Unique Flair!

- Lots of special touches add a fascinating charm to this dynamic two-story home. Its unique flair will bring a bold, bright outlook to your life!
- You'll find windows virtually everywhere! They add a glorious shine to the home's exterior while creating a warm, sunny glow in the interior.
- Guests pass a pair of stately columns at the covered entry. The foyer, with its dramatic 16-ft., 10-in. ceiling, offers a grand welcome.
- Distinctive features abound in the main-floor living areas, as well. The sunken living room, with a 9-ft. ceiling, makes a quaint but spacious place to gather

friends after a formal dinner in the beautiful dining room. Its cozy fireplace adds cheer to any occasion.
- A bay-windowed nook with access to a back patio gives you a pleasant spot for casual dining.
- Nearby, the large family room offers a second handsome fireplace and space enough for all your relatives!
- From the stunning master suite, look out through a huge arched window. This incredible room also boasts a sizable walk-in closet and a brilliant private bath highlighted by a spa tub nestled into a pretty bay window.
- Three more bedrooms and a full bath on the upper floor provide room for overnight guests or growing families.

Plan WH-9422

Bedrooms: 4	**Baths:** 2½

Living Area:	
Upper floor	1,126 sq. ft.
Main floor	1,090 sq. ft.
Total Living Area:	**2,216 sq. ft.**
Standard basement	1,067 sq. ft.
Garage	418 sq. ft.
Exterior Wall Framing:	2x6

Foundation Options:

Standard basement
(All plans can be built with your choice of foundation and framing. A generic conversion diagram is available. See order form.)

BLUEPRINT PRICE CODE:	C

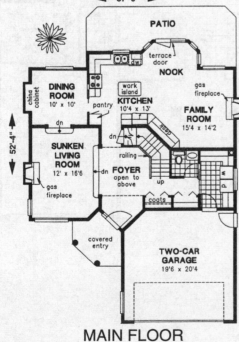

MAIN FLOOR

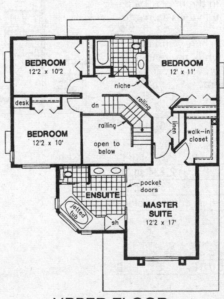

UPPER FLOOR

New Traditions

- Giving nostalgic design features a contemporary flair, this home will inspire you to create new traditions for your family.
- Opening from the foyer, the brilliant living room hosts any formal affair with style. Step into the elegant dining room to feast on a culinary masterpiece.
- The caual areas of the home are as versatile as they are expansive. Multiple angled walls create open and inviting spaces for virtually any type of entertainment.
- The sensational kitchen is a gourmet's delight with lots of cabinets and a generous walk-in pantry.
- Hidden treasures lie within the tremendous master suite. On one end, a bright sitting area accents the tray-ceilinged bedroom. In the master bath, a beautiful soaking tub views a private garden.
- Two more bedrooms share a full bath just off the kitchen, while the rear bedroom, with its own bath, would be perfect as a guest room.

Plan HDS-99-318

Bedrooms: 4	Baths: 3
Living Area:	
Main floor	2,224 sq. ft.
Total Living Area:	**2,224 sq. ft.**
Garage	554 sq. ft.
Exterior Wall Framing:	8-in. concrete block

Foundation Options:

Slab

(All plans can be built with your choice of foundation and framing. A generic conversion diagram is available. See order form.)

BLUEPRINT PRICE CODE:	**C**

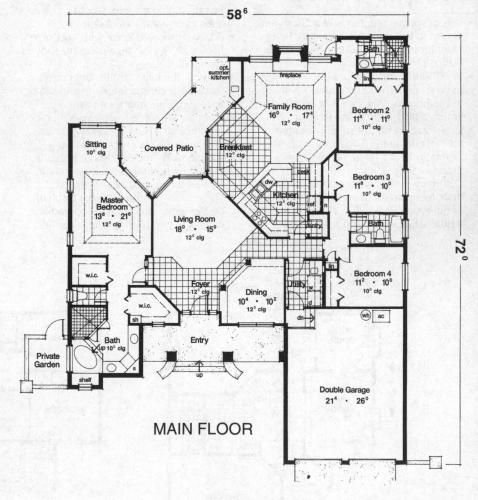

MAIN FLOOR

Plan HDS-99-318

PRICES AND DETAILS
ON PAGES 13-15

Transomed Treasure

- A striking facade, showcasing breathtaking transom windows, lures you to this one-story treasure.
- The huge family room is the center of attention for all your festive occasions. It offers easy access to the other living areas as well as to the delightful covered porch out back.
- A sunny breakfast nook is just one of the highlights of the spacious kitchen, which also sports a snack bar, a handy island and a walk-in pantry.
- The formal dining room's coffered ceiling and fabulous transom window add class to special meals.
- Prepare to be pampered in the dreamy master suite. Double doors hide a lavish bath with a whirlpool tub, dual vanities and a seated shower. The large walk-in closet offers convenient access to the utility room's washer and dryer.
- Across the home, two large bedrooms share a compartmentalized bath designed for multiple users. The front room can be used as a private study or a fourth bedroom.

Plan KLF-972

Bedrooms: 3+	Baths: 2
Living Area:	
Main floor	2,230 sq. ft.
Total Living Area:	**2,230 sq. ft.**
Garage	501 sq. ft.
Exterior Wall Framing:	2x4

Foundation Options:

Slab
(All plans can be built with your choice of foundation and framing. A generic conversion diagram is available. See order form.)

BLUEPRINT PRICE CODE: C

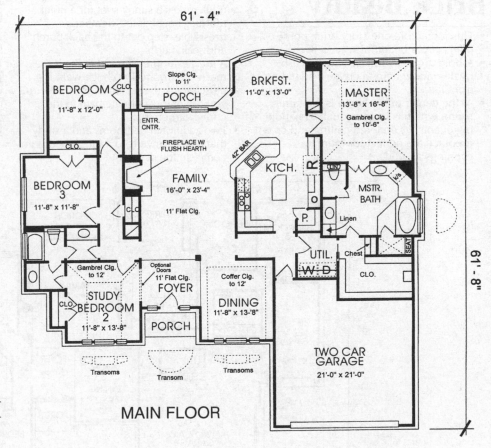

MAIN FLOOR

ORDER BLUEPRINTS ANYTIME!
CALL TOLL-FREE 1-888-626-2026

Plan KLF-972

PRICES AND DETAILS
ON PAGES 13-15

155

Incredible Brick Beauty

- This incredible one-story brick home offers you a beautiful way to live.
- A bold arched window and a stylish, oval window help to create a sparkling front facade.
- At the center of the home is the family room, which is large enough to handle big events. Its coffered ceiling and cozy fireplace are perfect for intimate evenings as well.

- The spacious island kitchen boasts a handy corner pantry and a convenient eating bar. A bay-windowed breakfast nook makes a sunny spot for a quick morning bagel; if the weather's irresistible, step out to the back porch and soak it up!
- A great example of grand living is the master bedroom. Two huge walk-in closets flank the secluded bath, where you can enjoy a private bath in the corner garden tub.
- Two additional bedrooms and a study that easily converts to a fourth bedroom complete the design.

Plan KLF-973	
Bedrooms: 3+	**Baths:** 2
Living Area:	
Main floor	2,244 sq. ft.
Total Living Area:	**2,244 sq. ft.**
Garage	791 sq. ft.
Exterior Wall Framing:	2x4

Foundation Options:

Slab
(All plans can be built with your choice of foundation and framing. A generic conversion diagram is available. See order form.)

BLUEPRINT PRICE CODE: C

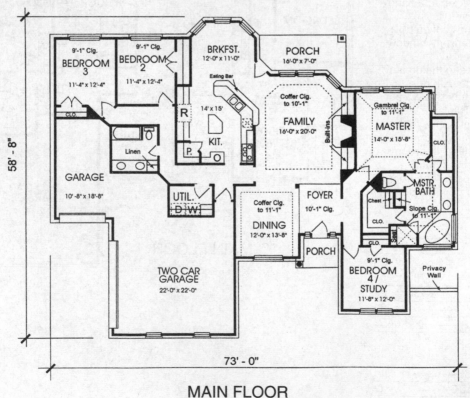

MAIN FLOOR

Plan KLF-973

PRICES AND DETAILS
ON PAGES 13-15

Stop Looking!

- Stop your search for the perfect home! With every imaginable amenity and the right combination of separation and openness, this plan is for you.
- Two octagonal ceilings anchor a playful floor plan. The left octagonal area is brightened by a skylight.
- To the right of the skylighted foyer, a fireplace and an arched window arrangement enhance the living room.
- The island kitchen is nicely situated for easy service to both the dining room and the bayed breakfast nook.
- A corner fireplace warms the large family room. Sliding glass doors open to an inviting backyard patio.
- Need a moment to collect your thoughts or curl up with a good book? Try the quiet study. This room could also be used to put up overnight guests.
- The skylighted laundry room will amaze you! A drop-down ironing board and a two-way linen closet are nice features.
- The master suite is the stuff of dreams. A French door gives easy backyard access. The whirlpool tub will often call you away from the stresses of daily life.
- Two good-sized secondary bedrooms share a skylighted hall bath.

Plan TS-9616

Bedrooms: 3+	Baths: 2
Living Area:	
Main floor	2,255 sq. ft.
Total Living Area:	**2,255 sq. ft.**
Garage	710 sq. ft.
Exterior Wall Framing:	2x6

Foundation Options:
Crawlspace
(All plans can be built with your choice of foundation and framing. A generic conversion diagram is available. See order form.)

BLUEPRINT PRICE CODE: C

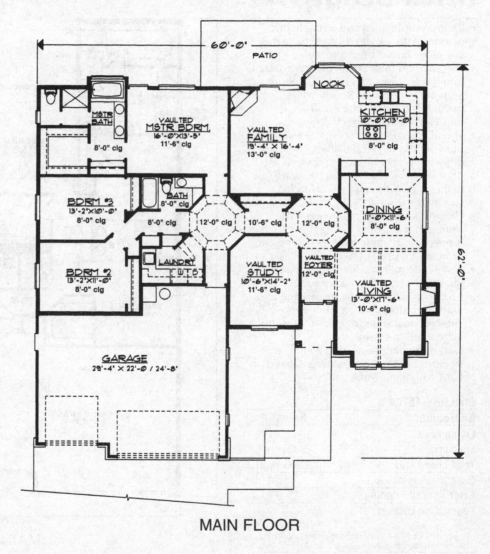

MAIN FLOOR

Brick Beauty

- Clean, simple lines and a stately brick exterior with louvered vents make this one-story home a real beauty.
- The covered front porch escorts guests into the gracious foyer. Here, columns announce the Great Room, which features a cozy fireplace and an impressive Palladian window.
- The modern kitchen shares an eating bar with the bayed breakfast nook, allowing plenty of serving options. A door from the nook to the backyard makes it easy to call the kids in for summertime meals!
- Elegant occasions find the perfect setting in the formal dining room, topped by an attractive tray ceiling and lit by an expanse of windows.
- A separate hallway leads to the sleeping quarters, where the master suite offers luxurious escape and a private bath with a whirlpool tub, a sit-down shower, dual sinks, a private toilet and a large walk-in closet.
- Two more bedrooms, one with a walk-in closet, share a compartmentalized bath with a dual-sink vanity.

Plan NBV-10796

Bedrooms: 3	Baths: 2½
Living Area:	
Main floor	2,265 sq. ft.
Total Living Area:	**2,265 sq. ft.**
Garage and storage	704 sq. ft.
Exterior Wall Framing:	2x4

Foundation Options:

Slab

(All plans can be built with your choice of foundation and framing. A generic conversion diagram is available. See order form.)

BLUEPRINT PRICE CODE:	C

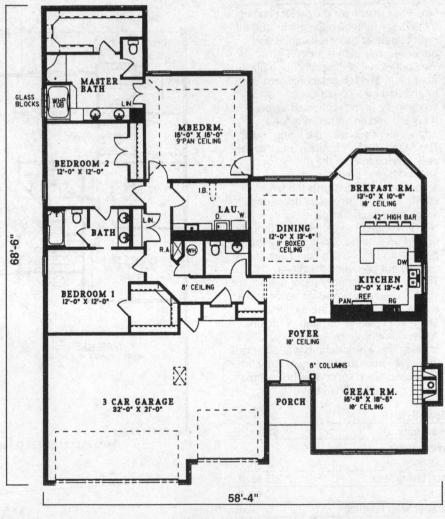

MAIN FLOOR

Soulful Enclosure

- This home's warm country accents and delightful interior appointments combine to bring peace to your soul and comfort to your days.
- The high entry introduces the bayed dining room to the left; straight ahead, the expansive living room beckons. Here, radiant windows bathe the space in natural light. A French door leads to a backyard porch. For romantic weekend nights, the fireplace is perfect.

- A boxed-out window brightens the breakfast nook. A raised bar smoothly joins the nook to the walk-through kitchen. There is plenty of room for two cooks here, plus a young apprentice!
- Sublime quietude reigns in the secluded master suite. A cute window seat provides a sweet spot for reading or needlepoint. The private bath spoils you with two big walk-in closets and a stunning oval tub.
- The upper floor is no less tempting. It offers two additional bedrooms with a shared bath, and a vast bonus room that could become a media room or a suite for your boomerang child.

Plan RD-2000	
Bedrooms: 3+	**Baths: 2½**
Living Area:	
Upper floor	560 sq. ft.
Main floor	1,440 sq. ft.
Bonus room	267 sq. ft.
Total Living Area:	**2,267 sq. ft.**
Standard basement	1,430 sq. ft.
Garage	424 sq. ft.
Exterior Wall Framing:	**2x4**

Foundation Options:

Standard basement
Crawlspace
Slab
(All plans can be built with your choice of foundation and framing. A generic conversion diagram is available. See order form.)

BLUEPRINT PRICE CODE:	**C**

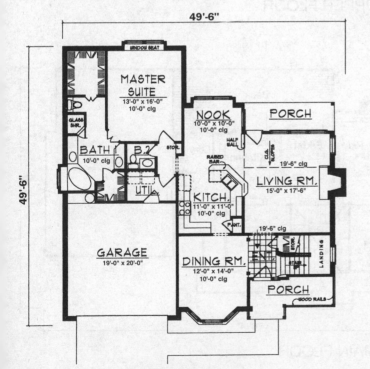

MAIN FLOOR

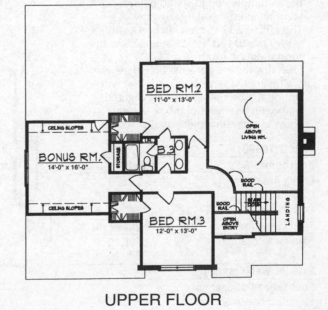

UPPER FLOOR

Victorian Reprise

- Intricate detailing, a pointed turret and a gracious entry with an oval-glassed door herald this delightful reprise of the Victorian style.
- The striking two-story foyer greets family and friends. To the side, the old-fashioned parlor features a bright octagonal sitting area and creates the perfect atmosphere for enjoying afternoon tea or keeping up correspondence with far-away friends.
- Double doors open to the cozy family room, warmed by several sunny windows and the glow of a charming fireplace. A door to the wraparound porch tempts you to spend balmy summer evenings stargazing.
- The efficient U-shaped kitchen easily serves the bayed breakfast nook and the formal dining room.
- Upstairs, the master suite boasts a sweet sitting area, a large walk-in closet with optional attic space, and a skylighted bath with a whirlpool tub, a separate shower and convenient dual sinks.

Plan G-10690

Bedrooms: 3	Baths: 2½
Living Area:	
Upper floor	1,021 sq. ft.
Main floor	1,260 sq. ft.
Total Living Area:	**2,281 sq. ft.**
Standard basement	1,186 sq. ft.
Garage	840 sq. ft.
Exterior Wall Framing:	2x4 or 2x6
Foundation Options:	

Standard basement

(All plans can be built with your choice of foundation and framing. A generic conversion diagram is available. See order form.)

BLUEPRINT PRICE CODE:	**C**

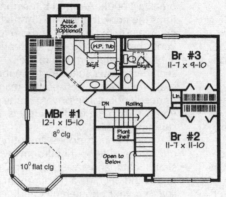

UPPER FLOOR

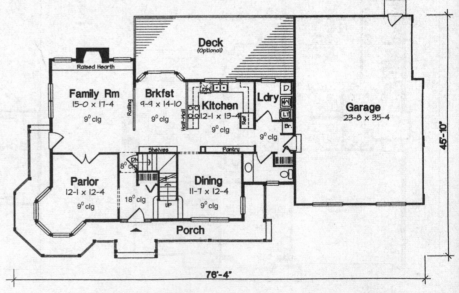

MAIN FLOOR

Plan G-10690

PRICES AND DETAILS ON PAGES 13-15

The Total Package!

- Traditional country charm mixed with brilliant, modern design produces this remarkably sophisticated two-story package of amenities!
- The covered porch has practical and pleasurable functions—it protects on rainy days and is a grand spot for games or a good book when it's sunny out.
- The dining room is large enough for those extra long dinner-guest lists. After dinner, the huge living room is waiting just across the 17-ft.-high foyer to help complete the evening.
- Enjoyment is the theme in the spacious family room, where a handsome fireplace warms nearby spirits and double doors lead to the backyard for outdoor fun.
- All four bedrooms, including the sizable master suite, are found upstairs.

Plan CH-150-A

Bedrooms: 4	Baths: 2½
Living Area:	
Upper floor	1,139 sq. ft.
Main floor	1,147 sq. ft.
Total Living Area:	**2,286 sq. ft.**
Basement	1,158 sq. ft.
Garage	462 sq. ft.
Exterior Wall Framing:	2x4

Foundation Options:

Daylight basement
Standard basement
Crawlspace
(All plans can be built with your choice of foundation and framing. A generic conversion diagram is available. See order form.)

BLUEPRINT PRICE CODE: C

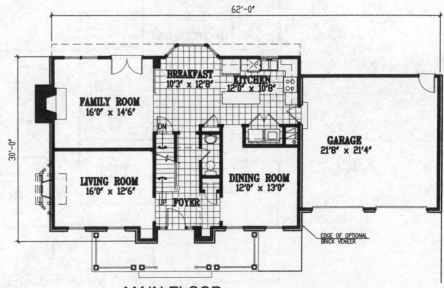

UPPER FLOOR

MAIN FLOOR

ORDER BLUEPRINTS ANYTIME!
CALL TOLL-FREE 1-888-626-2026

Plan CH-150-A

PRICES AND DETAILS
ON PAGES 13-15

161

Family Ties

- This home's wonderful design, both inside and out, will enhance the ties that bind your family together.
- Decorative columns frame the entry of the living room, where a soaring 14-ft. vaulted ceiling crowns the space.
- Special occasions call for special meals in the formal dining room.
- Topped by a 14-ft. ceiling, the family room begs you to relax beside a glowing fire. Step out to the backyard deck through a sliding glass door to enjoy a bright summer day.
- The roomy kitchen easily accesses both the formal dining room and the sunny breakfast nook. All three spaces boast 11-ft. ceilings.
- Retreat to the stunning master suite, where a 14-ft. vaulted ceiling brightens the space. A bayed sitting area unfolds beyond a private deck access, and the luxurious bath offers a relaxing spa tub.
- Create another bedroom or a rec room in the bonus area above the garage.
- Unless specified otherwise, this home features 9-ft ceilings.

Plan APS-2219	
Bedrooms: 3	**Baths:** 2½
Living Area:	
Main floor	2,290 sq. ft.
Total Living Area:	**2,290 sq. ft.**
Bonus room	234 sq. ft.
Daylight basement	2,290 sq. ft.
Garage	504 sq. ft.
Exterior Wall Framing:	2x4

Foundation Options:

Daylight basement

(All plans can be built with your choice of foundation and framing. A generic conversion diagram is available. See order form.)

BLUEPRINT PRICE CODE: C

MAIN FLOOR

Plan APS-2219

The Great Outdoors

- This home's wraparound porch and expansive backyard deck, complete with a built-in barbecue and room for a relaxing spa, will lure you to the great outdoors.
- After a long day outside, warm your toes beside a roaring fire in the spacious Great Room.
- Two wonderful living spaces frame the sidelighted entry. To the left, the sunny, formal dining room is ideal for intimate meals with good friends. To the right,

the large study provides a quiet place to finish that novel you've been putting off for years.
- A steaming cup of coffee and a beautiful sunrise are great ways to start your day in the island kitchen's bayed morning room.
- Secluded on the main floor, the spacious master bedroom offers a whirlpool tub and a dual-sink vanity.
- For a roomier feel, the first floor features 9-ft. ceilings.
- A children's paradise is waiting upstairs. Two large bedrooms access a compartmentalized bath, and the playroom promises countless hours of fun-filled activity.

Plan DD-2298-1	
Bedrooms: 3+	**Baths:** 2½
Living Area:	
Upper floor	782 sq. ft.
Main floor	1,517 sq. ft.
Total Living Area:	**2,299 sq. ft.**
Upper floor storage	112 sq. ft.
Standard basement	1,517 sq. ft.
Garage and storage	456 sq. ft.
Exterior Wall Framing:	2x4

Foundation Options:
Standard basement
Crawlspace
Slab
(All plans can be built with your choice of foundation and framing. A generic conversion diagram is available. See order form.)

BLUEPRINT PRICE CODE: C

REAR VIEW

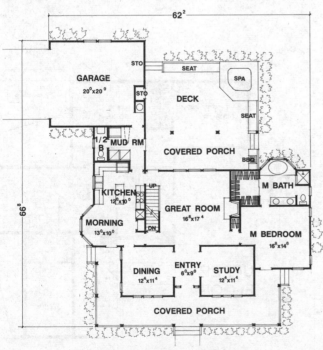

MAIN FLOOR

UPPER FLOOR

Plan DD-2298-1

PRICES AND DETAILS
ON PAGES 13-15

A New Look

- Unique angles, a varied roofline and clean lines give this home its bold, contemporary look. Sweeping expanses of glass brighten the exterior.
- Beyond the air-lock entry, a stunning 17-ft. ceiling in the dramatic foyer will draw endless compliments from visitors.
- On the left, the sunken living room, which also features a 17-ft. ceiling, accommodates gatherings of any nature. Built-in shelves and cabinets by the fireplace easily hold media equipment and books. Above, a pretty plant shelf displays lush greenery.

- The nearby dining room is set off by columns. French doors expand dining options to a sprawling backyard deck.
- For the gourmet chef, the kitchen will never cease to delight. A large pantry stores reserves of your favorite cooking supplies, while a window above the sink brings sunshine to daily chores.
- Skylights and a 14½-ft. ceiling create an enhanced sense of space in the posh master bedroom. French doors lead to an inviting hot tub on the deck.
- Upstairs, a loft overlooking the living room would be great as a reading nook or a fourth bedroom. A large storage room could serve as a studio.

Plan B-92021

Bedrooms: 3+	Baths: 3½
Living Area:	
Upper floor	841 sq. ft.
Main floor	1,487 sq. ft.
Bonus room/storage	126 sq. ft.
Total Living Area:	**2,454 sq. ft.**
Garage	527 sq. ft.
Exterior Wall Framing:	2x4

Foundation Options:

Crawlspace
(All plans can be built with your choice of foundation and framing. A generic conversion diagram is available. See order form.)

BLUEPRINT PRICE CODE: C

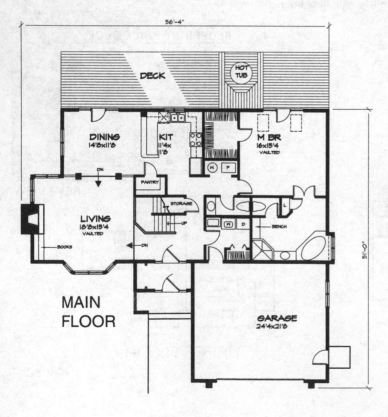

MAIN FLOOR

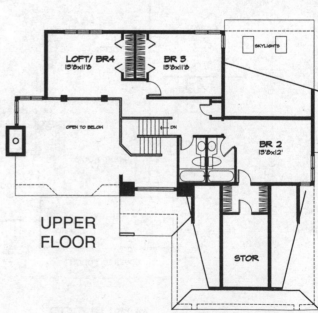

UPPER FLOOR

Warm Welcome

- Warm welcomes that start in the spacious foyer are followed by evenings long on good conversation in the living room. When a few friends becomes a houseful, open the pocket door to the family room.
- Fine dining is only steps away in the formal dining room, which offers convenient access to the kitchen.
- The island kitchen includes a large dinette and a handy built-in desk for planning your weekly menu.
- Slide the latest new release into the VCR, pop a batch of popcorn and gather with your kids as a warm fire glows in the fireplace of the comfortable family room.
- Upstairs, the master suite is bursting with special features. The bath offers a soothing garden tub, a dual-sink vanity and a large walk-in closet. A neat, alcove could function as a private study, sitting area or hobby room.
- The other two bedrooms are nicely sized with ample closet space and a shared full bath.

Plan LS-97849-RE

Bedrooms: 3	Baths: 2½
Living Area:	
Upper floor	1,102 sq. ft.
Main floor	1,233 sq. ft.
Total Living Area:	**2,335 sq. ft.**
Standard basement	1,233 sq. ft.
Garage	755 sq. ft.
Exterior Wall Framing:	2x6

Foundation Options:

Standard basement

(All plans can be built with your choice of foundation and framing. A generic conversion diagram is available. See order form.)

BLUEPRINT PRICE CODE:	**C**

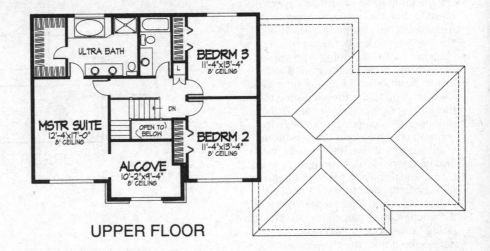

UPPER FLOOR

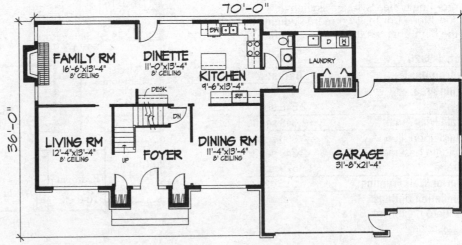

MAIN FLOOR

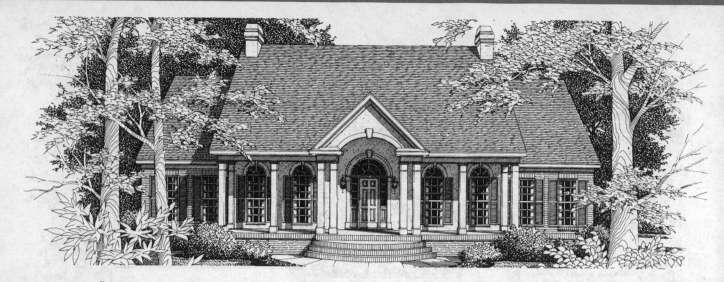

Better by Design

- For the family that values an easygoing lifestyle, but also wants to impress friends with a beautiful home, this Southern-style design fits the bill.
- Hanging baskets dripping with vibrant flowers will dress up the front porch.
- Inside, handsome columns lend a look of distinction to the formal dining room, the ideal spot for classy meals. After dinner, guests can drift into the living room to continue their conversation. Plant shelves above display lush florals and greenery for all to admire.
- Casual meals have a place of their own in the kitchen and breakfast nook. While Mom and Dad prepare dinner in the kitchen, they can chat with the kids doing homework in the nook.
- Across the home, the master suite's sitting room provides an oasis of peace and quiet. The handy wet bar there puts you steps closer to that first cup of morning coffee, while a skylight lets sunshine pour in. Two more skylights in the bath brighten this space as well.

Plan J-9320

Bedrooms: 3+	Baths: 2½
Living Area:	
Main floor	2,348 sq. ft.
Total Living Area:	**2,348 sq. ft.**
Future upper floor	860 sq. ft.
Standard basement	2,348 sq. ft.
Garage	579 sq. ft.
Exterior Wall Framing:	2x4

Foundation Options:

Standard basement
Crawlspace
Slab

(All plans can be built with your choice of foundation and framing. A generic conversion diagram is available. See order form.)

BLUEPRINT PRICE CODE:	C

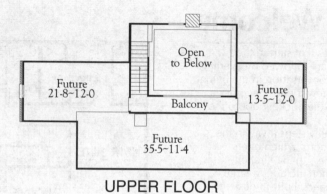

UPPER FLOOR

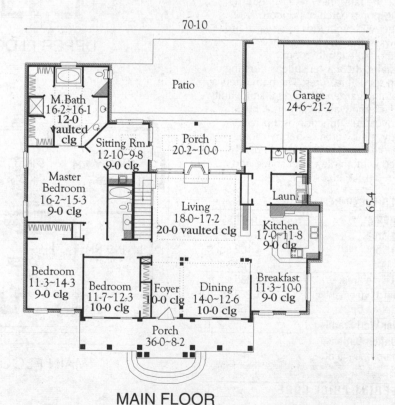

MAIN FLOOR

ORDER BLUEPRINTS ANYTIME!
CALL TOLL-FREE 1-888-626-2026

Plan J-9320

PRICES AND DETAILS
ON PAGES 13-15

Great Features, Great Design

- A covered front porch that is roomy enough for your rocking chair fronts this delightful country home.
- To the right of the foyer, double doors swing wide to grant passage to a quiet study. If you wish, this room could easily serve as an extra bedroom.
- The joined living and dining rooms spread out beneath a breathtaking cathedral ceiling. A crackling fireplace and bright windows paint the scene with vibrant light.
- At the back of the home, a big family room offers perfection in both design and function. A second fireplace and a TV nook make this room the obvious choice for weekend fun.
- On hot summer days, the pleasant terrace is a great spot to unwind.
- The secluded master suite boasts a skylighted bath and a private terrace!

Plan AHP-9616

Bedrooms: 5+	Baths: 3½
Living Area:	
Upper floor	798 sq. ft.
Main floor	1,570 sq. ft.
Total Living Area:	**2,368 sq. ft.**
Standard basement	1,570 sq. ft.
Garage and storage	502 sq. ft.
Exterior Wall Framing:	2x4 or 2x6

Foundation Options:

Standard basement

Crawlspace

Slab

(All plans can be built with your choice of foundation and framing. A generic conversion diagram is available. See order form.)

BLUEPRINT PRICE CODE: **C**

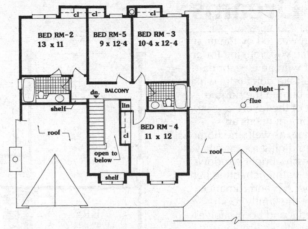

UPPER FLOOR

MAIN FLOOR

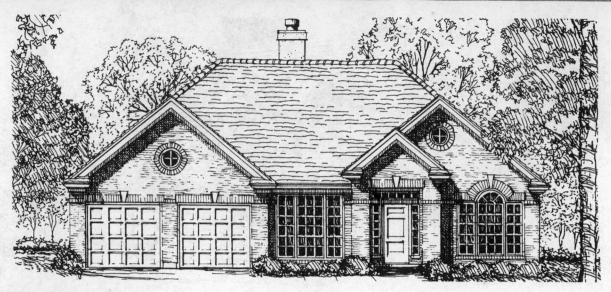

Fed by Dreams

- This cozy design was fed by the dreams of people just like you, longing for an oasis of comfort with an elegant flair.
- Who doesn't desire a quiet refuge like the study found behind the double doors to the left of the foyer?
- Formal entertainment needs an appropriate venue, as well; the home's joined living and dining rooms answer the need effortlessly. Bright windows splash the scene with enchanting light.
- A perfect blend of fun and romance may be found in the family room, which hosts media and book shelves separated by a soothing fireplace.
- The jewel in the home's crown is the master bedroom. Its sleeping chamber is finished with a bayed sitting area. The private bath includes an oval garden tub, a zesty shower and a dual-sink vanity. No more jockeying for position!
- You'll welcome each morning in the sun-splashed breakfast nook. A French door leads to a cute patio, in case you prefer fresh air with your fresh fruit.
- Meal preparation is simplified in the walk-through kitchen, where you'll find a step-in pantry and a serving counter for Sunday afternoon ball games.

Plan BRF-2371

Bedrooms: 3+	Baths: 2
Living Area:	
Main floor	2,371 sq. ft.
Total Living Area:	**2,371 sq. ft.**
Garage	420 sq. ft.
Exterior Wall Framing:	2x4

Foundation Options:

Slab

(All plans can be built with your choice of foundation and framing. A generic conversion diagram is available. See order form.)

BLUEPRINT PRICE CODE: **C**

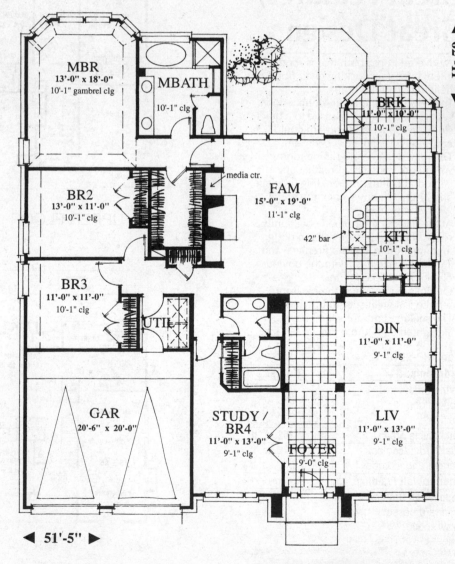

MAIN FLOOR

- MBR 13'-0" x 18'-0" 10'-1" gambrel clg
- MBATH 10'-1" clg
- BRK 11'-0" x 10'-0" 10'-1" clg
- BR2 13'-0" x 11'-0" 10'-1" clg
- media ctr.
- FAM 15'-0" x 19'-0" 11'-1" clg
- 42" bar
- KIT 10'-1" clg
- BR3 11'-0" x 11'-0" 10'-1" clg
- UTIL
- DIN 11'-0" x 11'-0" 9'-1" clg
- GAR 20'-6" x 20'-0"
- STUDY / BR4 11'-0" x 13'-0" 9'-1" clg
- LIV 11'-0" x 13'-0" 9'-1" clg
- FOYER 9'-0" clg
- 62'-11"
- 51'-5"

TO ORDER THIS BLUEPRINT, CALL TOLL-FREE 1-888-626-2026

Plan BRF-2371

PRICES AND DETAILS ON PAGES 13-15

Sweet Symmetry

- Enjoy the sweet symmetry of this four-bedroom Colonial-style home as its bay windows flank a grand columned entry.
- The formal spaces on either side of the 18-ft.-high foyer display this same pleasant balance to your arriving guests.
- When relaxation is in the cards, unwind in the spacious casual areas at the rear of the home. The family room's orientation to the kitchen means you won't have to miss the flickering flames of the fireplace or your favorite sitcom while preparing dinner or dining in the breakfast room.
- A butler's pantry and a laundry closet efficiently utilize the space between the kitchen, dining room and garage.
- Unless otherwise mentioned, the main-floor rooms have 9-ft. ceilings.
- Upstairs, four nice-sized bedrooms unfold from the stairway. The master bedroom's private suite includes a skylighted bath and a garden tub.

Plan CH-127-A

Bedrooms: 4	Baths: 2½
Living Area:	
Upper floor	1,149 sq. ft.
Main floor	1,244 sq. ft.
Total Living Area:	**2,393 sq. ft.**
Basement	1,237 sq. ft.
Garage	452 sq. ft.
Exterior Wall Framing:	2x4

Foundation Options:

Daylight basement

Standard basement

Crawlspace

(All plans can be built with your choice of foundation and framing. A generic conversion diagram is available. See order form.)

BLUEPRINT PRICE CODE:	C

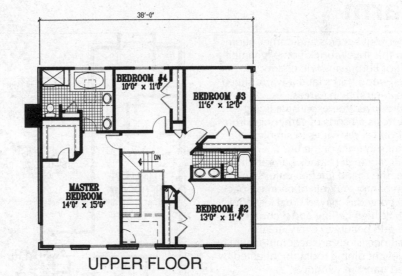

UPPER FLOOR

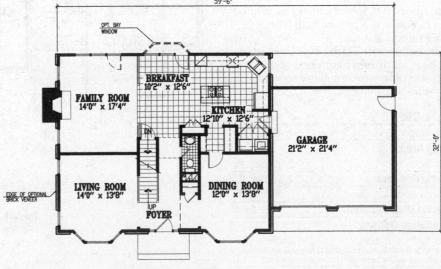

MAIN FLOOR

Old World Charm

- Copper roof accents and corner quoins adorn this lovely brick home, giving it a touch of European-style charm.
- Inside, wood floors lend a warm sheen to the central living areas.
- Past the foyer, the expansive living room hosts all sorts of gatherings, from gala holiday festivities to simple evenings in front of the fire.
- Sharing an angled snack bar with this space, the island kitchen enjoys an ample pantry and lots of counter space.
- In the gorgeous, bayed breakfast nook, an 11-ft.-high ceiling and a corner niche add beauty to every meal.
- Formal occasions are accommodated by the elegant dining room, highlighted by arched transom windows.
- Across the home, the master bedroom boasts a 10-ft. raised ceiling, two walk-in closets and a private bath with dual sinks and a spa tub.
- The extra room nearby may be used as a cozy study or a fourth bedroom.
- Unless otherwise noted, all rooms feature 9-ft. ceilings.

Plan L-395-FB

Bedrooms: 3+	Baths: 3
Living Area:	
Main floor	2,397 sq. ft.
Total Living Area:	**2,397 sq. ft.**
Garage and storage	537 sq. ft.
Exterior Wall Framing:	2x4
Foundation Options:	

Slab

(All plans can be built with your choice of foundation and framing. A generic conversion diagram is available. See order form.)

BLUEPRINT PRICE CODE:	**C**

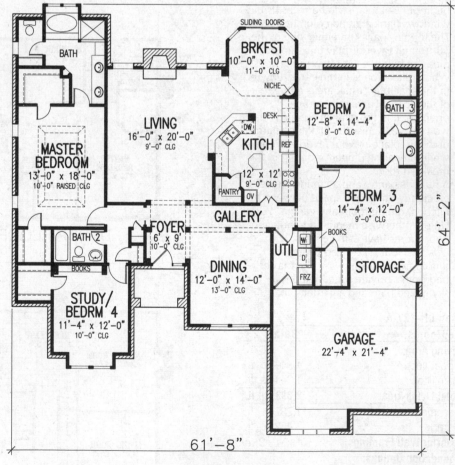

MAIN FLOOR

ORDER BLUEPRINTS ANYTIME!
CALL TOLL-FREE 1-888-626-2026

Plan L-395-FB

PRICES AND DETAILS
ON PAGES 13-15

Dream Weaver

- A calm invitation exudes from this country-style home's delightful front porch, where you'll often find yourself whiling away the evening hours and dreaming of a rewarding future.
- Formal spaces greet dinner guests as they step into the foyer: to the left, a charming dining room; to the right, a cozy living room with a fireplace.
- Airy spaces bless the remainder of the first floor. The family room opens to a sweet breakfast nook and an island kitchen, where you'll find a step-in pantry and windows above the sink.
- From the nook, a fun patio is just steps away. Who's up for some barbecue?
- Upstairs, a stunning master suite delivers plenty of room in the sleeping chamber; its private bath includes a large walk-in closet, a tub and a dual-sink vanity with lots of elbow room.
- Your future needs are addressed with the inclusion of a large bonus room. You make the call: a game room? Home office? Bedroom?

Plan TS-9661

Bedrooms: 3+	Baths: 2½
Living Area:	
Upper floor	946 sq. ft.
Main floor	1,094 sq. ft.
Bonus room	375 sq. ft.
Total Living Area:	**2,415 sq. ft.**
Garage	519 sq. ft.
Exterior Wall Framing:	2x6

Foundation Options:

Crawlspace
(All plans can be built with your choice of foundation and framing. A generic conversion diagram is available. See order form.)

BLUEPRINT PRICE CODE: C

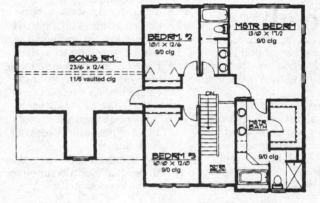

UPPER FLOOR

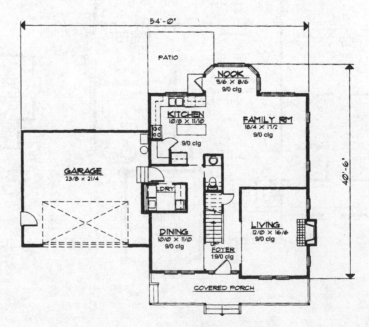

MAIN FLOOR

ORDER BLUEPRINTS ANYTIME!
CALL TOLL-FREE 1-888-626-2026

Plan TS-9661

PRICES AND DETAILS
ON PAGES 13-15

171

Raised to New Heights

- The distinctive raised foyer of this gorgeous European-style two-story will impress your guests, elevating them to new heights.
- With a soaring fireplace framed by dazzling windows, the living room is poised to make a good impression.
- A lovely bay window enhances the elegance of the formal dining room.
- The whole family will want to help prepare meals in the spacious kitchen, which offers ample cupboard and counter space.
- A cozy breakfast nook, open to the kitchen, features an attractive boxed-out window for additional seating, plus a set of French doors to the backyard.
- The secluded main floor master bedroom flaunts an exquisite bath, complete with a relaxing garden tub and a stylish dual-sink vanity.
- Upstairs, a raised game room generates a host of possibilities for your children's entertainment.
- Two bedrooms share a dual sink bath; an optional fourth bedroom offers expansion potential.

Plan L-2269-C	
Bedrooms: 3+	**Baths:** 2½
Living Area:	
Upper floor	790 sq. ft.
Main floor	1,479 sq. ft.
Optional fourth bedroom	185 sq. ft.
Total Living Area:	**2,454 sq. ft.**
Detached garage	552 sq. ft.
Exterior Wall Framing:	2x4
Foundation Options:	
Slab	
(All plans can be built with your choice of foundation and framing. A generic conversion diagram is available. See order form.)	
BLUEPRINT PRICE CODE:	C

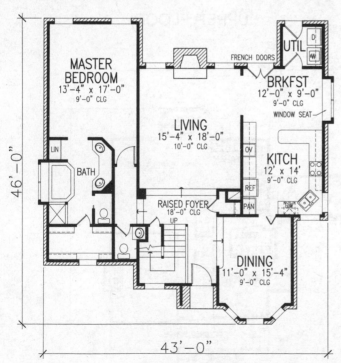

MAIN FLOOR

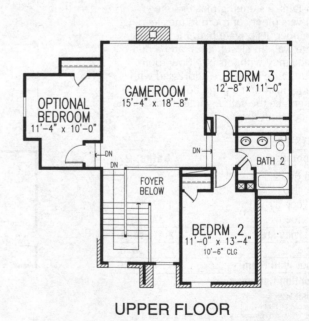

UPPER FLOOR

Plan L-2269-C

PRICES AND DETAILS *ON PAGES 13-15*

Power Play

- Power and prestige await those who choose this stunning Victorian home. Its wide-open interior spaces invite both serious and playful interaction.
- The two-story foyer ushers guests directly into the breathtaking living room, where dazzling windows admit natural light and views to a cute backyard porch.
- A see-through fireplace draws the eye into a lovely octagonal breakfast nook. On busy mornings or lazy, this is the spot to start your day off right!

- Any cooks in the family? They'll fall in love with the big kitchen, with its step-in pantry. A nearby desk helps them to plan their meals—a week at a time.
- When it's time to get away from the world's hubbub, retreat to the master bedroom. Here, you'll find a cozy bayed sitting area and a master bath that boasts a raised tub, a separate shower and a pair of sinks with lots of elbow room for the two of you.
- Weekends were made for the upper-floor's future game room. There's plenty of room for several card tables and a rousing game of bingo!

Plan BOD-24-2A	
Bedrooms: 4+	**Baths:** 3
Living Area:	
Upper floor	558 sq. ft.
Main floor	1,880 sq. ft.
Total Living Area:	**2,438 sq. ft.**
Future game room	287 sq. ft.
Garage	472 sq. ft.
Exterior Wall Framing:	2x4

Foundation Options:
Crawlspace
Slab
(All plans can be built with your choice of foundation and framing. A generic conversion diagram is available. See order form.)

BLUEPRINT PRICE CODE:	C

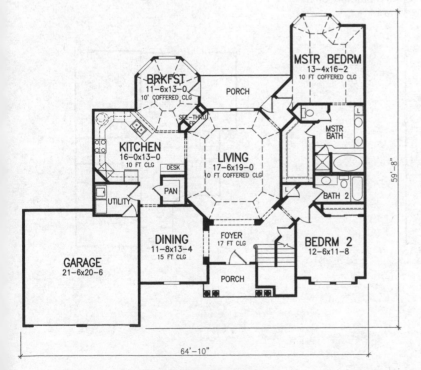

MAIN FLOOR

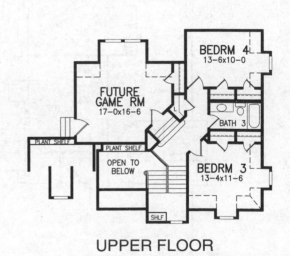

UPPER FLOOR

Plan BOD-24-2A

PRICES AND DETAILS
ON PAGES 13-15

French Beauty

- This French-style beauty boasts an exquisite brick facade, plus a floor plan with a sensible traffic flow.
- An 18-ft. ceiling lends drama to the open foyer. A handy powder room with an 8-ft. ceiling is just around the corner.
- Striking columns introduce the fabulous Great Room, which is warmed by a fireplace, brightened by a Palladian window arrangement and expanded by a ceiling that slopes up to 18 feet. Built-in bookshelves and cabinets hold all of your entertainment needs.
- The right wing of the home caters to your growling stomach, with its island kitchen, formal dining room and casual breakfast room. A Jenn-Air cooktop, a sizable pantry and a convenient eating bar are highlights here.
- Tired after a long day at work? Soak your cares away in the master suite's corner tub. After that, the flickering stars will call you out to the covered porch for a moment of quiet reflection before turning in.
- For added spaciousness, all main-floor rooms have 9-ft. ceilings unless otherwise noted.
- Upstairs, two bedrooms with walk-in closets share a hall bath and two linen closets. A railed balcony offers sweeping views.

Plan BOD-24-6A	
Bedrooms: 3	**Baths:** 2½
Living Area:	
Upper floor	632 sq. ft.
Main floor	1,831 sq. ft.
Total Living Area:	**2,463 sq. ft.**
Garage and storage	525 sq. ft.
Exterior Wall Framing:	2x4

Foundation Options:

Crawlspace
Slab
(All plans can be built with your choice of foundation and framing. A generic conversion diagram is available. See order form.)

BLUEPRINT PRICE CODE:	C

WIDTH 50'-7"

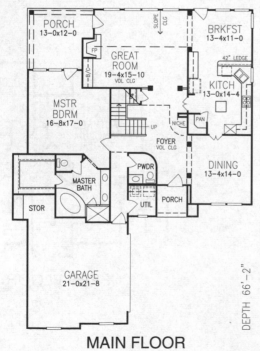

MAIN FLOOR

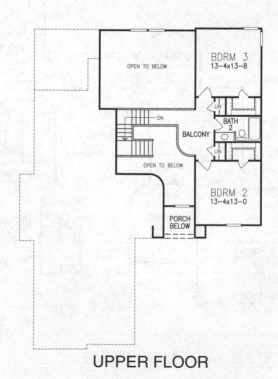

UPPER FLOOR

DEPTH 66'-2"

Architecturally Astounding!

- Neighbors and friends will be astounded by this wonderful architectural masterpiece!
- If you want, you can spend the whole day on the beautiful front porch. Bring a good book, a favorite beverage and your best rocking chair and just relax.
- The huge family room is topped by a ceiling with exposed beams. The exposed beams, coupled with a marvelous fireplace and access to the covered patio in back, create a room that's soothing and cozy.
- Ready for anything on the menu, the efficient island kitchen can serve gourmet meals in the dining room or simple snacks in the breakfast room with equal alacrity!
- The dramatic master suite occupies the entire "west" wing; a pretty coffered ceiling and an unbelievably big private bath top its list of features.
- Upstairs, you'll find three additional bedrooms and a great game room.

Plan KD-2463-2

Bedrooms: 4+	Baths: 2½
Living Area:	
Upper floor	810 sq. ft.
Main floor	1,645 sq. ft.
Total Living Area:	**2,455 sq. ft.**
Garage and storage	542 sq. ft.
Exterior Wall Framing:	2x4

Foundation Options:

Crawlspace

Slab

(All plans can be built with your choice of foundation and framing. A generic conversion diagram is available. See order form.)

BLUEPRINT PRICE CODE: C

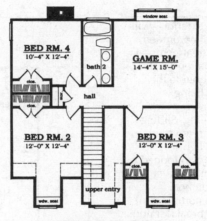

UPPER FLOOR

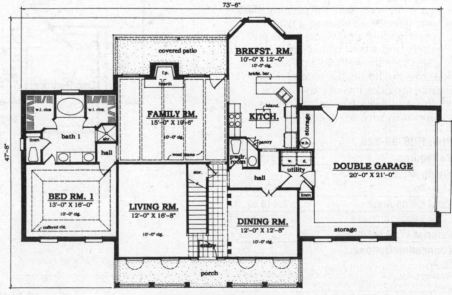

MAIN FLOOR

ORDER BLUEPRINTS ANYTIME!
CALL TOLL-FREE 1-888-626-2026

Plan KD-2463-2

PRICES AND DETAILS
ON PAGES 13-15

175

Terrific Times Two

- This home's outstanding exterior—with a stucco finish, a graceful columned entry and fresh window treatments—is echoed on the inside by a terrific floor plan. Two master suites double the possibilities for gracious living.
- Ahead of the foyer, the living room resides under a 12-ft. ceiling. Sliding glass doors open to a rear, covered porch illuminated by skylights.
- The formal dining room, also topped by a 12-ft. ceiling, is efficiently served by the huge walk-through kitchen.
- Expansive window walls complement the family room and the breakfast nook.
- A den/extra bedroom overlooks the front yard and accesses a nice half-bath.
- In a wing of its own, the primary master suite offers a sitting area, a walk-in closet, sliding glass doors to the rear porch, and a bath with a corner spa tub, a separate shower and a private toilet.
- Across the home, the second master suite provides lots of closet space.
- Unless otherwise noted, all rooms are topped by airy, 10-ft. ceilings.

Plan HDS-99-320

Bedrooms: 2+	Baths: 2½
Living Area:	
Main floor	2,470 sq. ft.
Total Living Area:	**2,470 sq. ft.**
Garage and storage	664 sq. ft.
Exterior Wall Framing:	2x4
Foundation Options:	

Slab
(All plans can be built with your choice of foundation and framing. A generic conversion diagram is available. See order form.)

BLUEPRINT PRICE CODE:	C

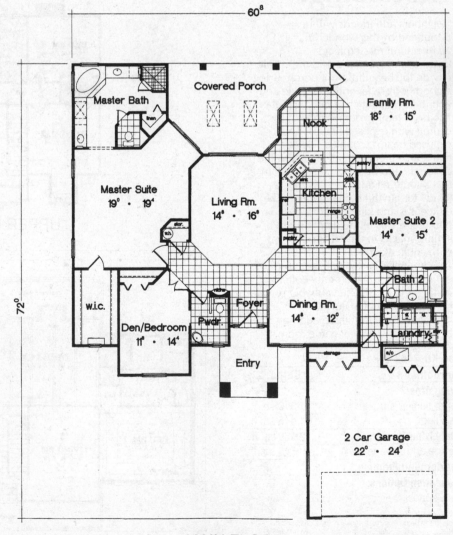

MAIN FLOOR

Elegant Facade

- Eye-catching windows and columns add elegance to both the front and rear of this appealing ranch-style home.
- The columns of the covered front porch are repeated inside, defining the spacious gallery. The central section soars to a height of 20 ft., 4 in., basking in sunlight from a windowed dormer.
- The gorgeous Great Room features a cozy fireplace flanked by built-ins. Two sets of sliding glass doors with elliptical transoms open to a backyard terrace.
- The gourmet kitchen offers a handy snack bar, while the breakfast room expands to a columned rear porch.
- The peaceful dining room boasts a stepped ceiling that rises to 10 ft. at the stunning front window.
- The secluded master suite provides a sitting area, porch access and a private whirlpool bath with dual sinks and wardrobe closets.
- The second bedroom is brightened by an arched window arrangement under a 12½-ft.-high vaulted area.
- Ceilings are at least 9½ ft. high throughout the home.

Plan AX-4315

Bedrooms: 3	Baths: 2
Living Area:	
Main floor	2,018 sq. ft.
Total Living Area:	**2,018 sq. ft.**
Basement	2,018 sq. ft.
Garage/storage/utility	474 sq. ft.
Exterior Wall Framing:	2x4

Foundation Options:

Daylight basement
Standard basement
Crawlspace
Slab

(All plans can be built with your choice of foundation and framing. A generic conversion diagram is available. See order form.)

BLUEPRINT PRICE CODE: C

VIEW INTO GREAT ROOM

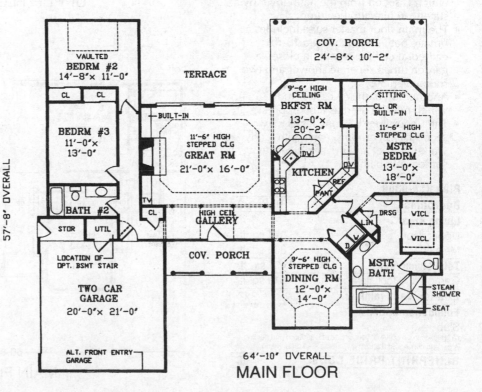

MAIN FLOOR

Plan AX-4315

Magnificent Masonry Arch

- This beautiful brick home attracts the eye with its magnificent arch high above the recessed entry.
- The two-story-high foyer is highlighted by a huge half-round transom as it radiates between a bayed study and the elegant formal dining room.
- The fabulous kitchen boasts a walk-in pantry, a snack bar and a sunny bayed breakfast nook with backyard access.
- A fireplace flanked by windows brings comfort to the adjoining family room, which is set off from the main foyer by a stately architectural column.
- The main-floor master suite includes a private bath enhanced by a 13-ft. cathedral ceiling, a walk-in closet, a garden tub, a separate shower and two roomy vanities.
- Another full bath serves the study, which may be used as a bedroom.
- The upper-floor balcony leads to two secondary bedrooms, each with a tidy walk-in closet and private access to a shared split bath.

Plan KLF-9309

Bedrooms: 3+	Baths: 3
Living Area:	
Upper floor	574 sq. ft.
Main floor	1,863 sq. ft.
Total Living Area:	**2,437 sq. ft.**
Garage and tool storage	519 sq. ft.
Exterior Wall Framing:	2x4

Foundation Options:

Slab

(All plans can be built with your choice of foundation and framing. A generic conversion diagram is available. See order form.)

BLUEPRINT PRICE CODE:	C

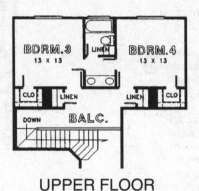

UPPER FLOOR

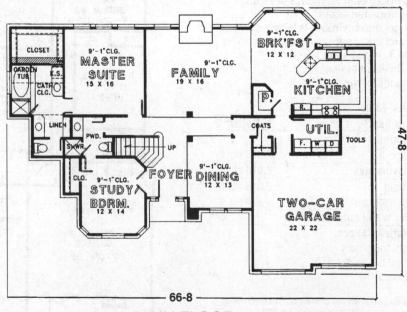

MAIN FLOOR

Plan KLF-9309

PRICES AND DETAILS
ON PAGES 13-15

Family Farmhouse

- There's more to this house than its charming front porch, steeply pitched roof and dormer windows.
- A feeling of spaciousness is emphasized by the open floor plan, with the living room adjoining the kitchen and bayed breakfast area. A snack bar allows easy service to the living room.
- The back door leads from the carport to the utility room, which is convenient to the kitchen and half-bath.
- The secluded main-floor master bedroom offers a large walk-in closet and a private bathroom.
- Upstairs, two bedrooms share another full bath. One includes dormer windows and the other a window seat. A door at the top of the stairs provides access to attic space that could be turned into an extra bedroom.

Plan J-86133

Bedrooms: 3	Baths: 2½
Living Area:	
Upper floor	559 sq. ft.
Main floor	1,152 sq. ft.
Total Living Area:	**1,711 sq. ft.**
Standard basement	1,152 sq. ft.
Carport	387 sq. ft.
Storage	85 sq. ft.
Exterior Wall Framing:	2x4

Foundation Options:

Standard basement
Crawlspace
Slab

(All plans can be built with your choice of foundation and framing. A generic conversion diagram is available. See order form.)

BLUEPRINT PRICE CODE:	B

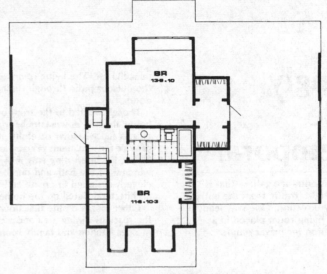

UPPER FLOOR

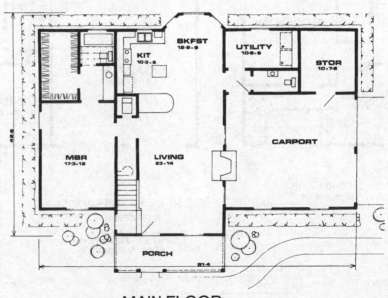

MAIN FLOOR

ORDER BLUEPRINTS ANYTIME!
CALL TOLL-FREE 1-888-626-2026

Plan J-86133

PRICES AND DETAILS
ON PAGES 13-15

179

FRONT VIEW

Strikingly Simple Contemporary

From its spacious entrance gallery that is two stories in height, traffic from the entry radiates in every direction. One way leads to the 20' x 15' living room placed in a sequestered location for privacy and peaceful use. The living room also joins the outdoor patio through sliding glass doors.

Though located to the front of the home, the two downstairs bedrooms have closets and windows carefully placed to provide for maximum privacy and quiet. Notice the interesting way in which the windows of the bath and one bedroom are cleverly designed to create an interesting architectural detail on the home's exterior.

Other rooms on the first floor include the spacious dining area and a combination of open kitchen and family room. A corner fireplace opening is established in the family room as a part of the central masonry wall common to the living room. The well equipped laundry room with two storage closets and built-in appliances completes the first floor.

The open and interesting semi-circular staircase is used to connect with the second story bedroom arrangement. Here, the 616 sq. ft. of floor space includes a complete bathroom. From the uppermost landing of the staircase common to both bedrooms, one may overlook the balustrade into the open entry hall below.

SECOND FLOOR
616 SQUARE FEET

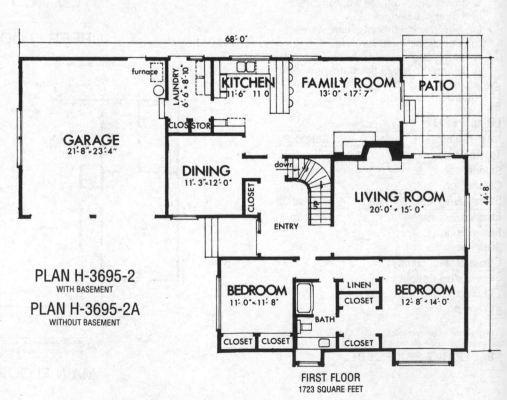

PLAN H-3695-2
WITH BASEMENT

PLAN H-3695-2A
WITHOUT BASEMENT

FIRST FLOOR
1723 SQUARE FEET

First floor: 1,723 sq. ft.
Second floor: 616 sq. ft.

Total living area: 2,339 sq. ft.
(Not counting basement or garage)

ORDER BLUEPRINTS ANYTIME!
CALL TOLL-FREE 1-888-626-2026

Blueprint Price Code C
Plans H-3695-2 &-2A

PRICES AND DETAILS
ON PAGES 13-15

Design Fits Narrow Lot

- This compact, cozy and dignified plan makes great use of a small lot, while also offering an exciting interior design.
- In from the covered front porch, the living room features a warm fireplace and a 13-ft., 6-in. cathedral ceiling.
- The bay-windowed dining room joins the living room to provide a spacious area for entertaining.
- The galley-style kitchen has easy access to a large pantry closet, the utility room and the carport.
- The master suite includes a deluxe bath and a roomy walk-in closet.
- Two secondary bedrooms share another bath off the hallway.
- A lockable storage area is located off the rear patio.

Plan J-86161

Bedrooms: 3	Baths: 2
Living Area:	
Main floor	1,626 sq. ft.
Total Living Area:	**1,626 sq. ft.**
Standard basement	1,626 sq. ft.
Carport	410 sq. ft.
Storage	104 sq. ft.
Exterior Wall Framing:	2x4

Foundation Options:

Standard basement
Crawlspace
Slab
(All plans can be built with your choice of foundation and framing. A generic conversion diagram is available. See order form.)

BLUEPRINT PRICE CODE: B

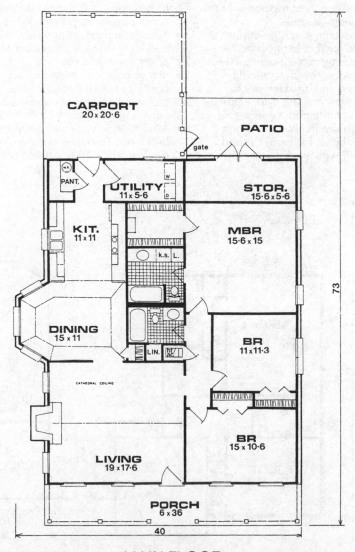

MAIN FLOOR

ORDER BLUEPRINTS ANYTIME!
CALL TOLL-FREE 1-888-626-2026

Plan J-86161

PRICES AND DETAILS
ON PAGES 13-15

181

Memories in the Making

- You will enjoy years of memories in this peaceful country home.
- A tranquil covered porch opens into the foyer, where regal columns introduce the formal dining room. Soaring 10-ft. ceilings enhance the foyer, dining room, kitchen and breakfast nook.
- Past two closets, a 15-ft., 4-in. cathedral ceiling adds glamour to the living room. A grand fireplace flanked by French doors under beautiful quarter-round transoms will wow your guests! The

French doors open to an inviting porch that is great for afternoon get-togethers.
- The sunny breakfast bay merges with the gourmet kitchen, which includes a large pantry and an island snack bar. Bi-fold doors above the sink create a handy pass-through to the living room.
- A neat computer room nearby allows the kids to do their homework under a parent's watchful eye.
- Across the home, a stylish 10-ft. tray ceiling crowns the master suite. The skylighted master bath features a refreshing whirlpool tub.
- A hall bath services two additional bedrooms. The larger bedroom is expanded by a 10-ft. vaulted ceiling.

Plan J-9294	
Bedrooms: 3	**Baths:** 2
Living Area:	
Main floor	2,018 sq. ft.
Total Living Area:	**2,018 sq. ft.**
Standard basement	2,018 sq. ft.
Garage and storage	556 sq. ft.
Exterior Wall Framing:	2x4
Foundation Options:	
Standard basement	
Crawlspace	
Slab	

(All plans can be built with your choice of foundation and framing. A generic conversion diagram is available. See order form.)

BLUEPRINT PRICE CODE:	C

74-11

49-2

Porch
17'10"~10'0"

M.Bath

Master Bedroom
13'0"~17'1"

Bath

Living
21'0"~16'3"

Breakfast
13'3"~8'11"

Comp. Room

Laun.

Storage
8'1"~7'1"

Kitchen
13'0"~14'0"

Garage
20'11"~21'5"

Bedroom
13'0"~11'3"

Bedroom
13'1"~14'1"

Foyer

Dining
13'0"~10'11"

Porch
22'11"~5'10"

MAIN FLOOR

ORDER BLUEPRINTS ANYTIME!
CALL TOLL-FREE 1-888-626-2026

Plan J-9294

PRICES AND DETAILS
ON PAGES 13-15

Spacious Kitchen, Open Living/Dining Area

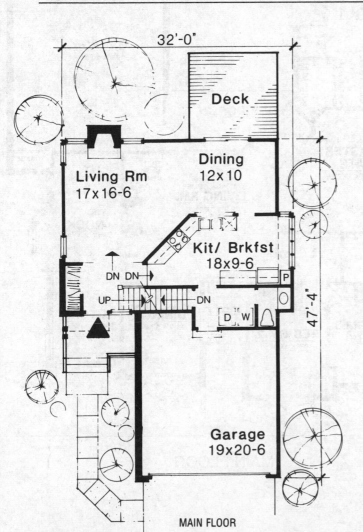

32'-0"

Deck

Dining
12 x 10

Living Rm
17 x 16-6

Kit/ Brkfst
18 x 9-6

DN DN

UP   DN

D W

47'-4"

Garage
19 x 20-6

MAIN FLOOR

PLAN B-112-86
WITH BASEMENT

Main floor:	775 sq. ft.
Upper floor:	727 sq. ft.
Total living area:	1,502 sq. ft.

(Not counting basement or garage)

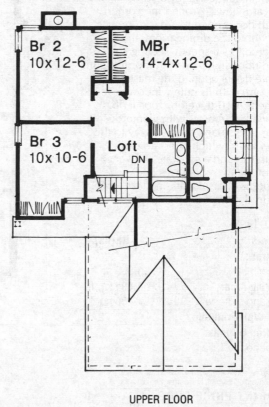

Br 2
10 x 12-6

MBr
14-4 x 12-6

Br 3
10 x 10-6

Loft

DN

UPPER FLOOR

Blueprint Price Code B
Plan B-112-86

ORDER BLUEPRINTS ANYTIME!
CALL TOLL-FREE 1-888-626-2026

PRICES AND DETAILS
ON PAGES 13-15
183

Ultimate French Comfort

- Delightful interior touches coupled with a striking French facade make this home the ultimate in one-story comfort.
- In the sidelighted entry, an attractive overhead plant ledge captures the eye.
- The entry opens to the formal dining and living rooms—both of which boast 10-ft. ceilings.
- In the living room, a handy wet bar and a media center flank a handsome fireplace. Large windows frame wide backyard views. Around the corner, French doors open to a back porch.
- Adjacent to the dining room, the kitchen offers a speedy serving bar. A bayed nook lights up with morning sun.
- Double doors open to the master bedroom, with its cute window seat and TV shelf. A 10-ft. ceiling tops it off.
- Two walk-in closets with glamorous mirror doors flank the walkway to the master bath, which offers an exotic garden tub and a separate shower.
- One of the two roomy secondary bedrooms offers a walk-in closet, a built-in desk and a gorgeous window.

Plan RD-1895

Bedrooms: 3	Baths: 2
Living Area:	
Main floor	1,895 sq. ft.
Total Living Area:	**1,895 sq. ft.**
Garage and storage	485 sq. ft.
Exterior Wall Framing:	2x4

Foundation Options:

Crawlspace
Slab

(All plans can be built with your choice of foundation and framing. A generic conversion diagram is available. See order form.)

BLUEPRINT PRICE CODE: B

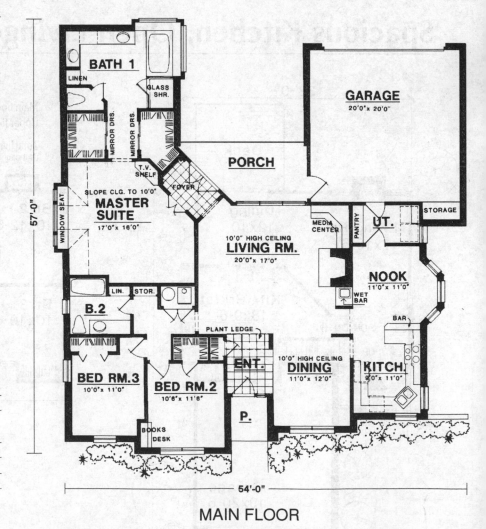

MAIN FLOOR

Plan RD-1895

PRICES AND DETAILS
ON PAGES 13-15

Affordable Luxury

- This stylish and enticing home combines luxury and affordability in one compact package.
- The foyer offers an immediate view of the living room's impressive fireplace and the wraparound deck beyond. The spacious living room also features a dramatic 15-ft. vaulted ceiling.
- The adjoining formal dining room is outlined by decorative wood columns. Sliding glass doors access the deck.
- A corner sink framed by a half-wall keeps the well-planned kitchen open to the sunny breakfast nook.
- The master suite is spectacular, with a bright sitting area and a distinctive ceiling that slopes up to 10 feet. A large walk-in closet and a sumptuous master bath with a dual-sink vanity, a whirlpool tub and a corner shower are other highlights.
- The third bedroom, with its beautiful Palladian window and vaulted ceiling, would serve equally well as a den or an impressive home office.

Plan B-89020

Bedrooms: 2+	Baths: 2
Living Area:	
Main floor	1,642 sq. ft.
Total Living Area:	**1,642 sq. ft.**
Standard basement	1,642 sq. ft.
Garage	455 sq. ft.
Exterior Wall Framing:	2x4

Foundation Options:

Standard basement
(All plans can be built with your choice of foundation and framing. A generic conversion diagram is available. See order form.)

BLUEPRINT PRICE CODE: **B**

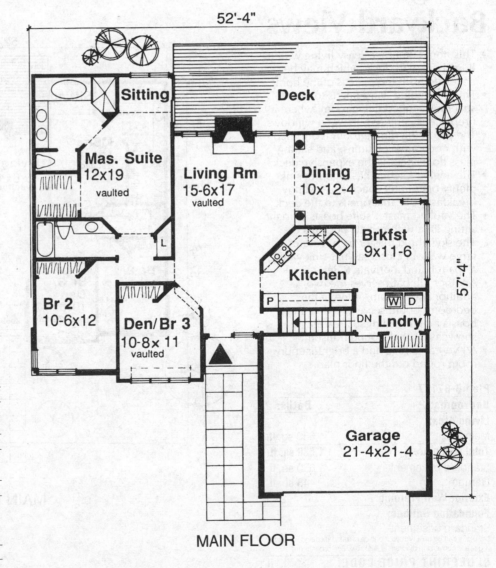

MAIN FLOOR

ORDER BLUEPRINTS ANYTIME!
CALL TOLL-FREE 1-888-626-2026

Plan B-89020

PRICES AND DETAILS
ON PAGES 13-15

185

Delightful Backyard Views

- This home embraces easy living with its huge backyard deck, which may be accessed from three areas of the home.
- The sidelighted entry opens to the spacious vaulted living room, where a fireplace is centered between windows.
- The adjoining dining room is adorned with decorative columns, and sliding glass doors access the expansive deck.
- The angled kitchen has a corner sink, plenty of counter space and a sunny breakfast nook that opens to the deck.
- The vaulted master suite boasts a bright sitting area with private deck access. The skylighted master bath features a large walk-in closet, a dual-sink vanity, a spa tub and a private toilet.
- Another full bath serves the two additional bedrooms. One of the bedrooms could serve as a den and boasts a high-ceilinged area that showcases a half-round transom.
- A two-car garage and a bright laundry room round out the floor plan.

Plan B-87127

Bedrooms: 2+	Baths: 2
Living Area:	
Main floor	1,630 sq. ft.
Total Living Area:	**1,630 sq. ft.**
Standard basement	1,630 sq. ft.
Garage	448 sq. ft.
Exterior Wall Framing:	2x4

Foundation Options:

Standard basement
(All plans can be built with your choice of foundation and framing. A generic conversion diagram is available. See order form.)

BLUEPRINT PRICE CODE:	**B**

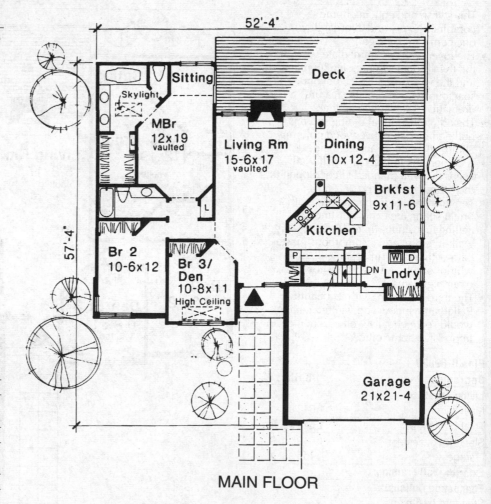

MAIN FLOOR

ORDER BLUEPRINTS ANYTIME!
CALL TOLL-FREE 1-888-626-2026

Plan B-87127

PRICES AND DETAILS
ON PAGES 13-15

FRONT VIEW

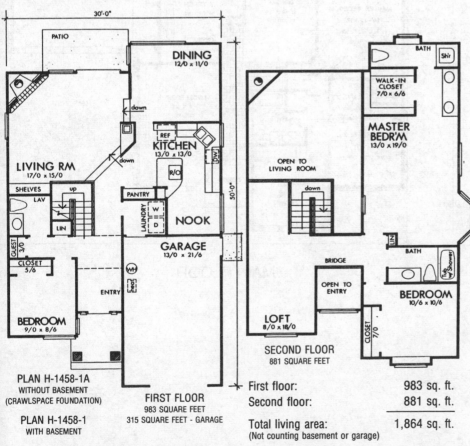

30'-0"

PATIO

DINING
12/0 x 11/0

KITCHEN
13/0 x 13/0

REF

DW

R/O

PANTRY

LIVING RM
17/0 x 15/0

SHELVES

LAV

up

down

down

LIN

W
D

LAUNDRY

NOOK

50'-0"

GUEST
3/0

CLOSET
5/6

ENTRY

GARAGE
13/0 x 21/6

W

BEDROOM
9/0 x 8/6

PLAN H-1458-1A
WITHOUT BASEMENT
(CRAWLSPACE FOUNDATION)

PLAN H-1458-1
WITH BASEMENT

FIRST FLOOR
983 SQUARE FEET
315 SQUARE FEET - GARAGE

BATH

Shr

WALK-IN
CLOSET
7/0 x 6/6

MASTER
BEDR'M
13/0 x 19/0

OPEN TO
LIVING ROOM

down

LIN

BATH

Tub
n'
Shower

BRIDGE

OPEN TO
ENTRY

BEDROOM
10/6 x 10/6

LOFT
8/0 x 18/0

CLOSET
7/0

SECOND FLOOR
881 SQUARE FEET

First floor: 983 sq. ft.
Second floor: 881 sq. ft.

Total living area: 1,864 sq. ft.
(Not counting basement or garage)

Queen Anne with Contemporary Interior

This gracious home offers numerous features for convenience and charm:

- 1,864 sq. ft. of living area.
- 2 bedrooms, plus den.
- Traditional exterior style.
- 30' wide at first floor, 32' wide at second floor.
- Versatile kitchen with range/oven/eating bar combination.
- Practical spice cabinet, pantry and nook.
- Sunken living room with vaulted ceiling, fireplace, French doors, wet bar and built-in shelves.
- Dramatic open staircase.
- Interesting entry open to bridge above.
- 2½ baths.
- Cozy loft open to living area.
- Spacious and elegant master bedroom with bay window, walk-in closet, separate shower, double-sink vanity and window overlooking living/loft area.
- Energy-efficient specifications throughout, including 2x6 wall framing.

Blueprint Price Code B

Plans H-1458-1 & 1A

*PRICES AND DETAILS
ON PAGES 13-15*

Three to One

- This stunning brick-clad home harbors three cozy bedrooms in its spacious one-story design.
- A masterpiece of comfort, the master bedroom unfolds, beckoning you to sweet relaxation after tiresome days. Double doors introduce the sanctuary of the bath, where you'll find a zesty shower and a soothing tub. On warm nights, slip through the French doors and enjoy the night sky's starry dance.
- When the evening calls for fun, stage your gathering in the family room. Here, window seats provide comfort for larger crowds, and a cheery fireplace adds to the spirit of the night.
- Do you prefer a more sophisticated setting? The living room easily fills the bill, with its welcoming angles and handsome fireplace.
- The dining room is a marvel, too. There's plenty of room for in-laws and grandkids, and dazzling French doors to a back porch add elegant intrigue.
- Not surprisingly, the kitchen is placed to serve as the hub of the home. Its walk-through configuration smoothly handles large traffic levels while maintaining a decidedly casual appeal.

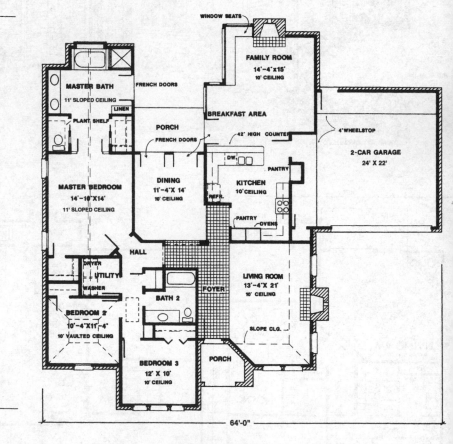

MAIN FLOOR

Plan L-62-FAB	
Bedrooms: 3	**Baths:** 2
Living Area:	
Main floor	2,060 sq. ft.
Total Living Area:	**2,060 sq. ft.**
Garage	527 sq. ft.
Exterior Wall Framing:	2x4

Foundation Options:

Slab

(All plans can be built with your choice of foundation and framing. A generic conversion diagram is available. See order form.)

BLUEPRINT PRICE CODE: C

Lots of Style and Impact

- An exciting assortment of features gives this stylish design the volume and impact of a much larger home.
- Beyond the inviting covered entrance, the foyer opens to a charming bayed breakfast area and a modern kitchen.
- The vaulted Great Room flaunts a handsome fireplace and a view of the outdoors through corner windows. The adjoining dining room includes sliding glass doors to a backyard deck.
- The vaulted master bedroom is brightened by corner windows. The luxurious master bath has a corner spa tub, a separate shower and a roomy walk-in closet.
- Upstairs, a quiet bedroom is serviced by a bath and a linen closet. A cozy loft overlooking the Great Room can double as an extra bedroom.

Plan B-917

Bedrooms: 2+	Baths: 2½
Living Area:	
Upper floor	460 sq. ft.
Main floor	1,105 sq. ft.
Total Living Area:	**1,565 sq. ft.**
Standard basement	1,105 sq. ft.
Garage	387 sq. ft.
Exterior Wall Framing:	2x4

Foundation Options:

Standard basement

(All plans can be built with your choice of foundation and framing. A generic conversion diagram is available. See order form.)

BLUEPRINT PRICE CODE:	B

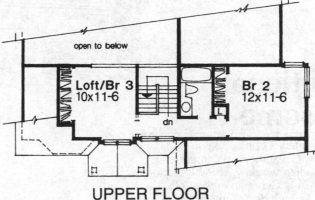

UPPER FLOOR

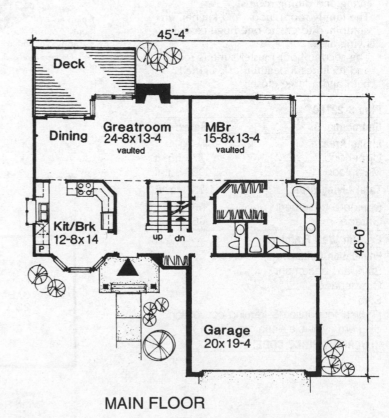

MAIN FLOOR

ORDER BLUEPRINTS ANYTIME!
CALL TOLL-FREE 1-888-626-2026

Plan B-917

PRICES AND DETAILS
ON PAGES 13-15

189

Elevation B

Elevation A

Traditional Twosome

- This plan offers a choice of two elevations. Elevation A has an upper-level Palladian window, while Elevation B has a stately Georgian entry. Both versions are included in the blueprints.
- A vaulted entry foyer leads to formal living and dining rooms.
- The family room, nook and kitchen are combined to create one huge casual living area.
- The second-floor master suite is roomy and includes a beautiful, skylighted bath and a large closet.

Plan S-22189

Bedrooms: 3	Baths: 2½

Living Area:	
Upper floor	774 sq. ft.
Main floor	963 sq. ft.
Total Living Area:	**1,737 sq. ft.**
Standard basement	963 sq. ft.
Garage	462 sq. ft.

Exterior Wall Framing: 2x6

Foundation Options:
Standard basement
Crawlspace
Slab
(Typical foundation & framing conversion diagram available—see order form.)

BLUEPRINT PRICE CODE: B

See this plan on our "Country & Traditional" Video Tour!
Order form on page 9

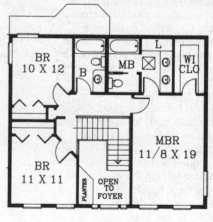

UPPER FLOOR

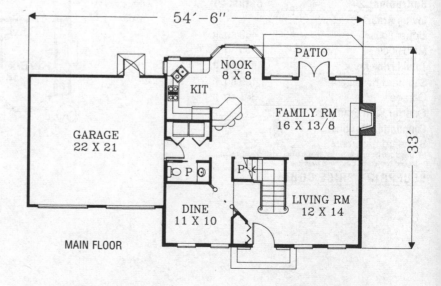

MAIN FLOOR

ORDER BLUEPRINTS ANYTIME!
CALL TOLL-FREE 1-888-626-2026

Plan S-22189

PRICES AND DETAILS
ON PAGES 13-15

Never Better!

- Safe and secure within the walls of this bold, brick design, you'll appreciate the comfort and fun it provides and soon realize that life has never been better.
- Corner quoins, soldier coursing and an arched window and entryway present a distinctive, meticulous image to visitors or passersby.
- Step into the foyer and view the splendors of the interior spaces.
- You've dreamt about master bedrooms like this one! Past its entry you'll find an incredibly spacious sleeping area, a huge walk-in closet and French doors to the backyard. A beautiful octagonal

sitting area with a gazebo ceiling leads to a peaceful, skylighted bath with a wonderfully soothing garden tub.
- The two additional bedrooms boast walk-in closets and share a large bath.
- The family room provides a great gathering place for big social events. It offers a pass-through to the kitchen's wet bar and a fireplace to keep you warm and happy.
- Designed to serve several areas at once, the island kitchen will see plenty of action. It's positioned smartly between the formal dining room and a breakfast nook with a comfy corner window seat.
- Unless otherwise noted, each room features a 9-ft. ceiling.

Plan L-2314-FTC	
Bedrooms: 3	**Baths:** 2
Living Area:	
Main floor	2,314 sq. ft.
Total Living Area:	**2,314 sq. ft.**
Exterior Wall Framing:	2x4

Foundation Options:

Slab

(All plans can be built with your choice of foundation and framing. A generic conversion diagram is available. See order form.)

BLUEPRINT PRICE CODE:	C

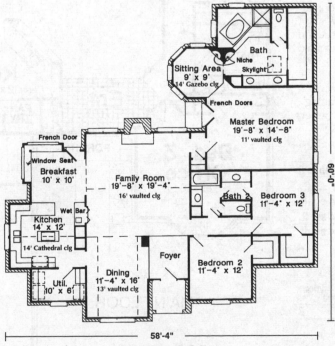

MAIN FLOOR

ORDER BLUEPRINTS ANYTIME!
CALL TOLL-FREE 1-888-626-2026

Plan L-2314-FTC

PRICES AND DETAILS
ON PAGES 13-15

191

Large, Stylish Spaces

- This stylish brick home greets guests with a beautiful entry court that leads to the recessed front porch.
- Beyond the porch, the bright entry flows into the Great Room, which features an 11-ft. sloped ceiling. This airy space also offers a fireplace, a sunny dining area and sliding glass doors to a backyard patio.
- The kitchen has a walk-in pantry, an open serving counter above the sink and convenient access to the laundry facilities and the garage.
- Isolated from the secondary bedrooms, the master suite boasts a 9-ft. tray ceiling, an oversized walk-in closet and an exquisite bath with two distinct sink areas, a corner garden tub and a separate shower.
- The third bedroom, which features lovely double doors and a front-facing bay window, would also make a perfect home office.

Plan SDG-91188

Bedrooms: 2+	Baths: 2
Living Area:	
Main floor	1,704 sq. ft.
Total Living Area:	**1,704 sq. ft.**
Garage	484 sq. ft.
Exterior Wall Framing:	2x4

Foundation Options:

Slab
(All plans can be built with your choice of foundation and framing. A generic conversion diagram is available. See order form.)

BLUEPRINT PRICE CODE:	B

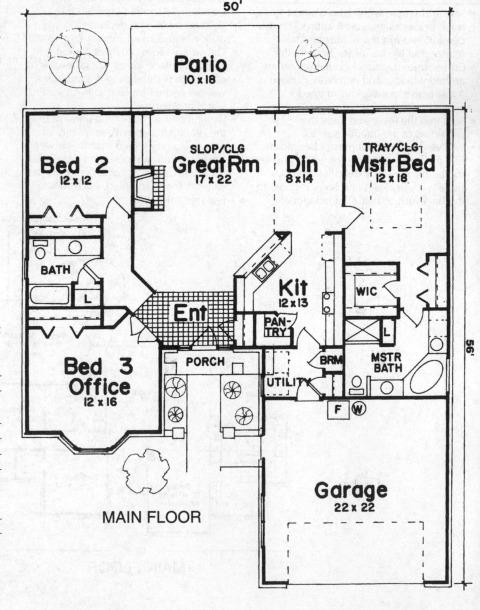

MAIN FLOOR

Plan SDG-91188

Sun-Splashed One-Story

- This unique angled design offers spectacular backyard views, a delightful sun room and two enticing terraces.
- The high-ceilinged reception hall is open to the huge combination living and dining area. Here, more high ceilings, a stone fireplace and walls of glass add to the expansive look and the inviting atmosphere.

See this plan on our "One-Story" VideoGraphic Tour! Order form on page 9

- The adjoining family room, kitchen and nook are just as appealing. The family room features a built-in entertainment center and sliding glass doors that access the energy-saving sun room. The comfortable kitchen has a handy snack counter facing the sunny dinette.
- The sleeping wing offers three bedrooms and two baths. The master suite boasts a sloped ceiling, a private terrace, a large walk-in closet and a personal bath with a whirlpool tub. The two remaining bedrooms are just steps away from another full bath.

Plan AHP-9330	
Bedrooms: 3	**Baths:** 2
Living Area:	
Main floor	1,626 sq. ft.
Sun room	146 sq. ft.
Total Living Area:	**1,772 sq. ft.**
Standard basement	1,542 sq. ft.
Garage	427 sq. ft.
Exterior Wall Framing:	2x4 or 2x6

Foundation Options:
Standard basement
Crawlspace
Slab
(All plans can be built with your choice of foundation and framing. A generic conversion diagram is available. See order form.)

BLUEPRINT PRICE CODE: B

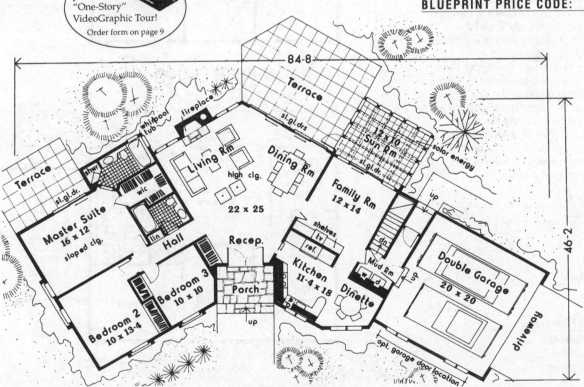

MAIN FLOOR

ORDER BLUEPRINTS ANYTIME!
CALL TOLL-FREE 1-888-626-2026

Plan AHP-9330

PRICES AND DETAILS
ON PAGES 13-15

193

Contemporary Colonial

- A Palladian window and a half-round window above the entry door give this Colonial a new look. Inside, the design maximizes space while creating an open, airy atmosphere.
- The two-story-high foyer flows between the formal areas at the front of the home. Straight ahead, the exciting family room features a built-in wet bar and a fireplace framed by French doors.
- A bay window brightens the adjoining breakfast nook and kitchen. An angled counter looks to the nook and the family room, keeping the cook in touch with the family activities.
- The four bedrooms on the upper floor include a luxurious master suite with an 11-ft. vaulted ceiling and a skylighted bathroom. The upper-floor laundry also makes this a great family home.
- The basement plan (not shown) has room for an optional den or bedroom, a recreation room with a fireplace, a storage room and a utility area.

Plan CH-320-A

Bedrooms: 4+	Baths: 3
Living Area:	
Upper floor	1,164 sq. ft.
Main floor	1,293 sq. ft.
Total Living Area:	**2,457 sq. ft.**
Basement	1,293 sq. ft.
Garage	462 sq. ft.
Exterior Wall Framing:	2x4

Foundation Options:

Daylight basement

Standard basement

Crawlspace

(All plans can be built with your choice of foundation and framing. A generic conversion diagram is available. See order form.)

BLUEPRINT PRICE CODE: C

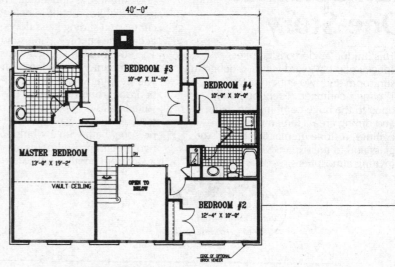

UPPER FLOOR

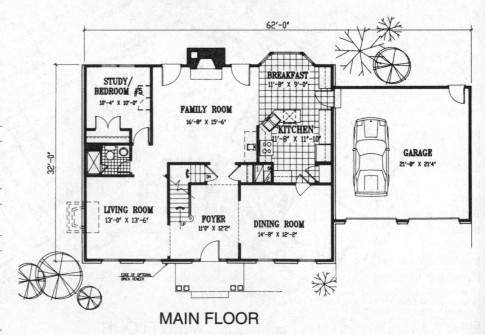

MAIN FLOOR

ORDER BLUEPRINTS ANYTIME!
CALL TOLL-FREE 1-888-626-2026

Plan CH-320-A

PRICES AND DETAILS
ON PAGES 13-15

Relax on the Front Porch

- With its wraparound covered porch, this quaint two-story home makes summer evenings a breeze.
- Inside, a beautiful open stairway welcomes guests into the vaulted foyer, which connects the formal areas. The front-facing living and dining rooms have views of the covered front porch.
- French doors open from the living room to the family room, where a fireplace and corner windows warm and brighten this spacious activity area.
- The breakfast nook, set off by a half-wall, hosts a handy work desk and opens to the back porch.
- The country kitchen offers an oversized island, a pantry closet and illuminating windows flanking the corner sink.
- The upper-floor master suite boasts two walk-in closets and a private bath with a tub and a separate shower. Two more bedrooms, another full bath and a laundry room are also included.

Plan AGH-1997

Bedrooms: 3	Baths: 2½
Living Area:	
Upper floor	933 sq. ft.
Main floor	1,064 sq. ft.
Total Living Area:	**1,997 sq. ft.**
Standard basement	1,064 sq. ft.
Garage	662 sq. ft.
Exterior Wall Framing:	2x6

Foundation Options:

Standard basement
(All plans can be built with your choice of foundation and framing. A generic conversion diagram is available. See order form.)

BLUEPRINT PRICE CODE: B

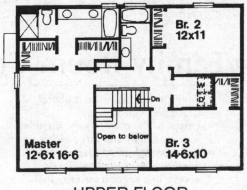

UPPER FLOOR

See this plan on our "Country & Traditional" Video Tour!
Order form on page 9

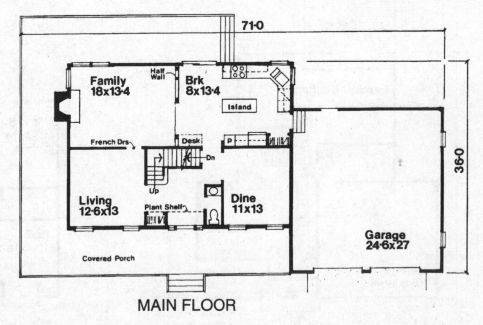

MAIN FLOOR

ORDER BLUEPRINTS ANYTIME!
CALL TOLL-FREE 1-888-626-2026

Plan AGH-1997

PRICES AND DETAILS
ON PAGES 13-15

195

Open Kitchen/Family Room Combination

- This compact plan is designed to provide maximum casual living space for a small but busy family.
- A large family room/kitchen combination opens onto a large deck.
- The great room features an impressive corner fireplace and a vaulted ceiling and adjoins the

dining room to create a liberal space for entertaining.
- Upstairs, the master suite includes a private bath and large closet.
- Bedroom 2 boasts a large gable window, two closets and easy access to a second upstairs bath.
- The loft area is available for study, play, an exercise area or third bedroom.

Plan B-88006	
Bedrooms: 2-3	**Baths:** 2½
Space:	
Upper floor:	732 sq. ft.
Main floor:	818 sq. ft.
Total living area:	**1,550 sq. ft.**
Basement:	818 sq. ft.
Garage:	374 sq. ft.
Exterior Wall Framing:	2x4

Foundation options:
Standard basement only.
(Foundation & framing conversion diagram available — see order form.)

Blueprint Price Code: B

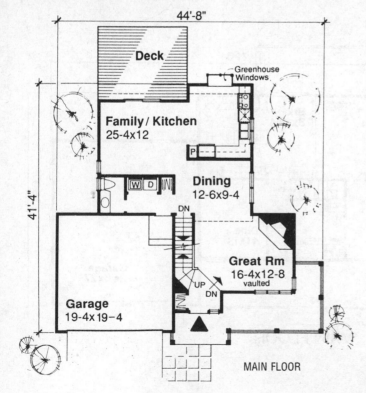

MAIN FLOOR

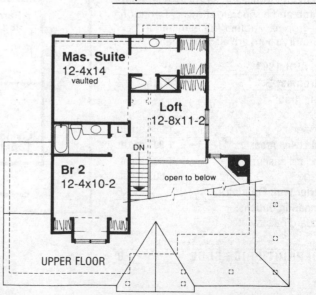

UPPER FLOOR

Plan B-88006
PRICES AND DETAILS
ON PAGES 13-15

Morning Room with a View

- This modern-looking ranch is stylishly decorated with a pair of arched-window dormers, handsome brick trim and a covered front porch.
- Inside, the dining room is set off by columns, as it merges with the entry.
- The main living areas are oriented to the rear, where a huge central family room offers a patio view and a fireplace that may also be enjoyed from the bayed morning room and adjoining kitchen.
- The walk-through kitchen features a pantry, a snack bar to the family room and easy service to the formal dining room across the hall.
- The secluded master suite boasts a wide window seat and a private bath with a walk-in closet, a corner garden tub and a separate shower.
- Across the home, the three secondary bedrooms share another full bath. The fourth bedroom may double as a study.
- High 10-ft. ceilings are found throughout the home, except in the secondary bedrooms.

Plan DD-1962-1

Bedrooms: 3+	Baths: 2
Living Area:	
Main floor	1,962 sq. ft.
Total Living Area:	**1,962 sq. ft.**
Standard basement	1,962 sq. ft.
Garage	386 sq. ft.
Exterior Wall Framing:	2x4

Foundation Options:

Standard basement
Crawlspace
Slab

(All plans can be built with your choice of foundation and framing. A generic conversion diagram is available. See order form.)

BLUEPRINT PRICE CODE:	B

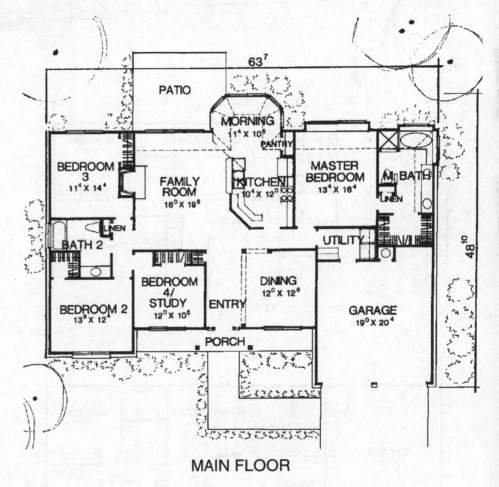

MAIN FLOOR

FRONT VIEW

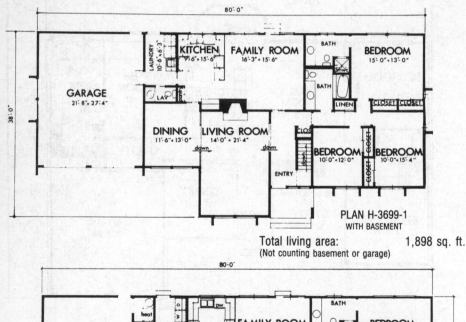

PLAN H-3699-1
WITH BASEMENT

Total living area: 1,898 sq. ft.
(Not counting basement or garage)

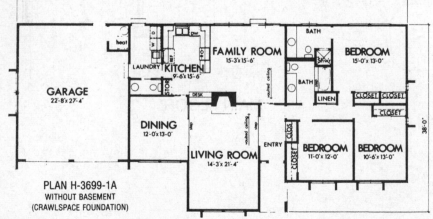

PLAN H-3699-1A
WITHOUT BASEMENT
(CRAWLSPACE FOUNDATION)

Total living area: 1,851 sq. ft.
(Not counting garage)

Popular Floor Plan, Contemporary Exterior

A contemporary beauty, this excellent family-oriented home will be an asset to any neighborhood setting. Clerestory windows peek out along the ridge lines of the front and rear of the roof to create light for the kitchen, inside bath, living room and entry hall. Other contemporary details include extended bay windows and wing walls, to give the window areas desirable shade covering and privacy.

Revolving around a central entry hall, all the living spaces function independently without any traffic congestion. A dramatic vaulted ceiling covers the family room, living room and entry hall. One step down from the entry into the sunken living room, and the cabaret-type dining area comes into view.

An efficient U-shaped kitchen serves the dining room or family room, with a separate two-thirds bath near the kitchen. The other wing includes an efficient three-bedroom sleeping area served by two bathrooms.

Blueprint Price Code B

Plans H-3699-1 & -1A

PRICES AND DETAILS
ON PAGES 13-15

Modern Elegance

- Half-round transom windows and a barrel-vaulted porch with paired columns lend elegance to the facade of this post-modern design.
- Inside, the two-story-high foyer leads past a den and a diagonal, open-railed stairway to the sunken living room.
- A 17-ft. vaulted ceiling and a striking fireplace enhance the living room, while square columns introduce the adjoining formal dining room.
- The adjacent kitchen is thoroughly modern, including an island cooktop and a large pantry. A sunny bay window defines the breakfast area, where a sliding glass door opens to the angled backyard deck.
- Columns preface the sunken family room, which also sports a 17-ft.-high vaulted ceiling and easy access to the deck. A half-bath, a laundry room and access to the garage are nearby.
- Upstairs, the master suite features a 10-ft. vaulted ceiling, a private bath and a large walk-in closet.

Plan B-89005

Bedrooms: 4	Baths: 2½
Living Area:	
Upper floor	1,083 sq. ft.
Main floor	1,380 sq. ft.
Total Living Area:	**2,463 sq. ft.**
Standard basement	1,380 sq. ft.
Garage	483 sq. ft.
Exterior Wall Framing:	2x4

Foundation Options:

Standard basement

(All plans can be built with your choice of foundation and framing. A generic conversion diagram is available. See order form.)

BLUEPRINT PRICE CODE:	C

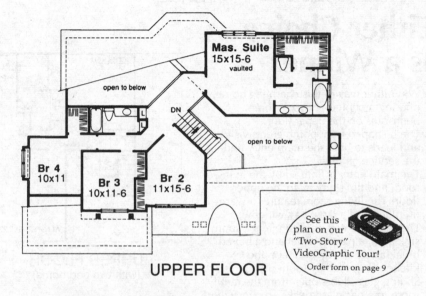

UPPER FLOOR

See this plan on our "Two-Story" VideoGraphic Tour! Order form on page 9

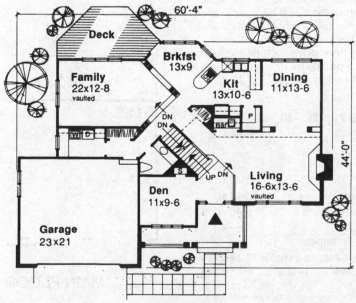

MAIN FLOOR

ORDER BLUEPRINTS ANYTIME!
CALL TOLL-FREE 1-888-626-2026

Plan B-89005

PRICES AND DETAILS
ON PAGES 13-15

199

Either Choice Is a Winner

- Win either way in this charming home, offering a choice of two or three bedrooms on the upper floor.
- The L-shaped front porch greets visitors and leads to both the main entry and the service entry.
- The main entry is flanked by the living room and the stairway to the upper floor. The living room features a warm fireplace and a large bay window.
- The rear-oriented kitchen offers a sunny sink area, a pantry closet and a bayed breakfast nook that connects the kitchen to the family room.
- Sliding glass doors open from the family room to a backyard deck. An oversized laundry room and a half-bath are convenient to the family living area as well as to the service entry.
- Both upper floor plans include a master suite with a private bath, a second full bath and a railing overlooking the front entry below.

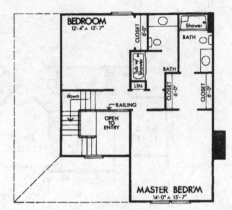

UPPER FLOOR
(with two bedrooms)

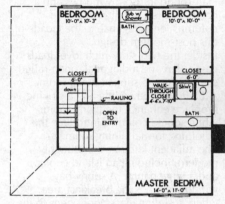

UPPER FLOOR
(with three bedrooms)

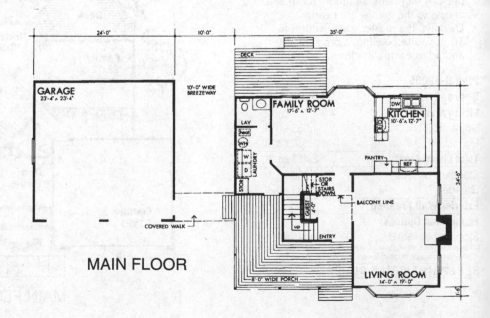

MAIN FLOOR

Plans H-1439-2D, -2E, -3D, -3E

Bedrooms: 2+	Baths: 2½
Living Area:	
Upper floor	678 sq. ft.
Main floor	940 sq. ft.
Total Living Area:	**1,618 sq. ft.**
Standard basement	940 sq. ft.
Garage	544 sq. ft.
Exterior Wall Framing:	2x6

Foundation Options:	2-bedroom	3-bedroom
Standard basement	H-1439-2E	H-1439-3E
Crawlspace	H-1439-2D	H-1439-3D

(All plans can be built with your choice of foundation and framing. A generic conversion diagram is available. See order form.)

BLUEPRINT PRICE CODE:	B

Garden Home with a View

- This clever design proves that privacy doesn't have to be compromised even in high-density urban neighborhoods. From within, views are oriented to a beautiful, lush entry courtyard and a covered rear porch.
- The exterior appearance is sheltered, but warm and welcoming.
- The innovative interior design centers on a unique kitchen, which directs traffic away from the working areas while still serving the entire home.
- The sunken family room features a 14-ft. vaulted ceiling and a warm fireplace.
- The master suite is highlighted by a sumptuous master bath with an oversized shower and a whirlpool tub, plus a large walk-in closet.
- The formal living room is designed and placed in such a way that it can become a third bedroom, a den, or an office or study room, depending on family needs and lifestyles.

Plan E-1824

Bedrooms: 2+	Baths: 2
Living Area:	
Main floor	1,891 sq. ft.
Total Living Area:	**1,891 sq. ft.**
Garage	506 sq. ft.
Storage	60 sq. ft.
Exterior Wall Framing:	2x4

Foundation Options:

Crawlspace
Slab
(All plans can be built with your choice of foundation and framing. A generic conversion diagram is available. See order form.)

BLUEPRINT PRICE CODE: B

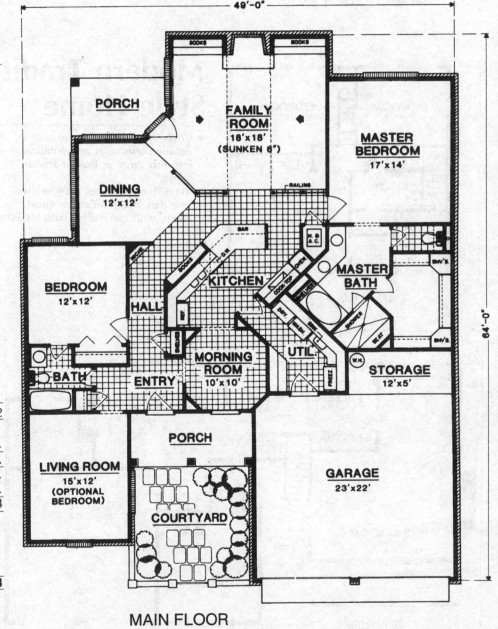

MAIN FLOOR

ORDER BLUEPRINTS ANYTIME!
CALL TOLL-FREE 1-888-626-2026

Plan E-1824

**PRICES AND DETAILS
ON PAGES 13-15**

201

UPPER FLOOR

BEDROOM 12/0×10/6
BEDROOM 14/5×11/7
CLOSET 4/0
CLOSET 4/0
LIN
BATH
down
Tub w/ Shower
BATH
5/3 CLOSET
5/0 CLOSET
BEDROOM 16/0×13/6

30'-0"
28'-9"

Modern Traditional-Style Home

- Covered porch and decorative double doors offer an invitation into this three or four bedroom home.
- Main floor bedroom may be used as a den, home office, or guest room, with convenient bath facilities.

- Adjoining dining room makes living room seem even more spacious; breakfast nook enlarges the look of the attached kitchen.
- Brick-size concrete block veneer and masonry tile roof give the exterior a look of durability.

REF
SHELVES
4/0 CLOSET
CLOS. 3/0

PLAN H-1351-M1A
WITHOUT BASEMENT
(CRAWLSPACE FOUNDATION)

Plans H-1351-M1 & -M1A

Bedrooms: 3-4	Baths: 3
Space:	
Upper floor:	862 sq. ft.
Main floor:	1,383 sq. ft.
Total living area:	**2,245 sq. ft.**
Basement:	1,383 sq. ft.
Garage:	413 sq. ft.
Exterior Wall Framing:	**2x6**

Foundation options:
Standard basement (Plan H-1351-M1).
Crawlspace (Plan H-1351-M1A).
(Foundation & framing conversion diagram available — see order form.)

Blueprint Price Code: C

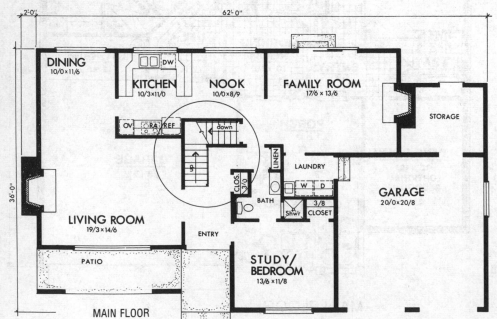

DINING 10/0×11/6
KITCHEN 10/3×11/0
NOOK 10/0×8/9
FAMILY ROOM 17/6×13/6
STORAGE
DW
OV RA REF
down
LINEN
LAUNDRY
W D
BATH
CLOS. 3/0
Shwr 3/8 CLOSET
GARAGE 20/0×20/8
LIVING ROOM 19/3×14/6
ENTRY
PATIO
STUDY/ BEDROOM 13/6×11/8

MAIN FLOOR

2'-0"
62'-0"
36'-0"

ORDER BLUEPRINTS ANYTIME!
CALL TOLL-FREE 1-888-626-2026

Plans H-1351-M1 & -M1A

PRICES AND DETAILS ON PAGES 13-15

Economical Plan for Narrow Lot

- Designed to accommodate a narrow lot, this economical plan still provides the amenities wanted by today's families.
- An efficient foyer distributes traffic in several directions, including the formal dining room on the right, living room on the left and the family room straight ahead.
- The kitchen is designed with efficiency in mind, and features an angled snack counter and a sunny breakfast nook.
- Upstairs, a deluxe master suite includes a private bath and large walk-in closet.
- Three secondary bedrooms and another full bath are also found upstairs.

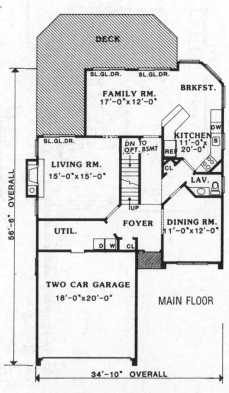

MAIN FLOOR

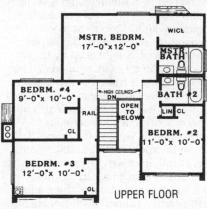

UPPER FLOOR

Plan AX-98821

Bedrooms: 4	Baths: 2½
Space:	
Upper floor	886 sq. ft.
Main floor	1,104 sq. ft.
Total Living Area	**1,990 sq. ft.**
Basement	1,013 sq. ft.
Garage	383 sq. ft.
Exterior Wall Framing	2x4

Foundation options:
Standard Basement
Slab
(Foundation & framing conversion diagram available—see order form.)

Blueprint Price Code	B

ORDER BLUEPRINTS ANYTIME!
CALL TOLL-FREE 1-888-626-2026

Plan AX-98821

PRICES AND DETAILS
ON PAGES 13-15

203

Delightful Great Room

- An expansive Great Room with a 10-ft. vaulted ceiling, a warm corner fireplace and an angled wet bar highlights this tastefully appointed home.
- On the exterior, decorative plants thrive in the lush wraparound planter that leads to the sheltered entry. The foyer is brightened by a sidelight and a skylight.
- To the left, the kitchen offers an island cooktop with lots room for food preparation and serving. The bayed breakfast nook is enhanced by bright windows and a 12½-ft. vaulted ceiling.
- Formal dining is hosted in the space adjoining the Great Room. Graced by a lovely bay window, the room also offers French doors to a covered patio.
- In the sleeping wing of the home, the master bedroom features a sitting area and a walk-in closet. The private master bath boasts a relaxing Jacuzzi tub.
- Two secondary bedrooms share a full bath nearby. Laundry facilities are also convenient.

Plan S-52394

Bedrooms: 3	Baths: 2
Living Area:	
Main floor	1,841 sq. ft.
Total Living Area:	**1,841 sq. ft.**
Standard basement	1,789 sq. ft.
Garage	432 sq. ft.
Exterior Wall Framing:	2x6

Foundation Options:

Standard basement

Crawlspace

Slab

(All plans can be built with your choice of foundation and framing. A generic conversion diagram is available. See order form.)

BLUEPRINT PRICE CODE: B

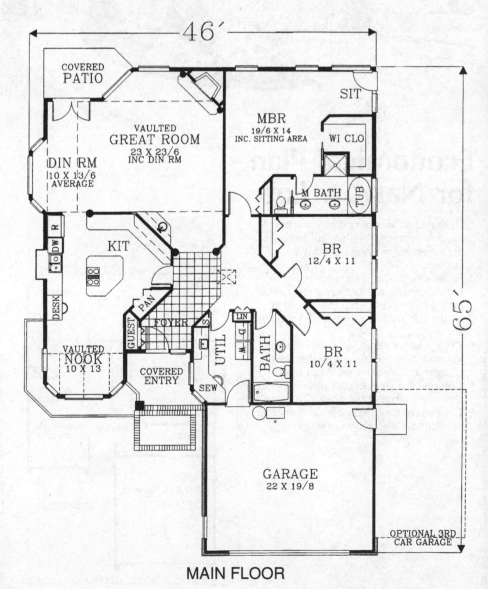

MAIN FLOOR

Plan S-52394

PRICES AND DETAILS
ON PAGES 13-15

Appealing and Well-Appointed

- A feature-filled interior and a warm, appealing exterior are the keynotes of this spacious two-story home.
- Beyond the charming front porch, the foyer is brightened by sidelights and an octagonal window. To the right, a cased opening leads into the open living room and dining room. Plenty of windows, including a beautiful boxed-out window, bathe the formal area in light.
- The casual area consists of an extra-large island kitchen, a sizable breakfast area and a spectacular family room with a corner fireplace and a skylighted cathedral ceiling that slopes from 11 ft. to 17 ft. high.
- The upper floor hosts a superb master suite, featuring a skylighted bath with an 11-ft. sloped ceiling, a platform spa tub and a separate shower.
- A balcony hall leads to two more bedrooms, a full bath and an optional bonus room that would make a great loft, study or extra bedroom.

Plan AX-8923-A

Bedrooms: 3+	Baths: 2½
Living Area:	
Upper floor	853 sq. ft.
Main floor	1,199 sq. ft.
Optional loft/bedroom	180 sq. ft.
Total Living Area:	**2,232 sq. ft.**
Standard basement	1,184 sq. ft.
Garage	420 sq. ft.
Exterior Wall Framing:	2x4

Foundation Options:

Standard basement

Slab

(All plans can be built with your choice of foundation and framing. A generic conversion diagram is available. See order form.)

BLUEPRINT PRICE CODE: C

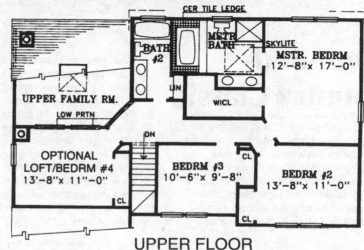

UPPER FLOOR

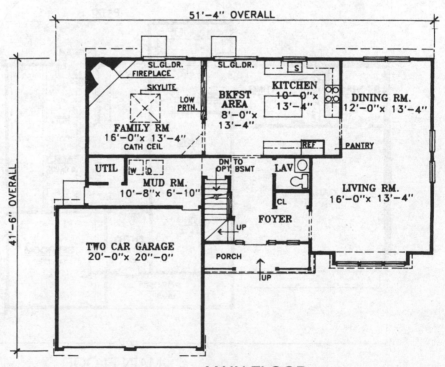

MAIN FLOOR

ORDER BLUEPRINTS ANYTIME!
CALL TOLL-FREE 1-888-626-2026

Plan AX-8923-A

PRICES AND DETAILS
ON PAGES 13-15

205

Town-and-Country Classic

- A railed front porch, a charming cupola and stylish shutters add town and country flair to this classic one-story.
- The welcoming entry flows into the vaulted family room, which boasts a 14-ft. vaulted ceiling with exposed beams, a handsome fireplace and a French door to a backyard patio.

- The living room and the formal dining room are separated by a half-wall with decorative wooden spindles. The adjoining kitchen features wraparound counter space. The eating nook has a laundry closet and garage access.
- The master bedroom enjoys a private bath with a separate dressing and a roomy walk-in closet.
- Two additional bedrooms are serviced by a compartmentalized hallway bath.
- The two-car garage includes a separate storage area at the back.

Plan E-1815

Bedrooms: 3	Baths: 2
Living Area:	
Main floor	1,898 sq. ft.
Total Living Area:	**1,898 sq. ft.**
Garage and storage	513 sq. ft.
Exterior Wall Framing:	2x4

Foundation Options:
Crawlspace
Slab
(All plans can be built with your choice of foundation and framing. A generic conversion diagram is available. See order form.)

BLUEPRINT PRICE CODE: B

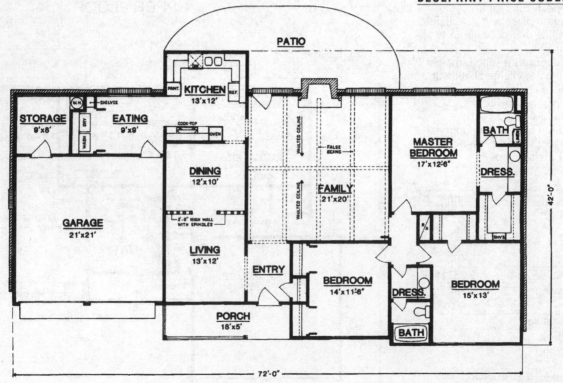

MAIN FLOOR

Plan E-1815

PRICES AND DETAILS
ON PAGES 13-15

Captivating Showpiece

- This design is sure to be the showpiece of the neighborhood, with its captivating blend of traditional and contemporary features.
- The angled front porch creates an eye-catching look. Inside, the foyer, the dining room and the Great Room are expanded by 9-ft., 4-in. tray ceilings and separated by columns.
- The dining room features a spectacular arched window, while the spacious Great Room hosts a fireplace framed by windows overlooking the rear terrace.
- The glass-filled breakfast room is given added impact by a 9-ft., 4-in. tray ceiling. The adjoining kitchen offers an expansive island counter with an eating bar and a cooktop.
- A wonderful TV room or home office views out to the front porch.
- The master suite is highlighted by a 9-ft., 10-in. tray ceiling and a sunny sitting area with a large picture window topped by an arched transom.

Plan AX-92322

Bedrooms: 3+	Baths: 2
Living Area:	
Main floor	1,699 sq. ft.
Total Living Area:	**1,699 sq. ft.**
Standard basement	1,740 sq. ft.
Garage	480 sq. ft.
Exterior Wall Framing:	2x4

Foundation Options:

Standard basement
Crawlspace
Slab

(All plans can be built with your choice of foundation and framing. A generic conversion diagram is available. See order form.)

BLUEPRINT PRICE CODE: B

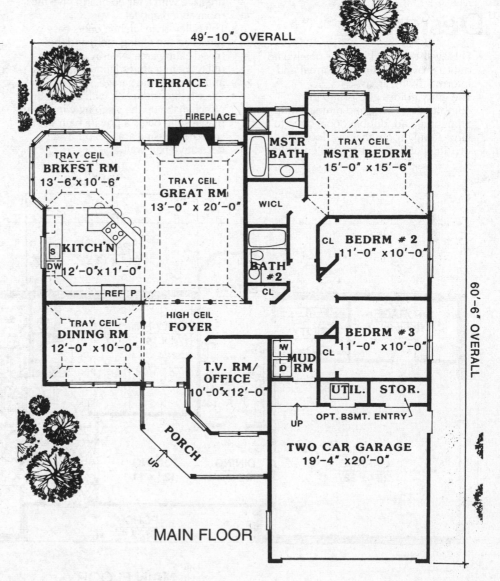

MAIN FLOOR

ORDER BLUEPRINTS ANYTIME!
CALL TOLL-FREE 1-888-626-2026

Plan AX-92322

PRICES AND DETAILS
ON PAGES 13-15

207

Distinctive Design

- This well-designed home is neatly laid out to provide distinctive formal and informal living areas.
- The entry guides guests into the combination living and dining room. Straight ahead, double doors open to a large family room that overlooks an inviting patio. An 11-ft. vaulted ceiling

with exposed beams and a dramatic fireplace with a raised hearth give the room added appeal.

- The galley-style kitchen offers easy service to the dining room and the bayed eating area. Nearby, a deluxe utility room features laundry facilities and access to the garage.
- Three bedrooms, each with a walk-in closet, make up the sleeping wing. The master suite offers a private bath with a separate dressing area set off by a decorative half-wall.

Plan E-1601

Bedrooms: 3	**Baths:** 2
Living Area:	
Main floor	1,630 sq. ft.
Total Living Area:	**1,630 sq. ft.**
Garage and storage	610 sq. ft.
Exterior Wall Framing:	2x4

Foundation Options:

Crawlspace
Slab
(All plans can be built with your choice of foundation and framing. A generic conversion diagram is available. See order form.)

BLUEPRINT PRICE CODE: **B**

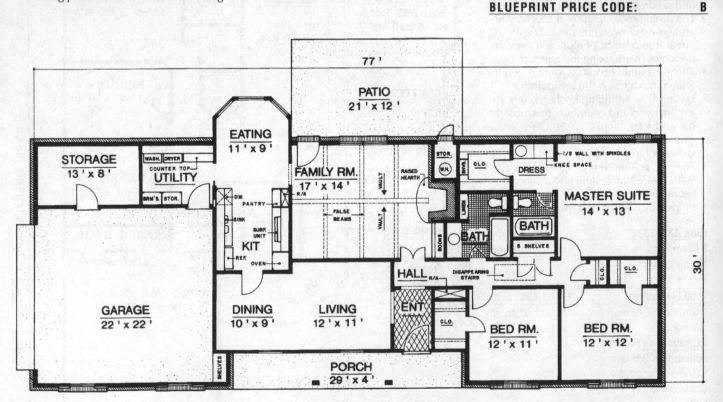

MAIN FLOOR

Impressive Columns

- Impressive columns and striking stucco give this home a distinguished look.
- Inside, a 14-ft. ceiling extends above the foyer, the formal living and dining rooms and the inviting family room.
- The stunning raised dining room is set off by decorative wood columns that support a wraparound overhead plant shelf. A two-way fireplace is shared with the family room, which also features built-in shelves and arched windows that overlook a large deck.
- The study includes built-in bookshelves and a ceiling that vaults to 13½ feet.
- The kitchen has an angled counter bar and a corner pantry while the breakfast nook provides deck access. Both rooms are enhanced by 10-ft. ceilings.
- The large master suite shows off a bayed sitting area and a roomy, private bath. Ceilings heights here are 10 ft. in the sleeping area and 9 ft. in the bath.
- Two secondary bedrooms with 12-ft. vaulted ceilings share a nice hall bath.

Plan DW-2342

Bedrooms: 3+	Baths: 2
Living Area:	
Main floor	2,342 sq. ft.
Total Living Area:	**2,342 sq. ft.**
Standard basement	2,342 sq. ft.
Garage	460 sq. ft.
Exterior Wall Framing:	2x4

Foundation Options:
Standard basement
Crawlspace
Slab
(All plans can be built with your choice of foundation and framing. A generic conversion diagram is available. See order form.)

BLUEPRINT PRICE CODE:	C

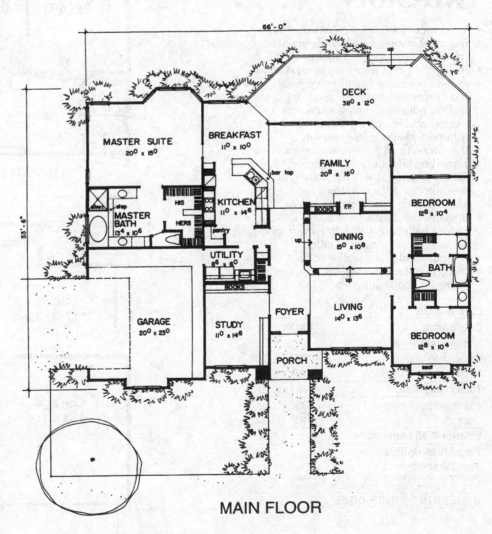

MAIN FLOOR

ORDER BLUEPRINTS ANYTIME!
CALL TOLL-FREE 1-888-626-2026

Plan DW-2342

PRICES AND DETAILS
ON PAGES 13-15
209

Clean-Cut Two-Story

- A clean-cut roofline, a recessed entry and eye-catching window treatments give this design its good looks.
- Inside, the Great Room is graced with a vaulted ceiling, an inviting fireplace and corner windows. An open staircase and the adjoining dining room with a wet bar accentuate the Great Room's volume and add to its versatility.
- The kitchen and the breakfast nook are framed by bright corner windows. Casual gatherings will naturally spill over into the adjacent family room, where sliding doors open to a deck.
- Upstairs, the master suite boasts a sunken bath with a skylighted whirlpool tub, a separate shower, a toilet compartment and a walk-in closet.
- The upper floor also houses a second bedroom and an all-purpose loft.

Plan B-8329

Bedrooms: 2+	Baths: 2½
Living Area:	
Upper floor	797 sq. ft.
Main floor	904 sq. ft.
Total Living Area:	**1,701 sq. ft.**
Standard basement	904 sq. ft.
Garage	405 sq. ft.
Exterior Wall Framing:	2x4

Foundation Options:

Standard basement

(All plans can be built with your choice of foundation and framing. A generic conversion diagram is available. See order form.)

BLUEPRINT PRICE CODE: B

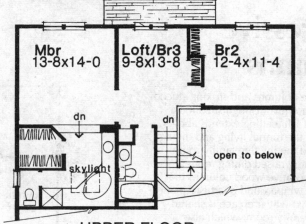

UPPER FLOOR

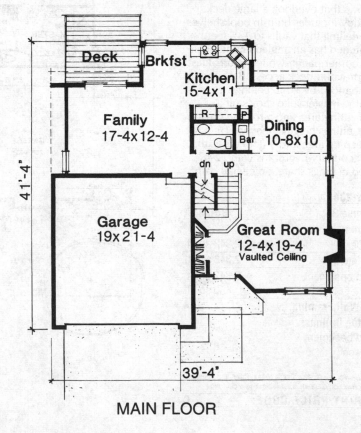

MAIN FLOOR

Tasteful Style

- Traditional lines and a contemporary floor plan combine to make this home a perfect choice for the '90s.
- The two-story-high entry introduces the formal living room, which is warmed by a fireplace and brightened by a round-top window arrangement. The living room's ceiling rises to 13 ft., 9 inches.
- A handy pocket door separates the formal dining room from the kitchen for special occasions. The U-shaped kitchen features an eating bar, a work desk and a bayed nook with access to an outdoor patio.
- The spacious family room includes a second fireplace and outdoor views.
- Ceilings in all main-floor rooms are at least 9 ft. high for added spaciousness.
- Upstairs, the master suite features a 12-ft. vaulted ceiling, two walk-in closets and a compartmentalized bath with a luxurious tub in a window bay.
- Two additional bedrooms share a split bath. A versatile bonus room could serve as an extra bedroom or as a sunny area for hobbies or paperwork.

Plan S-8389

Bedrooms: 3+	Baths: 2½
Living Area:	
Upper floor	932 sq. ft.
Main floor	1,290 sq. ft.
Bonus room	228 sq. ft.
Total Living Area:	**2,450 sq. ft.**
Standard basement	1,290 sq. ft.
Garage	429 sq. ft.
Exterior Wall Framing:	**2x6**

Foundation Options:
Standard basement
Crawlspace
Slab
(All plans can be built with your choice of foundation and framing. A generic conversion diagram is available. See order form.)

BLUEPRINT PRICE CODE: C

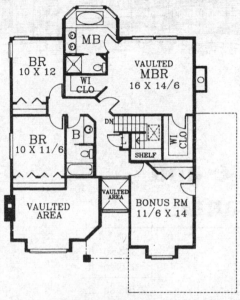

UPPER FLOOR

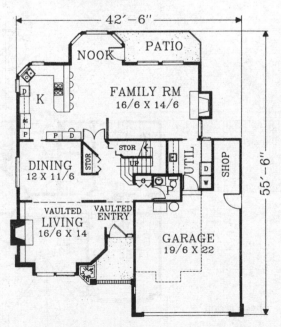

MAIN FLOOR

ORDER BLUEPRINTS ANYTIME!
CALL TOLL-FREE 1-888-626-2026

Plan S-8389

PRICES AND DETAILS
ON PAGES 13-15

211

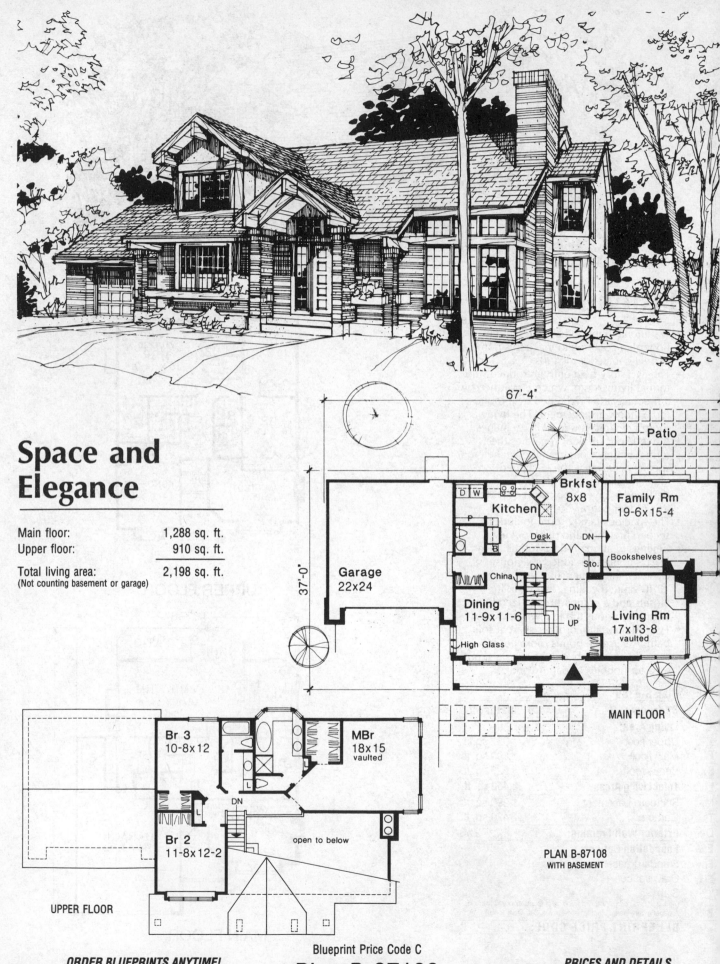

Space and Elegance

Main floor:	1,288 sq. ft.
Upper floor:	910 sq. ft.
Total living area: (Not counting basement or garage)	2,198 sq. ft.

67'-4"

Patio

D W

Kitchen

Brkfst
8x8

Family Rm
19-6x15-4

P

B

Desk

DN

Bookshelves

Sto.

China

DN

Garage
22x24

37'-0"

Dining
11-9x11-6

DN
UP

Living Rm
17x13-8
vaulted

High Glass

MAIN FLOOR

Br 3
10-8x12

MBr
18x15
vaulted

L

DN

L

Br 2
11-8x12-2

open to below

UPPER FLOOR

PLAN B-87108
WITH BASEMENT

Blueprint Price Code C
Plan B-87108

PRICES AND DETAILS
ON PAGES 13-15

Room to Boast

- You'll have plenty to boast about if you choose to make this brick-clad French charmer your home!
- Serving as the hub of the home, the centralized living room flaunts cheery windows, a high ceiling and a stunning fireplace that spreads its flickering warmth as far as the kitchen.
- Here, corner windows brighten the sink, and service to both the formal and informal meal areas is a simple matter of a step or two.
- Like fresh air with your Wheaties? French doors open from the breakfast nook to a lovely covered porch.
- The master bedroom is breathtaking in its simplicity. Private access to a covered porch will have you thinking romantic thoughts when midnight rolls around, and the sprawling bath allows for two people to prepare for bedtime without bumping elbows.
- The two remaining bedrooms each have their own walk-in closet, plus a shared bath between them.
- Placing the laundry facilities near the kids' bedrooms is a stroke of genius that you'll come to appreciate when the weekend arrives!

Plan L-1943

Bedrooms: 3	Baths: 2
Living Area:	
Main floor	1,943 sq. ft.
Total Living Area:	**1,943 sq. ft.**
Detached 2-car garage	506 sq. ft.
Exterior Wall Framing:	2x4

Foundation Options:

Slab

(All plans can be built with your choice of foundation and framing. A generic conversion diagram is available. See order form.)

BLUEPRINT PRICE CODE: B

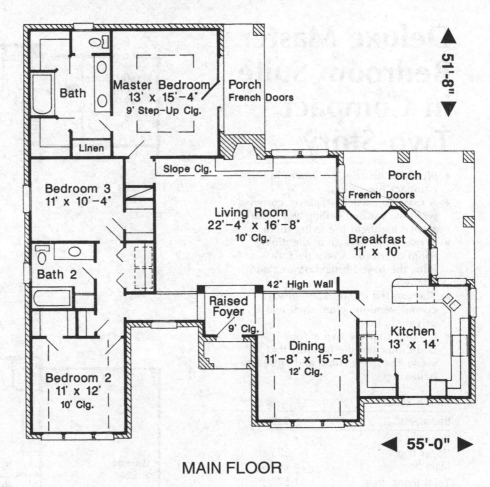

MAIN FLOOR

◀ 51'-8" ▶

◀ 55'-0" ▶

Bath

Master Bedroom
13' x 15'-4"
9' Step-Up Clg.

Porch
French Doors

Linen

Slope Clg.

Porch
French Doors

Bedroom 3
11' x 10'-4"

Living Room
22'-4" x 16'-8"
10' Clg.

Breakfast
11' x 10'

Bath 2

42" High Wall

Raised Foyer
9' Clg.

Kitchen
13' x 14'

Dining
11'-8" x 15'-8"
12' Clg.

Bedroom 2
11' x 12'
10' Clg.

ORDER BLUEPRINTS ANYTIME!
CALL TOLL-FREE 1-888-626-2026

Plan L-1943

PRICES AND DETAILS
ON PAGES 13-15

213

Deluxe Master Bedroom Suite in Compact Two-Story

- Plenty of luxuries are found in this compact two-story.
- A massive corner fireplace, corner window, vaulted ceiling and library alcove highlight the living room.
- A rear window wall in the dining room overlooks a rear deck that joins the bayed breakfast area and kitchen.
- The vaulted master suite offers corner window, plant shelf and a private bath.
- Up one step are two extra bedrooms and the hall loft that views the living room and entryway below.

Plan B-88002

Bedrooms: 3	Baths: 2½

Space:	
Upper floor:	833 sq. ft.
Main floor:	744 sq. ft.
Total living area:	**1,577 sq. ft.**
Garage:	528 sq. ft.

Exterior Wall Framing:	2x4

Foundation options:
Standard basement.
(Foundation & framing conversion diagram available — see order form.)

Blueprint Price Code:	B

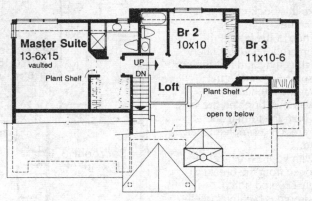

UPPER FLOOR

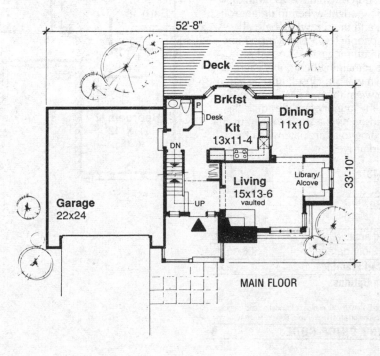

MAIN FLOOR

Plan B-88002

PRICES AND DETAILS
ON PAGES 13-15

Tradition Recreated

- Classic traditional styling is recreated in this home with its covered porch, triple dormers and half-round windows.
- A central hall stems from the two-story-high foyer and accesses each of the main living areas.
- A large formal space is created with the merging of the living room and the dining room. The living room boasts a fireplace and a view of the front porch.
- The informal spaces merge at the rear of the home. The kitchen features an oversized cooktop island. The sunny dinette is enclosed with a circular glass wall. The family room boasts a media center and access to the rear terrace.
- A convenient main-floor laundry room sits near the garage entrance.
- The upper floor includes three secondary bedrooms that share a full bath, and a spacious master bedroom that offers dual walk-in closets and a large private bath.

Plan AHP-9393

Bedrooms: 4+	Baths: 3
Living Area:	
Upper floor	989 sq. ft.
Main floor	1,223 sq. ft.
Total Living Area:	**2,212 sq. ft.**
Standard basement	1,223 sq. ft.
Garage and storage	488 sq. ft.
Exterior Wall Framing:	2x4 or 2x6

Foundation Options:

Standard basement

Crawlspace

Slab

(Typical foundation & framing conversion diagram available—see order form.)

BLUEPRINT PRICE CODE:	C

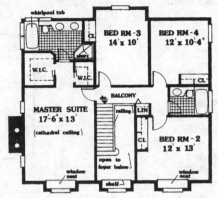

UPPER FLOOR

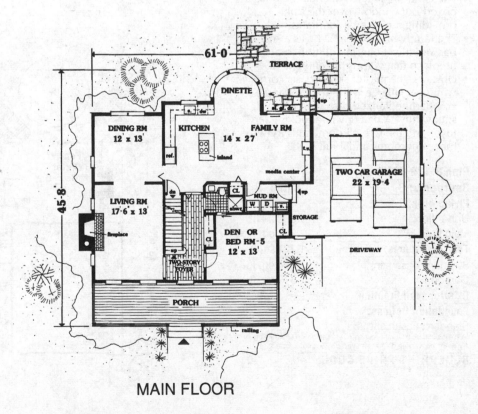

MAIN FLOOR

ORDER BLUEPRINTS ANYTIME!
CALL TOLL-FREE 1-888-626-2026

Plan AHP-9393

PRICES AND DETAILS
ON PAGES 13-15

215

Windows of Opportunity

- This handsome home features a wide assortment of windows, flooding the interior with light and accentuating the open, airy atmosphere.
- The two-story-high entry is brightened by a beautiful Palladian window above. Just ahead, the vaulted Great Room also showcases a Palladian window. The adjoining dining area offers sliding glass doors that open to a large deck.
- The centrally located kitchen includes a boxed-out window over the sink, providing a nice area for plants.
- The family/breakfast area hosts a snack bar and a wet bar, in addition to a fireplace that warms the entire area.
- Upstairs, the master suite boasts corner windows, a large walk-in closet and a compartmentalized bath with a dual-sink vanity. A balcony overlooking the foyer and the Great Room leads to two more bedrooms and a full bath.

Plan B-129-8510

Bedrooms: 3	Baths: 2½
Living Area:	
Upper floor	802 sq. ft.
Main floor	922 sq. ft.
Total Living Area:	**1,724 sq. ft.**
Standard basement	924 sq. ft.
Garage	579 sq. ft.
Exterior Wall Framing:	2x4

Foundation Options:

Standard basement

(All plans can be built with your choice of foundation and framing. A generic conversion diagram is available. See order form.)

BLUEPRINT PRICE CODE: B

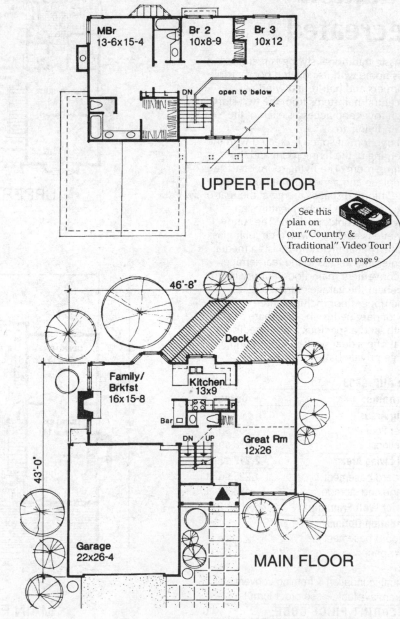

UPPER FLOOR

MBr 13-6x15-4
Br 2 10x8-9
Br 3 10x12
DN open to below

See this plan on our "Country & Traditional" Video Tour! Order form on page 9

MAIN FLOOR

46'-8"
Deck
Family/Brkfst 16x15-8
Kitchen 13x9
Bar
DN UP
Great Rm 12x26
43'-0"
Garage 22x26-4

Contemporary Elegance

- This striking contemporary design combines vertical siding with elegant traditional overtones.
- Inside, an expansive activity area is created with the joining of the vaulted living room, the family/dining room and the kitchen. The openness of the rooms creates a spacious, dramatic feeling, which extends to an exciting two-story sun space and a patio beyond.

- A convenient utility/service area near the garage includes a clothes-sorting counter, a deep sink and ironing space.
- Two bedrooms share a bright bath to round out the main floor.
- Upstairs, the master suite includes a sumptuous skylighted bath with two entrances. The tub is positioned on an angled wall, while the shower and toilet are secluded behind a pocket door. An optional overlook provides views down into the sun space, which is accessed by a spiral staircase.
- A versatile loft area and a large bonus room complete this design.

Plan LRD-1971

Bedrooms: 3+	Baths: 2
Living Area:	
Upper floor	723 sq. ft.
Main floor	1,248 sq. ft.
Sun space	116 sq. ft.
Bonus room	225 sq. ft.
Total Living Area:	**2,312 sq. ft.**
Standard basement	1,248 sq. ft.
Garage	483 sq. ft.
Exterior Wall Framing:	2x6

Foundation Options:

Standard basement
Crawlspace
(All plans can be built with your choice of foundation and framing. A generic conversion diagram is available. See order form.)

BLUEPRINT PRICE CODE: C

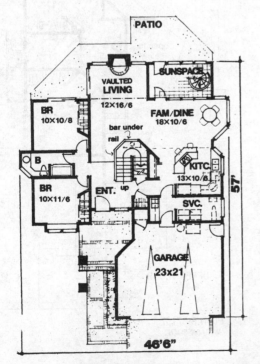

MAIN FLOOR

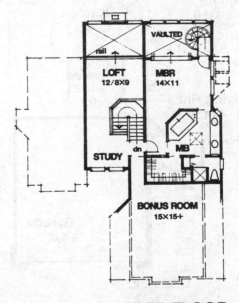

UPPER FLOOR

ORDER BLUEPRINTS ANYTIME!
CALL TOLL-FREE 1-888-626-2026

Plan LRD-1971

PRICES AND DETAILS
ON PAGES 13-15

217

Cozy, Rustic Comfort

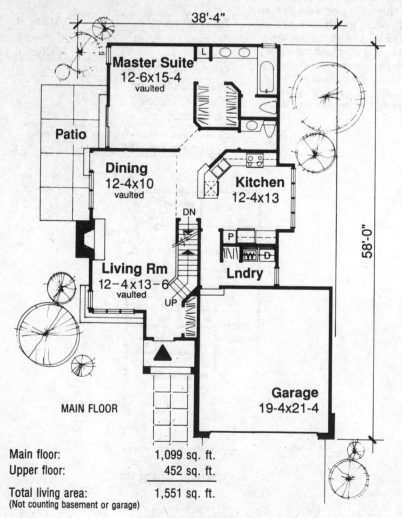

38'-4"

Master Suite
12-6x15-4
vaulted

Patio

Dining
12-4x10
vaulted

Kitchen
12-4x13

DN

P

Living Rm
12-4x13-6
vaulted

Lndry

W D

UP

58'-0"

Garage
19-4x21-4

MAIN FLOOR

Main floor: 1,099 sq. ft.
Upper floor: 452 sq. ft.
Total living area: 1,551 sq. ft.
(Not counting basement or garage)

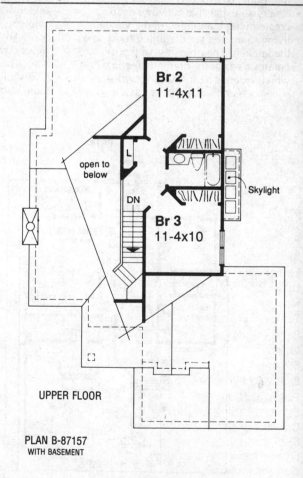

Br 2
11-4x11

open to
below

L

DN

Br 3
11-4x10

Skylight

UPPER FLOOR

PLAN B-87157
WITH BASEMENT

Blueprint Price Code B
Plan B-87157

PRICES AND DETAILS
ON PAGES 13-15

Five-Bedroom Traditional

- This sophisticated traditional home makes a striking statement both inside and out.
- The dramatic two-story foyer is flanked by the formal living spaces. The private dining room overlooks the front porch, while the spacious living room has outdoor views on two sides.
- A U-shaped kitchen with a snack bar, a sunny dinette area and a large family room flow together at the back of the home. The family room's fireplace warms the open, informal expanse, while sliding glass doors in the dinette access the backyard terrace.
- The second floor has five roomy bedrooms and two skylighted bathrooms. The luxurious master suite has a high ceiling with a beautiful arched window, a dressing area and a huge walk-in closet. The private bath offers dual sinks, a whirlpool tub and a separate shower.
- Attic space is located above the garage.

Plan AHP-9392

Bedrooms: 5	Baths: 2½
Living Area:	
Upper floor	1,223 sq. ft.
Main floor	1,193 sq. ft.
Total Living Area:	**2,416 sq. ft.**
Standard basement	1,130 sq. ft.
Garage	509 sq. ft.
Storage	65 sq. ft.
Exterior Wall Framing:	2x4 or 2x6

Foundation Options:
Standard basement
Crawlspace
Slab
(Typical foundation & framing conversion diagram available—see order form.)

BLUEPRINT PRICE CODE:	C

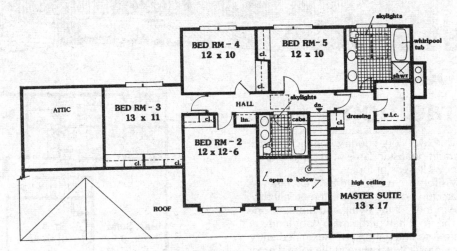

UPPER FLOOR

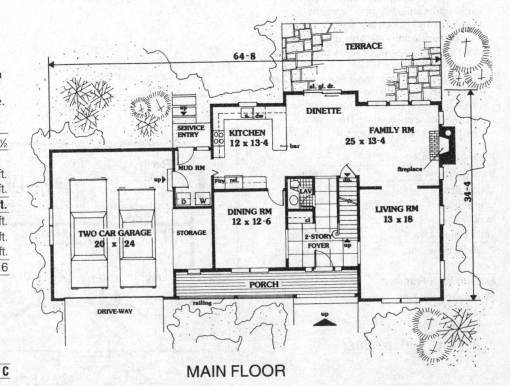

MAIN FLOOR

Today's Tradition

- This two-story country home combines traditional standards with the exciting new designs of today.
- Visitors are welcomed by the wrap-around porch and the symmetrical bay windows of the living and dining rooms.
- The front half of the main floor lends itself to entertaining as the angled entry creates a flow between the formal areas.
- French doors lead from the living room to the spacious family room, which boasts a beamed ceiling, a warm fireplace and porch access.
- The super kitchen features an island cooktop with a snack bar. A nice-sized laundry room is nearby.
- The spacious upper level hosts a master suite with two walk-in closets and a large bath with a dual-sink vanity, a tub and a separate shower. Three more bedrooms share another full bath.

Plan AGH-2143

Bedrooms: 4	Baths: 2½
Living Area:	
Upper floor	1,047 sq. ft.
Main floor	1,096 sq. ft.
Total Living Area:	**2,143 sq. ft.**
Daylight basement	1,096 sq. ft.
Garage	852 sq. ft.
Exterior Wall Framing:	2x6

Foundation Options:

Daylight basement

(All plans can be built with your choice of foundation and framing. A generic conversion diagram is available. See order form.)

BLUEPRINT PRICE CODE: **C**

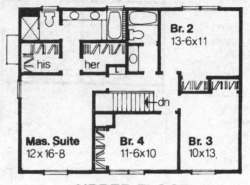

UPPER FLOOR

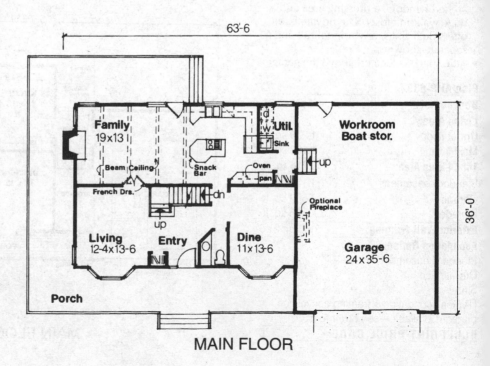

MAIN FLOOR

220

ORDER BLUEPRINTS ANYTIME!
CALL TOLL-FREE 1-888-626-2026

Plan AGH-2143

PRICES AND DETAILS
ON PAGES 13-15

Exemplary Colonial

- Inside this traditionally designed home is an exciting floor plan for today's lifestyles.
- The classic center-hall arrangement of this Colonial allows easy access to each of the living areas.
- Plenty of views are possible from the formal rooms at the front of the home, as well as from the informal areas at the rear.
- The spacious kitchen offers lots of counter space, a handy work island, a laundry closet and a sunny bayed breakfast nook.
- The adjoining family room shows off a fireplace and elegant double doors to the rear. An optional set of double doors opens to the living room.
- The beautiful master suite on the upper level boasts a 10-ft., 10-in. vaulted ceiling, two closets, dual sinks, a garden tub and a separate shower.

Plan CH-100-A

Bedrooms: 4	Baths: 2½
Living Area:	
Upper floor	923 sq. ft.
Main floor	965 sq. ft.
Total Living Area:	**1,888 sq. ft.**
Basement	952 sq. ft.
Garage	462 sq. ft.
Exterior Wall Framing:	2x4

Foundation Options:

Daylight basement

Standard basement

Crawlspace

(All plans can be built with your choice of foundation and framing. A generic conversion diagram is available. See order form.)

BLUEPRINT PRICE CODE: **B**

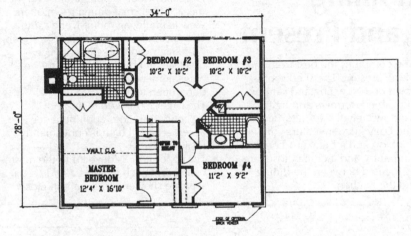

UPPER FLOOR

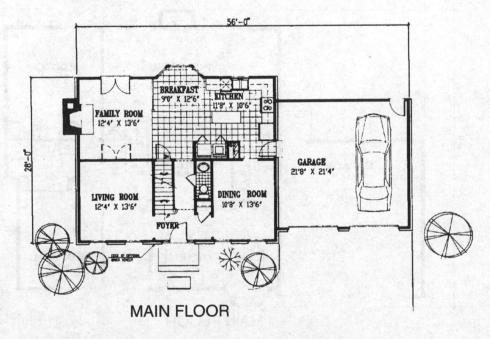

MAIN FLOOR

ORDER BLUEPRINTS ANYTIME!
CALL TOLL-FREE 1-888-626-2026

Plan CH-100-A

PRICES AND DETAILS
ON PAGES 13-15

221

Combining Past and Present

- This home combines the best from the past and the present. The shed roof is reminiscent of a New England saltbox, while the gabled dormers and half-circle windows recall the Victorian era.
- Inside, the cozy kitchen features an island cooktop and a breakfast counter. A built-in pantry and a china closet are centrally located between the dining room and the kitchen.

- The sunny nook is popular for everyday meals. The formal dining room offers a view to the living room over a railing.
- The sunken living room boasts a soaring 25-ft.-high vaulted ceiling, a nice fireplace and built-in shelves for an entertainment center. Sliding glass doors open to a backyard deck.
- The larger of the two main-floor bedrooms provides additional deck access. The full bath is conveniently located nearby.
- The upper floor is devoted to the master bedroom, which features a hydro-spa, a separate shower and a walk-in closet.

Plan H-1453-1A	
Bedrooms: 3	**Baths:** 2
Living Area:	
Upper floor	386 sq. ft.
Main floor	1,385 sq. ft.
Total Living Area:	**1,771 sq. ft.**
Garage	438 sq. ft.
Exterior Wall Framing:	2x6

Foundation Options:

Crawlspace
(All plans can be built with your choice of foundation and framing. A generic conversion diagram is available. See order form.)

BLUEPRINT PRICE CODE: B

MAIN FLOOR

DECK

LIVING ROOM
24/6x14/0
SLOPED CEILING

BEDROOM
13/0x13/0

SHELVES

W/H furn

UTILITY

DINING
11/6x10/0

CLOSET
9/6

LIN

tub w/sh

BATH

down

up

CLOSET
7/9

LIN

GARAGE
19/0x21/6

D W

PAN.

NOOK
7/6x11/0

KITCHEN
10/0x12/0

REF

R/O

GUEST

P.W.

ENTRY

BEDROOM
11/0x11/0

up

58'-0"

41'-7"

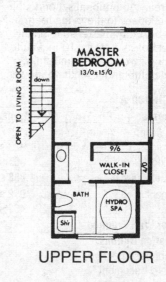

UPPER FLOOR

MASTER BEDROOM
13/0x15/0

OPEN TO LIVING ROOM

down

9/6

WALK-IN CLOSET

BATH

Shr

HYDRO SPA

ORDER BLUEPRINTS ANYTIME! CALL TOLL-FREE 1-888-626-2026   Plan H-1453-1A   *PRICES AND DETAILS ON PAGES 13-15*

A Real Original

- This home's round window, elegant entry and transom windows create an eye-catching, original look.
- Inside, high ceilings and tremendous views let the eyes wander. The foyer provides an exciting look at an expansive deck and inviting spa through the living room's tall windows. The windows frame a handsome fireplace, while a 10-ft. ceiling adds volume and interest.
- To the right of the foyer is a cozy den or home office with its own fireplace, 10-ft. ceiling and dramatic windows.
- The spacious kitchen/breakfast area features an oversized snack bar island and opens to a large screen porch. Within easy reach are the laundry room and the entrance to the garage.
- The bright formal dining room overlooks the deck and boasts a ceiling that vaults up to 10 feet.
- The secluded master suite looks out to the deck as well, with access through a patio door. The private bath features a dynamite corner spa tub, a separate shower and a large walk-in closet.
- A second bedroom and bath complete the main floor.

Plan B-90065

Bedrooms: 2+	Baths: 2
Living Area:	
Main floor	1,889 sq. ft.
Total Living Area:	**1,889 sq. ft.**
Screen porch	136 sq. ft.
Standard basement	1,889 sq. ft.
Garage	406 sq. ft.
Exterior Wall Framing:	2x6
Foundation Options:	
Standard basement	

(All plans can be built with your choice of foundation and framing. A generic conversion diagram is available. See order form.)

BLUEPRINT PRICE CODE:	B

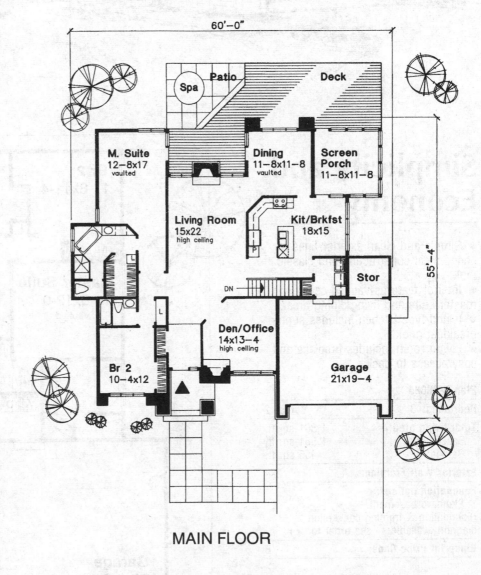

MAIN FLOOR

ORDER BLUEPRINTS ANYTIME!
CALL TOLL-FREE 1-888-626-2026

Plan B-90065

PRICES AND DETAILS
ON PAGES 13-15

223

Simplicity and Economy

- Simple and clean exterior lines for economical construction and classic look.
- Interior features vaulted ceilings in master suite and living/dining area.
- Island-type kitchen includes sunny breakfast nook.
- Living room includes fireplace and easy access to deck.

Plan B-88085

Bedrooms: 3	Baths: 2
Total living area:	1,561 sq. ft.
Basement:	1,561 sq. ft.
Garage:	455 sq. ft.
Exterior Wall Framing:	2x4

Foundation options:
Standard basement.
(Foundation & framing conversion diagram available — see order form.)

Blueprint Price Code: B

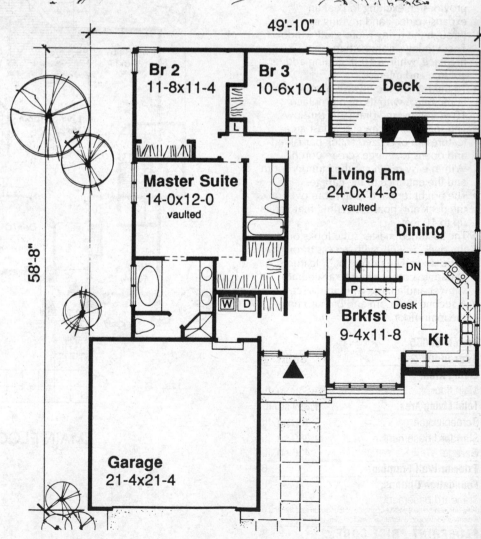

49'-10"

58'-8"

Br 2 11-8x11-4	Br 3 10-6x10-4	Deck
Master Suite 14-0x12-0 vaulted		Living Rm 24-0x14-8 vaulted
		Dining
	W D	Brkfst 9-4x11-8 Kit
Garage 21-4x21-4		

Updated Tudor

- Updated Tudor styling gives this home an extra-appealing exterior. Inside, the bright and open living spaces are embellished with a host of wonderfully contemporary details.
- An inviting brick arch frames the front door, which opens directly into the living room. Here, a 14-ft. sloped ceiling, a fireplace and a view to the covered rear porch provide an impressive welcome.
- The octagonal dining area is absolutely stunning—the perfect complement for the skylighted kitchen, which boasts an angled cooktop/snack bar and a 12-ft. sloped ceiling. Double doors in the kitchen lead to a roomy utility area and the cleverly disguised side-entry garage.
- No details were left out in the sumptuous master suite, which features access to a private porch with a 14-ft. sloped ceiling and skylights. The luxurious bath offers a platform tub, a sit-down shower, his-and-hers vanities and lots of storage and closet space.
- Two more bedrooms are situated at the opposite side of the home and share a hall bath. One bedroom features a window seat, while the other has direct access to the central covered porch.

Plan E-1912

Bedrooms: 3	Baths: 2
Living Area:	
Main floor	1,946 sq. ft.
Total Living Area:	**1,946 sq. ft.**
Garage and storage	562 sq. ft.
Exterior Wall Framing:	2x6

Foundation Options:

Crawlspace

Slab

(All plans can be built with your choice of foundation and framing. A generic conversion diagram is available. See order form.)

BLUEPRINT PRICE CODE: C

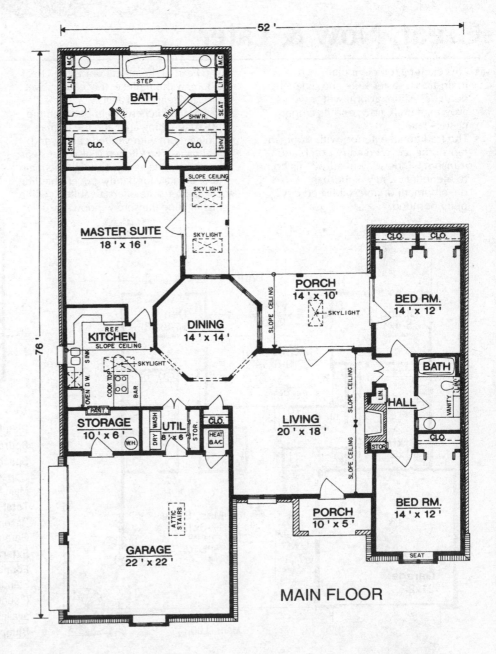

MAIN FLOOR

Plan E-1912

Great, Now & Later

- This exciting, efficient plan, with a main-floor master suite and adjacent den/guest/sitting room, will serve its growing family now, and its empty-nesters later.
- The traditional exterior, with stone and lap siding, covered entry porch and transom windows, will allow this home to blend into a new suburban development or an established city neighborhood.

- The heart of the main floor is the Great Room, with fireplace, tray ceiling, wet bar, and rear patio access.
- The island kitchen lies in-between the breakfast eating area and the formal dining room with vaulted ceiling and rear patio. The kitchen is also just steps away from the garage through the main-floor laundry for handy grocery hauling.
- The master suite offers a vaulted ceiling highlighting transom windows, a

spacious walk-in closet and private bath with dual vanities and separate tub and shower.
- The den/guest room has a vaulted ceiling, a quaint window seat and built-in shelves, as well as an adjacent, full bath.
- Older kids will enjoy the privacy of the two upstairs bedrooms, with a shared, full bath and plenty of closet and storage space.

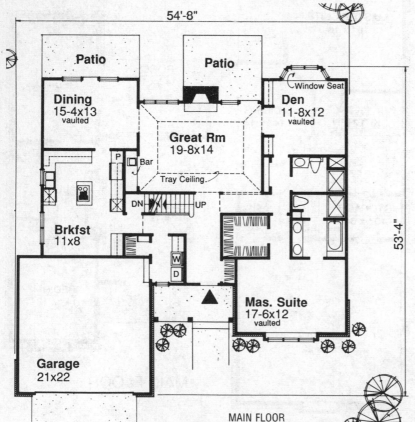

MAIN FLOOR

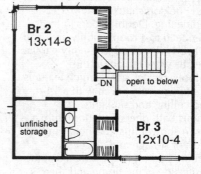

UPPER FLOOR

Plan B-89060	
Bedrooms: 3-4	**Baths:** 3
Space:	
Upper floor	502 sq. ft.
Main floor	1,698 sq. ft.
Total Living Area	**2,200 sq. ft.**
Basement	1,698 sq. ft.
Garage	462 sq. ft.
Exterior Wall Framing	2x4
Foundation options:	
Standard Basement	
(Foundation & framing conversion diagram available—see order form.)	
Blueprint Price Code	C

Light and Bright

- This outstanding home features a light, inviting facade with arched windows, unique transoms and twin dormers.
- The sheltered front porch opens to an airy entry, which is flanked by a quiet study and the formal dining room. Straight ahead, the living room offers backyard views through three windows.
- The well-designed island kitchen is brightened by fluorescent lighting and enhanced by a nice corner window and a step-in pantry. The adjoining morning room features a lovely window seat, a built-in hutch and a snack bar.
- An inviting fireplace with a tile hearth is the focal point of the cozy family room. French doors open to a large deck.
- Walk-in closets are featured in each of the three bedrooms. The master suite includes deck access and a private bath with a garden tub, a separate shower and a dual-sink vanity.
- In the second bedroom, the ceiling slopes up to 11½ ft., accenting the elegant front window. The third bedroom has a standard 8-ft. ceiling.
- Unless otherwise specified, all rooms have high 10-ft. ceilings.

Plan DD-2372

Bedrooms: 3+	Baths: 2½
Living Area:	
Main floor	2,376 sq. ft.
Total Living Area:	**2,376 sq. ft.**
Standard basement	2,376 sq. ft.
Garage	473 sq. ft.
Exterior Wall Framing:	2x4

Foundation Options:
Standard basement
Crawlspace
Slab
(All plans can be built with your choice of foundation and framing. A generic conversion diagram is available. See order form.)

BLUEPRINT PRICE CODE: C

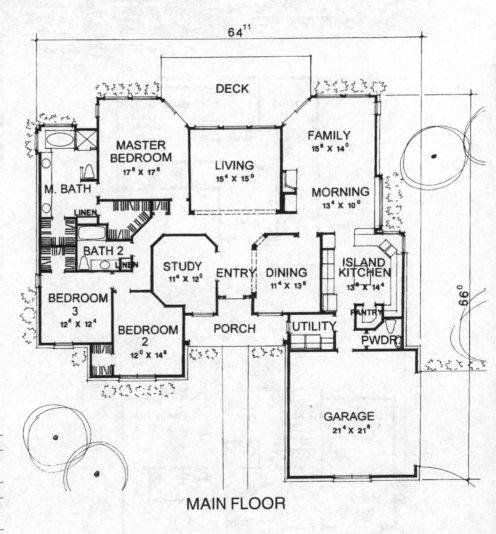

MAIN FLOOR

ORDER BLUEPRINTS ANYTIME!
CALL TOLL-FREE 1-888-626-2026

Plan DD-2372

PRICES AND DETAILS
ON PAGES 13-15

227

Decorative Columns, Outside & In

- Decorative columns adorn the front outside entrance and the inside living and dining room entryways of this updated traditional.
- The living room also features a boxed front window, fireplace and vaulted ceiling.
- An open kitchen and sunny breakfast area join the large family room with fireplace and wet bar to form a stretch of dining and relaxing pleasure; both areas overlook a rear deck.
- A beautiful master suite with tray ceiling, his 'n her walk-in closets, and a private bath with windowed garden tub and two secondary bedrooms share the upper level.

Plan B-90009

Bedrooms: 3	**Baths:** 2 ½
Space:	
Upper floor	918 sq. ft.
Main floor	1,349 sq. ft.
Total Living Area	**2,267 sq. ft.**
Basement	1,349 sq. ft.
Garage	420 sq. ft.
Exterior Wall Framing	2x4
Foundation options:	
Standard Basement	
(Foundation & framing conversion diagram available—see order form.)	
Blueprint Price Code	**C**

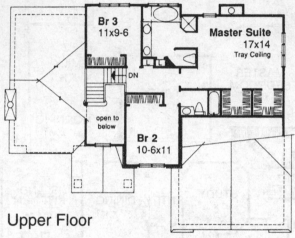

Upper Floor

Br 3
11x9-6

Master Suite
17x14
Tray Ceiling

DN

open to below

Br 2
10-6x11

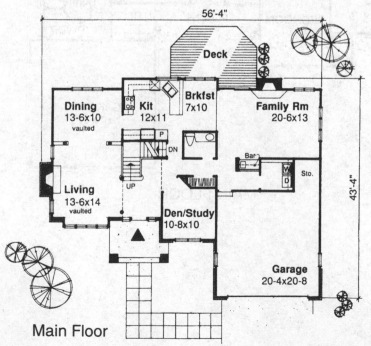

Main Floor

56'-4"

Deck

Dining
13-6x10
vaulted

Kit
12x11

Brkfst
7x10

Family Rm
20-6x13

P

DN

Bar

Living
13-6x14
vaulted

UP

Den/Study
10-8x10

W D Sto.

43'-4"

Garage
20-4x20-8

228

ORDER BLUEPRINTS ANYTIME!
CALL TOLL-FREE 1-888-626-2026

Plan B-90009

PRICES AND DETAILS
ON PAGES 13-15

A Spanish Classic for Today

The romance of Spanish culture is well captured in this classic hacienda. An inner courtyard completely surrounded by arched masonry walls, decorative wrought iron accents, adobe-type brick facing clay tile roofs, and even a roof ventilator masquerading as a dove cote, all contribute to the old world charm of this home.

Passing through the protective iron gates, one crosses the paved courtyard and approaches the heavy double entrance door. For beauty and convenience, the entry is paved with tile in soft shades of sepia and umber.

Four distinct dining options allow for any occasion: a formal dining room adjoining the living room; a convenient kitchen nook for normal daily family use; a four seat bar for quick "get-away" breakfasts or late evening snacks; and a huge family room where a long table can be set for celebrations.

A feature of the sleeping wing is the connecting hallway, a naturally lighted passage flanked by 200 cubic feet of closet space. A master suite and two other bedrooms with nearly wall-length wardrobe closets complete the picture.

Total living area: 2,377 sq. ft.
(Not counting garage)

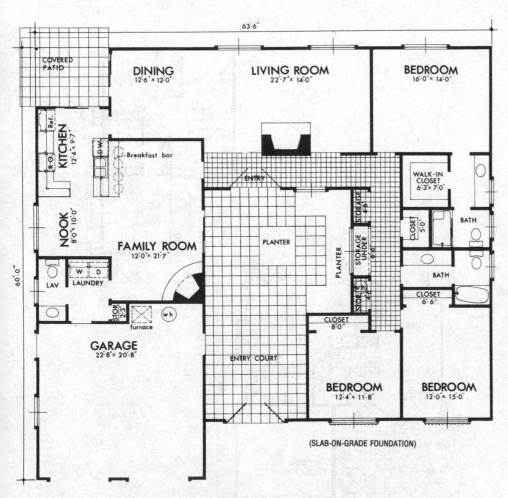

DINING
12'-6" x 12'-0"

LIVING ROOM
22'-7" x 14'-0"

BEDROOM
16'-0" x 14'-0"

COVERED PATIO

KITCHEN
12'-4" x 9'-7"

Ref.
R-O
DW
Breakfast bar

NOOK
8'-0" x 10'-0"

FAMILY ROOM
12'-0" x 21'-7"

LAV
W D
LAUNDRY

STOR
2'-3"
wh
furnace

GARAGE
22'-8" x 20'-8"

ENTRY

PLANTER

PLANTER

STORAGE UNDER
6'-0"

STORAGE
4'-6"

ENTRY COURT

CLOSET
8'-0"

WALK-IN CLOSET
6'-3" x 7'-0"

CLOSET
5'-0"

BATH

BATH

CLOSET
6'-6"

BEDROOM
12'-4" x 11'-8"

BEDROOM
12'-0" x 15'-0"

63'-6"

60'-0"

(SLAB-ON-GRADE FOUNDATION)

Blueprint Price Code C
Plan H-1422-M1A

PRICES AND DETAILS
ON PAGES 13-15

Economical Traditional

- This compact traditional design reflects a thrifty attitude toward life, while still providing the necessities and amenities proper for today's families.
- Main floor is devoted to informal family living, with a large family room and Great Room with a more formal dining area.
- Also note the large foyer, an impressive feature not often found in homes of this size.
- Upstairs, you'll find three bedrooms with good closet space, plus two baths.

Plan B-906

Bedrooms: 3	Baths: 2½

Space:

Upper floor:	816 sq. ft.
Main floor:	1,075 sq. ft.
Total living area:	**1,891 sq. ft.**
Basement:	1,075 sq. ft.
Garage:	386 sq. ft.

Exterior Wall Framing:	2x4

Foundation options:
Standard basement.
(Foundation & framing conversion diagram available — see order form.)

Blueprint Price Code:	B

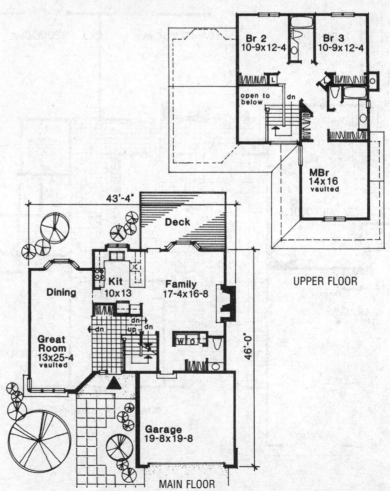

FRONT VIEW

Tradition with Modern Touch

- Dining room and master bedroom offer access to rear patio.
- Entryway approaches large living room with sloped ceilings and built-in fireplace, both exposed to second-level loft.
- Roomy kitchen has corner pantry and convenient nearby laundry facilities.
- First floor master bedroom includes generous walk-in closet and "his 'n hers" vanities.

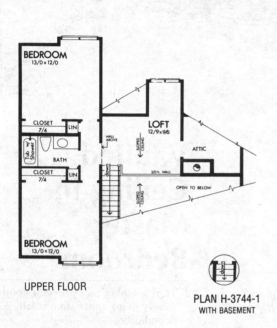

UPPER FLOOR

BEDROOM
13/0 x 12/0

CLOSET 7/4 — LIN

BATH — Tub w/ Shower

CLOSET 7/4 — LIN

LOFT 12/9 x 9/6

SLOPED CEILING

ATTIC

WALL ABOVE

OPEN TO BELOW

2/0 h. wall

BEDROOM
13/0 x 12/0

down

PLAN H-3744-1
WITH BASEMENT

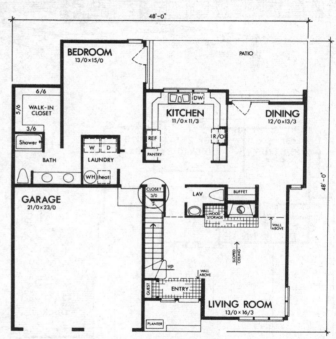

MAIN FLOOR

48'-0"

BEDROOM
13/0 x 15/0

PATIO

WALK-IN CLOSET 6/6 / 5/0

3/6 Shower

BATH

KITCHEN
11/0 x 11/3

DW

DINING
12/0 x 13/3

REF

PANTRY

R/O

W D

LAUNDRY

WH — heat

GARAGE
21/0 x 23/0

CLOSET 3/0

WOOD STORAGE

LAV

BUFFET

WALL ABOVE

up

SLOPED CEILING

GUEST

ENTRY

WALL ABOVE

LIVING ROOM
13/0 x 16/3

PLANTER

48'-0"

Plans H-3744-1 & -1A

Bedrooms: 3	Baths: 2½

Space:

Upper floor:	660 sq. ft.
Main floor:	1,300 sq. ft.

Total living area:	**1,960 sq. ft.**
Basement:	approx. 1,300 sq. ft.
Garage:	483 sq. ft.

Exterior Wall Framing:	2x6

Foundation options:
Standard basement (Plan H-3744-1).
Crawlspace (Plan H-3744-1A).
(Foundation & framing conversion diagram available — see order form.)

Blueprint Price Code:	B

REAR VIEW

ORDER BLUEPRINTS ANYTIME!
CALL TOLL-FREE 1-888-626-2026

Plans H-3744-1 & -1A

PRICES AND DETAILS
ON PAGES 13-15

231

MBr
13-6x15-4
vaulted

Br 2
10-8x10-2

Br 3
10x12

DN

open to below

plant shelf

UPPER FLOOR

Plan B-87102

Bedrooms: 3	Baths: 2½

Space:

Upper floor:	806 sq. ft.
Main floor:	926 sq. ft.
Total living area:	**1,732 sq. ft.**
Basement:	926 sq. ft.
Garage:	579 sq. ft.

Exterior Wall Framing:	2x4

Foundation options:
Standard basement only.
(Foundation & framing conversion diagram available — see order form.)

Blueprint Price Code:	B

47'-0"

Deck

Brkfst
7-6x9-6

Kit

Dining
11-2x12

Family Rm
14x15-9

P

Bar

DN UP

Living Rm
16-6x14
vaulted

46'-4"

▲

Garage
22x26-4

MAIN FLOOR

Vaulted Ceiling in Master Bedroom

- Here's a plan that provides good family living space on a small foundation.
- A protected entry leads into a vaulted living room with an adjoining dining area.
- The kitchen/breakfast area and family room combination is large and includes a pantry, bar, fireplace and easy access to the outdoors.
- The master bedroom upstairs includes a private bath and large walk-in closet.
- Two secondary bedrooms share another full bath and open onto a balcony hallway overlooking the living room below.
- The deep garage allows storage space in front of the vehicles.

ORDER BLUEPRINTS ANYTIME!
CALL TOLL-FREE 1-888-626-2026

Plan B-87102

PRICES AND DETAILS
ON PAGES 13-15

Classic Homestead

SECOND FLOOR

- WALK IN CLOSET
- LAV
- W.C.
- sh'w'r
- BEDROOM 11'-0" × 11'-5"
- CLOSET
- CLOSET
- BEDROOM 10'-0" × 11'-5"
- LINEN
- down
- BEDROOM 13'-0" × 15'-0"
- BATH
- LAV
- W.C.
- CLOSET
- BEDROOM 10'-0" × 11'-5"

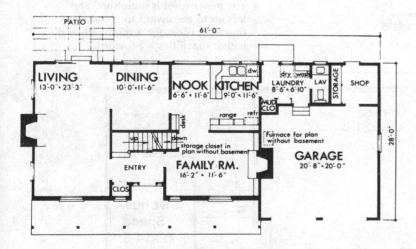

FIRST FLOOR

- PATIO
- 61'-0"
- LIVING 13'-0" × 23'-3"
- DINING 10'-0" × 11'-6"
- NOOK 6'-6" × 11'-6"
- KITCHEN 9'-0" × 11'-6"
- dw
- desk
- up
- down
- storage closet in plan without basement
- range
- refr
- LAUNDRY 8'-6" × 6'-10"
- dry
- wash
- LAV
- STORAGE
- SHOP
- MUD CLO
- Furnace for plan without basement
- ENTRY
- FAMILY RM. 16'-2" × 11'-6"
- CLOS
- GARAGE 20'-8" × 20'-0"
- 28'-0"

Plans H-3678-3 & H-3678-3A	
Bedrooms: 4	**Baths:** 2½

Finished space:

Upper floor:	960 sq. ft.
Main floor:	1,036 sq. ft.

Total living area:	**1,996 sq. ft.**
Basement:	900 sq. ft.
Garage:	413 sq. ft.

Features:
Spacious living room and large family room.
Convenient nook/kitchen/laundry arrangement.
Inviting porch and roomy entry area.

Exterior Wall Framing:	2x4

Foundation options: (Specify)
Standard Basement: Plan H-3678-3
Crawlspace: Plan H-3678-3A
(Foundation & framing conversion diagram available — see order form.)

Blueprint Price Code:
Without finished basement design: B
With finished basement design: D

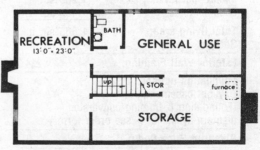

BASEMENT

- RECREATION 13'-0" × 23'-0"
- BATH
- GENERAL USE
- up
- STOR
- furnace
- STORAGE

Split Entry with Country Kitchen

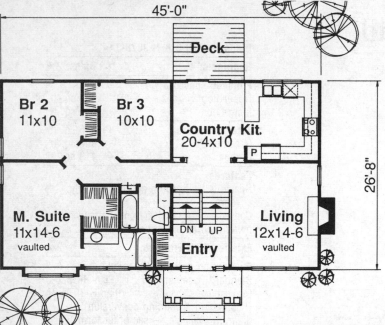

45'-0"

Deck

Br 2
11x10

Br 3
10x10

Country Kit.
20-4x10

P

M. Suite
11x14-6
vaulted

DN   UP

Living
12x14-6
vaulted

Entry

26'-8"

MAIN FLOOR

- The split entry of this updated traditional opens up to a large vaulted living room with fireplace and a lovely country kitchen with sliders to a deck.
- Down the hall you'll find the vaulted master suite with large walk-in closet and private bath.
- Two additional bedrooms and a second bath are also included.
- The lower level is unfinished and left up to the owner to choose its function; room for a third bath and laundry facilities is provided.

Plan B-90012

Bedrooms: 3	Baths: 2-3

Space:

Main/upper level:	1,203 sq. ft.
Basement:	460 sq. ft.

Total living area:	1,663 sq. ft.
Garage:	509 sq. ft.

Exterior Wall Framing:	2x4

Foundation options:
Daylight basement.
(Foundation & framing conversion diagram available — see order form.)

Blueprint Price Code:	B

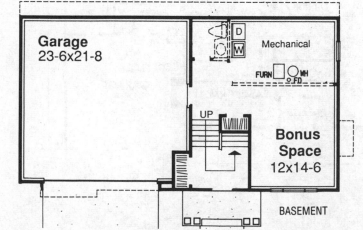

Garage
23-6x21-8

Mechanical

D
W

FURN   WH
FD

UP

Bonus
Space
12x14-6

BASEMENT

Plan B-90012

PRICES AND DETAILS
ON PAGES 13-15

PLAN H-2107-1B

Solarium for Sloping Lots

This plan is available in two versions. Plan H-2107-1B, shown above, is most suitable for a lot sloping upward from front to rear, providing a daylight front for the lower floor. The other version, Plan H-2107-1 (at right), is more suitable for a lot that slopes from side to side.

Either way, this moderately sized home has a number of interesting and imaginative features. Of these, the passive sun room will provoke the most comment. Spanning two floors between recreation and living rooms, this glass-enclosed space serves the practical purpose of collecting, storing and redistributing the sun's natural heat, while acting as a conservatory for exotic plants, an exercise room, or any number of other uses. A link between the formal atmosphere of the living room and the carefree activities of the recreation area is created by this two-story solarium by way of an open balcony railing. Living, dining, and entry blend together in one huge space made to seem even larger by the vaulted ceiling spanning the entire complex of rooms.

PLAN H-2107-1

MAIN FLOOR
1505 SQUARE FEET

PLAN H-2107-1B
DAYLIGHT BASEMENT

PLAN H-2107-1
WITH STANDARD BASEMENT
(BOTH VERSIONS INCLUDE
2X6 EXTERIOR WALL CONSTRUCTION)

Main floor:	1,505 sq. ft.
Lower level:	779 sq. ft.
Total living area: (Not counting garage)	2,284 sq. ft.

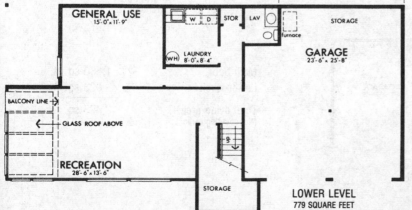

LOWER LEVEL
779 SQUARE FEET

Blueprint Price Code C

ORDER BLUEPRINTS ANYTIME!
CALL TOLL-FREE 1-888-626-2026

Plans H-2107-1 & -1B

**PRICES AND DETAILS
ON PAGES 13-15**

235

Gracious Living on a Grand Scale

Well suited to either a gently sloping or flat building site, this home is also geared to a conservative building budget. First, it saves money through the partial enclosure of the lower level with foundation walls. A portion of the lower level that is surrounded by concrete walls is devoted to a 15'-10" x 13'-0" bedroom or optional den with wardrobe closet, a spacious recreation room with fireplace, and a third complete bathroom along with an abundance of storage space.

The balance of the area at this level is devoted to a two-car garage. Access from this portion of the home to the floor directly above is via a central staircase.

In Plan H-2082-2, a formal dining room and large kitchen provide two places for family eating.

Plan H-2082-1 includes a combination family room and U-shaped kitchen in one open area. Spatial continuity is further extended into the cantilevered deck that projects over the garage driveway below and is accessible through sliding glass doors off the family room.

This system of multi-level planning offers economy in building where grading would otherwise be required.

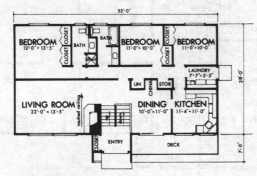

PLAN H-2082-2
MAIN FLOOR
1500 SQUARE FEET

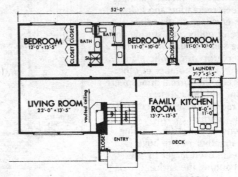

PLAN H-2082-1
MAIN FLOOR
1500 SQUARE FEET

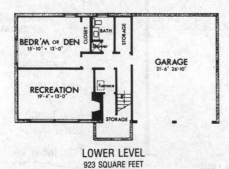

LOWER LEVEL
923 SQUARE FEET

Main floor:	1,500 sq. ft.
Lower level:	923 sq. ft.
Total living area: (Not counting garage)	2,423 sq. ft.

Blueprint Price Code C
Plans H-2082-1 & -2

PRICES AND DETAILS
ON PAGES 13-15

Suite Trio

- This gorgeous home's symmetrical facade conceals a sleeping wing with three separate suites—giving luxurious privacy to all family members!
- The bayed master bedroom boasts a high 11-ft. ceiling, a walk-in closet, a whirlpool bath and two linen closets.
- The exterior of the home features an elegant combination of brick and stucco, accented by half-round transoms, keystones and shutters.
- In from the gracious, columned front porch, the sidelighted foyer shows off an 11-ft. ceiling as it welcomes guests. A lovely staircase ascends to future expansion space on the upper floor.

- The bright and spacious Great Room is warmed by a fireplace, making it a great spot for entertaining or relaxing.
- A curved serving bar highlights the open kitchen, where a china hutch, stacked ovens and a handy pantry line the right wall.
- Casual meals will be delightful in the adjacent breakfast nook; French doors expand the charming experience to a columned porch and a brick patio.
- Facing the door to the two-car garage, a computer desk offers a special area to work on the budget or write letters.
- A powder room and cheery laundry facilities round out the floor plan.
- Where not otherwise specified, ceilings are 9 ft. high for added spaciousness.

Plan J-9307	
Bedrooms: 3+	**Baths:** 3½
Living Area:	
Main floor	2,497 sq. ft.
Total Living Area:	**2,497 sq. ft.**
Future upper floor	966 sq. ft.
Standard basement	2,497 sq. ft.
Garage and storage	587 sq. ft.
Exterior Wall Framing:	2x4

Foundation Options:

Standard basement
Crawlspace
Slab

(All plans can be built with your choice of foundation and framing. A generic conversion diagram is available. See order form.)

BLUEPRINT PRICE CODE:	C

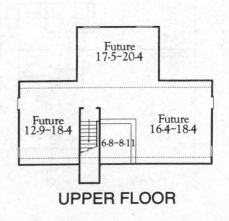

MAIN FLOOR

87-0

57-3

Master Bedroom 16-0~21-0
Bedroom 11-0~14-3
Great Room 18-0~21-1
Patio 18-0~14-6
Porch 13-0~8-0
Breakfast 11-6~12-7
Stor.
Laun.
Kitchen 11-10~15-6
M. Bath
Bedroom 12-9~10-10
Foyer
Dining 17-1~13-2
Garage 21-8~23-3
Porch 43-0~7-0

UPPER FLOOR

Future 17-5~20-4
Future 12-9~18-4
Future 16-4~18-4
6-8~8-11

ORDER BLUEPRINTS ANYTIME!
CALL TOLL-FREE 1-888-626-2026

Plan J-9307

PRICES AND DETAILS
ON PAGES 13-15

237

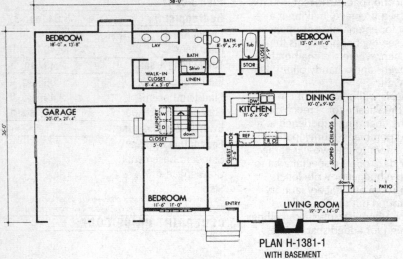

PLAN H-1381-1
WITH BASEMENT

Total living area: 1,596 sq. ft.
(Not counting basement or garage)

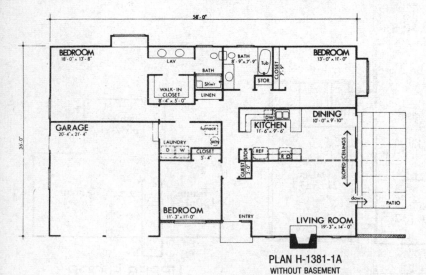

PLAN H-1381-1A
WITHOUT BASEMENT
(CRAWLSPACE FOUNDATION)

Total living area: 1,587 sq. ft.
(Not counting garage)

Popular Contemporary

This low-slung contemporary design contains a lot more space than is apparent from the outside. Oriented towards the outdoor sideyard, it features a pair of sliding glass doors offering outside access from both the living and dining room.

Effective zoning is the rule here: Bedrooms are secluded on one side to the rear; living areas and active kitchen space are grouped on the opposite side of the home.

All of these rooms are easily reached from a central hallway that provides excellent traffic flow, precluding unnecessary cross-room traffic.

Note the convenient location of the laundry room and staircase to the basement. Access to the garage is also available from the interior of the home. A generous assortment of plumbing facilities is grouped at the rear of the home. One bath serves the master bedroom privately. Another complete unit serves the balance of the house.

The attractive low silhouette is embellished with architectural touches such as the interesting window seats, the extension of the masonry wall that shields the side patio, and the low pitched roof.

Overall width of the home is 58' and greatest depth measures 36'. Exterior walls are 2x6 construction.

Blueprint Price Code B

Plans H-1381-1 & -1A

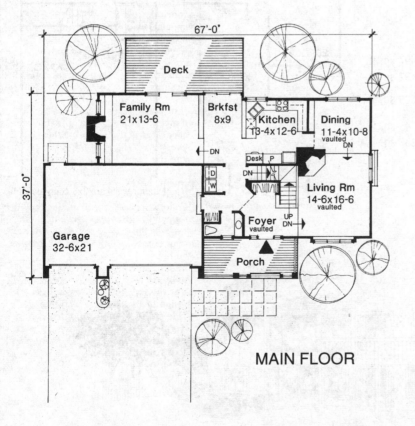

UPPER FLOOR

Br 2
11x12-6

Br 3
10-2x11-4

Br 4/
Den
11x11-4

DN

Loft

open to below

MBr
13-2x19-2

Skylights

vaulted area

67'-0"

37'-0"

Deck

Family Rm
21x13-6

Brkfst
8x9

Kitchen
13-4x12-6

Dining
11-4x10-8
vaulted

DN

Desk P

DN

DN

Living Rm
14-6x16-6
vaulted

D

W

UP
DN

Foyer
vaulted

Garage
32-6x21

Porch

MAIN FLOOR

Two-Story for Today

- The charm and character of yesterday are re-created in this two-story design for today. The quaint exterior is highlighted by half-round windows, planter boxes and a covered front porch.
- The dramatic skylighted entry preludes a formal, sunken living room with a stunning corner fireplace and an adjoining formal dining room with a built-in hutch. Both rooms are also enhanced by vaulted ceilings.
- A large kitchen with a built-in desk and a pantry opens to a sunny breakfast room and a large, sunken family room at the rear of the home. The family room features an exciting fireplace wall and French doors that open to the rear deck.
- The upstairs loft leads to a luxurious master bedroom with a vaulted ceiling, angled walk-in closet and private bath. Two to three additional bedrooms and a second bath are also included.

Plan B-159-86

Bedrooms: 3-4	**Baths:** 2½

Living Area:	
Upper floor	1,155 sq. ft.
Main floor	1,290 sq. ft.
Total Living Area:	**2,445 sq. ft.**
Standard basement	1,290 sq. ft.
Garage	683 sq. ft.
Exterior Wall Framing:	2x4

Foundation Options:

Standard basement

(Typical foundation & framing conversion diagram available—see order form.)

BLUEPRINT PRICE CODE:	C

ORDER BLUEPRINTS ANYTIME!
CALL TOLL-FREE 1-888-626-2026

Plan B-159-86

PRICES AND DETAILS
ON PAGES 13-15

239

Garden Room Enhances Contemporary

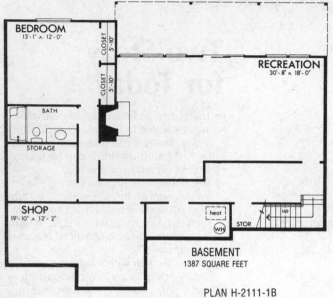

BEDROOM
13'-1" x 12'-0"

CLOSET 5'-10"

CLOSET 5'-10"

RECREATION
30'-8" x 18'-0"

BATH

STORAGE

SHOP
19'-10" x 12'-2"

heat
WH

STOR

up

BASEMENT
1387 SQUARE FEET

PLAN H-2111-1B
WITH DAYLIGHT BASEMENT

Main floor:	1,497 sq. ft.
Garden room:	92 sq. ft.
Total living area: (Not counting basement or garage)	**1,589 sq. ft.**
Airlock entry:	45 sq. ft.
Basement:	1,387 sq. ft.

FAMILY ROOM

D | W | heat | **WH**

STORAGE

GARAGE

PLAN H-2111-1A
WITHOUT BASEMENT
(CRAWLSPACE FOUNDATION)

Main floor:	1,448 sq. ft.
Garden room:	92 sq. ft.
Total living area: (Not counting garage)	**1,540 sq. ft.**
Airlock entry:	45 sq. ft.

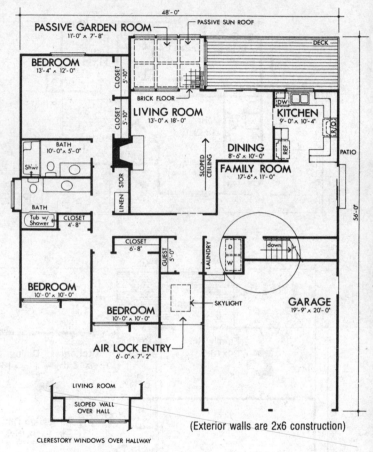

48'-0"

PASSIVE GARDEN ROOM
11'-0" x 7'-8"

PASSIVE SUN ROOF

DECK

BEDROOM
13'-4" x 12'-0"

CLOSET 5'-10"

CLOSET 5'-10"

BRICK FLOOR

LIVING ROOM
13'-0" x 18'-0"

DW

KITCHEN
9'-0" x 10'-4"

R/O

REF

PATIO

BATH
10'-0" x 5'-0"

Sh'wr

SLOPED CEILING

DINING
8'-6" x 10'-0"

FAMILY ROOM
17'-6" x 11'-0"

BATH

Tub w/
Shower

CLOSET
4'-8"

LINEN **STOR**

56'-0"

CLOSET
6'-8"

down

GUEST 5'-0"

LAUNDRY

D | W

BEDROOM
10'-0" x 10'-0"

BEDROOM
10'-0" x 10'-0"

SKYLIGHT

GARAGE
19'-9" x 20'-0"

AIR LOCK ENTRY
6'-0" x 7'-2"

LIVING ROOM

SLOPED WALL OVER HALL

CLERESTORY WINDOWS OVER HALLWAY

(Exterior walls are 2x6 construction)

REAR VIEW

Blueprint Price Code B

Plans H-2111-1A & -1B

PRICES AND DETAILS ON PAGES 13-15

Rural and Refined

- This refined and graceful two-story is at home in the country or in the city, offering a covered front porch with fine detailing to welcome visitors.
- Inside, the foyer flows into the dining room and back to a dramatic two-story living room with its warm fireplace and adjoining rear porch.

- The adjoining bayed eating area looks to the kitchen over a handy snack bar. The gourmet kitchen also features a built-in desk, a large butler's pantry and easy service to the formal dining room.
- An enormous walk-in closet is found in the isolated master suite. The master bath has an enticing garden tub, a separate shower and two vanities.
- A hall bath with an oversized shower is shared by two additional bedrooms.
- Upstairs, a quiet balcony library overlooks the living room.

Plan THD-220-0	
Bedrooms: 3	**Baths:** 2
Living Area:	
Upper floor	96 sq. ft.
Main floor	2,159 sq. ft.
Total Living Area:	**2,255 sq. ft.**
Daylight basement	2,159 sq. ft.
Garage and storage	664 sq. ft.
Future expansion space	878 sq. ft.
Exterior Wall Framing:	2x6

Foundation Options:

Daylight basement
Crawlspace
Slab
(All plans can be built with your choice of foundation and framing. A generic conversion diagram is available. See order form.)

BLUEPRINT PRICE CODE:	C

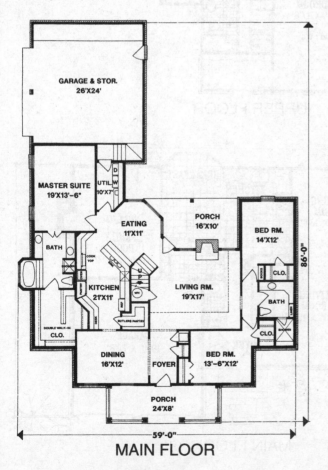

MAIN FLOOR

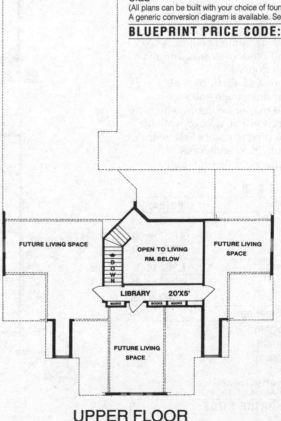

UPPER FLOOR

ORDER BLUEPRINTS ANYTIME!
CALL TOLL-FREE 1-888-626-2026

Plan THD-220-0

PRICES AND DETAILS
ON PAGES 13-15

241

CH-210-A

CH-210-B

Outstanding Options

- A functional floor plan and the option of two exteriors make this traditional home an outstanding choice.
- Guests will be impressed by the large, light-filled living room, with its classic columns and optional fireplace. The adjoining dining room offers an optional bay window.
- The adjacent kitchen offers an island work area and a sunny breakfast nook tucked into a large bay window.
- An open railing separates the nook from the skylighted family room, which boasts a 10½-ft. vaulted ceiling, a cozy fireplace and outdoor access through triple French doors.
- A utility room and a half-bath are located near the garage entrance.
- Upstairs, the master bedroom flaunts a 10-ft. vaulted ceiling, a huge walk-in closet and a private luxury bath with a whirlpool tub. Two additional bedrooms share another full bath.

Plans CH-210-A & -B

Bedrooms: 3	Baths: 2½
Living Area:	
Upper floor	823 sq. ft.
Main floor	1,079 sq. ft.
Total Living Area:	**1,902 sq. ft.**
Basement	978 sq. ft.
Garage	400 sq. ft.
Exterior Wall Framing:	2x4

Foundation Options:

Daylight basement

Standard basement

Crawlspace

(All plans can be built with your choice of foundation and framing. A generic conversion diagram is available. See order form.)

BLUEPRINT PRICE CODE:	**B**

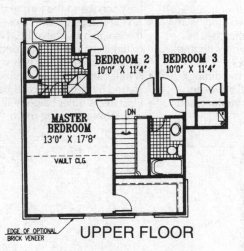

UPPER FLOOR

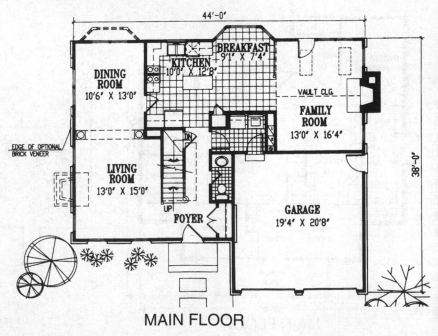

MAIN FLOOR

ORDER BLUEPRINTS ANYTIME!
CALL TOLL-FREE 1-888-626-2026

Plans CH-210-A & -B

PRICES AND DETAILS
ON PAGES 13-15

Essential Peace

- This home's nostalgic porch and charming interior wrap you up in peace and comfort.
- On a warm summer night, you can rig up a hammock on the porch and enjoy a cold drink while watching fireflies, the air around you so quiet you can hear the ice in your drink settling.
- Inside, a wide passageway joins the formal living room to the strikingly angled kitchen and dining room. An island greatly simplifies your food preparation efforts. Sliding glass doors let you deliver that potato salad to hungry picnickers in the backyard!
- A design option included with the blueprints for this home substitutes one main-floor bedroom for a greatly expanded master bedroom with an amenity-laden bath.
- Upstairs, two secondary bedrooms are placed at each end of a balcony hall for privacy. Dormer windows grace each room, and a third dormer between them houses an optional third bath.
- All rooms have 9-ft. ceilings.

VIEW INTO KITCHEN AND DINING ROOM

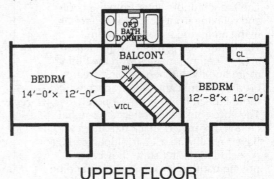

UPPER FLOOR

Plan AX-94341

Bedrooms: 4+	Baths: 1½-3
Living Area:	
Upper floor	597 sq. ft.
Main floor	1,040 sq. ft.
Total Living Area:	**1,637 sq. ft.**
Standard basement	1,040 sq. ft.
Exterior Wall Framing:	2x4

Foundation Options:

Standard basement
Crawlspace
Slab

(All plans can be built with your choice of foundation and framing. A generic conversion diagram is available. See order form.)

BLUEPRINT PRICE CODE:	**B**

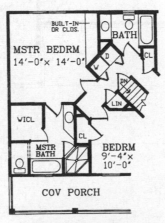

ALTERNATE MAIN FLOOR

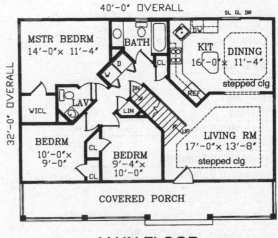

MAIN FLOOR

ORDER BLUEPRINTS ANYTIME!
CALL TOLL-FREE 1-888-626-2026

Plan AX-94341

PRICES AND DETAILS
ON PAGES 13-15

243

Updated Creole

- This Louisiana-style raised cottage features a tin roof, shuttered windows and three pairs of French doors, all of which add to the comfort and nostalgic appeal of this Creole classic.
- The French doors enter from the cool and relaxing front porch to the formal living areas and a front bedroom.
- The central living room, which features a 12-ft. ceiling, merges with the dining room and the kitchen's eating area. A fireplace warms the whole space while more French doors access a porch.
- The efficient kitchen offers a 12-ft. flat ceiling, an angled snack bar and a bayed nook with a 12-ft. sloped ceiling.
- A secluded master suite showcases a private bath, fit for the most demanding tastes. Across the home, the secondary bedrooms include abundant closet space and share a full bath.
- This full-featured, energy-efficient design also includes a large utility room and extra storage space in the garage.

Plan E-1823

Bedrooms: 3	Baths: 2
Living Area:	
Main floor	1,800 sq. ft.
Total Living Area:	**1,800 sq. ft.**
Garage	550 sq. ft.
Exterior Wall Framing:	2x6
Foundation Options:	
Crawlspace	
Slab	

(All plans can be built with your choice of foundation and framing. A generic conversion diagram is available. See order form.)

BLUEPRINT PRICE CODE:	B

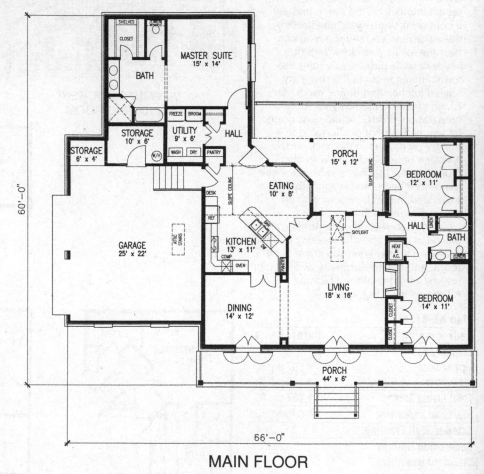

MAIN FLOOR

Plan E-1823

**PRICES AND DETAILS
ON PAGES 13-15**

Spectacular One-Story!

- The angled, covered entry of this spectacular one-story home opens into its thoroughly up-to-date interior.
- Past the inviting foyer, the spacious dining area shares a soaring 13-ft. ceiling with the adjoining Great Room.
- Brightened by sliding glass doors to a covered backyard patio, the Great Room also includes an extensive built-in media center.
- The gourmet kitchen has a 13-ft. ceiling and serves a sunny bay-windowed breakfast area over an angled counter. A convenient laundry/utility area with garage access is nearby.
- Enhanced by a 10-ft. ceiling and windows on three sides, the master bedroom has an air of elegance. The lavish master bath boasts a spa tub, a separate shower, a dual-sink vanity and a roomy walk-in closet.
- Two additional bedrooms are expanded by 11-ft. ceilings and share a full bath.
- Featuring an enormous front window and a walk-in closet, the study would make a fantastic fourth bedroom.

Plan HDS-99-143

Bedrooms: 3+	Baths: 2
Living Area:	
Main floor	1,865 sq. ft.
Total Living Area:	**1,865 sq. ft.**
Garage	377 sq. ft.
Exterior Wall Framing:	2x4

Foundation Options:

Slab

(All plans can be built with your choice of foundation and framing. A generic conversion diagram is available. See order form.)

BLUEPRINT PRICE CODE: B

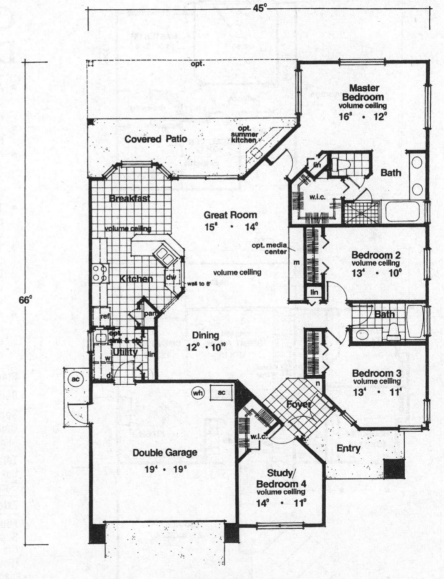

MAIN FLOOR

ORDER BLUEPRINTS ANYTIME!
CALL TOLL-FREE 1-888-626-2026

Plan HDS-99-143

PRICES AND DETAILS
ON PAGES 13-15

245

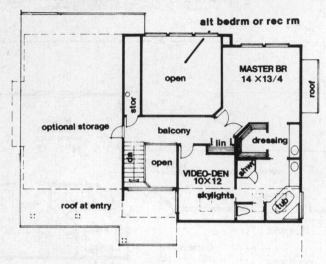

alt bedrm or rec rm

optional storage

open

stor

MASTER BR
14 × 13/4

roof

balcony

lin

dressing

den

open

VIDEO-DEN
10 × 12

shwr

tub

roof at entry

skylights

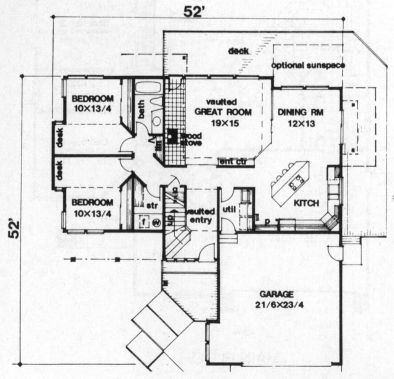

52'

52'

deck

optional sunspace

BEDROOM
10 × 13/4

bath

vaulted
GREAT ROOM
19 × 15

DINING RM
12 × 13

desk

wood
stove

ent ctr

BEDROOM
10 × 13/4

str

util

KITCH

vaulted
entry

up

GARAGE
21/6 × 23/4

Convenient Contemporary Design

- A thoroughly contemporary front elevation includes a sheltered porch as a traditional, homey touch.
- A vaulted Great Room makes this home look extra spacious.
- A large, open kitchen gives plenty of working space and avoids the confined feeling often found in kitchens.
- The second floor is really an "adult retreat," with its master bedroom, video/den area and balcony hallway.
- The master suite features a walk-through closet and dressing area leading to a generous master bath, which is also accessible from the video room.
- As an alternate, the vaulted area over the Great Room can be enclosed to make a fourth bedroom or upstairs rec room.

Plan S-72485

Bedrooms: 3-4	Baths: 2

Space:

Upper floor:	650 sq. ft.
Main floor:	1,450 sq. ft.
Total living area:	**2,100 sq. ft.**
Basement:	1,450 sq. ft.
Garage:	502 sq. ft.

Exterior Wall Framing:	2x6

Foundation options:
Standard basement.
Crawlspace.
(Foundation & framing conversion diagram available — see order form.)

Blueprint Price Code:	C

246

ORDER BLUEPRINTS ANYTIME!
CALL TOLL-FREE 1-888-626-2026

Plan S-72485

PRICES AND DETAILS
ON PAGES 13-15

Colonial Has Modern Features

- This stately Colonial is as distinguished on the inside as it is on the outside.
- The dramatic entrance reveals a spacious living room with a big fireplace and a front bay window and an adjoining family room separated only by a decorative see-through wood divider. A sloped ceiling and French doors to the rear terrace are highlights in the family room.
- The high-tech kitchen has an island work area, a pantry, a handy laundry closet and a sunny, circular dinette.
- Featured in the private main-floor master suite is a cathedral ceiling and a private terrace accessed through French doors. A walk-in closet and a personal bath with whirlpool tub are other extras.
- Three other bedrooms share the upper level, which also offers a balcony that views the family room below.

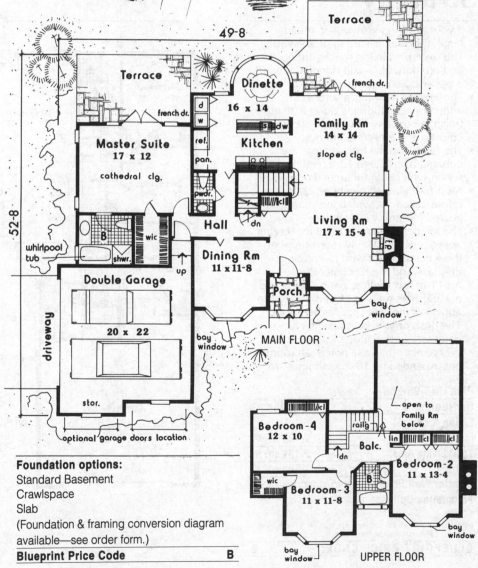

Plan AHP-9121	
Bedrooms: 4	**Baths:** 2 ½
Space:	
Upper floor	557 sq. ft.
Main floor	1,183 sq. ft.
Total Living Area	**1,740 sq. ft.**
Basement	1,183 sq. ft.
Garage	440 sq. ft.
Exterior Wall Framing	2x4 or 2x6

Foundation options:

Standard Basement

Crawlspace

Slab

(Foundation & framing conversion diagram available—see order form.)

Blueprint Price Code   B

ORDER BLUEPRINTS ANYTIME!
CALL TOLL-FREE 1-888-626-2026

Plan AHP-9121

PRICES AND DETAILS
ON PAGES 13-15

247

Large-Scale Strategy

- If your family is growing or already large, this plan is sure to please you!
- The oversized living spaces are open and comfortable—and oriented toward a backyard covered patio.
- The exterior also has a surplus of attractions, including a durable textured finish, a concrete tile roof, a stately column and elegant windows.
- The foyer and the formal areas are enhanced with high 12-ft. ceilings and set off with beautiful arched openings.
- An 8-ft.-high wall nicely separates the informal spaces, which are strategically geared for family interaction.
- The kitchen's island is ideal for serving appetizers. The family room supplies the entertainment with its enticing fireplace and media center duo.
- An 11-ft. tray ceiling, patio access and his-and-hers walk-in closets add to the appeal of the quiet master bedroom. The posh private bath features a gorgeous garden tub.
- Where not otherwise noted, all rooms are expanded by 10-ft. ceilings.

Plan HDS-99-256

Bedrooms: 4	Baths: 3
Living Area:	
Main floor	2,131 sq. ft.
Total Living Area:	**2,131 sq. ft.**
Garage	595 sq. ft.
Exterior Wall Framing:	8-in. concrete block
Foundation Options:	

Slab

(All plans can be built with your choice of foundation and framing. A generic conversion diagram is available. See order form.)

BLUEPRINT PRICE CODE:	C

MAIN FLOOR

Captivating Facade

- This home attracts the eye with stately columns, half-round transoms and a sidelighted entry.
- A tall, barrel-vaulted foyer flows between the radiant formal areas at the front of the home.
- The barrel vault opens from the foyer to an overwhelming 14½-ft. vaulted family room, where a striking fireplace and a media center are captivating features.
- The central kitchen offers a dramatic 14½-ft. vaulted ceiling and a snack bar to the breakfast nook and family room. The nook's bay window overlooks a covered backyard patio.
- Formal occasions are hosted in the dining room, which boasts its own bay window and a 10½-ft. vaulted ceiling.
- The secluded master bedroom opens to the patio and flaunts an 11-ft. vaulted ceiling. A large walk-in closet and a posh bath with a step-up garden tub and a separate shower are also featured. On the other side of the home are three additional vaulted bedrooms and two more full baths.

Plan HDS-90-807

Bedrooms: 4	**Baths:** 3

Living Area:

Main floor	2,171 sq. ft.
Total Living Area:	**2,171 sq. ft.**
Garage	405 sq. ft.

Exterior Wall Framing:

2x4 and 8-in. concrete block

Foundation Options:

Slab
(All plans can be built with your choice of foundation and framing. A generic conversion diagram is available. See order form.)

BLUEPRINT PRICE CODE: C

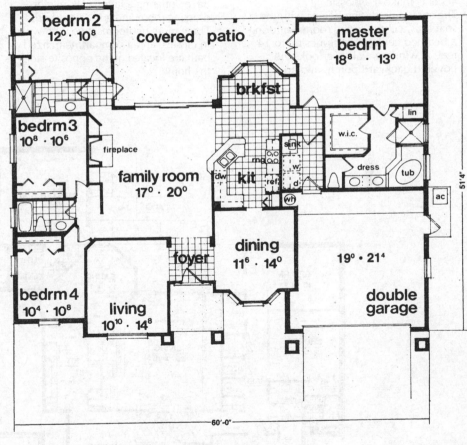

MAIN FLOOR

Plan HDS-90-807

PRICES AND DETAILS
ON PAGES 13-15

Classic Styling

- This handsome one-story traditional would look great in town or in the country. The shuttered and paned windows, narrow lap siding and brick accents make it a classic.
- The sprawling design begins with the spacious, central living room, featuring a beamed ceiling that slopes up to 14 feet. A window wall overlooks the covered backyard porch, and an inviting fireplace includes an extra-wide hearth and built-in bookshelves.
- The galley-style kitchen features a snack bar to the sunny eating area and a raised-panel door to the dining room.
- The isolated master suite is a quiet haven offering a large walk-in closet, a dressing room and a spacious bath.
- Three more bedrooms, two with walk-in closets, and a compartmentalized bath are located at the opposite side of the home.

Plan E-2206

Bedrooms: 4	Baths: 2
Living Area:	
Main floor	2,200 sq. ft.
Total Living Area:	**2,200 sq. ft.**
Standard basement	2,200 sq. ft.
Garage and storage	624 sq. ft.
Exterior Wall Framing:	2x6

Foundation Options:
Standard basement
Crawlspace
Slab
(All plans can be built with your choice of foundation and framing. A generic conversion diagram is available. See order form.)

BLUEPRINT PRICE CODE: C

MAIN FLOOR

Plan E-2206

***PRICES AND DETAILS
ON PAGES 13-15***

Charming Simplicity

- This home boasts a covered front porch and a simple floor plan, each enhancing the home's charming appeal.
- In the living room, the cozy fireplace offers warmth and drama. Built-in bookcases are featured on either side.
- The adjoining dining room flows into the bright island kitchen and opens to the backyard. Laundry facilities and a carport entrance are nearby.
- The secluded master bedroom offers a sloped ceiling, a corner window, a walk-in closet, a dressing area and a separate bath.
- Two nice-sized bedrooms share a full bath at the opposite end of the home.

Plan J-8670

Bedrooms: 3	Baths: 2
Living Area:	
Main floor	1,522 sq. ft.
Total Living Area:	**1,522 sq. ft.**
Standard basement	1,522 sq. ft.
Carport and storage	436 sq. ft.
Exterior Wall Framing:	**2x4**

Foundation Options:

Standard basement

Crawlspace

Slab

(All plans can be built with your choice of foundation and framing. A generic conversion diagram is available. See order form.)

BLUEPRINT PRICE CODE:	**B**

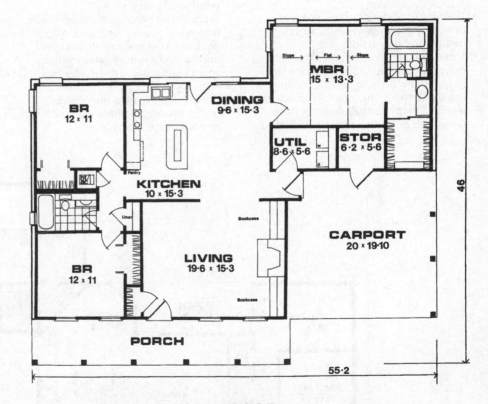

MAIN FLOOR

See this plan on our "Country & Traditional" Video Tour! Order form on page 9

ORDER BLUEPRINTS ANYTIME!
CALL TOLL-FREE 1-888-626-2026

Plan J-8670

PRICES AND DETAILS
ON PAGES 13-15

251

Luxurious Living on One Level

- The elegant exterior of this spacious one-story presents a classic air of quality and distinction.
- Three French doors brighten the inviting entry, which flows into the spacious living room. Boasting a 13-ft. ceiling, the living room enjoys a fireplace with a wide hearth and adjoining built-in bookshelves. A wall of glass, including a French door, provides views of the sheltered backyard porch.
- A stylish angled counter joins the spacious kitchen to the sunny bay-windowed eating nook.
- Secluded for privacy, the master suite features a nice dressing area, a large walk-in closet and private backyard access. A convenient laundry/utility room is adjacent to the master bath.
- At the opposite end of the home, double doors lead to three more bedrooms, a compartmentalized bath and lots of closet space.

Plan E-2208

Bedrooms: 4	**Baths: 2**

Living Area:	
Main floor	2,252 sq. ft.
Total Living Area:	**2,252 sq. ft.**
Standard basement	2,252 sq. ft.
Garage and storage	592 sq. ft.
Exterior Wall Framing:	2x6

Foundation Options:

Standard basement
Crawlspace
Slab
(All plans can be built with your choice of foundation and framing. A generic conversion diagram is available. See order form.)

BLUEPRINT PRICE CODE:	C

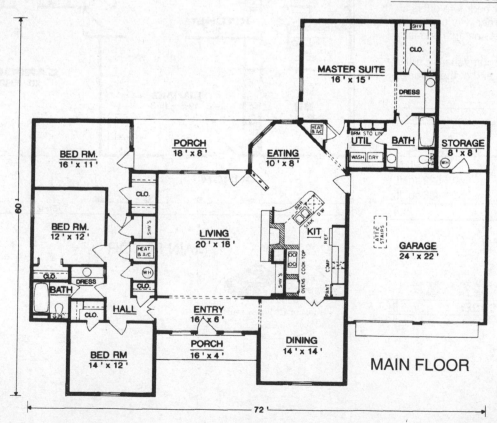

MAIN FLOOR

Striking One-Story Home

- Eye-catching angles, both inside and out, are the keynotes of this luxurious one-story home.
- The striking double-door entry is illuminated by a skylight. The foyer is just as impressive, with its cathedral ceiling and skylight.
- The sunken living room also features a cathedral ceiling, and a bay-window alcove faces the front.
- A low partition separates the living room from the formal dining room. Here, too, a cathedral ceiling and bay windows add interesting angles and spaciousness to the room.
- The open family room, breakfast room and kitchen offer plenty of space for casual family living. The family room includes a corner fireplace with adjacent built-in shelves. The bayed breakfast area boasts a cathedral ceiling and French doors to the backyard. An angled snack counter faces the U-shaped kitchen.
- The master bedroom also has a bay window facing the backyard, plus a large walk-in closet. Also included is a private bath with a whirlpool tub.
- Two more bedrooms, another full bath and a utility area complete the design.

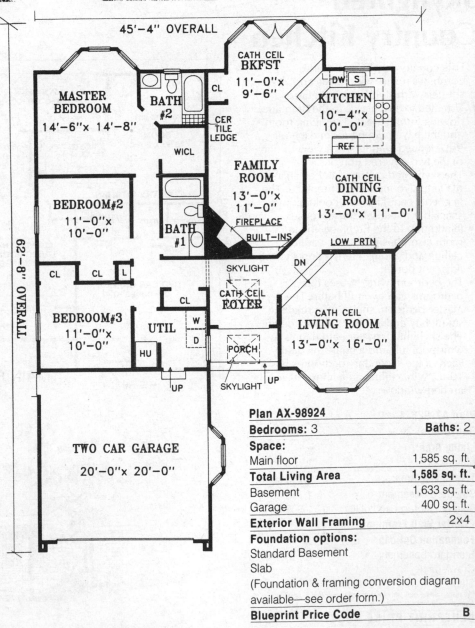

Plan AX-98924

Bedrooms: 3	Baths: 2
Space:	
Main floor	1,585 sq. ft.
Total Living Area	**1,585 sq. ft.**
Basement	1,633 sq. ft.
Garage	400 sq. ft.
Exterior Wall Framing	2x4

Foundation options:
Standard Basement
Slab
(Foundation & framing conversion diagram available—see order form.)

Blueprint Price Code	B

ORDER BLUEPRINTS ANYTIME!
CALL TOLL-FREE 1-888-626-2026

Plan AX-98924

PRICES AND DETAILS
ON PAGES 13-15

253

Skylighted Country Kitchen

- This country ranch-style home combines rustic wood posts and shutters with stylish curved glass.
- The tiled foyer unfolds to the dramatic, flowing formal areas. The living room and the bayed dining room each offer a 9-ft. stepped ceiling and a view of one of the two covered porches.
- The skylighted country kitchen shares the family room's warm fireplace. The kitchen's central island cooktop and snack bar make serving a breeze!
- In addition to the fireplace, the family room also boasts an 11-ft. vaulted ceiling and gliding French doors to the adjacent porch.
- The bedroom wing houses three bedrooms and two full baths. The master bedroom shows off a relaxing sitting bay and a 9-ft., 9-in. tray ceiling. The skylighted master bath flaunts a whirlpool tub and a dual-sink vanity.
- Each of the secondary bedrooms has a 10-ft., 9-in. ceiling area above its lovely arched window.

Plan AX-92321

Bedrooms: 3	Baths: 2
Living Area:	
Main floor	1,735 sq. ft.
Total Living Area:	**1,735 sq. ft.**
Standard basement	1,735 sq. ft.
Garage, storage and utility	505 sq. ft.
Exterior Wall Framing:	2x4

Foundation Options:
Standard basement
Crawlspace
Slab
(All plans can be built with your choice of foundation and framing. A generic conversion diagram is available. See order form.)

BLUEPRINT PRICE CODE:	B

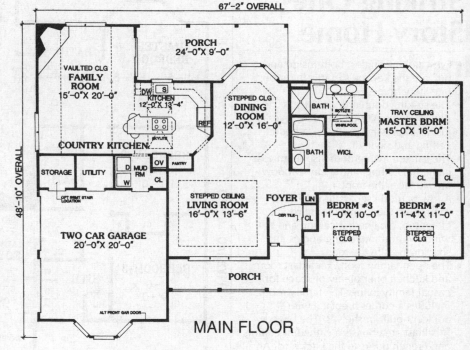

MAIN FLOOR

REAR VIEW

ORDER BLUEPRINTS ANYTIME!
CALL TOLL-FREE 1-888-626-2026

Plan AX-92321

PRICES AND DETAILS
ON PAGES 13-15

Elegance
Inside and Out

- The raised front porch of this home is finely detailed with wood columns, railings, moldings, and French doors with half-round transoms.
- The living room, dining room and entry have 12-ft.-high ceilings. Skylights illuminate the living room, which offers a fireplace and access to a roomy deck.
- The efficient kitchen permits easy service to both the dining room and the casual eating area.
- The master suite features a raised tray ceiling and an enormous skylighted bath with a walk-in closet, dual vanities and a large quarter-circle spa tub surrounded by a mirror wall.
- On the left, two secondary bedrooms are insulated from the more active areas of the home by an efficient hallway, and also share another full bath.

Plan E-1909

Bedrooms: 3	Baths: 2
Living Area:	
Main floor	1,936 sq. ft.
Total Living Area:	**1,936 sq. ft.**
Garage	484 sq. ft.
Storage	132 sq. ft.
Exterior Wall Framing:	2x6

Foundation Options:

Crawlspace

Slab

(All plans can be built with your choice of foundation and framing. A generic conversion diagram is available. See order form.)

BLUEPRINT PRICE CODE:	B

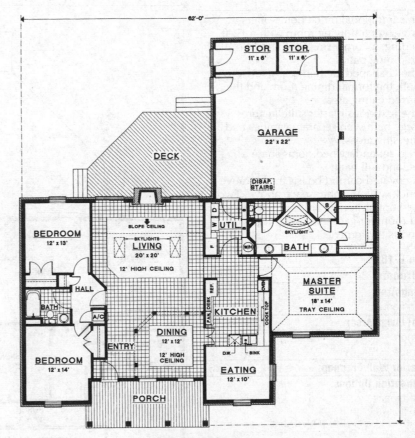

MAIN FLOOR

ORDER BLUEPRINTS ANYTIME!
CALL TOLL-FREE 1-888-626-2026

Plan E-1909

PRICES AND DETAILS
ON PAGES 13-15

255

Attainable Luxury

- This traditional ranch home offers a large, central living room with a 12-ft. ceiling, a corner fireplace and an adjoining patio.
- The U-shaped kitchen easily services both the formal dining room and the bayed eating area.
- The luxurious master suite features a large bath with separate vanities and dressing areas.
- Two secondary bedrooms share a second full bath.
- A covered carport boasts a decorative brick wall and attic space above. Two additional storage areas provide plenty of room for gardening supplies and sports equipment.

Plan E-1812

Bedrooms: 3	Baths: 2

Living Area:

Main floor	1,860 sq. ft.
Total Living Area:	**1,860 sq. ft.**
Carport	484 sq. ft.
Storage	132 sq. ft.

Exterior Wall Framing: 2x6

Foundation Options:

Crawlspace

Slab

(All plans can be built with your choice of foundation and framing. A generic conversion diagram is available. See order form.)

BLUEPRINT PRICE CODE: B

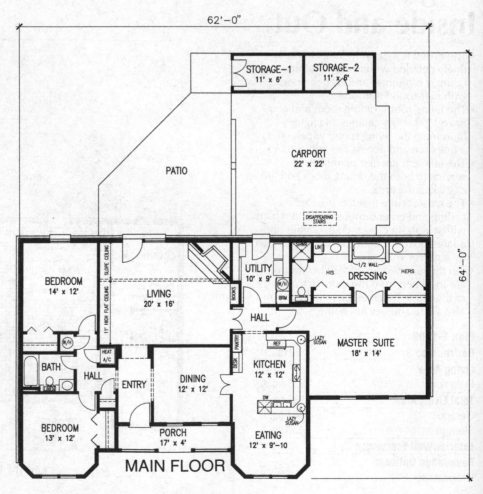

MAIN FLOOR

Plan E-1812

PRICES AND DETAILS
ON PAGES 13-15

Country Charm, Cottage Look

- An interesting combination of stone and stucco gives a charming cottage look to this attactive country home.
- Off the inviting sidelighted entry, the formal dining room is defined by striking columns.
- The dining room expands into the living room, which boasts a fireplace and built-in shelves. A French door provides access to a cute backyard patio.
- The galley-style kitchen unfolds to a sunny morning room.
- All of the living areas are expanded by 10-ft. ceilings.
- The master bedroom features a 10-ft. ceiling and a nice bayed sitting area. The luxurious master bath boasts an exciting garden tub and a glass-block shower, as well as a big walk-in closet and a dressing area with two sinks.
- Across the home, two additional bedrooms with walk-in closets and private dressing areas share a tidy compartmentalized bath.

Plan DD-1790

Bedrooms: 3	Baths: 2½
Living Area:	
Main floor	1,790 sq. ft.
Total Living Area:	**1,790 sq. ft.**
Standard basement	1,790 sq. ft.
Garage	438 sq. ft.
Exterior Wall Framing:	2x4

Foundation Options:

Standard basement

Crawlspace

Slab

(All plans can be built with your choice of foundation and framing. A generic conversion diagram is available. See order form.)

BLUEPRINT PRICE CODE: B

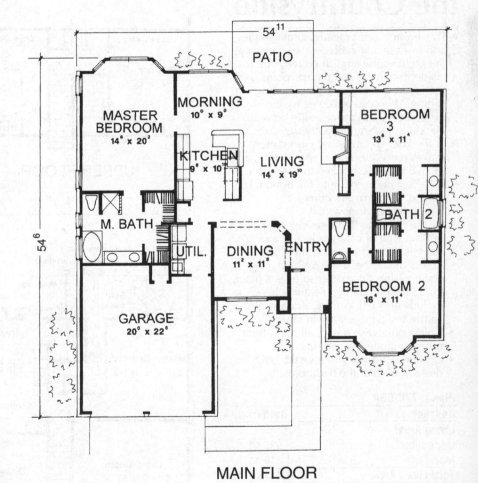

MAIN FLOOR

ORDER BLUEPRINTS ANYTIME!
CALL TOLL-FREE 1-888-626-2026

Plan DD-1790

PRICES AND DETAILS
ON PAGES 13-15

257

Dreaming of the Countryside

- This home's brick facade, gentle angles and front-facing gables evoke images of the picturesque English countryside.
- Inside, the living and dining rooms flank the foyer, creating an open, inviting setting. When guests come by for dinner, they can move easily between cocktails and the main course.
- In the kitchen, an island workstation makes room for helpers. At the rear, an alcove is perfectly sized to serve as a breakfast nook. Without the optional garage, the alcove becomes a wraparound window seat.
- By the entrance to the nearby garage, a built-in wall of cabinets keeps boots, scarves and mittens neat and tidy.
- Across the home, a deluxe bath distinguishes the master suite as a place for a little pampering. Features here include an 11-ft. ceiling, a dual-sink vanity and a huge walk-in closet.
- Unless otherwise noted, all main-floor rooms include 9-ft. ceilings.
- Upstairs, students will love the built-in desks in both of the bedrooms.

Plan L-778-CSA

Bedrooms: 3	Baths: 2½
Living Area:	
Upper floor	525 sq. ft.
Main floor	1,319 sq. ft.
Total Living Area:	**1,844 sq. ft.**
Garage	451 sq. ft.
Exterior Wall Framing:	2x4

Foundation Options:

Slab
(All plans can be built with your choice of foundation and framing. A generic conversion diagram is available. See order form.)

BLUEPRINT PRICE CODE:	**B**

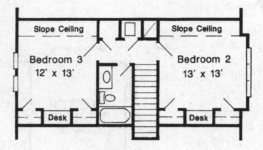

UPPER FLOOR

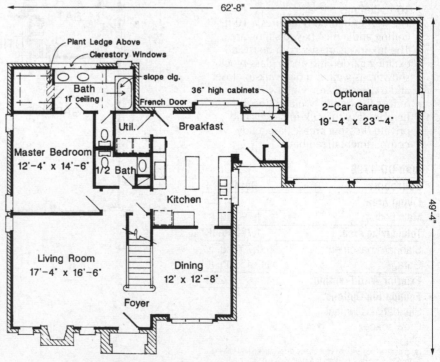

MAIN FLOOR

ORDER BLUEPRINTS ANYTIME!
CALL TOLL-FREE 1-888-626-2026

Plan L-778-CSA

PRICES AND DETAILS ON PAGES 13-15

Distinctive and Elegant

- A distinctive look is captured in the exterior of this elegant one-story. Half-round transoms grace the three glass doors that open to the columned, covered front porch.

- The spacious living room at the center of the homer commands attention, with its 15-ft. ceiling and inviting fireplace. A glass door flanked by windows opens to a skylighted porch, which is also accessible from the secondary bedroom at the back of the home.

- The unique dining room overlooks the two backyard porches and boasts an elegant octagonal design, shaped by columns and cased openings.

- A 14-ft. sloped, skylighted ceiling adds drama to the gourmet kitchen, which also showcases an angled cooktop bar and a windowed sink. Laundry facilities and storage space are nearby.

- The luxurious master suite is secluded at the rear of the home, with private access to the porch. The sumptuous master bath features an oval spa tub, a separate shower, dual vanities and a huge walk-in closet.

Plan E-1628

Bedrooms: 3	Baths: 2
Living Area:	
Main floor	1,655 sq. ft.
Total Living Area:	**1,655 sq. ft.**
Garage and storage	549 sq. ft.
Exterior Wall Framing:	2x6

Foundation Options:

Crawlspace

Slab

(All plans can be built with your choice of foundation and framing. A generic conversion diagram is available. See order form.)

BLUEPRINT PRICE CODE: B

MAIN FLOOR

ORDER BLUEPRINTS ANYTIME!
CALL TOLL-FREE 1-888-626-2026

Plan E-1628

PRICES AND DETAILS
ON PAGES 13-15

259

Live It Up!

- While this home's square footage is modest, its features and amenities are far from it. After years of taking care of others, an older couple will find that this easy-to-manage design makes the days fun and memorable.

- Out front, a brick exterior presents a stately image to the neighborhood. For the more practical minded, it will also withstand the tests of time and the elements with ease.

- Inside, the dining room awaits formal meals. When you want to put your best foot forward, you can't go wrong in this beautiful setting. A pretty niche in the corner displays artwork.

- At the rear of the home, a handsome fireplace anchors the living room. Whether quietly chatting with colleagues, or relaxing with a classic novel, your comfort is ensured.

- Coffee and cereal take on a whole new look in the sun-drenched breakfast nook. The adjacent kitchen includes plenty of room to maneuver.

- At day's end, the master suite gives you the fine treatment you deserve. Enjoy the refreshing garden tub, and then step outside to the patio to let your hair dry naturally in the breeze.

Plan L-793-NAA

Bedrooms: 2+	Baths: 2
Living Area:	
Main floor	1,795 sq. ft.
Total Living Area:	**1,795 sq. ft.**
Garage	500 sq. ft.
Exterior Wall Framing:	2x4

Foundation Options:

Slab
(All plans can be built with your choice of foundation and framing. A generic conversion diagram is available. See order form.)

BLUEPRINT PRICE CODE: B

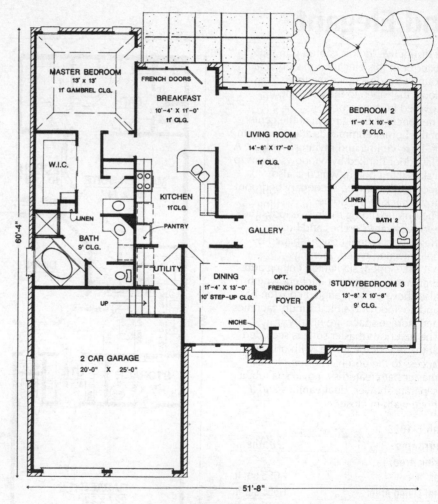

MAIN FLOOR

Plan L-793-NAA

PRICES AND DETAILS
ON PAGES 13-15

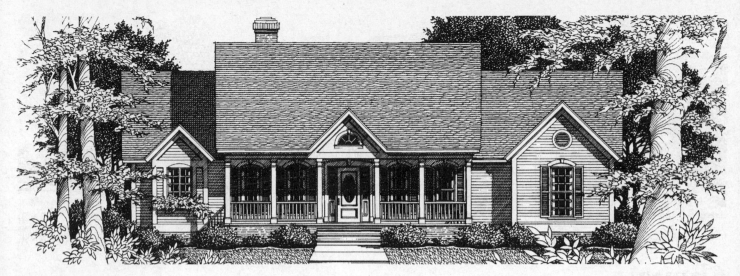

Gracious
Demeanor

- Elegant windows and a covered porch adorn the facade of this country-style home, giving it a gracious demeanor.
- Directly ahead of the ornate foyer, the skylighted living room boasts a cozy fireplace flanked by shelves and cabinets. An impressive 12-ft., 5-in. vaulted ceiling rises overhead, while oversized windows provide great backyard views.
- The adjoining dining room is topped by an elaborate 10-ft. vaulted ceiling and offers a door to a skylighted porch. The porch unfolds to a large patio and accesses the huge garage.
- Behind double doors, the master bedroom presents a 12-ft., 5-in. vaulted ceiling. The master bath flaunts a garden tub and a private toilet.
- At the front of the home, two good-sized bedrooms share a full bath near the laundry room. The den or study may be used as an extra bedroom.

Plan J-9421

Bedrooms: 3+	Baths: 2
Living Area:	
Main floor	1,792 sq. ft.
Total Living Area:	**1,792 sq. ft.**
Standard basement	1,792 sq. ft.
Garage and storage	597 sq. ft.
Exterior Wall Framing:	2x4

Foundation Options:

Standard basement
Crawlspace
Slab
(All plans can be built with your choice of foundation and framing. A generic conversion diagram is available. See order form.)

BLUEPRINT PRICE CODE:	B

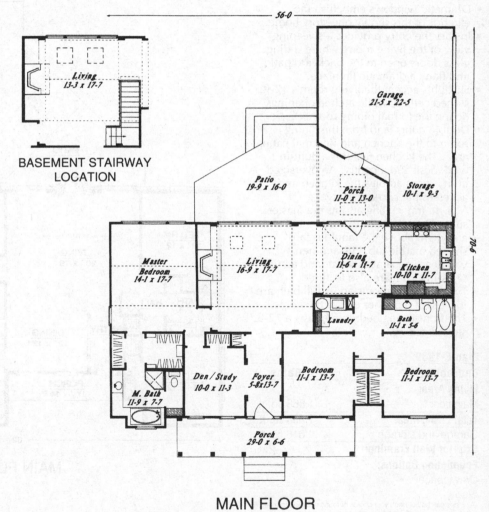

BASEMENT STAIRWAY LOCATION

MAIN FLOOR

ORDER BLUEPRINTS ANYTIME!
CALL TOLL-FREE 1-888-626-2026

Plan J-9421

PRICES AND DETAILS
ON PAGES 13-15

261

Showy One-Story

- Dramatic windows embellish the exterior of this showy one-story home.
- Inside, the entry provides a sweeping view of the living room, where sliding glass doors open to the backyard patio and flank a dramatic fireplace.
- Skylights accent the living room's 12-ft. sloped ceiling, while arched openings define the formal dining room.
- Double doors lead from the dining room to the kitchen and informal eating area. The kitchen features a built-in work desk and a pantry. An oversized utility room adjoins the kitchen and accesses the two-car garage.
- A 10-ft. tray ceiling adorns the master suite. The private bath is accented with a skylight above the fabulous fan-shaped marble tub. His-and-hers vanities, a separate shower and a huge walk-in closet are also featured.
- Two more bedrooms and a full bath are located at the other end of the home.
- The front-facing bedroom boasts a 12-ft. sloped ceiling.

Plan E-1830

Bedrooms: 3	Baths: 2
Living Area:	
Main floor	1,868 sq. ft.
Total Living Area:	**1,868 sq. ft.**
Garage and storage	616 sq. ft.
Exterior Wall Framing:	2x6

Foundation Options:

Crawlspace

Slab

(All plans can be built with your choice of foundation and framing. A generic conversion diagram is available. See order form.)

BLUEPRINT PRICE CODE: B

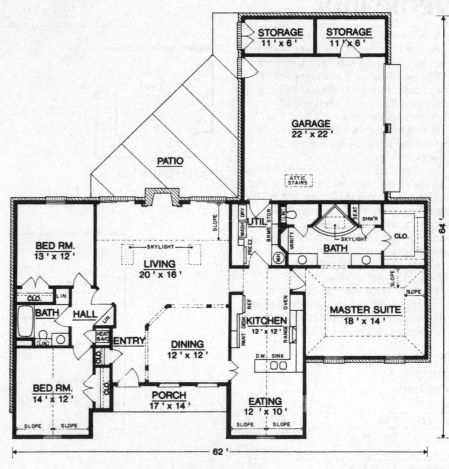

MAIN FLOOR

Tasteful Charm

- Columned covered porches lend warmth and charm to the front and rear of this tasteful traditional home.
- Sidelight and transom glass brightens the entry foyer, which shares a 10-ft. ceiling with the elegant dining room.
- The dining room provides a quiet spot for formal meals, while a Palladian window arrangement adds light and flair.
- The spacious living room offers a warm fireplace and an adjacent TV cabinet. The dramatic ceiling vaults to a height of 11 ft., 8 inches. French doors give way to the skylighted rear porch, which is finished with lovely brick pavers.

Two brick steps descend to the adjoining patio, which is also beautifully paved with brick.
- The gourmet kitchen offers a built-in oven/microwave cabinet, a separate cooktop and an island snack bar with a sink. Its 10-ft. ceiling extends into the sunny breakfast nook.
- The oversized laundry room includes a handy half-bath, a wall-to-wall storage cabinet, a hanging rod, a large sink and nearby porch access.
- The secluded master bedroom boasts a 12-ft. vaulted ceiling and a large walk-in closet. In the private master bath, a glass-block divider separates the whirlpool tub from the shower stall.

Plan J-9414	
Bedrooms: 3	**Baths: 2½**
Living Area:	
Main floor	1,974 sq. ft.
Total Living Area:	**1,974 sq. ft.**
Standard basement	1,974 sq. ft.
Garage and storage	518 sq. ft.
Exterior Wall Framing:	2x4

Foundation Options:

Standard basement
Crawlspace
Slab
(All plans can be built with your choice of foundation and framing. A generic conversion diagram is available. See order form.)

BLUEPRINT PRICE CODE: **B**

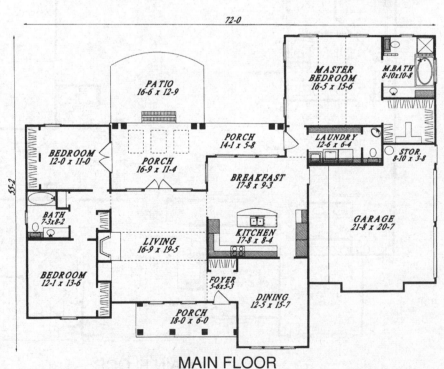

BASEMENT STAIRWAY LOCATION

MAIN FLOOR

ORDER BLUEPRINTS ANYTIME!
CALL TOLL-FREE 1-888-626-2026

Plan J-9414

PRICES AND DETAILS
ON PAGES 13-15

263

Sprawling Brick Beauty

- Exquisite exterior details hint at the many exciting features you'll find inside this sprawling brick beauty.
- The raised foyer boasts a neat display niche above the coat closet to spark interest for your guests.
- Attractive formal spaces unfold from the foyer and share a lofty 11-ft. ceiling.

The fireplace to the left is creatively nestled between built-in book cabinets. French doors whisk you to a lavish backyard covered porch.

- The kitchen and breakfast area flow together near the garage and laundry room for maximum mobility.
- Three bedrooms and two convenient dual-sink baths make up the sleeping wing. Entered through elegant double doors, the master suite offers the owners of the home a private library, garden bath and outdoor access.

Plan L-998-FA	
Bedrooms: 3	**Baths:** 2
Living Area:	
Main floor	1,996 sq. ft.
Total Living Area:	**1,996 sq. ft.**
Garage	449 sq. ft.
Exterior Wall Framing:	2x4
Foundation Options:	

Slab
(All plans can be built with your choice of foundation and framing. A generic conversion diagram is available. See order form.)

BLUEPRINT PRICE CODE:	**B**

MAIN FLOOR

71'-4"

51'-8"

BATH
10' CLG.
SLOPE CLG.

PLANT SHELF ABOVE

LINEN

FRENCH DOOR

2 – CAR GARAGE
20'-4" x 19'-4"

MASTER BEDROOM
15'-4" x 15'
9' STEP-UP CLG.

FRENCH DOORS

PORCH
23' x 10'

UTIL.

PANTRY

KITCHEN
15' x 10'
11' CLG.
SLOPE CLG.

DESK/BOOKS

BATH 2

10' CLG.

PLANT SHELF ABOVE

FRENCH DOORS

BREAKFAST
10' x 10'

HUTCH

DINING
13' x 11'
11' CLG.

BOOKS/CABINETS

BEDROOM 3
11'-4" x 12'
10' CLG.

BEDROOM 2
10'-8" x 13'-4"

LIVING ROOM
15'-4" x 19'-8"
11' CLG.

BOOKS/CABINETS

RAISED FOYER

PORCH

Plan L-998-FA

PRICES AND DETAILS
ON PAGES 13-15

Ever-Popular Floor Plan

- Open living spaces that are well integrated with outdoor areas give this plan its popularity.
- The covered porch ushers guests into a roomy entry that separates the formal entertaining areas.
- Double doors open to the huge family room, which boasts a 13-ft. vaulted ceiling accented by rustic beams, a raised-hearth fireplace and built-in bookshelves. Glass doors lead to a covered porch and an adjoining patio, creating a perfect poolside setting.
- A bayed eating area is open to the family room, separated only by a decorative half-wall, and features a large china hutch and great views. The adjacent kitchen has an angled sink for easy service to the family room and the eating area. The utility room and the garage are close by.
- The master suite is secluded to the rear of the home, with a private bath and access to the patio. The two remaining bedrooms share a dual-access bath.

Plan E-2000

Bedrooms: 3		**Baths:** 2	
Living Area:			
Main floor		2,009 sq. ft.	
Total Living Area:		**2,009 sq. ft.**	
Garage and storage		550 sq. ft.	
Exterior Wall Framing:		2x4	

Foundation Options:

Crawlspace
Slab
(All plans can be built with your choice of foundation and framing. A generic conversion diagram is available. See order form.)

BLUEPRINT PRICE CODE: C

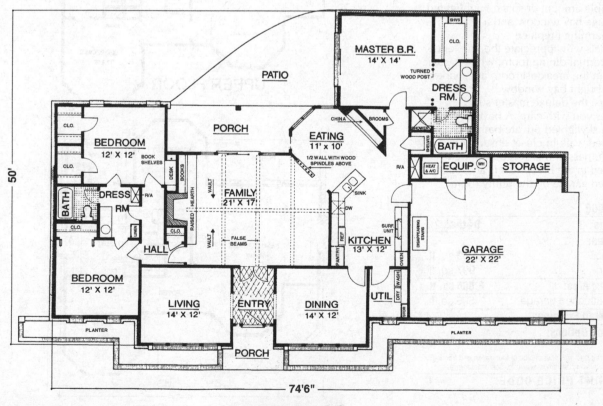

MAIN FLOOR

ORDER BLUEPRINTS ANYTIME!
CALL TOLL-FREE 1-888-626-2026

Plan E-2000

**PRICES AND DETAILS
ON PAGES 13-15**

265

Some Romantic Feeling

- Seemingly saved from some romantic era, this picturesque Victorian-style home will capture your heart.
- You can spend almost the entire day outside if you want; a great wraparound veranda in front and a covered porch in back are nice spots to while away a sunny day.
- Indoors, the family room offers an incredible amount of space, highlighted by a huge bay window and a heartwarming fireplace.
- Gourmets will appreciate the ambience of the formal dining room, while casual meals in the breakfast room are sparked by the bright bay window.
- Upstairs, the deluxe master suite handles you with care. A bayed sitting area, a skylighted private bath and an L-shaped walk-in closet ensure the peacefulness of this gorgeous retreat.
- Included in the blueprints is an optional attached garage off the utility room.

Plan L-2066

Bedrooms: 3	Baths: 2½
Living Area:	
Upper floor	1,069 sq. ft.
Main floor	997 sq. ft.
Total Living Area:	**2,066 sq. ft.**
Optional attached garage	506 sq. ft.
Exterior Wall Framing:	2x4
Foundation Options:	

Slab
(All plans can be built with your choice of foundation and framing. A generic conversion diagram is available. See order form.)

BLUEPRINT PRICE CODE: **C**

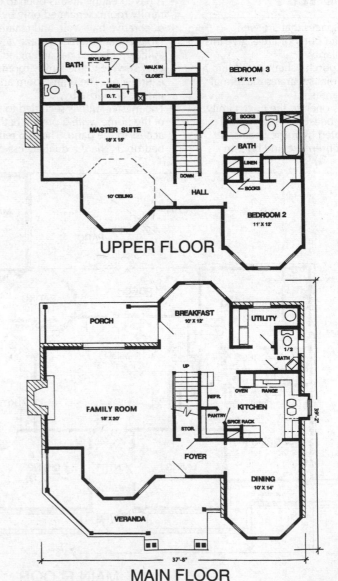

UPPER FLOOR

MAIN FLOOR

ORDER BLUEPRINTS ANYTIME!
CALL TOLL-FREE 1-888-626-2026

Plan L-2066

PRICES AND DETAILS
ON PAGES 13-15

Symmetry and Style

- This appealing one-story home boasts a striking facade with symmetrical rooflines, stately columns and terrific transoms.
- The formal living spaces have a classic split design, perfect for quiet times and conversation.
- The unique design of the bedroom wing gives each bedroom easy access to a full bath. The rear bedroom also enjoys pool and patio proximity.
- The huge family room, which opens up to the patio with 12-ft. pocket sliding doors, has plenty of space for a fireplace and media equipment.
- The master suite just off the kitchen and nook is private yet easily accessible. One unique feature is its bed wall with high glass above. The master bath offers a walk-in closet, a corner tub, a step down shower and a private toilet room.
- Throughout the home, volume ceilings to a height of at least ten feet increase the spacious, airy feeling.

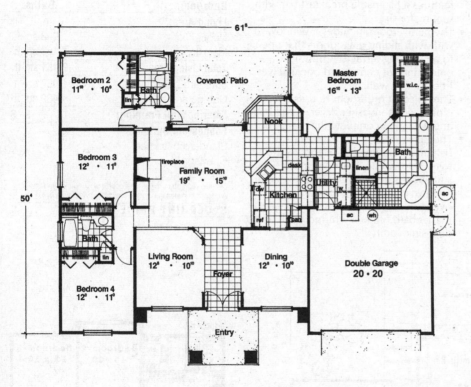

MAIN FLOOR

Plan HDS-99-147	
Bedrooms: 4	**Baths:** 3
Living Area:	
Main floor	2,089 sq. ft.
Total Living Area:	**2,089 sq. ft.**
Garage	415 sq. ft.
Exterior Wall Framing:	2x4
Foundation Options:	
Slab	
(Typical foundation & framing conversion diagram available—see order form.)	
BLUEPRINT PRICE CODE:	C

ORDER BLUEPRINTS ANYTIME!
CALL TOLL-FREE 1-888-626-2020

Plan HDS-99-147

*PRICES AND DETAILS
ON PAGES 13-15*

267

Colonial for Today

- Designed for a growing family, this handsome traditional home offers four bedrooms plus a den and three complete baths. The Colonial exterior is updated by a covered front entry porch with a fanlight window above.
- The dramatic tiled foyer is two stories high and provides direct access to all of the home's living areas. The spacious living room has an inviting brick fireplace and sliding pocket doors to the adjoining dining room.
- Overlooking the backyard, the huge combination kitchen/family room is the

home's hidden charm. The kitchen features a peninsula breakfast bar with seating for six.
- The family room includes a window wall with sliding glass doors that open to an enticing terrace. A built-in entertainment center and bookshelves line another wall.
- The adjacent mudroom houses a pantry closet and the washer/dryer. A full bath and a big den complete the main floor.
- The upper floor is highlighted by a beautiful balcony that overlooks the foyer below. The luxurious master suite boasts a skylighted dressing area and two closets, including an oversized walk-in closet. The private master bath offers a whirlpool tub and a dual-sink vanity.

Plan AHP-7050

Bedrooms: 4+	Baths: 3
Living Area:	
Upper floor	998 sq. ft.
Main floor	1,153 sq. ft.
Total Living Area:	**2,151 sq. ft.**
Standard basement	1,067 sq. ft.
Garage and storage	439 sq. ft.
Exterior Wall Framing:	2x6

Foundation Options:

Standard basement
Crawlspace
Slab

(All plans can be built with your choice of foundation and framing. A generic conversion diagram is available. See order form.)

BLUEPRINT PRICE CODE:	C

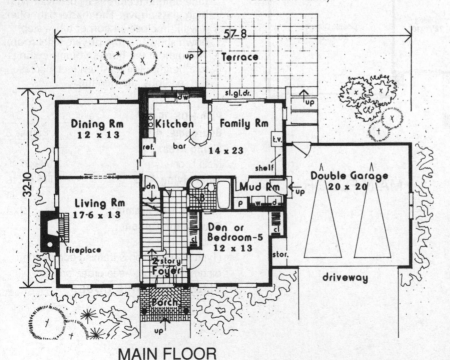

MAIN FLOOR

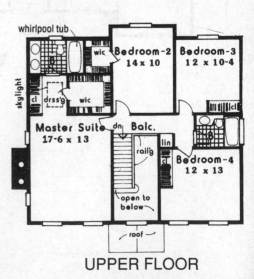

UPPER FLOOR

Plan AHP-7050

PRICES AND DETAILS
ON PAGES 13-15

Down-Home Country Flavor!

- Open living areas, decorative dormers and a spacious wraparound porch give this charming home its country feel.
- The main entrance opens into an enormous living room, which boasts a handsome fireplace flanked by bright windows and built-in cabinets.
- The adjoining dining room is brightened by windows on three sides. A rear French door opens to the porch.
- The modern kitchen serves the dining room over an eating bar. A half-bath and a laundry/utility area with access to the garage and porch are nearby.
- The removed master bedroom includes a roomy walk-in closet and a private bath with a corner shower and a dual-sink vanity with knee space.
- All main-floor rooms have 9-ft. ceilings.
- Two upper-floor bedrooms share a hallway bath, which is enhanced by one of three dormer windows.

Plan J-90013

Bedrooms: 3	Baths: 2½
Living Area:	
Upper floor	823 sq. ft.
Main floor	1,339 sq. ft.
Total Living Area:	**2,162 sq. ft.**
Standard basement	1,339 sq. ft.
Garage	413 sq. ft.
Storage	106 sq. ft.
Exterior Wall Framing:	2x4

Foundation Options:

Standard basement

Crawlspace

Slab

(All plans can be built with your choice of foundation and framing. A generic conversion diagram is available. See order form.)

BLUEPRINT PRICE CODE: C

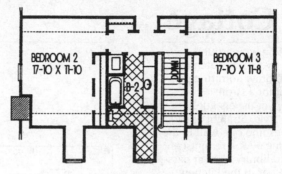

UPPER FLOOR

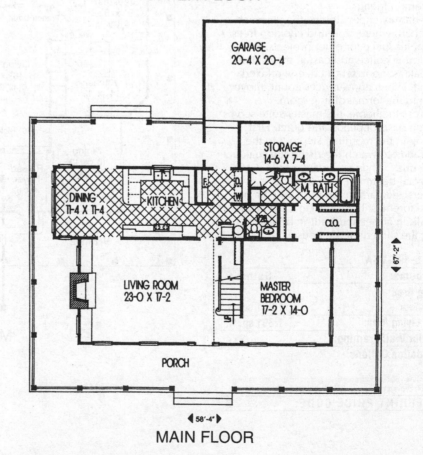

MAIN FLOOR

ORDER BLUEPRINTS ANYTIME!
CALL TOLL-FREE 1-888-626-2026

Plan J-90013

PRICES AND DETAILS
ON PAGES 13-15

269

Quite a Cottage

- This cottage's inviting wraparound veranda is topped by an eye-catching metal roof that will draw admiring gazes from neighbors out for a stroll.
- Inside, the raised foyer ushers guests into your home in style. Straight ahead, built-in bookshelves line one wall in the living room, creating a look reminiscent of an old-fashioned library. A neat pass-through to the wet bar in the kitchen saves trips back and forth when you entertain friends.
- The family chef will love the gourmet kitchen, where an island cooktop frees counter space for other projects. For morning coffee and casual meals, the breakfast nook sets a cheery, relaxed tone. When appearances count, move out to the formal dining room.
- Across the home, the master suite serves as an oasis of peace and quiet. First thing in the morning, step out to the veranda to watch the rising sun soak up the mist. When you want a little extra special treatment, sink into the oversized garden tub for a long bath.
- The foremost bedroom boasts a large walk-in closet and built-in bookshelves for the student of the house.

Plan L-893-VSA

Bedrooms: 3	Baths: 2

Living Area:

Main floor	1,891 sq. ft.
Total Living Area:	**1,891 sq. ft.**
Exterior Wall Framing:	2x4

Foundation Options:

Slab

(All plans can be built with your choice of foundation and framing. A generic conversion diagram is available. See order form.)

BLUEPRINT PRICE CODE:	B

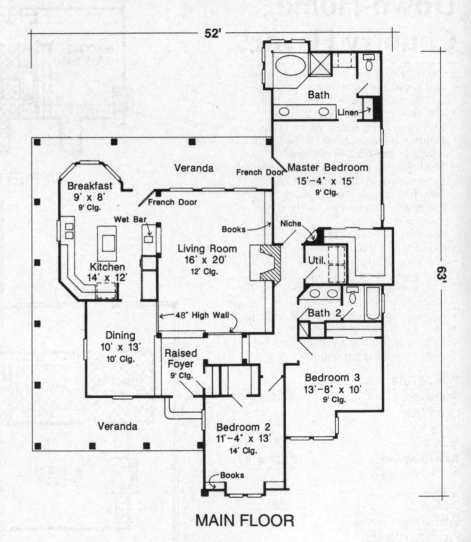

MAIN FLOOR

A Move Up

- Narrow lap siding and repeated round-top windows with divided panes give this traditional home a different look.
- The roomy interior offers space for the upwardly mobile family, with four to five bedrooms and large activity areas.
- The two-story foyer welcomes guests into a spacious formal area that combines the living and dining rooms. The rooms share a dramatic 13-ft. cathedral ceiling, while a handsome fireplace adds a peaceful glow.
- Behind double doors is a cozy study or fifth bedroom.
- A second fireplace and a media center make the family room a fun retreat. French doors open to a lovely terrace.
- Adjoining the family room is a well-designed kitchen with a bayed dinette.
- Double doors introduce the secluded master suite, which boasts a 12-ft. sloped ceiling and a quiet terrace. The private bath offers an invigorating whirlpool tub under a skylight.
- Three more bedrooms and another bath occupy the upper floor.

Plan AHP-9396

Bedrooms: 4+	Baths: 2½
Living Area:	
Upper floor	643 sq. ft.
Main floor	1,553 sq. ft.
Total Living Area:	**2,196 sq. ft.**
Standard basement	1,553 sq. ft.
Garage and storage	502 sq. ft.
Exterior Wall Framing:	2x4 or 2x6

Foundation Options:

Standard basement

Crawlspace

Slab

(All plans can be built with your choice of foundation and framing. A generic conversion diagram is available. See order form.)

BLUEPRINT PRICE CODE: C

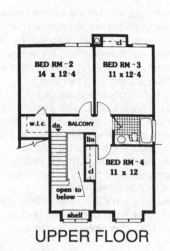

UPPER FLOOR

VIEW INTO LIVING AND DINING ROOMS

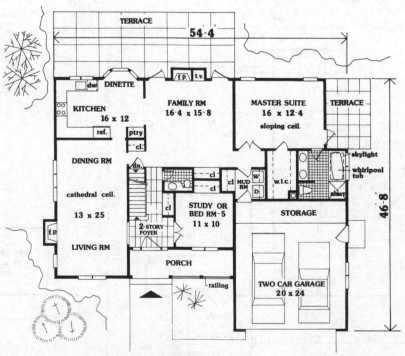

MAIN FLOOR

ORDER BLUEPRINTS ANYTIME!
CALL TOLL-FREE 1-888-626-2026

Plan AHP-9396

PRICES AND DETAILS
ON PAGES 13-15

271

Sweet Communion

- With easy access to the front and rear porches, and a private exit from the master bedroom to the great outdoors, this heartwarming home encourages communion with nature.
- The wide foyer allows guests to freely enter the dining and living rooms.
- In the living room, a prominent fireplace charms the eye and a battery of windows admits light. French doors lead from the living room to a quaint library, complete with a window seat.

- Mornings were made for the breakfast room and kitchen combo. French doors lead from the breakfast room to the front and rear porches, because that first meal of the day tastes better when it's drenched with fresh air!
- If you're concerned about getting a good night's sleep, rest assured you'll enjoy sweet slumber in the master bedroom. French doors let you take in the night sky before turning in.
- The master bath pampers you with a gorgeous oval tub, a separate shower and a dual-sink vanity.
- Upstairs, a balcony hall ushers you past a bookshelf to one of two bedrooms. A full bath completes the scene.

Plan L-268-VSB	
Bedrooms: 3+	**Baths:** 2½
Living Area:	
Upper floor	613 sq. ft.
Main floor	1,653 sq. ft.
Total Living Area:	**2,266 sq. ft.**
Detached garage	521 sq. ft.
Exterior Wall Framing:	2x4
Foundation Options:	

Slab
(All plans can be built with your choice of foundation and framing. A generic conversion diagram is available. See order form.)

BLUEPRINT PRICE CODE:	C

REAR VIEW

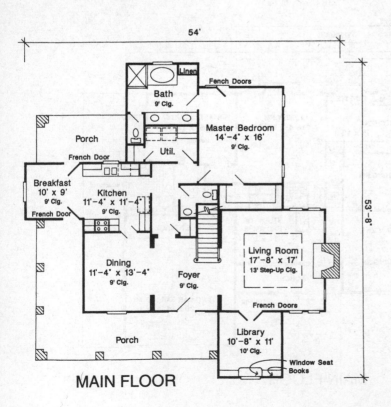

MAIN FLOOR

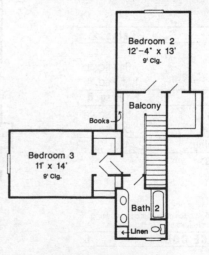

UPPER FLOOR

Grand Colonial Home

- This grand Colonial home boasts a porch entry framed by bay windows and gable towers.
- The two-story foyer flows to the dining room on the left and adjoins the bayed living room on the right, with its warm fireplace and flanking windows.
- At the rear, the family room features a 17-ft. ceiling, a media wall, a bar and terrace access through French doors.
- Connected to the family room is a high-tech kitchen with an island work area, a pantry, a work desk and a circular dinette.
- A private terrace, a romantic fireplace, a huge walk-in closet and a lavish bath with a whirlpool tub are featured in the main-floor master suite.
- Three bedrooms and two full baths share the upper floor.

Plan AHP-9120

Bedrooms: 4	Baths: 3½
Living Area:	
Upper floor	776 sq. ft.
Main floor	1,551 sq. ft.
Total Living Area:	**2,327 sq. ft.**
Standard basement	1,580 sq. ft.
Garage	440 sq. ft.
Exterior Wall Framing:	2x4 or 2x6

Foundation Options:

Standard basement
Crawlspace
Slab
(All plans can be built with your choice of foundation and framing. A generic conversion diagram is available. See order form.)

BLUEPRINT PRICE CODE: C

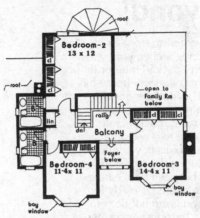

UPPER FLOOR

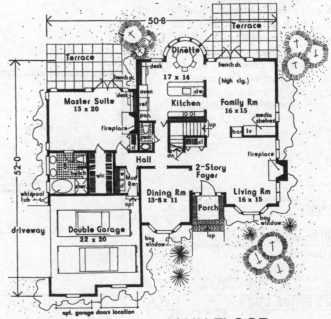

MAIN FLOOR

ORDER BLUEPRINTS ANYTIME!
CALL TOLL-FREE 1-888-626-2026

Plan AHP-9120

PRICES AND DETAILS
ON PAGES 13-15

273

Above and Beyond!

- The strong brick exterior, front-facing gables, eye-catching arched entryway and open, amenity-packed interior let you know that this two-story home has gone above and beyond the norm!
- At the foyer, you're met by the two stunning formal areas; the spacious living room boasts a two-way fireplace while the dining room's bay window adds elegance during dressy meals.
- Smartly situated between both eating areas, the corner kitchen is ready for any culinary mood, from hot dogs to filet mignon. The breakfast area's bay window adds sunshine to your morning.
- For large events, take advantage of the family room's expansiveness, as well as its fireplace, built-in media center and handy access to the backyard.
- An extra sense of openness results from the main floor's 9-ft. ceilings.
- The master suite anchors the upper floor; a cozy sitting area and an enormous private bath are highlights.

Plan L-295-NA

Bedrooms: 3	**Baths:** 2½

Living Area:	
Upper floor	1,066 sq. ft.
Main floor	1,208 sq. ft.
Total Living Area:	**2,274 sq. ft.**
Garage	568 sq. ft.
Exterior Wall Framing:	2x4

Foundation Options:

Slab
(All plans can be built with your choice of foundation and framing. A generic conversion diagram is available. See order form.)

BLUEPRINT PRICE CODE:	**C**

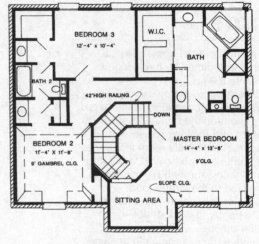

UPPER FLOOR

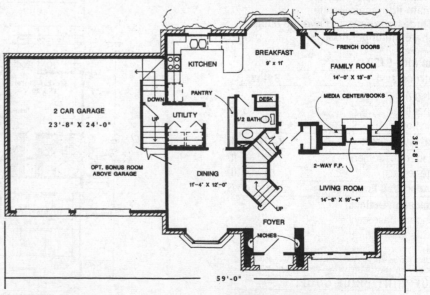

MAIN FLOOR

ORDER BLUEPRINTS ANYTIME!
CALL TOLL-FREE 1-888-626-2026

Plan L-295-NAB

PRICES AND DETAILS
ON PAGES 13-15

Ultra-Modern Mediterranean

- Soaring ceilings, a luxurious master suite and a clean stucco exterior with stylish arched windows give this nouveau-Mediterranean home its unique appeal.

- The magnificent living room and the elegant dining room combine to form one large, open area. The dining room has a tall, arched window and a 12-ft. coffered ceiling. The living room boasts a flat ceiling that is over 12 ft. high, a convenient wet bar and sliding glass doors to the covered patio.

- The informal family room is warmed by a fireplace and shares a soaring 12-ft. flat ceiling with the sunny breakfast area and the large, modern kitchen.

- The kitchen is easily accessible from the family area and the formal dining room, and features an eating bar and a spacious pantry.

- The luxurious master suite offers patio access and is enhanced by an elegant 11-ft., 6-in. tray ceiling and his-and-hers walk-in closets. The huge master bath features a dual-sink vanity, a large tiled shower and a whirlpool tub.

Plan HDS-99-158

Bedrooms: 4	Baths: 3

Living Area:

Main floor	2,352 sq. ft.
Total Living Area:	**2,352 sq. ft.**
Garage	440 sq. ft.

Exterior Wall Framing:
8-in. concrete block and 2x4

Foundation Options:

Slab
(All plans can be built with your choice of foundation and framing. A generic conversion diagram is available. See order form.)

BLUEPRINT PRICE CODE: C

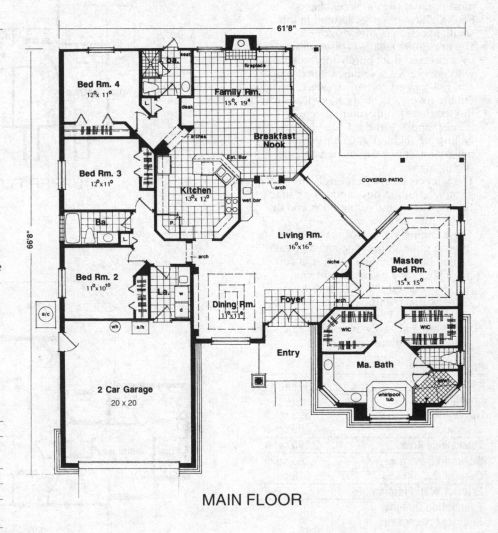

MAIN FLOOR

ORDER BLUEPRINTS ANYTIME!
CALL TOLL-FREE 1-888-626-2026

Plan HDS-99-158

PRICES AND DETAILS
ON PAGES 13-15

275

One More Time!

- The character and excitement of our most popular plan in recent years, E-3000, have been recaptured in this smaller version of the design.
- The appealing facade is distinguished by a covered front porch and accented with decorative columns, triple dormers and rail-topped corner windows.
- Off the foyer, a central gallery leads to the spacious family room, where a corner fireplace and a 17-ft. vaulted ceiling are highlights. Columns in the gallery introduce the kitchen and the dining areas.
- The kitchen showcases a walk-in pantry, a built-in desk and a long snack bar that serves the eating nook and the dining room.
- The stunning main-floor master suite offers a quiet sitting area and a private angled bath with dual vanities, a corner garden tub and a separate shower.
- A lovely curved stairway leads to a balcony that overlooks the family room and the foyer. Two large bedrooms, a split bath and easily accessible attics are also found upstairs.

Plan E-2307-A

Bedrooms: 3	Baths: 2½
Living Area:	
Upper floor	595 sq. ft.
Main floor	1,765 sq. ft.
Total Living Area:	**2,360 sq. ft.**
Standard basement	1,765 sq. ft.
Garage and storage	528 sq. ft.
Exterior Wall Framing:	2x6

Foundation Options:

Standard basement

Crawlspace

Slab

(All plans can be built with your choice of foundation and framing. A generic conversion diagram is available. See order form.)

BLUEPRINT PRICE CODE:	C

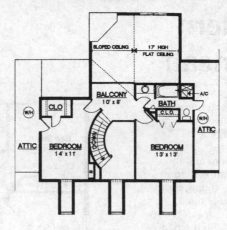

UPPER FLOOR

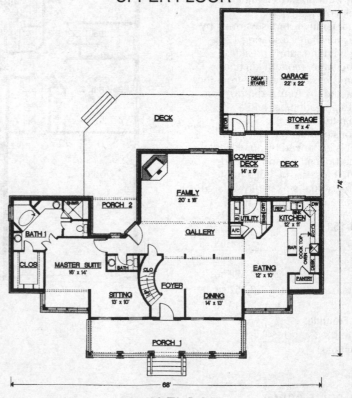

MAIN FLOOR

Plan E-2307-A

PRICES AND DETAILS
ON PAGES 13-15

Rich Victorian

- The deep, rich tradition of Queen Anne Victorian homes is easily understood after close inspection of this marvel.
- Oohs and aahs and envious sighs will come from passersby upon viewing its columned, railed veranda, turrets and fishscale shingles.
- Equally impressive is the interior. The enormous family room anchors the main floor, and features a bay window, a media/book center by a mighty fireplace and windows overlooking the back porch.
- Carefully positioned to serve the bay-windowed breakfast nook and the formal dining room, the island kitchen stands ready for any sort of meal.
- Separated somewhat from the main living area is the recreation room; enter via French doors and enjoy its special sense of privacy. It includes a bay window and access to a third bath which walks out to the back porch.
- Upstairs, the master bedroom will take you back to some noble, romantic era. The dome ceiling in the sitting area, the skylighted bath and the roomy walk-in closet treat you like royalty.
- The two nice-sized secondary bedrooms each boast bookshelves and walk-in closets, and also share a full-sized bath.

Plan L-2412	
Bedrooms: 3+	**Baths: 3**
Living Area:	
Upper floor	1,086 sq. ft.
Main floor	1,326 sq. ft.
Total Living Area:	**2,412 sq. ft.**
Detached garage	576 sq. ft.
Exterior Wall Framing:	2x4

Foundation Options:

Slab
(All plans can be built with your choice of foundation and framing. A generic conversion diagram is available. See order form.)

BLUEPRINT PRICE CODE:	**C**

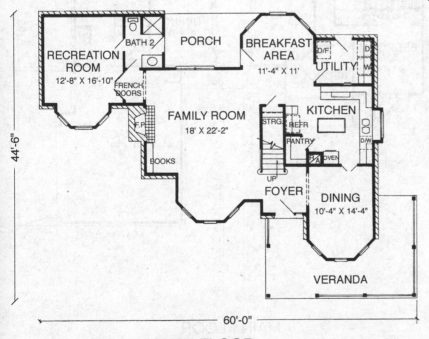

MAIN FLOOR

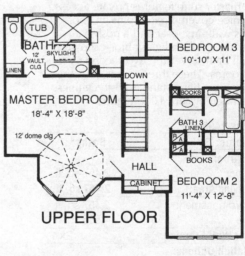

UPPER FLOOR

ORDER BLUEPRINTS ANYTIME!
CALL TOLL-FREE 1-888-626-2026

Plan L-2412

PRICES AND DETAILS
ON PAGES 13-15

277

Sophisticated One-Story

- Beautiful windows accentuated by elegant keystones highlight the exterior of this sophisticated one-story design.
- An open floor plan is the hallmark of the interior, beginning with the foyer that provides instant views of the study as well as the dining and living rooms.
- The spacious living room boasts a fireplace with built-in bookshelves and a rear window wall that stretches into the morning room.
- The sunny morning room has a snack bar to the kitchen. The island kitchen includes a walk-in pantry, a built-in desk and easy access to the utility room and the convenient half-bath.
- The master suite features private access to a nice covered patio, plus an enormous walk-in closet and a posh bath with a spa tub and glass-block shower.
- A hall bath serves the two secondary bedrooms. These three rooms, plus the utility area, have standard 8-ft. ceilings. Other ceilings are 10 ft. high.

Plan DD-2455

Bedrooms: 3+	**Baths:** 2½
Living Area:	
Main floor	2,457 sq. ft.
Total Living Area:	**2,457 sq. ft.**
Standard basement	2,457 sq. ft.
Garage	585 sq. ft.
Exterior Wall Framing:	2x4

Foundation Options:

Standard basement

Crawlspace

Slab

(All plans can be built with your choice of foundation and framing. A generic conversion diagram is available. See order form.)

BLUEPRINT PRICE CODE: C

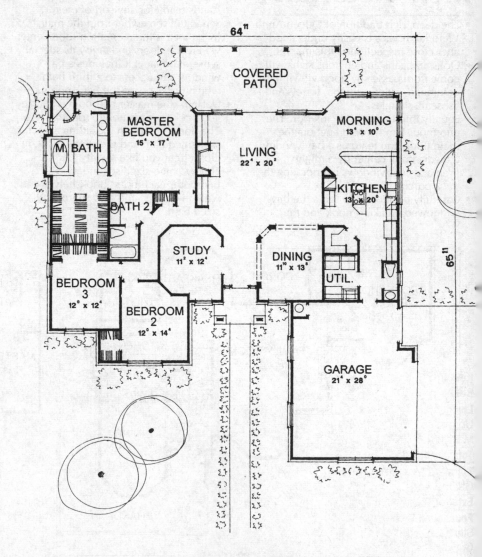

MAIN FLOOR

ORDER BLUEPRINTS ANYTIME!
CALL TOLL-FREE 1-888-626-2026

Plan DD-2455

PRICES AND DETAILS
ON PAGES 13-15

Comfortable Contemporary

- This home's contemporary facade and roofline give way to an impressive Great Room for ultimate comfort.
- The sidelighted two-story foyer unfolds directly to the spectacular sunken Great Room, which is highlighted by a 10-ft., open-beam ceiling. A wood-burning stove, a pair of ceiling fans and two French doors that open to a rear wraparound deck are also showcased.
- Sharing the Great Room's 10-ft. ceiling, the open kitchen boasts an eating bar and a pass-through to the dining area.
- The secluded master bedroom features a TV wall with his-and-hers dressers. A French door provides access to a covered deck. The master bath flaunts a relaxing whirlpool tub and two vanities.
- Where not otherwise noted, the main-floor rooms have 9-ft. ceilings.
- A long balcony on the second level overlooks the foyer. Two good-sized bedrooms offer nice views of the backyard and share a full bath.

Plan LRD-22994

Bedrooms: 3	Baths: 2½
Living Area:	
Upper floor	692 sq. ft.
Main floor	1,777 sq. ft.
Total Living Area:	**2,469 sq. ft.**
Standard basement	1,655 sq. ft.
Garage	550 sq. ft.
Exterior Wall Framing:	2x6

Foundation Options:

Standard basement
Crawlspace
Slab
(All plans can be built with your choice of foundation and framing. A generic conversion diagram is available. See order form.)

BLUEPRINT PRICE CODE: C

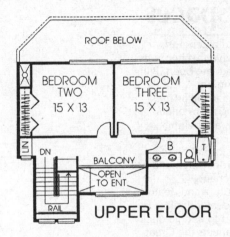

UPPER FLOOR

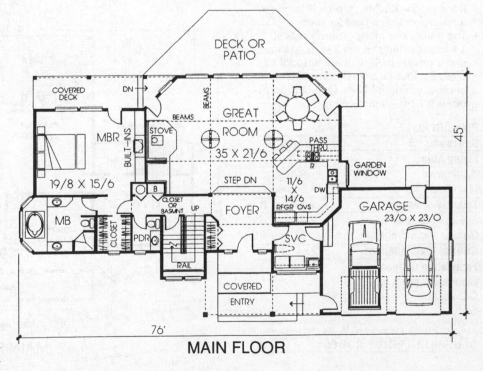

MAIN FLOOR

ORDER BLUEPRINTS ANYTIME!
CALL TOLL-FREE 1-888-626-2026

Plan LRD-22994

PRICES AND DETAILS
ON PAGES 13-15

279

Fantastic Facade, Stunning Spaces

- Matching dormers and a generous covered front porch give this home its fantastic facade. Inside, the open living spaces are just as stunning.

- A two-story foyer bisects the formal living areas. The living room offers three bright windows, an inviting fireplace and sliding French doors to the Great Room. The formal dining room overlooks the front porch and has easy access to the kitchen.

- The Great Room is truly grand, featuring a fireplace and a TV center flanked by French doors that lead to a large deck.

- A circular dinette connects the Great Room to the kitchen, which is handy to a mudroom and a powder room.

- The main-floor master suite boasts a 14-ft. cathedral ceiling, a walk-in closet and a private bath with a whirlpool tub.

- Upstairs, four large bedrooms share another whirlpool bath. One bedroom offers a 12-ft. sloped ceiling.

Plan AHP-9397

Bedrooms: 5	Baths: 2½
Living Area:	
Upper floor	928 sq. ft.
Main floor	1,545 sq. ft.
Total Living Area:	**2,473 sq. ft.**
Standard basement	1,545 sq. ft.
Garage and storage	432 sq. ft.
Exterior Wall Framing:	2x4 or 2x6

Foundation Options:

Standard basement

Crawlspace

Slab

(All plans can be built with your choice of foundation and framing. A generic conversion diagram is available. See order form.)

BLUEPRINT PRICE CODE: C

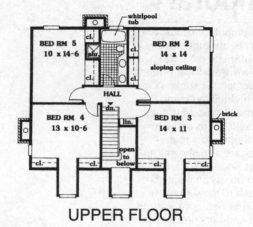

UPPER FLOOR

MAIN FLOOR

Plan AHP-9397

PRICES AND DETAILS
ON PAGES 13-15

Genteel Luxury

- This extraordinary home offers countless details and genteel luxury.
- In the foyer, an elegant marble floor and an 11-ft. ceiling define the sunny space.
- A fireplace serves as the focal point of the living room, which extends to the dining room to isolate formal affairs. The dining room features a bay window and a French door to a lush courtyard. Both rooms feature 11-ft. ceilings.
- A columned serving counter separates the kitchen from the breakfast nook and the family room. A convenient built-in desk to the right is a great place to jot down a grocery list.
- A 14-ft. ceiling soars over the versatile family room, where a corner fireplace and a French door to the backyard are great additions.
- A 10-ft. stepped ceiling, a romantic fireplace, a quiet desk and access to the backyard make the master bedroom an inviting retreat. A luxurious raised tub and a sit-down shower highlight the master bath, which also includes a neat dressing table between two sinks.
- Two more bedrooms, one with an 11-ft. ceiling and a bay window, share a bath.
- Unless otherwise mentioned, each room includes a 9-ft. ceiling.

VIEW INTO KITCHEN

REAR VIEW

Plan L-483-HB

Bedrooms: 3	Baths: 2
Living Area:	
Main floor	2,481 sq. ft.
Total Living Area:	**2,481 sq. ft.**
Garage	706 sq. ft.
Exterior Wall Framing:	2x4

Foundation Options:

Slab

(All plans can be built with your choice of foundation and framing. A generic conversion diagram is available. See order form.)

BLUEPRINT PRICE CODE:	C

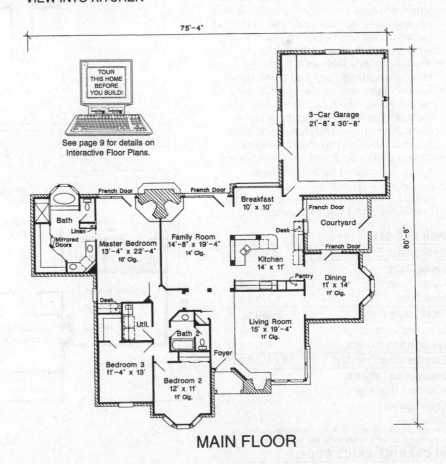

TOUR THIS HOME BEFORE YOU BUILD!

See page 9 for details on Interactive Floor Plans.

75'-4"

80'-8"

3-Car Garage
21'-8" x 30'-8"

French Door   French Door

Bath

Linen

Mirrored Doors

Master Bedroom
13'-4" x 22'-4"
10' Clg.

Family Room
14'-8" x 19'-4"
14' Clg.

Breakfast
10' x 10'

French Door

Courtyard

French Door

Desk

Kitchen
14' x 11'

Pantry

Dining
11' x 14'
1' Clg.

Desk

Utll.

Bath 2

Living Room
15' x 19'-4"
1' Clg.

Foyer

Bedroom 3
11'-4" x 13'

Bedroom 2
12' x 11'
1' Clg.

MAIN FLOOR

ORDER BLUEPRINTS ANYTIME!
CALL TOLL-FREE 1-888-626-2026

Plan L-483-HB

PRICES AND DETAILS
ON PAGES 13-15

281

Picture-Perfect

- Those tall, cold glasses of summertime lemonade will taste even better when enjoyed on the shady front porch of this picture-perfect home.
- Inside, the two-story, sidelighted foyer unfolds to the formal living areas and the Great Room beyond.
- Fireplaces grace the living room and the Great Room, which are separated by French pocket doors. A TV nook borders the fireplace in the Great Room, letting the kids catch their favorite show while Mom and Dad fix dinner in the kitchen. Two sets of French doors swing wide to reveal a backyard deck.
- A glassy dinette with an 8-ft. ceiling makes breakfasts cozy and comfortable.
- Restful nights will be the norm in the master suite, which boasts a 14-ft. cathedral ceiling. Next to the walk-in closet, the private bath has a whirlpool tub in a fabulous boxed-out window.
- Unless otherwise noted, all main-floor rooms are topped by 9-ft. ceilings.
- At day's end, guests and children may retire to the upper floor, where four big bedrooms and a full bath await them.

Plan AHP-9512

Bedrooms: 5	Baths: 2½
Living Area:	
Upper floor	928 sq. ft.
Main floor	1,571 sq. ft.
Total Living Area:	**2,499 sq. ft.**
Standard basement	1,571 sq. ft.
Garage and storage	420 sq. ft.
Exterior Wall Framing:	2x4 or 2x6

Foundation Options:

Standard basement
Crawlspace
Slab

(All plans can be built with your choice of foundation and framing. A generic conversion diagram is available. See order form.)

BLUEPRINT PRICE CODE: C

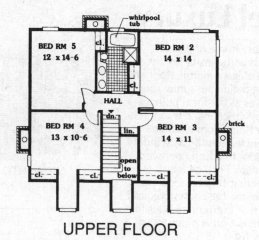

UPPER FLOOR

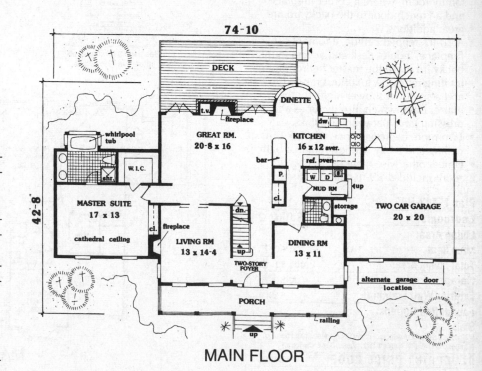

MAIN FLOOR

Plan AHP-9512

PRICES AND DETAILS
ON PAGES 13-15

Practicality, Plus!

- Impressive looks and volume define this delightful and practical home.
- The 17-ft.-high vaulted entry and living room create an immediate and exciting spatial dimension. The addition of an open stairway, a soaring fireplace and a view of the upper loft make the living area seem double its size.
- You'll appreciate the separation of formal dining and everyday dining when your home is hosting a special event. Both the dining room and the eat-in kitchen have plenty of table and chair space. The kitchen expands to a side patio through sliding glass doors.
- Double closets and a personal dressing area offer a measure of privacy to the home owners in the spacious main-floor master bedroom.
- Upstairs, two more bedrooms share a second full bath.
- The loft that overlooks the living room and entry could be used as a homework, TV or play area for the kids.

Plan B-7947

Bedrooms: 3	Baths: 2
Living Area:	
Upper floor	639 sq. ft.
Main floor	1,065 sq. ft.
Total Living Area:	**1,704 sq. ft.**
Standard basement	1,065 sq. ft.
Garage	440 sq. ft.
Exterior Wall Framing:	2x4

Foundation Options:

Standard basement

(All plans can be built with your choice of foundation and framing. A generic conversion diagram is available. See order form.)

BLUEPRINT PRICE CODE: B

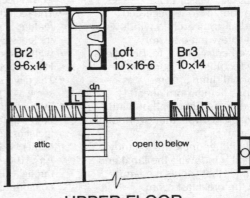

UPPER FLOOR

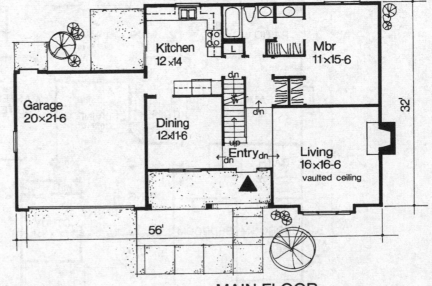

MAIN FLOOR

ORDER BLUEPRINTS ANYTIME!
CALL TOLL-FREE 1-888-626-2026

Plan B-7947

PRICES AND DETAILS
ON PAGES 13-15

283

Sprawling One-Story

- A high hip roof, a stone-accented facade and alluring arched windows adorn this sprawling one-story.
- The recessed entry opens to the foyer, where regal columns introduce the elegant formal dining room.
- The spacious living room ahead is highlighted by a bright wall of windows and sliding glass doors that overlook the covered lanai.
- The island kitchen includes a handy pass-through window to the lanai and a snack counter that serves the family room and the breakfast room.

- The family room warms the entire area with a handsome fireplace and opens to a cozy covered patio.
- A French door from the sunny breakfast nook accesses the lanai.
- The secluded master bedroom also features a great view of the lanai, and includes a dressing room, an enormous walk-in closet and a private bath with French-door lanai access.
- The quiet study off the foyer could also serve as a guest bedroom.
- Two additional bedrooms share a hall bath with a dual-sink vanity. Laundry facilities are just steps away. The cozy corner bedroom has an 8-ft. ceiling. Airy 10-ft. ceilings are found throughout the rest of this delightfully comfortable home.

Plan DD-2241-1	
Bedrooms: 3+	Baths: 2
Living Area:	
Main floor	2,256 sq. ft.
Total Living Area:	**2,256 sq. ft.**
Standard basement	2,256 sq. ft.
Garage	469 sq. ft.
Exterior Wall Framing:	2x4

Foundation Options:

Standard basement
Crawlspace
Slab
(All plans can be built with your choice of foundation and framing. A generic conversion diagram is available. See order form.)

BLUEPRINT PRICE CODE: **C**

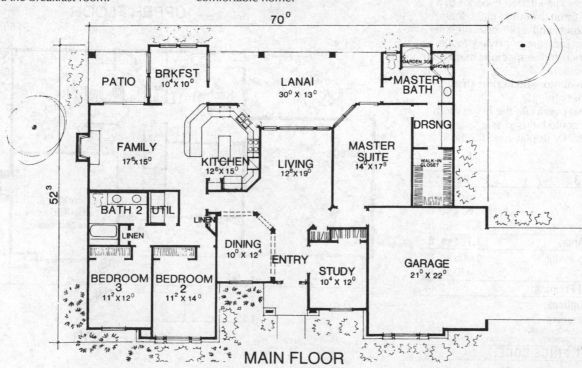

MAIN FLOOR

Plan DD-2241-1

PRICES AND DETAILS
ON PAGES 13-15

Tastefully Appointed

- Cheery dormer windows and a wide, columned front porch greet guests to this tastefully appointed home.
- Inside, the inviting living room boasts a 17-ft. vaulted ceiling and a neat TV nook for casual entertainment.
- A classy, three-sided fireplace warms both the living room and the adjoining formal dining room. Sliding glass doors open onto a nice deck, which is bordered on two sides by a large patio.
- The contemporary island kitchen offers a nifty nook for quick snacks or relaxed breakfasts. A sliding glass door leads to the patio, and a built-in desk is perfect for recording favorite recipes.
- The master bedroom shows off a large walk-in closet and a private bath with a whirlpool tub and a dual-sink vanity.
- Upstairs, eye-catching stepped plant shelves and an impressive loft space overlook the living room below.
- Two secondary bedrooms—one with a walk-in closet—share a full bath.

Plan B-93017

Bedrooms: 3+	Baths: 2½
Living Area:	
Upper floor	672 sq. ft.
Main floor	1,327 sq. ft.
Total Living Area:	**1,999 sq. ft.**
Standard basement	1,327 sq. ft.
Garage	400 sq. ft.
Exterior Wall Framing:	2x4

Foundation Options:

Standard basement
(All plans can be built with your choice of foundation and framing. A generic conversion diagram is available. See order form.)

BLUEPRINT PRICE CODE: B

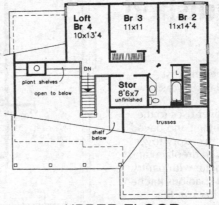

UPPER FLOOR

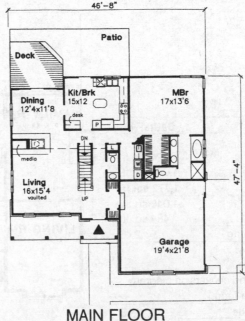

MAIN FLOOR

x

x

A Distinguished Solution

- Distinguishing describes the first impression of this updated two-story traditional.
- A brilliant entry and foyer rises to the upper level; a formal living and bayed dining room flank the two-story foyer.
- A large family room with fireplace and rear view, a bayed dinette with pantry and rear sliders, and a spacious kitchen are all oriented to the back of the home.
- A master bedroom with tray ceiling, plus two secondary bedrooms share the upper floor.

UPPER FLOOR

BR. #3
11-0 X 10-8

BR. #1
16-0 X 13-0
TRAY CLG

CLOS

BATH

TC

HALL

DN

BALC

CLOS

W.I.C.

BR. #2
12-0 X 10-0

MAIN FLOOR

56-0

FAMILY RM
12-0 X 16-0

DINETTE
10-8 X 9-6

DW

CLOS

LAUN

KITCHEN
11-6 X 11-0

MUD

REF

PDR

BC

PAN

DN

UP

CLOS

LIVING RM
12-0 X 14-0

FOYER

DINING RM
12-0 X 13-0

GARAGE
22-0 X 22-0

PORCH

33-6

Plan A-2238-DS	
Bedrooms: 3	**Baths: 1 ½**
Space:	
Upper floor	724 sq. ft.
Main floor	1,048 sq. ft.
Total Living Area	**1,772 sq. ft.**
Basement	1,048 sq. ft.
Garage	484 sq. ft.
Exterior Wall Framing	**2x6**
Foundation options:	
Standard Basement	
(Foundation & framing conversion diagram available—see order form.)	
Blueprint Price Code	**B**

286

ORDER BLUEPRINTS ANYTIME!
CALL TOLL-FREE 1-888-626-2026

Plan A-2238-DS

PRICES AND DETAILS
ON PAGES 13-15

French Charm

- The exterior of this charming French home displays great details, including attractive keystones, neat quoins and huge arched window arrangements.
- Inside the home, a high plant ledge adorns the tiled foyer, which boasts a dramatic 13-ft. ceiling.
- To the left, the elegant formal dining room extends to the huge living room, which boasts a warm fireplace and neat built-in bookshelves above functional cabinets. A striking 10-ft. ceiling soars above both rooms.
- A convenient serving bar links the gourmet kitchen to the sunny bayed breakfast nook. The adjacent utility room includes a handy pantry closet.
- Across the home, a tiled foyer features access to a covered porch and the luxurious master suite. The master suite boasts a sloped 10-ft. ceiling, a window seat and a lush private bath, which is highlighted by a marble tub set into a boxed-out window.
- Two more bedrooms share a hall bath. One bedroom features a sloped 10-ft. ceiling and a nice built-in desk.

Plan RD-1714

Bedrooms: 3	**Baths:** 2

Living Area:	
Main floor	1,714 sq. ft.
Total Living Area:	**1,714 sq. ft.**
Garage and storage	470 sq. ft.
Exterior Wall Framing:	2x4

Foundation Options:
Crawlspace
Slab
(All plans can be built with your choice of foundation and framing. A generic conversion diagram is available. See order form.)

BLUEPRINT PRICE CODE: **B**

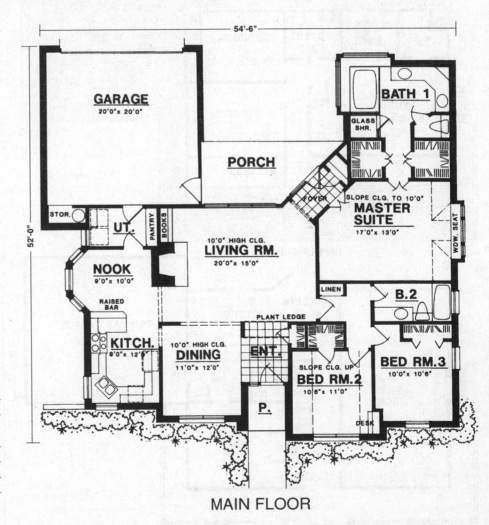

MAIN FLOOR

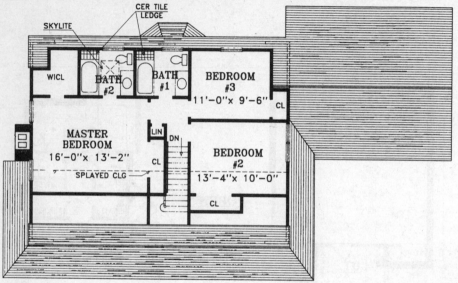

UPPER FLOOR

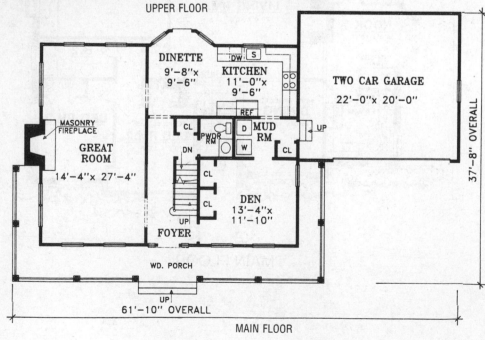

MAIN FLOOR

Quaint Country Design

- The renewed "country" look is evident in this simply designed two-story with wrap-around front porch.
- Functional living areas flank the entryway and stairs.
- A beautiful and spacious Great Room, with masonry fireplace and wrap-around windows, is to the left, and a nice-sized den which could serve as a library, office, guest room or fourth bedroom is to the right.
- The kitchen is a lovely space with two separate areas, an efficient work area and a distinct bay windowed dining area with center door leading to the rear yard.
- The second floor includes a master bedroom with full private bath and two large closets, plus two secondary bedrooms.

Plan AX-89311

Bedrooms: 3	Baths: 2½

Space:	
Upper floor:	736 sq. ft.
Main floor:	1,021 sq. ft.

Total living area:	**1,757 sq. ft.**
Basement:	approx. 1,021 sq. ft.
Garage:	440 sq. ft.

Exterior Wall Framing:	2x4

Foundation options:
Standard basement.
Slab.
(Foundation & framing conversion diagram available — see order form.)

Blueprint Price Code:	B

Plan AX-89311

PRICES AND DETAILS
ON PAGES 13-15

Style and Affordability

- This attractive family home offers affordability with style and openness.
- A brick planter accents the inviting covered porch. Inside, the sidelighted entry flows into the bright and spacious living room, with its 16½-ft. sloped ceiling and heat-circulating fireplace. Next to the fireplace, a wood bin is located beneath TV and stereo shelves.
- The sizable dining room opens to a backyard patio through French doors. The efficient U-shaped kitchen shares a serving counter with the dining room, for easy entertaining.
- On the upper floor, a railed balcony overlooks the entry and the living room.
- The bright master bedroom boasts a private bath, a walk-in closet and a handy linen closet.
- Two nice secondary bedrooms share a full bath with a large linen closet. A hallway closet provides additional storage space.

Plans H-3741-1 & -1A

Bedrooms: 3	Baths: 2½
Living Area:	
Upper floor	900 sq. ft.
Main floor	853 sq. ft.
Total Living Area:	**1,753 sq. ft.**
Standard basement	853 sq. ft.
Garage	520 sq. ft.
Exterior Wall Framing:	2x6
Foundation Options:	**Plan #**
Standard basement	H-3741-1
Crawlspace	H-3741-1A
(All plans can be built with your choice of foundation and framing. A generic conversion diagram is available. See order form.)	
BLUEPRINT PRICE CODE:	**B**

UPPER FLOOR

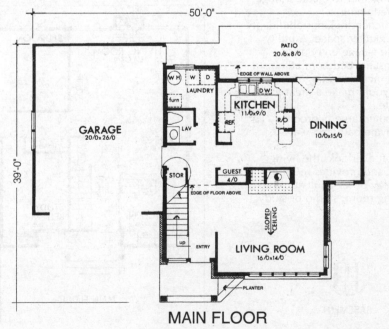

MAIN FLOOR

BASEMENT STAIRWAY LOCATION

ORDER BLUEPRINTS ANYTIME!
CALL TOLL-FREE 1-888-626-2026

Plans H-3741-1 & -1A

PRICES AND DETAILS
ON PAGES 13-15

289

Clean, Stylish Lines

- The sweeping roofline and arched windows give this home plenty of "presence", even though it is fairly modest in size.
- Besides being stylish, the plan is also sturdy and energy-efficient, with 2x6 walls, R-19 perimeter insulation and R-38 in the ceilings.
- The sheltered entry leads to an effective foyer which in turn leads visitors to the dining area or living room. These two spaces flow together to create a huge space for entertaining.
- The roomy kitchen includes abundant cabinet and counter space. A utility room is in the garage entry area.
- A large downstairs bedroom adjoins a full bath and includes a large walk-in closet. This would make a great guest or in-law suite.
- Upstairs, another large bedroom features a private bath and walk-in closet.
- A versatile loft overlooks the living room below, and provides room for children to play or for adults to keep a library, sewing room, studio or study.

UPPER FLOOR

BASEMENT

Plans H-1448-1 & -1A	
Bedrooms: 2-3	**Baths:** 2
Space:	
Upper floor	487 sq. ft.
Main floor	1,278 sq. ft.
Total Living Area	**1,765 sq. ft.**
Basement	1,278 sq. ft.
Garage	409 sq. ft.
Exterior Wall Framing	2x6
Foundation options:	Plan #
Standard Basement	H-1448-1
Crawlspace	H-1448-1A
(Foundation & framing conversion diagram available—see order form.)	
Blueprint Price Code	B

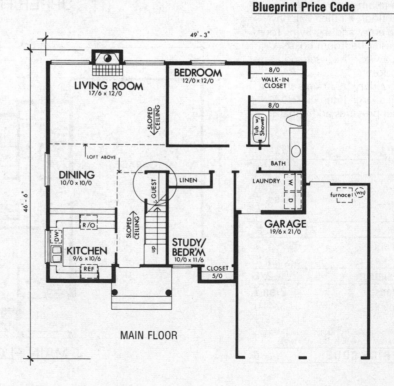

MAIN FLOOR

New Traditional

- A lovely front porch and an open floor plan give this new traditional its modern appeal.
- The foyer opens to a fabulous living room with a 16-ft. vaulted ceiling, a fireplace and an open staircase. Railings introduce the bayed breakfast area. The efficient galley-style kitchen leads to a covered back porch.
- The sizable master suite is enhanced by a 10-ft. raised ceiling and a cozy bay window. The compartmentalized bath includes a dual-sink vanity and a walk-in closet. Another bedroom is nearby, along with a convenient laundry closet.
- Upstairs, a third bedroom has private access to a full bath. A large future area provides expansion space.

Plan J-8636

Bedrooms: 3	Baths: 3
Living Area:	
Upper floor	270 sq. ft.
Main floor	1,253 sq. ft.
Bonus room	270 sq. ft.
Total Living Area:	**1,793 sq. ft.**
Standard basement	1,287 sq. ft.
Garage	390 sq. ft.
Exterior Wall Framing:	2x4

Foundation Options:
Standard basement
Crawlspace
Slab
(All plans can be built with your choice of foundation and framing. A generic conversion diagram is available. See order form.)

BLUEPRINT PRICE CODE: B

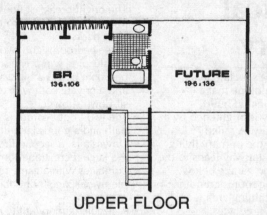

UPPER FLOOR

See this plan on our "Country & Traditional" Video Tour! Order form on page 9

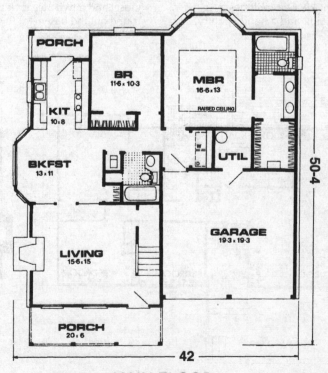

MAIN FLOOR

ORDER BLUEPRINTS ANYTIME!
CALL TOLL-FREE 1-888-626-2026

Plan J-8636

PRICES AND DETAILS
ON PAGES 13-15

291

Economical Split-Entry

- This split-entry home's rectangular shape and straight roofline make it simple and economical to build.
- The sidelighted entry is brightened by a large transom window. A railed stairway leads up to the primary living areas and a second stairway leads to the recreation spaces and garage below.
- The living and dining rooms combine for a spacious entertaining area, featuring a fabulous fireplace.
- The efficient kitchen includes a windowed sink and a handy pantry.

The bright breakfast nook gives access to a backyard deck through sliding glass doors.
- Three bedrooms and two baths occupy the sleeping wing. The secluded master bedroom boasts a big walk-in closet and a private bath with an oversized, sit-down shower.
- The two front bedrooms share the main bath and a good-sized linen closet.
- Downstairs, a second fireplace warms the large recreation room, which combines with a game room to provide plenty of space for hobbies and relaxation.
- A sizable laundry/utility room, a storage closet and a two-car, tuck-under garage round out the basement level.

Plan H-1332-5	
Bedrooms: 3	**Baths:** 2
Living Area:	
Main floor	1,262 sq. ft.
Daylight basement	576 sq. ft.
Total Living Area:	**1,838 sq. ft.**
Tuck-under garage	576 sq. ft.
Exterior Wall Framing:	2x6

Foundation Options:

Daylight basement
(All plans can be built with your choice of foundation and framing. A generic conversion diagram is available. See order form.)

BLUEPRINT PRICE CODE: B

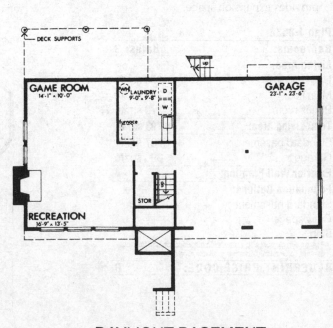

MAIN FLOOR

DAYLIGHT BASEMENT

Indoor/Outdoor Pleasure

- For a sloping, scenic lake or mountain lot, this spectacular design hugs the hill and takes full advantage of the views.
- A three-sided wraparound deck makes indoor/outdoor living a pleasure.
- The sunken living room—with a 19-ft. cathedral ceiling, a skylight, a beautiful fireplace and glass galore—is the heart of the floor plan.
- The formal dining room and the kitchen both overlook the living room and the surrounding deck beyond.
- The main-floor master bedroom has a 12-ft. cathedral ceiling and private access to the deck and hall bath.
- Two more bedrooms upstairs share a skylighted bath and flank a dramatic balcony sitting area overlooking the living room below.

Plan AX-98607

Bedrooms: 3	Baths: 2
Living Area:	
Upper floor	531 sq. ft.
Main floor	1,098 sq. ft.
Total Living Area:	**1,629 sq. ft.**
Standard basement	894 sq. ft.
Garage	327 sq. ft.
Exterior Wall Framing:	2x4

Foundation Options:

Standard basement

Slab

(All plans can be built with your choice of foundation and framing. A generic conversion diagram is available. See order form.)

BLUEPRINT PRICE CODE: B

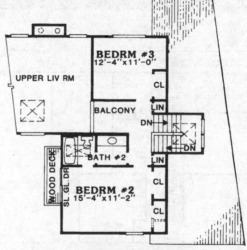

UPPER FLOOR

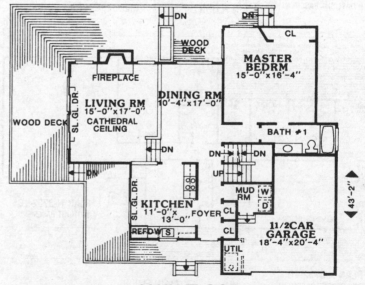

MAIN FLOOR

Plan AX-98607

PRICES AND DETAILS
ON PAGES 13-15

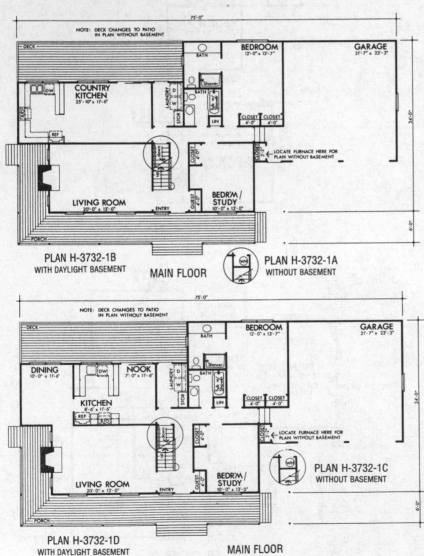

NOTE: DECK CHANGES TO PATIO IN PLAN WITHOUT BASEMENT

75'-0"

DECK

COUNTRY KITCHEN
25'-10" x 11'-6"

BEDROOM
12'-0" x 13'-7"

GARAGE
21'-7" x 23'-3"

BATH
BATH
LAUNDRY
STOR
LIN

CLOSET 4'-0"
CLOSET 4'-0"

LOCATE FURNACE HERE FOR PLAN WITHOUT BASEMENT

LIVING ROOM
20'-0" x 13'-0"

GUEST

BEDR'M / STUDY
10'-0" x 13'-0"

ENTRY

PORCH

34'-0"

6'-0"

PLAN H-3732-1B
WITH DAYLIGHT BASEMENT

MAIN FLOOR

PLAN H-3732-1A
WITHOUT BASEMENT

NOTE: DECK CHANGES TO PATIO IN PLAN WITHOUT BASEMENT

75'-0"

DECK

DINING
10'-0" x 11'-6"

NOOK
7'-0" x 11'-6"

KITCHEN
8'-6" x 11'-6"

REF

BEDROOM
12'-0" x 13'-7"

GARAGE
21'-7" x 23'-3"

BATH
BATH
LAUNDRY
STOR
LIN

CLOSET 4'-0"
CLOSET 4'-0"

LOCATE FURNACE HERE FOR PLAN WITHOUT BASEMENT

LIVING ROOM
20'-0" x 13'-0"

GUEST

BEDR'M / STUDY
10'-0" x 13'-0"

ENTRY

PORCH

34'-0"

6'-0"

PLAN H-3732-1C
WITHOUT BASEMENT

PLAN H-3732-1D
WITH DAYLIGHT BASEMENT

MAIN FLOOR

Old Homestead

Almost everyone has a soft place in his heart for a certain home in his childhood. A home like this one, with understated farmhouse styling and wrap-around porch, may be the image of "Home" that your children remember.

Two versions of the first floor plan provide a choice between a country kitchen and a more formal dining room.

All versions feature 2x6 exterior wall framing.

Upper floor: 626 sq. ft.
Main floor: 1,359 sq. ft.

Total living area: 1,985 sq. ft.

(Not counting basement or garage)
(Non-basement versions designed with crawlspace)

Garage: 528 sq. ft.

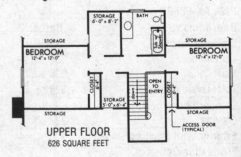

STORAGE
6'-0" x 8'-2"
BATH

STORAGE

BEDROOM
12'-4" x 12'-0"

STORAGE

BEDROOM
12'-4" x 12'-0"

STORAGE

OPEN TO ENTRY

STORAGE
5'-0" x 6'-4"

STORAGE

ACCESS DOOR (TYPICAL)

UPPER FLOOR
626 SQUARE FEET

Blueprint Price Code B

Plans H-3732-1A,-1B,-1C & -1D

PRICES AND DETAILS
ON PAGES 13-15

Space-Saving Floor Plan

- Easy, affordable living is the basis for this great town and country design.
- The welcoming porch and the graceful arched window give the home its curb appeal. Inside, the floor plan provides large, highly livable spaces rather than several specialized rooms.
- The foyer opens to the spacious living room. A column separates the foyer from the formal dining room, which features a bay window and an alcove that is perfect for a china hutch. The country kitchen is large enough to accommodate family and guests alike.
- A beautiful open staircase leads to the second floor, where there are three bedrooms and two baths. The master bedroom offers a tray ceiling and a luxurious bath with a sloped ceiling and a corner shower.

Plan AX-92320

Bedrooms: 3	Baths: 2½
Living Area:	
Upper floor	706 sq. ft.
Main floor	830 sq. ft.
Total Living Area:	**1,536 sq. ft.**
Standard basement	754 sq. ft.
Garage	510 sq. ft.
Exterior Wall Framing:	2x6

Foundation Options:

Standard basement

Slab

(Typical foundation & framing conversion diagram available—see order form.)

BLUEPRINT PRICE CODE: B

FRONT VIEW

REAR VIEW

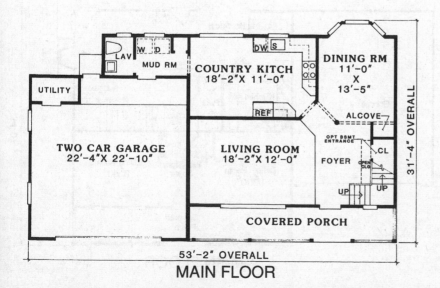

MAIN FLOOR

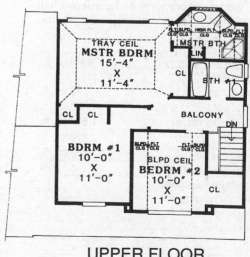

UPPER FLOOR

ORDER BLUEPRINTS ANYTIME!
CALL TOLL-FREE 1-888-626-2026

Plan AX-92320

PRICES AND DETAILS
ON PAGES 13-15

295

Luxury and Livability

- Big on style, this modest-sized home features a quaint Colonial exterior and an open interior.
- The covered front porch leads to a two-story foyer that opens to the formal living and dining rooms. A coat closet, an attractive display niche and a powder room are centrally located, as is the stairway to the upper floor.
- The kitchen, breakfast nook and family room are designed so that each room has its own definition yet also functions as part of a whole. The angled sink separates the kitchen from the breakfast nook, which is outlined by a bay window. The large family room includes a fireplace.
- The upper floor has an exceptional master suite, featuring an 8-ft., 6-in. tray ceiling in the sleeping area and an 11-ft. vaulted ceiling in the spa bath.
- Two more bedrooms and a balcony hall add to this home's luxury and livability.

Plan FB-1600

Bedrooms: 3	Baths: 2½
Living Area:	
Upper floor	772 sq. ft.
Main floor	828 sq. ft.
Total Living Area:	**1,600 sq. ft.**
Daylight basement	828 sq. ft.
Garage	473 sq. ft.
Exterior Wall Framing:	2x4

Foundation Options:
Daylight basement
Crawlspace
Slab
(All plans can be built with your choice of foundation and framing. A generic conversion diagram is available. See order form.)

BLUEPRINT PRICE CODE: B

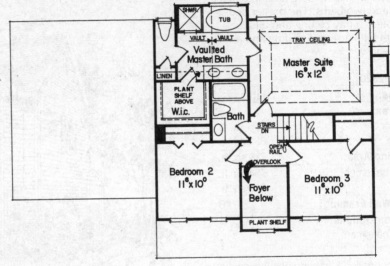

UPPER FLOOR

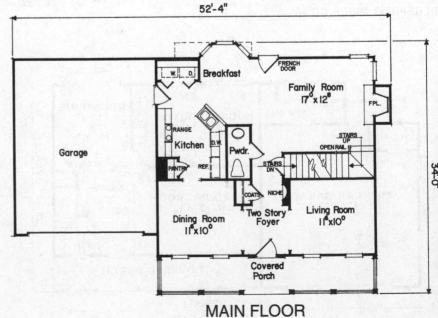

MAIN FLOOR

Plan FB-1600

PRICES AND DETAILS ON PAGES 13-15

Attractive Details

- This appealing ranch offers dramatic 12-foot ceilings in the foyer, living room, dining room and kitchen.
- Half-round windows add excitement to the sunken living room. Half-round windows are also found above the kitchen sink and above the patio doors in the dining room.
- The roomy kitchen is situated between the family room and the dining room for easy food service and efficient traffic flow; it features a pantry, and an eating bar overlooking the family room with fireplace.
- Railings around the living room and plant ledges off the foyer and hallway add decorative touches.
- Secluded to the rear of the home, the master suite has a private dressing area, walk-in closet and compartmentalized toilet and shower.

Plan U-87-101

Bedrooms: 3	Baths: 2
Space:	
Main floor without basement	1,546 sq. ft.
Main floor with basement	1,588 sq. ft.
Total Living Area	**1,546/1,588 sq. ft.**
Basement	1,588 sq. ft.
Garage	564 sq. ft.
Exterior Wall Framing	**2x6**

Foundation options:

Standard Basement
Crawlspace
Slab

(Foundation & framing conversion diagram available—see order form.)

Blueprint Price Code	**B**

STAIR LOCATION
FOR BASEMENT OPTION

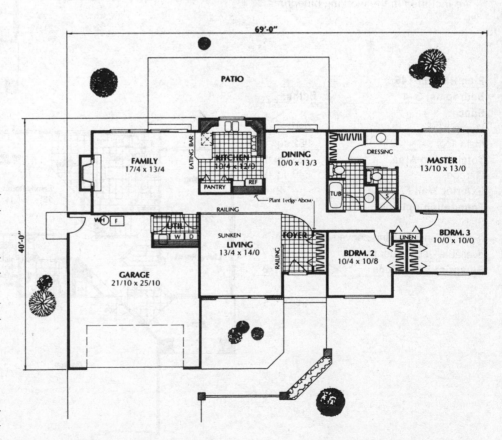

ORDER BLUEPRINTS ANYTIME!
CALL TOLL-FREE 1-888-626-2026

Plan U-87-101

PRICES AND DETAILS
ON PAGES 13-15

297

Exploding Views

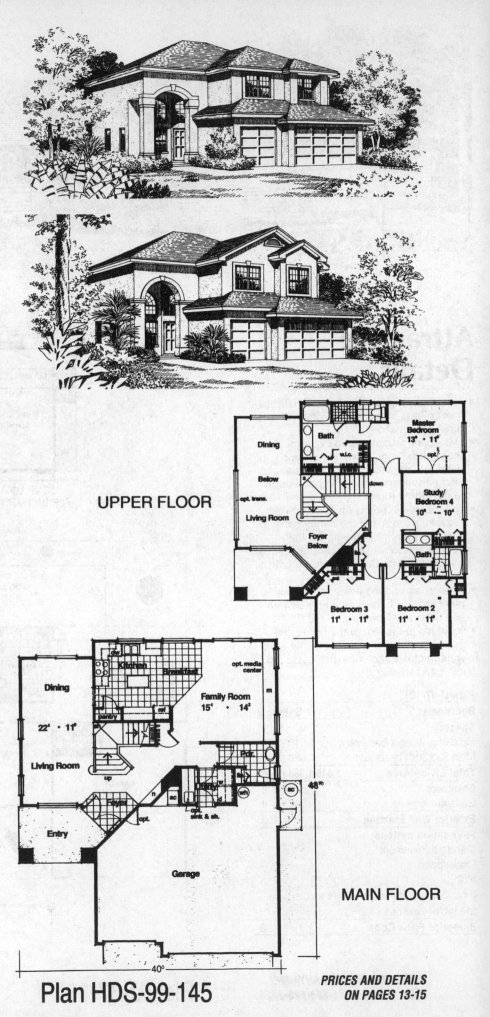

- This spectacular two-story has it all!
- An exploding view from the two-story foyer is just a preview of the excitement that follows.
- Every major living space on the main floor has a view of the outdoors, whether it be a pool area or a fifth tee.
- The formal living and dining area is perfect for seclusion or candlelight dinners.
- The modern island kitchen overlooks the breakfast area and the family room, which boasts an exciting and functional media wall.
- A half-bath and a laundry room are conveniently located near the garage entrance.
- Luxurious double doors open to the master bedroom on the upper level. An optional second set of doors could access a nursery or private study. Or, this room could be used as a conventional fourth bedroom.
- The home also offers your choice of elevation. Both elevations shown above are included in the working blueprints.

UPPER FLOOR

MAIN FLOOR

Plan HDS-99-145

Bedrooms: 3-4	Baths: 2 ½
Space:	
Upper floor	982 sq. ft.
Main floor	982 sq. ft.
Total Living Area	**1,964 sq. ft.**
Garage	646 sq. ft.
Exterior Wall Framing	2x4
Foundation options:	
Slab	

(Foundation & framing conversion diagram available—see order form.)

Blueprint Price Code	B

Plan HDS-99-145

PRICES AND DETAILS
ON PAGES 13-15

FRONT VIEW

Sun Room
Adds Warmth

At first glance this seems like just another very nice home, with crisp contemporary lines, a carefully conceived traffic flow and generous bedroom and living areas. What sets this home apart from most other houses is its passive sun room, a 13' x 11'6" solarium that collects, stores and distributes solar energy to warm the home, conserving fossil fuel and cutting energy costs. Adding to the energy efficiency of the design are 2x6 stud walls, allowing use of R-19 insulation batts, R-30 insulation in the ceiling, and an air-tight wood stove in the family room.

The passive sun room has glazing on three walls as it juts out from the home, and has a fully glazed ceiling to capture the maximum solar energy. A masonry tile floor stores the collected heat which is distributed to the family and living rooms through sliding glass doors. The wall adjoining the dining area also is glazed. With hanging plants, the sun room can be a visually stunning greenhouse extension of the vaulted-ceilinged living room. A French door from the sun room and sliding glass doors from the family room open onto a wood deck, for outdoor entertaining and relaxing.

First floor:	2,034 sq. ft.
Sun room:	159 sq. ft.
Total living area:	2,193 sq. ft.

(Not counting basement or garage)

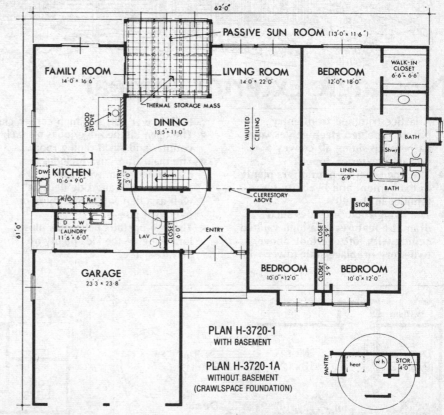

PASSIVE SUN ROOM (13'0" x 11'6")

FAMILY ROOM 14'0" x 16'6"

THERMAL STORAGE MASS

WOOD STOVE

DINING 13'5" x 11'0"

KITCHEN 10'6" x 9'0"

DW

R/O Ref

D W

LAUNDRY 11'6" x 6'0"

PANTRY

down

LAV

CLOSET 6'0"

GARAGE 23'3" x 23'8"

LIVING ROOM 14'0" x 22'0"

VAULTED CEILING

CLERESTORY ABOVE

ENTRY

BEDROOM 12'0" x 18'0"

WALK-IN CLOSET 6'6" x 6'6"

BATH

Shwr

LINEN 6'9"

BATH

STOR

CLOSET 5'9"

BEDROOM 10'0" x 12'0"

CLOSET 5'9"

BEDROOM 10'0" x 12'0"

62'0"

61'0"

PLAN H-3720-1
WITH BASEMENT

PLAN H-3720-1A
WITHOUT BASEMENT
(CRAWLSPACE FOUNDATION)

PANTRY

heat

w h

STOR 4'0"

REAR VIEW

Blueprint Price Code C

ORDER BLUEPRINTS ANYTIME!
CALL TOLL-FREE 1-888-626-2026

Plans H-3720-1 & -1A

PRICES AND DETAILS
ON PAGES 13-15

299

Nostalgic Exterior Appeal

- A lattice-trimmed front entry porch, repeated steep gables, and narrow lap siding all convey a nostalgic exterior appeal.
- The open-feeling plan offers plenty of excitement and livability for families in the 90's.
- The living room includes such dramatic features as a high-vaulted ceiling with loft overlook above, a two-story fireplace/stair tower with

built-in wet bar, and high corner glass.
- The open kitchen overlooks a snack counter and skylit dining room.
- The main floor also includes a master bedroom with access to a dramatic bath and side deck as well as a den for TV watching or overnight guests.
- The two upstairs bedrooms plus loft will give the kids plenty of private space.

UDG-90009	
Bedrooms: 3-4	**Baths:** 2

Space:

Upper floor:	554 sq. ft.
Main floor:	1,123 sq. ft.
Total living area:	**1,677 sq. ft.**
Basement:	1,123 sq. ft.
Garage:	544 sq. ft.

Exterior Wall Framing: 2x4

Foundation options:
Standard Basement.
(Foundation & framing conversion diagram available — see order form.)

Blueprint Price Code: B

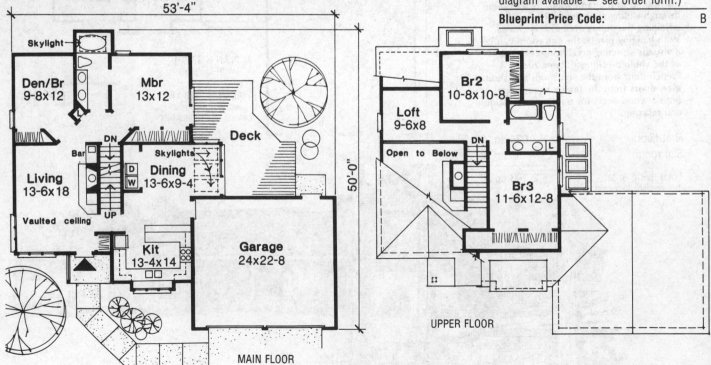

MAIN FLOOR

UPPER FLOOR

Plan UDG-90009

PRICES AND DETAILS
ON PAGES 13-15

Traditional Heritage

- A distinctive roofline and a covered wraparound porch reflect this charming home's traditional heritage.
- The roomy entry flows directly into the spacious, open living area. Enhanced by a cathedral ceiling, the living room is warmed by a fireplace and offers a French door to a backyard patio. A good-sized laundry room is nearby.

- The adjoining dining area shares porch access with the stylish gourmet kitchen, which includes an eating bar and a garden window over the sink.
- The master bedroom suite features a lavish private bath with a garden spa tub, a separate shower, a dual-sink vanity and a big walk-in closet.
- A second full bath, located at the end of the bedroom hallway, is convenient to the two remaining bedrooms.
- The double carport includes a separate lockable storage area.

Plan J-86142	
Bedrooms: 3	**Baths:** 2
Living Area:	
Main floor	1,536 sq. ft.
Total Living Area:	**1,536 sq. ft.**
Standard basement	1,536 sq. ft.
Carport and storage	520 sq. ft.
Exterior Wall Framing:	2x4

Foundation Options:

Standard basement
Crawlspace
Slab

(All plans can be built with your choice of foundation and framing. A generic conversion diagram is available. See order form.)

BLUEPRINT PRICE CODE: B

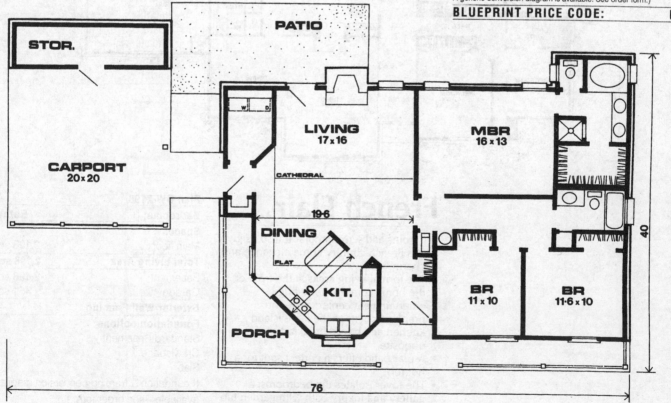

MAIN FLOOR

PRICES AND DETAILS
ON PAGES 13-15

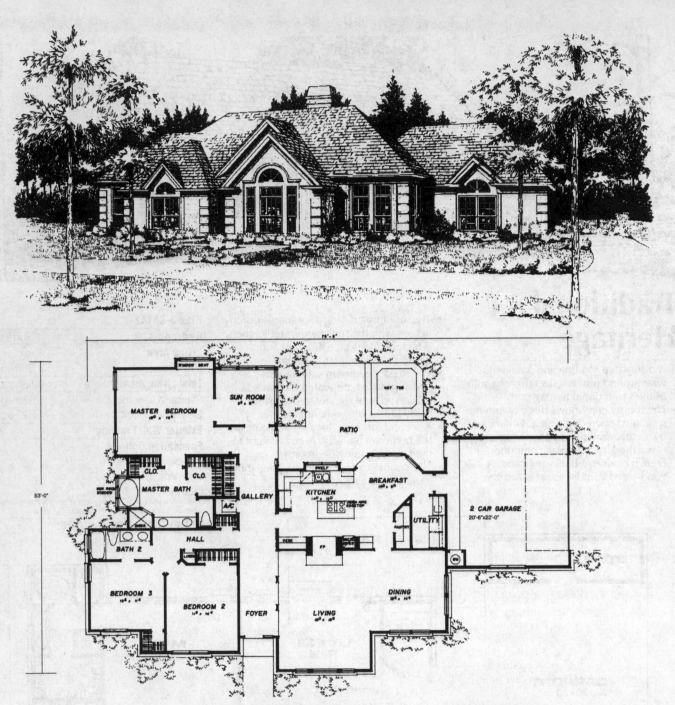

French Flair

- Quoins and semi-circular transoms give this French country home elegance and charm.
- The formal living areas at the front of the home combine for a huge entertainment center; a see-thru fireplace opens to the large island kitchen and bayed breakfast room, opposite.
- A rear patio offers a perfect spot for a hot tub.
- The foyer isolates the bedrooms; a gallery and luxury bath with garden tub and separate shower buffer the master suite and private sun room.

Plan DW-2198

Bedrooms: 3	Baths: 2
Space:	
Main floor	2,198 sq. ft.
Total Living Area	**2,198 sq. ft.**
Basement	2,198 sq. ft.
Garage	451 sq. ft.
Exterior Wall Framing	2x4

Foundation options:
Standard Basement
Crawlspace
Slab
(Foundation & framing conversion diagram available—see order form.)

Blueprint Price Code	C

Plan DW-2198

PRICES AND DETAILS
ON PAGES 13-15

Peace of Mind

- Peace and privacy were the inspiration for this tranquil home.
- Past the inviting columned entry, the bright foyer flows into the spacious 13½-ft.-high vaulted living room, which includes a wet bar.
- The gourmet kitchen enjoys a 14-ft. vaulted ceiling and includes an angled snack counter and a large pantry. Sliding glass doors in the adjoining breakfast nook lead to a covered patio with a functional summer kitchen.
- The adjacent family room boasts a 15-ft. vaulted ceiling and a handsome window-flanked fireplace.
- The master suite offers an 11½-ft. vaulted ceiling, a windowed sitting area and patio access. His-and-hers walk-in closets flank the entrance to the plush master bath, which is highlighted by a garden tub overlooking a privacy yard.
- Three more bedrooms have vaulted ceilings that are at least 11½ ft. high. With a nearby full bath and back door entrance, the rear bedroom could be made into a great guest or in-law suite.

Plan HDS-99-157

Bedrooms: 4	Baths: 3
Living Area:	
Main floor	2,224 sq. ft.
Total Living Area:	**2,224 sq. ft.**
Garage	507 sq. ft.

Exterior Wall Framing:
2x4 and concrete block

Foundation Options:
Slab
(All plans can be built with your choice of foundation and framing. A generic conversion diagram is available. See order form.)

BLUEPRINT PRICE CODE: C

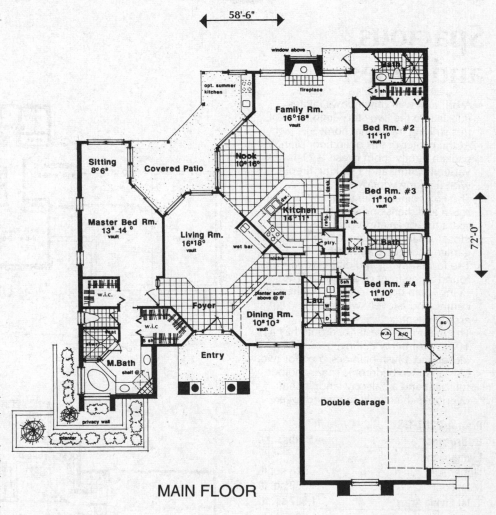

MAIN FLOOR

Spacious and Open

- A brilliant wall of windows invites guests into the two-story-high foyer of this striking traditional home.
- At the center of this open floor plan, the sunken family room boasts a 21-ft. vaulted ceiling and a striking fireplace with flanking windows.
- The cozy dinette merges with the family room and the island kitchen, creating a spacious, open atmosphere. A pantry closet, a laundry room, a half-bath and garage access are all nearby.
- The formal living and dining rooms are found at the front of the home. The living room boasts a 10½-ft. cathedral ceiling and a lovely window arrangement.
- The main-floor master bedroom has a 10-ft., 10-in. tray ceiling, a walk-in closet and a lush bath designed for two.
- Upstairs, two bedrooms share another full bath and a balcony landing that overlooks the family room and foyer.

Plan A-2207-DS

Bedrooms: 3	Baths: 2½
Living Area:	
Upper floor	518 sq. ft.
Main floor	1,389 sq. ft.
Total Living Area:	**1,907 sq. ft.**
Standard basement	1,389 sq. ft.
Garage	484 sq. ft.
Exterior Wall Framing:	2x6

Foundation Options:

Standard basement

(All plans can be built with your choice of foundation and framing. A generic conversion diagram is available. See order form.)

BLUEPRINT PRICE CODE:	B

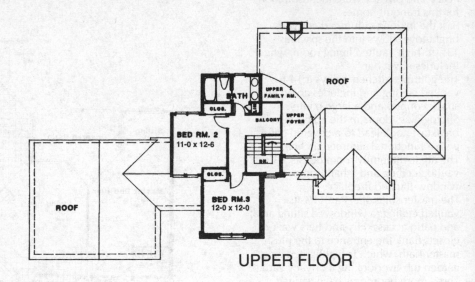

UPPER FLOOR

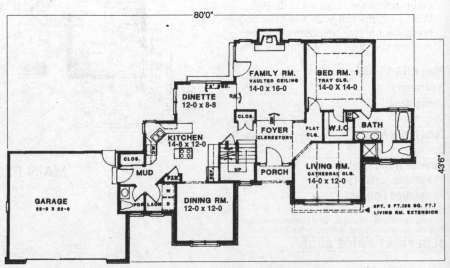

MAIN FLOOR

Plan A-2207-DS

PRICES AND DETAILS
ON PAGES 13-15